MW01088885

"This latest addition to the Foundations of Evangelical Theology series maintains the high standard already set. Graham Cole has written the widest-ranging text-book on pneumatology that currently exists. Meticulous and sharp in handling texts, and scrupulous on matters of method, he offers us cool, clear, sober answers to more questions about the Holy Spirit than probably any of us have hitherto thought to ask. New ground is not broken, but solid ground of a mainstream Reformed sort is set forth throughout. Well done, Dr. Cole!"

—J. I. Packer, Professor of Theology, Regent College

"Dr. Graham Cole's superbly written book is a wide-ranging biblical and theological study of the doctrine of the Holy Spirit that may well become a standard work on the subject. The volume is marked by careful exegesis of the scriptural references to the Spirit, each of which is interpreted within the salvation-historical flow of God's redemptive purposes. A convinced Trinitarian theologian, Dr. Cole listens carefully to the contributions made by earlier generations of Christian writers from a range of disciplines, including biblical studies, systematic theology, and historical theology. Authors from both the Eastern and Western traditions are drawn in as pertinent, and challenging questions for our generation are raised. Issues of doctrine, understanding, and experience are drawn together in this fine book as the author guides his readers in appropriate worship of the Triune God, Father, Son, and Spirit."

—Peter T. O'Brien, Senior Research Fellow in New Testament, Moore Theological College, Australia

HE WHO
GIVES LIFE

Foundations of Evangelical Theology Series
JOHN S. FEINBERG, GENERAL EDITOR

The Cross and Salvation
BRUCE DEMAREST

No One Like Him
JOHN S. FEINBERG

To Know and Love God
DAVID K. CLARK

HE WHO GIVES LIFE

THE DOCTRINE OF THE HOLY SPIRIT

GRAHAM A. COLE

CROSSWAY BOOKS

WHEATON, ILLINOIS

To my wife, Jules,
a bright patch of Aussie sunlight

CONTENTS

PART ONE:
THE MYSTERY OF THE SPIRIT

PART TWO:
THE MINISTRY OF THE SPIRIT—OLD TESTAMENT
PERSPECTIVES

PART THREE:
THE MINISTRY OF THE SPIRIT—NEW TESTAMENT
PERSPECTIVES

PART FOUR:
THE MAGNIFICENCE OF DIVINE SELFLESSNESS

Why another series of works on evangelical systematic theology? This is an especially appropriate question in light of the fact that evangelicals are fully committed to an inspired and inerrant Bible as their final authority for faith and practice. But since neither God nor the Bible changes, why is there a need to redo evangelical systematic theology?

Systematic theology is not divine revelation. Theologizing of any sort is a human conceptual enterprise. Thinking that it is equal to biblical revelation misunderstands the nature of both Scripture and theology! Insofar as our theology contains propositions that accurately reflect Scripture or match the world and are consistent with the Bible (in cases where the propositions do not come per se from Scripture), our theology is biblically based and correct. But even if all the propositions of a systematic theology are true, that theology would still not be equivalent to biblical revelation! It is still a human conceptualization of God and his relation to the world.

Although this may disturb some who see theology as nothing more than doing careful exegesis over a series of passages, and others who see it as nothing more than biblical theology, those methods of doing theology do not somehow produce a theology that is equivalent to biblical revelation either. Exegesis is a human conceptual enterprise, and so is biblical theology. All the theological disciplines involve human intellectual participation. But human intellect is finite, and hence there is always room for revision of systematic theology as knowledge increases. Though God and his Word do not change, human understanding of his revelation can grow, and our theologies should be reworked to reflect those advances in understanding.

Another reason for evangelicals to rework their theology is the nature of systematic theology as opposed to other theological disciplines. For example, whereas the task of biblical theology is more to describe biblical teaching on whatever topics Scripture addresses, systematics should make a special point to relate its conclusions to the issues of one's day. This does not mean that the systematician ignores the topics biblical writers address. Nor does it mean that theologians should warp Scripture to address issues it never intended to address. Rather it suggests that in addition to expounding what biblical writers teach, the theologian should attempt to take those biblical teachings (along with the biblical mind-set) and apply them to issues that are especially confronting the church in the theologian's own day. For example, 150 years ago, an evangelical theologian doing work on the doctrine of man would likely have discussed issues such as the creation of man and the constituent parts of man's being. Such a theology might even have included a discussion about human institutions such as marriage, noting in general the respective roles of husbands and wives in marriage. However, it is dubious that there would have been any lengthy discussion with various viewpoints about the respective roles of men and women in marriage, in society, and in the church. But at our point in history and in light of the feminist movement and the issues it has raised even among many conservative Christians, it would be foolish to write a theology of man (or, should we say, a "theology of humanity") without a thorough discussion of the issue of the roles of men and women in society, the home, and the church.

Because systematic theology attempts to address itself not only to the timeless issues presented in Scripture but also to the current issues of one's day and culture, each theology will to some extent need to be redone in each generation. Biblical truth does not change from generation to generation, but the issues that confront the church do. A theology that was adequate for a different era and different culture may simply not speak to key issues in a given culture at a given time. Hence, in this series we are reworking evangelical systematic theology, though we do so with the understanding that in future generations there will be room for a revision of theology again.

How, then, do the contributors to this series understand the nature of systematic theology? Systematic theology as done from an evangelical Christian perspective involves study of the person, works, and relationships of God. As evangelicals committed to the full inspiration, inerrancy, and final authority of Scripture, we demand that whatever appears in a systematic theology correspond to the way things are and must not contradict any claim taught in Scripture. Holy Writ is the touchstone of our theology, but we do not limit the source material for systematics to Scripture alone. Hence, whatever information from history, science, philosophy, and the like is relevant to our understanding of God and his relation to our world is fair game for systematics. Depending on the specific interests and expertise of the contributors to this series, their respective volumes will reflect interaction with one or more of these disciplines.

What is the rationale for appealing to other sources than Scripture and other disciplines than the biblical ones? Since God created the universe, there is revelation of God not only in Scripture but in the created order as well. There are many disciplines that study our world, just as does theology. But since the world studied by the non-theological disciplines is the world created by God, any data and conclusions in the so-called secular disciplines that accurately reflect the real world are also relevant to our understanding of the God who made that world. Hence, in a general sense, since all of creation is God's work, nothing is outside the realm of theology. The so-called secular disciplines need to be thought of in a theological context, because they are reflecting on the universe God created, just as is the theologian. And, of course, there are many claims in the non-theological disciplines that are generally accepted as true (although this does not mean that every claim in non-theological disciplines is true, or that we are in a position with respect to every proposition to know whether it is true or false). Since this is so, and since all disciplines are in one way or another reflecting on our universe, a universe made by God, any true statement in any discipline should in some way be informative for our understanding of God and his relation to our world. Hence, we have felt it appropriate to incorporate data from outside the Bible in our theological formulations.

As to the specific design of this series, our intention is to address all areas of evangelical theology with a special emphasis on key issues in each area. While other series may be more like a history of doctrine, this series purposes to incorporate insights from Scripture, historical theology, philosophy, etc., in order to produce an up-to-date work in systematic theology. Though all contributors to the series are thoroughly evangelical in their theology, embracing the historical orthodox doctrines of the church, the series as a whole is not meant to be slanted in the direction of one form of evangelical theology. Nonetheless, most of the writers come from a Reformed perspective. Alternate evangelical and non-evangelical options, however, are discussed.

As to style and intended audience, this series is meant to rest on the very best of scholarship while at the same time being understandable to the beginner in theology as well as to the academic theologian. With that in mind, contributors are writing in a clear style, taking care to define whatever technical terms they use.

Finally, we believe that systematic theology is not just for the understanding. It must apply to life, and it must be lived. As Paul wrote to Timothy, God has given divine revelation for many purposes, including ones that necessitate doing theology, but the ultimate reason for giving revelation and for theologians doing theology is that the people of God may be fitted for every good work (2 Tim. 3:16–17). In light of the need for theology to connect to life, each of the contributors not only formulates doctrines but also explains how those doctrines practically apply to everyday living.

It is our sincerest hope that the work we have done in this series will first glorify and please God, and, secondly, instruct and edify the people of God. May God be pleased to use this series to those ends, and may he richly bless you as you read the fruits of our labors.

John S. Feinberg
General Editor

PREFACE

For many years now there has been great popular interest and growing theological interest in the doctrine of the Holy Spirit or, technically put, pneumatology. The rise of modern Pentecostalism and the subsequent manifestation of Pentecostal phenomena and doctrine within mainline denominations through the charismatic movement are indicators of the fresh attention that is being given to the Third Person of the triune Godhead. For someone like myself who teaches in a divinity school, which attracts students from Pentecostal denominations as well as mainline churches, questions about how we are best to understand the Spirit's nature and work are inescapable. So the invitation to contribute to a theological series of monographs on key doctrines with my brief being the topic of pneumatology was irresistible though daunting. I have taught pneumatology classes in Australia, England, and now the United States. However, to teach systematically about the Holy Spirit, when Scripture itself does not present the story of the Spirit in that way, has always proved a considerable challenge. Moreover, if one believes the biblical testimony—which I do—then when I write about Holy Spirit, surely I ought to be *in* the Spirit. Moreover, as I write I am actually in the Spirit's own unseen presence, who may be grieved by what I say and do with the written page. Indeed, in human experience there is something odd, in fact impolite, about talking to a third party about someone else in that person's very presence and never directly addressing the person under discussion even though he or she is there. Likewise with the Spirit. Sobering!

Special thanks and acknowledgment need to be given to John Feinberg, my editor, for unfailing encouragement, and to two doctoral students for their research assistance, Steve Garrett and Jim Franks. In particular, I am grateful to the Board of Regents of Trinity International University for granting a sabbatical leave which was crucial for this work to progress.

A B B R E V I A T I O N S

AsTJ	*Asbury Theological Journal*
CCC	*Catechism of the Catholic Church*. Liguori, Mo.: Liguori, 1994.
CD	Karl Barth, *Church Dogmatics*. G. W. Bromiley and T. F. Torrance, eds. Edinburgh: T. & T. Clark, 1936–1977.
CJCC	*The Comprehensive John Calvin Collection*. Rio, Wis.: Ages Software, 2002. CD-Rom version.
CSR	*Christian Scholar's Review*
DJG	*Dictionary of Jesus and the Gospels* (EIRC)
DPHL	*Dictionary of Paul and His Letters* (EIRC)
EBC	*The Expositor's Bible Commentary*. Frank E. Gaebelein, ed. Grand Rapids, Mich.: Zondervan, 1976– . CD-Rom version.
EDT	*Evangelical Dictionary of Theology*. Walter A. Elwell, ed. Grand Rapids, Mich.: Baker, 1994.
EIRC	*The Essential IVP Reference Collection*. Leicester, UK: Inter-Varsity Press, 2001. CD-Rom version.
ESV	*English Standard Version Bible*
JETS	*Journal of the Evangelical Theological Society*
JSB	*Jewish Study Bible*
NBC	*New Bible Commentary, Twenty-first Century Edition*, G. J. Wenham et al., eds. Downers Grove, Ill.: InterVarsity Press, 1994.
NBCRev	*New Bible Commentary Revised* (EIRC)
NDBT	*New Dictionary of Biblical Theology* (EIRC)
NDOT	*New Dictionary of Theology* (EIRC)
NIDNTT	*The New International Dictionary of New Testament Theology*. Colin Brown, ed., 3 vols. Grand Rapids, Mich.: Zondervan, 1975–78. CD-Rom version.
NIV	*New International Version Bible*
NRSV	*New Revised Standard Version Bible*
RTR	*Reformed Theological Review*
TDNT	*Theological Dictionary of the New Testament*. G. Kittel and G. Friedrich, eds. G. W. Bromiley, trans. 10 vols. Grand Rapids, Mich.: Eerdmans, 1964–1976.
TrinJ	*Trinity Journal*
TS	*Theological Studies*
WBC	Word Biblical Commentary, Bruce M. Metzger, David A. Hubbard, and Glenn W. Barker, eds. Nelson Reference & Electronic, 2004. CD-Rom version.
WTJ	*Westminster Theological Journal*

ONE

INTRODUCTION

There is no higher pursuit than the worship of God. In fact we become like the God we adore and serve for good or ill. All depends upon the nature of the God or gods we follow. If we follow the living God of biblical revelation then we will image him. If we follow idols we will image them. A. W. Tozer saw this when he wrote,

> What comes into our minds when we think about God is the most important thing about us. . . . The history of mankind will probably show that no people has ever risen above its religion, and man's spiritual history will positively demonstrate that no religion has ever been greater than its idea of God. . . . Always the most revealing thing about the Church is her idea of God, just as her most significant message is what she says about Him or leaves unsaid, for her silence is often more eloquent than her speech. She can never escape the self-disclosure of her witness concerning God.[1]

Tozer was on solid biblical ground for his view. As the psalmist says of the worship of idols in Psalm 115:8, "Those who make them become like them; so do all who trust in them." This is a firm biblical principle.

SCRIPTURAL REVELATION

But where do we get our ideas of God? Evangelical theology prizes the Scriptures as the revelation of the only God there is. Without revelation from God our theology is blind and represents the best human guesses about the divine. Such guessing would make for an interesting chat show on late-night television but hardly a body of knowledge worth staking one's

---

1. A. W. Tozer, *The Knowledge of the Holy* (London: James Clarke, 1965), 9.

life on. Therefore this study will need to examine carefully the witness of Scripture. In so doing it assumes that Scripture ought to occupy a unique place in understanding God's relationship with creation and ourselves. The important doctrines that spell out that uniqueness include inspiration, inerrancy, sufficiency, clarity, and canon, to name a few. These are not the subject of this study but are presupposed by it. In other words, this study presupposes a high view of biblical authority, which is a defining characteristic of the evangelical tradition.

However, it is one thing to have such a high view of Scripture and quite another to interpret the Bible responsibly. A high view of Scripture requires a respectful hermeneutic. The Reformers had such a respectful and responsible interpretive approach summed up in the notion of the analogy of faith (*analogia fidei*), which took seriously the unity of the canon.[2] Scripture is to interpret Scripture, Scripture is not to be interpreted against Scripture, and the plain Scripture is to interpret the obscure Scripture. I would add to these a fourth principle: Scripture is to be interpreted genre by genre. However, sometimes conservatively minded Christians can read Scripture in a one-dimensional and wooden way. I recall talking to an elder in a church who insisted that if there wasn't an actual robbery informing Jesus' story of the Good Samaritan in Luke 10, then Jesus was not the Son of God. Why? Because Jesus would have attempted to teach truth by a lie. "But it is parable!" I insisted, to little effect.[3]

What then do the Scriptures tell us? As we shall see, the Scriptures reveal to us a God who is personal. Persons generate narratives or stories that can be told by them and not simply by us. Scripture contains much divine autobiography. God has his own stories. For example, God presents himself to the Israelites as the one who brought them out of the land of Egypt (Ex.

2. From a literary viewpoint Leland Ryken sees five kinds of unity in the Bible: "There is unity of national authorship, with only two books in the whole Bible (Luke and Acts) not having been written by Jews [better, "Israelites and Jews"]. There is a unity of subject matter, consisting most broadly of God's ways with people and the relationship of people to God and fellow humans. There is a unity of worldview and general theological outlook from book to book. There is unity of purpose underlying all biblical literature—the purpose of revealing God to people so that they might know how to order their lives. There is, finally, a unity of literary texture based on allusion. No other anthology of literature possesses the unified texture of allusions that biblical literature displays" (*The Literature of the Bible* [Grand Rapids, Mich.: Zondervan, 1980], 15–16).

3. When I teach the doctrine of Scripture in a seminary setting, I will start the class by saying that I am distressed because of the news. England has been invaded. The landscape is ablaze. There is mayhem everywhere. Surprised students want to know how come they haven't heard the news. I point out that it is in the paper and we even have the name of the invading leader in print, Hagar the Horrible. Of course, I am referring to a cartoon character and have turned the cartoon into a piece of foreign correspondence. A category mistake. For when it comes to the newspaper we recognize that the editorial is not the weather report, nor the TV guide, nor the feature article, and so forth. At times, however, the conservative Christian appears to read the daily newspaper with more sophistication than the Scriptures.

20:1–2). Unless our doctrine of the Spirit can be anchored firmly in the narratives of the self-presentation of the God of creation and redemption as found in the Bible, that doctrine has little, in fact, no claim on Christian allegiance.

OTHER SOURCES

Given that evangelical theologians have such a high regard for Scripture as God's Word written—albeit in human words—one might expect wrongly that other sources for theological reflection are thereby neglected. But in practice evangelical theologians work with tradition, or with what I call the witness of Christian thought, and do so also with a firm eye on the contemporary world of human predicament which we ourselves experience. We live outside of Eden. We live this side of the fall (Augustine's *lapsus*), or as French lay theologian Jacques Ellul (1912–1994) put it, "The Rupture" (*"La Rupture"*).[4] Thus the evangelical theologian seeks to connect the text and today, past and present, the Word and the world. To make these connections both truthful and fruitful requires wisdom and not simply intelligence. Wisdom is our intelligence exercised within the attitudinal framework of the fear of the Lord (Prov. 1:7). Doing theology ought to be therefore a wisdom activity embodying a particular attitude of reverence toward God. When done so it becomes part of the Christian's reasonable worship—that is to say, worship understood in that broad NT sense of life lived in response to the gospel (Rom. 12:1–2) and not in the traditional but narrower sense of the corporate acknowledgment of the grandeur of God (as in Revelation 4–5).

This study of the doctrine of the Holy Spirit will need then not only to respect Scripture but also to interact with the witness of Christian thought. By that I mean the study will need to be in conversation, as it were, with the creeds and with the great theologians of the past and present who have turned their attention to the person and work of the Spirit of God. Basil of Caesarea, Augustine, Aquinas, Calvin, Owen, Kuyper, Barth, Moltmann, and many others will need to be given their due. Doing theology is an ecclesiastical practice or it runs the risk of idiosyncrasy. Sometimes at a popular level evangelicals can act as though God has not been active in the world and in his people between St. Paul's conversion and their own. That trap we will need to avoid. Moreover this study will need to make connection with the issues surrounding the doctrine of the Spirit today in the world of human predicament. Last century, Dietrich Bonhoeffer (1906–1945) asked,

4. Jacques Ellul, *The Humiliation of the Word* (Grand Rapids, Mich.: Eerdmans, 1985), chapter 7.

Who is Christ for us *today*?[5] An analogous question may be asked of the Spirit: Who is the Holy Spirit for us *today*?

The theological enterprise, therefore, involves the foundational and normative Word of Revelation brought to bear on the World of Human Predicament with an awareness of the Witness of Christian Thought.[6] To do so responsibly is a Work of Wisdom predicated on the fear of the Lord and is to be conducted in the Way of Worship offered to the living God.

AN EVIDENCE-BASED APPROACH

In my view an evangelical approach to the doctrine of the Holy Spirit needs to be an evidence-based practice.[7] Philosophy offers a parallel. In their useful book *What Philosophers Think*, Julian Baggini and Jeremy Stangroom maintain,

> What regulates the flow of ideas in philosophy is rational argumenta-tion. Exactly what makes an argument rational is itself a philosophical question, but in general it is that any conclusions reached are based upon a combination of good evidence, good reasoning and self-evident basic principles of logic. (The 'evidence' philosophy draws upon is not usually the special data of science, but the kind of evidence which is available to all. These are facts which are established by every

5. See Keith Clements, "Bonhoeffer, Dietrich," in Adrian Hastings, Alister Mason, and Hugh Pyper, eds., *The Oxford Companion to Christian Thought* (Oxford: Oxford University Press, 2000), 79, emphasis mine.

6. Scripture, according to my view, because it is the Word of God, is the "norming norm" (*norma normans*) while other authorities (tradition, reason, and experience), although operative in Christian theology, are "ruled norms" (*norma normata*). Put another way, in any contest between authorities we appeal to Scripture since it is the touchstone and rules the others. As article 21 of *The Articles of Religion* of the Church of England of 1562 has it, "General Councils . . . may err, and sometimes have erred, even in things pertaining to God. Wherefore things ordained by them as necessary to salvation have neither strength nor authority, unless it may be declared that they be taken out of Holy Scripture" (see *An Australian Prayer Book: For Use Together with the Book of Common Prayer [1662]* [Sydney: AIO Press, 1978], 632). Likewise, reason (our discursive thought) may err and experience may be misdescribed.

7. Philosophically speaking, by "evidence" I mean "information bearing on the truth or falsity of a proposition," as Richard Feldman maintains in "Evidence," in Robert Audi, gen. ed., *The Cambridge Dictionary of Philosophy*, 2nd Ed. (Cambridge: Cambridge University Press, 1999), 293. There is another way worth noting to understand what constitutes evidence. R. G. Collingwood suggests, "Anything is evidence which enables you to answer your question—the question you are asking now" (*The Idea of History* [New York : Oxford University Press, 1961], 281). The fundamental questions asked in this study are: "What are we to believe about the Holy Spirit?" and "What are some of the implications of that belief for Christian thought and life?" To answer those questions, evidence drawn from Scripture will be essential. Hence there will be frequent reference to Scripture in this work.

day experience or established science. *In this way there is no special evidence-base for philosophy.*)[8]

Like philosophy, theology needs to have its ideas regulated. Like doing philosophy, doing theology is an evidence-based practice. Like philosophy, rational argument is a desideratum for theology as a discipline. But unlike philosophy, as Baggini and Stangroom conceive of it, theology does have a special evidence-base: namely, that provided by special revelation now crystallized as Holy Scripture and by general revelation as interpreted by that same Scripture.

Likewise any evidence provided by contemporary Christian experience needs to be viewed through the grid of Scripture and not the other way around, especially when the question of how best to describe the experience is under examination—a question to which we shall return in a later chapter.

The alternative to the above is to spin theological ideas out of our minds much like one of Francis Bacon's spiders which spins its web out of its own body.[9] In contrast to such self-sufficient spiders, Dietrich Bonhoeffer can still teach a fresh generation when he writes,

> We must learn to know the Scriptures again, as the Reformers and our fathers knew them. We must know the Scriptures first and foremost for the sake of our salvation. But besides this, there are ample reasons that make this requirement exceedingly urgent. How, for example, shall we ever attain certainty and confidence in our personal and church activity if we do not stand on solid biblical ground? It is not our heart that determines our course, but God's Word. But who in this day has any proper understanding of the need for scriptural proof? How often do we hear innumerable arguments 'from life' and 'from experience' put forward as the basis for the most crucial decisions *but the argument of Scripture is missing.* And this authority would perhaps point in exactly the opposite direction. It is not surprising, of course, that the person who attempts to cast discredit upon their wisdom should be the one who himself does not seriously read, know, and study the Scriptures. But one who will not learn to handle the Bible for himself is not an evangelical Christian.[10]

8. Julian Baggini and Jeremy Stangroom, eds., *What Philosophers Think* (London and New York: Continuum, 2003), 1–2, emphasis mine.

9. Francis Bacon (1561–1626), *The Advancement of Learning,* book 1:5: "For the wit and mind of man, if it work upon matter, which is the contemplation of the creatures of God, worketh according to the stuff, and is limited thereby; but if it worl [*sic*] upon itself, as the spider worketh his web, then it is endless, and brings forth indeed cobwebs of learning, admirable for the fineness of thread and work, but of no substance or profit" (see http://www.lewis.up.edu/efl/asarnow/eliza4.htm, accessed February 23, 2005).

10. Dietrich Bonhoeffer, *Life Together,* trans. John W. Doberstein (London: SCM, 1983), 39, emphasis mine.

Evidence-based theological practice provides scriptural support for its affirmations and denials.[11] Moreover, that scriptural support will be utilized in a way that is sensitive to the biblical text in its immediate context in its literary unit in its book in the canon in the light of the flow of redemptive history.[12]

This is not to say that there is no room for daring theological hypotheses. There is. But they need to be identified as such and offered to the church for debate as *theologoumena* (theological opinions) rather than as convictions. Some notion of dogmatic rank needs deployment when proposals are offered that far outrun the force of the scriptural evidence. If such proposals lead away from the body of divinity (teaching) found in Scripture then they are to be abandoned. If they are consistent with that body of divinity then they may be embraced heuristically until better are found.

The History of Pneumatological Discussion and Debate: A Sketch[13]

A conventional way to periodize the Christian past is to divide it into four periods.[14] The Patristic era covers late NT times to the eighth century, the Medieval Era covers the eighth century to the fifteenth, the Reformational one from the sixteenth to the seventeenth, and the Modern from the eigh-

---

11. A feature of this systematic treatment of the doctrine of the Holy Spirit will be the intentional use of biblical theologies as resources as well as, more traditionally, commentaries and works of systematic theology. Biblical theologies attempt to understand Scripture from within. Brian S. Rosner defines the biblical theology project in these terms: "To sum up, *biblical theology may be defined as theological interpretation of Scripture in and for the church. It proceeds with historical and literary sensitivity and seeks to analyse and synthesize the Bible's teaching about God and his relations to the world on its own terms, maintaining sight of the Bible's overarching narrative and Christocentric focus*" ("Biblical Theology," *NDBT,* 11, emphasis original). D. A Carson adds that, "biblical theology stands as a kind of bridge discipline between responsible exegesis and responsible systematic theology (even though each of these inevitably influences the other two)" (ibid., 94). Names of biblical theologians that will appear in the present work include Childs, Dumbrell, Goldsworthy, Scobie, and VanGemeren, to name a few.

12. Richard Lints, *The Fabric of Theology: A Prolegomenon to Evangelical Theology* (Grand Rapids, Mich.: Eerdmans, 1993), describes such an approach in terms of sensitivity to the textual horizon, the epochal horizon, and the canonical horizon (293–310). My use of biblical evidence will employ such an approach, although limitations of space preclude showing one's workings very often.

13. "Sketch" is the operative word. For far more extensive historical treatments see Jaroslav Pelikan, *The Christian Tradition: A History of the Development of Doctrine,* 5 vols. (Chicago and London: University of Chicago Press, 1971–1989), passim; and the three works by Stanley M. Burgess: *The Holy Spirit: Ancient Christian Traditions* (Peabody, Mass.: Hendrickson, 1984); *The Holy Spirit: Medieval Roman Catholic and Reformation Traditions* (Peabody, Mass.: Hendrickson, 1997); and *The Holy Spirit: Eastern Christian Traditions* (Peabody, Mass.: Hendrickson, 1989).

14. For example, Geoffrey W. Bromiley, "History of Theology," *NDOT,* 309–312.

teenth until today. Let's examine briefly each period in turn—albeit in broad strokes.[15]

The great topic of discussion and debate in the Patristic era concerned the ontology of the Spirit in relation to the essential Trinity rather than the work of the Spirit in the economy (administration) of salvation. Was the Spirit as much God as the Father is God and as the Son is God? The orthodox judgment—both East (Greek speaking) and West (Latin-speaking)—was strongly affirmative. The Spirit is to be worshiped with the Father and the Son, one God in three Persons. However, there is a plausible historical argument that despite the espoused equality of the Spirit with the Father and the Son in the Trinity there was operationally a "subordination" of the Spirit, especially in the West, as reflected in the somewhat minimal treatment of the Spirit in comparison with the Father and the Son in the great creeds of Christendom, whether Apostles', Nicene, or Athanasian.

The Medieval period saw further wrestling over the precise nature of the Spirit's relation to the Father and the Son within the triune Godhead with respect to the biblical ideas of the sending of the Spirit by the Father and the Son. Did these sendings reflect the inner life of God as Trinity or was the sending of the Spirit from the Son reflective only of an economic function? As Raymond E. Brown observes, "In the first millennium of Christianity at the great Councils the Churches could agree on God and, for the most part, on Jesus Christ; but East and West ultimately split apart over the Spirit."[16] The *filioque* ("from the Son also") controversy, which we will explore in more than one place in subsequent discussion, engendered much bitterness and is part of the story of the schism of Eastern and Western Christianity (A.D. 1054) which continues to this day. The West embraces *filioque*. The East rejects it.

With Reformational Christianity, the conclusions of the Patristic era concerning the ontology of the Spirit (the person of the Spirit) were maintained in their Western form (Luther, Calvin, and Cranmer). What does emerge is more attention given to the work of the Spirit. Brown contends, "The Reformation was a battle among Western Christians who were united in the belief that the Spirit had come forth from the Son (as well as from the Father) but who were divided over how the Spirit functioned in the church."[17] Luther (1483–1546) and Calvin (1509–1564), in particular, emphasized the work of the Spirit in conjunction with the Word to bring about faith both in response to the preached gospel and to Scripture whether taught or read. Both Reformers reacted strongly against

15. For this section I am very much indebted to the discussion of William W. Menzies, "The Holy Spirit in Christian Theology," in Kenneth S. Kantzer and Stanley S. Gundry, eds., *Perspectives on Evangelical Theology* (Grand Rapids, Mich.: Baker, 1979), 67–79.

16. Raymond E. Brown, "Diverse Views of the Spirit in the New Testament," *Worship* 77 no. 3 (May 1983): 226.

17. Ibid.

the Roman Catholic claim that the Spirit worked in some exclusive way through the official spokespersons of that church: namely, "the hierarchy of bishops" as "the interpreters of the Christian faith."[18] Likewise both Reformers reacted strongly against enthusiasts of the day with their stress on immediate Spirit experience. Calvin, in particular, contributed the lastingly fruitful notion of an inner witness of the Spirit in the believer to the objective Word of God (*testimonium internum Spiritus Sancti*). He is rightly described by J. I. Packer as *"the* theologian of the Holy Spirit," just as Athanasius (c. 296–373) is *"the* theologian of the incarnation" and Luther "of justification."[19] In the next century the great Puritan divine John Owen (1616–1683) did pioneering work on the Spirit's role in progressive sanctification or the believer's growth in godliness.[20]

The Modern period has witnessed a number of phases of interest in the Spirit's work. In the eighteenth and nineteenth centuries the experiential dimensions of the Spirit's work were especially to the fore. The mission of the Spirit is to regenerate and sanctify. George Whitefield (1714–1770) especially thematized the former and John Wesley (1703–1791) the latter. Subsequently, in the nineteenth century the topic of Spirit-impelled sanctification was understood in terms of the experience of a "higher Christian life" and holiness before the Lord. In the early twentieth century modern Pentecostalism arose against this holiness background and out of a concern to serve the Lord with power in what was perceived to be an increasingly hostile world. The concern for power to serve was not confined to the rising Pentecostal movement. Prominent evangelists such as R. A. Torrey (1856–1928) also accented the need for "a baptism in the Spirit." At the present time a number of pneumatological currents are at work. There is the continued growth of the Pentecostal movement worldwide, the influence of the charismatic movement within mainline churches, and the rise of "Third Wave" congregations.[21] There is continued interest in such issues as *filioque,* the Spirit and the power to serve, the Spirit and the gifting of today's church, the Spirit and the doctrine of

18. Ibid.

19. J. I. Packer, *Keep in Step with the Spirit* (Leicester, England: Inter-Varsity, 1984), 235, emphasis original.

20. Owen is a good example of Menzies' point about the historical shift of attention to the Spirit's work in the Reformational period while affirming the early church's legacy concerning the person of the Spirit. The full title of Owen's work is illustrative, as is the structure. The title runs: *The Holy Spirit, His Gifts and Power: Exposition of the Spirit's Name, Nature, Personality, Operations and Effects* (reprint, abridged, Grand Rapids, Mich.: Kregel, 1967). And as for the structure: book 1 consists of five chapters, two of which concern the person of the Spirit. Books 2 to 4 concern the operations of the Spirit, while book 4 focuses on progressive sanctification. Owen's work may be fruitfully contrasted with the fourth-century Basil of Caesarea, where discussion of the person of the Spirit predominates (Basil of Caesarea, *On the Holy Spirit,* St. Vladimir's Seminary Press Translation [New York: St. Vladimir's Seminary Press, 1980]).

21. For the distinctions between Pentecostal, charismatic, and Third Wave movements see the glossary.

the church (ecclesiology per se), the Spirit and the use of gendered language in addressing and describing God, the Spirit and the liberation of oppressed people, and finally the Spirit and claims of authentic religious experience in religions other than Christianity.[22] This list is indicative rather than exhaustive.

The Importance of Questions

Questions constitute the lifeblood of both conversation and critical inquiry. This is so with theological discussion and inquiry. Important questions for our study include:

- What does the Bible say about the Holy Spirit?
- How is the Spirit characterized?
- Is the Spirit a person?
- Is the Spirit God?
- If the Spirit is God, should we then pray to the Holy Spirit?
- How is the Spirit to be understood in Trinitarian terms?
- What are we to make of the elusiveness of the Spirit, who is like the wind?
- What role does the Spirit play in creation?
- How does the Spirit make the deep things of God known?
- What is the Spirit's relation to the institutions of Israel: prophets, priests, kings, tabernacle, and temple?
- How does the Spirit figure in the messianic hopes of Israel?
- Were OT believers regenerated and indwelt by the Spirit?
- What is the Spirit's relation to Jesus the Messiah?
- How does the Spirit connect to the life of the believer?
- What is the blasphemy against the Spirit?
- How does the Spirit connect to the life of the church?
- What is the role of the Spirit with regard to Scripture?
- Are all the gifts of the Spirit for today?
- Is the Spirit at work in other religions around the world?
- How are we to discern the Spirit at work today?
- What about ambiguous references to s/Spirit in Scripture?

22. Menzies, "Holy Spirit," 76–78, focuses on the Holy Spirit and the community of faith as the contemporary pneumatological issue. But as he acknowledges, applying theology to life involves "a shifting of the target" (67). In the quarter century since he wrote, the "targets"—not the most felicitous of terms now, post-9/11—have become multiple.

The list of questions is suggestive rather than exhaustive. This study will address to greater or lesser degrees each of these questions. Moreover it will look to theologians of the past and present to see how they have addressed some of these questions: for example, how Augustine (354–430) understood the Spirit as the bond of love in the triune Godhead; and how Calvin saw the Spirit's role as integral to our belief in the authority of Scripture; and how Moltmann (1926–), with his strong accent on the Spirit's relation to creation, understands the Holy Spirit as "the Spirit of Life."

However, systematically addressing such questions does raise a problem when it comes to the biblical testimony.

A PROBLEM TO FACE

Scripture is not systematic in its form in the way that traditional Western theology is. Scripture is like a garden richly filled with many plant varieties: trees, shrubs, cacti, flowers, and even reports of weeds. The reader of Scripture is not presented with books—or a canon, for that matter—dealing with the standard theological topics in neat order. Put another way, Scripture is not organized like Peter Lombard's *Sentences* or Aquinas's *Summa Theologica* or Calvin's *Institutes* or Barth's *Church Dogmatics* or Louis Berkhof's *Systematic Theology.* Story or narrative is a feature of Scripture: the story of creation, the story of the fall, the story of Abraham, the story of Israel, the story of the one God who is Father, Son, and Holy Spirit.

The challenge facing the systematician is to do his or her theology in an organized way that does not drain Scripture of its narrative color. This problem especially needs addressing when at issue is the discussion of the personal nature of the triune God in general or of one Person of the Godhead in particular. Otherwise a book on the doctrine of the Holy Spirit—the present task—risks becoming a mere collection of words, propositions, arguments, and conceptual gymnastics. All of these elements will feature in this work. But if only *they* feature then something is missing: namely, the drama of redemption and how the Spirit plays his role in the Trinity's reclamation of creation. J. S. Whale captured the problem vividly when he wrote of the doctrine of the atonement:

> Instead of putting off our shoes from our feet because the place whereon we stand is holy ground, we are taking nice photographs of the burning bush, from suitable angles: we are chatting about theories of the atonement [and I would add, chatting about interpretations of Pentecost] with our feet on the mantelpiece instead of kneeling down before the wounds of Christ [and I would add, without recognizing that the Spirit is here].[23]

23. J. S. Whale, *Christian Doctrine* (London and Glasgow: Fontana, 1958), 146.

According to Whale, we need a "living synthesis where those very facts [of doctrine], which the intellect dissects and coldly examines, are given back to us with the wholeness which belongs to life." But how can such a synthesis be achieved?

Two things are required to achieve the synthesis. First, the narrative nature of Scripture will need to be given its due weight. This study will need to rehearse the stories of the Spirit in the Scriptures and reflect on them as well as examine the didactic portions of Scripture that thematize the Spirit. Second, both the writer will need to write and the reader will need to read intentionally *coram Deo* (before God). Augustine knew this latter need. In terms of genre, Augustine's famous *Confessions* is in the form of a prayer, as is Anselm's *Proslogion*. Though this study will not be in prayer form it will presuppose the practice of prayer or paying attention to God, as Simone Weil has taught us.[24] After all, as the early church theologian Evagrius Pontus (346–399) observed, "If you are a theologian, you truly pray. If you truly pray, you are a theologian."[25]

THE SHAPE OF THE STUDY

In the first part of the book the mystery of the Spirit is addressed. As Daniel L. Migliore observes with regard to theology in general, "Christian theology begins, continues and ends with the inexhaustible mystery of God."[26] And as Richard B. Gaffin Jr. wisely suggests with regard to the Holy Spirit in particular, "Any sound theology of the Holy Spirit . . . will be left with a certain remainder, a surplus unaccounted for, an area of mystery."[27] More recently, Gordon Fee has described Paul's characterization of the Spirit as "God's empowering presence."[28] There is merit in Fee's expression and in his recognition of "the dynamic and experienced nature of the life of the Spirit."[29] In his view that experience at the beginning of the Christian's life was lost early on in the history of the church, to its hurt. Spontaneity gave way to performance.[30] The events that occurred on the first Pentecost after the resurrection of Christ provide a case in point. The Spirit's outpouring on that day was a dramatic and dynamic experience. But in his encounter

24. Simone Weil, *Waiting on God,* trans. Emma Craufurd (London: Routledge & Kegan Paul, 1951), 51.

25. Quoted in Bernard McGinn and Patricia Ferris McGinn, *Early Christian Mystics: The Divine Vision of the Spiritual Masters* (New York: Crossroad, 2003), 55.

26. Daniel L. Migliore, *Faith Seeking Understanding: An Introduction to Christian Theology,* 2nd ed. (Grand Rapids, Mich., and Cambridge: Eerdmans, 2004), 64.

27. Richard B. Gaffin Jr., *Perspectives on Pentecost: New Testament Teaching on the Gifts of the Holy Spirit* (Phillipsburg, N.J.: Presbyterian & Reformed, 1980), 25.

28. Gordon D. Fee, *God's Empowering Presence: The Holy Spirit in the Letters of Paul* (Peabody, Mass.: Hendrickson, 2005).

29. Ibid., 899–900.

30. Ibid.

with Nicodemus in the Fourth Gospel Jesus taught that the Spirit was like the wind (John 3:8). The wind is a mystery. It blows where it wills. It can be overwhelming as a storm wind (Ex. 14:21) or gentle as a breeze. Paul on the Damascus Road experienced the storm wind (Acts 9:1–19). Timothy, who grew up in the faith, may have experienced the breeze (2 Tim. 1:5; 3:14–15). As John Wesley wrote in his letter to Mary Cooke, "There is an irreconcilable variability in the operations of the Holy Spirit on the souls of men."[31] According to Wesley, "[m]any find Him rushing upon them like a torrent" while in Mary herself the Spirit's work had been "gentle." There is an epistemological elusiveness about the Spirit that this part of the study examines. An excursus looks at some of the ambiguities in the biblical text with regard to the Spirit. The issue is whether the issue in a given text is a reference to the Holy Spirit or to the human spirit or to the inanimate wind. Psalm 51, which has four references to "Spirit" or "spirit" (*rûach*), will provide the case in point. In this part of the discussion we also examine the personhood of the Spirit, the deity of the Spirit, the Spirit's relation to the triune Godhead. In addition, the question of our language about the Spirit and gender issues will be among those discussed. In particular, we will pursue the question of whether the Spirit should be spoken of as "he" or, as some are suggesting, "she." Another excursus will treat the debated question of whether the order (*taxis*) within the Trinity between Father, Son, and Holy Spirit is paradigmatic in some way for Christians' behavior today.

In the second part we turn our attention from the person of the Spirit to the ministry or the work of the Spirit in the OT presentation. In so doing we will be following the scholastic principle of *operari sequitur esse* ("operation follows being").[32] Or put another way, what we say of the work of the Spirit needs to be predicated on what can be said of the person of the Spirit.[33] Themes covered include: the Spirit and creation as the "Lord of

31. John Wesley, "Letter to Mary Cooke," in Robert W. Burtner and Robert E. Chiles, eds., *A Compend of Wesley's Theology* (New York and Nashville: Abingdon, 1954), 94. The letter is dated October 30, 1785.

32. See Thomas A. Smail, *The Forgotten Father: Rediscovering the Heart of the Christian Gospel* (London, Sydney, Auckland, and Toronto: Hodder & Stoughton, 1987), 96. Smail applies the principle to his discussion of Christology. However, the same principle usefully applies *mutatis mutandis* to a discussion of pneumatology. Stanley Grenz takes the opposite approach in his "The Holy Spirit: Divine Love Guiding Us Home," *Ex Auditu* 12 (1996): 1–13. He discusses "The Spirit in Salvation History" before "The Spirit in Trinitarian Life," arguing that, "We *must* retrace the steps the biblical people followed which eventually led to the trinitarian pneumatology of the Christian church" (ibid., 2, emphasis mine). "Must" is too strong.

33. Boyd Hunt appears critical of this approach (*Redeemed! Eschatological Redemption and the Kingdom of God* [Nashville: Broadman & Holman, 1993], 19). He calls it "standard Pneumatology," which, he maintains, is "too individualistic," "too subjective," and omits the discussion of the Spirit in a kingdom context. However, his complaint is not so much about the standard structure of first the person and then the work. Rather, his problem is that the work is construed too narrowly and without placement in the broad eschatological purposes of God. This study hopes to avoid the trap.

life"; the Spirit's role in making God known through revelation; the Spirit's role in the institutional life of God's OT people Israel; and the Spirit's part in the messianic hopes of Israel. In this part we will also begin to explore the biblical vocabulary for and symbols of the Holy Spirit (*passim*). An excursus will address the much debated question of whether OT believers were regenerated by the Spirit.

Part 3 continues the study of the Spirit's ministry, this time looking at the NT testimony. The Spirit's role in empowering the Messiah of Israel and then the Messiah's role in bestowing the Spirit upon God's NT people will be discussed. Next the Spirit's role in the corporate life of God's people will be examined. Here our themes, among others, will include Pentecost revisited, the making of God's children, the baptism and fullness of the Spirit, the Spirit's relation to water baptism and the Lord's Supper, the gifts of the Spirit given to the body of Christ, and the future of the church and cosmos in the light of pneumatology. Some readers may note at this point what may seem to be a strange omission. In this study there is no separate chapter on the Spirit and the Christian. Instead when the role of the Spirit in the life of the church is explored, so too will be the implications for the individual believer. The reasons for such an approach are to be found in the chapter itself. But to anticipate: since the rise of modern individualism it comes as so natural in the West to think first of the atom and next, if at all, of the molecule. Or put another way, we concern ourselves with the one and next, if at all, with the many. However, as we shall see, the accent in the scriptural revelation is otherwise. God is making a people for his name.[34] Finally, in the last chapter in this part, the question of revelation will again be raised as the Spirit's role in the inspiration and illumination of the Scriptures is canvassed. This chapter concerns the Spirit and our knowing God. This discussion could have come earlier. Indeed, it could have constituted the very first chapter. However, I have elected to place it last in the part dealing with the Spirit's ministry in NT perspective. My chief reason for doing so lies in the fact that the NT reveals so much more about the Spirit's role in epistemology than does the OT, especially Jesus' teaching about the ministry of the Spirit as the Paraclete in John 14–16 and Paul's teaching on the Spirit as the searcher of the depths in 1 Corinthians 2:6–16.

The third part also considers matters concerning the manifestation of the Spirit in today's world. The discussion of these practical questions and issues will flow out of the relevant NT material. Debated questions that will be addressed include the important—because so pastorally freighted—matter of blasphemy against the Spirit as well as whether the gifts of NT times

---

34. On the Spirit and the Christian see the excellent work in this series by Bruce Demarest, *The Cross and Salvation: The Doctrine of Salvation* (Wheaton, Ill.: Crossway, 1997). In his work Demarest lucidly covers such theological themes in the *ordo salutis* (order of salvation) as salvation, grace, election, calling, conversion, regeneration, union, sanctification, preservation and perseverance, and glorification, with appropriate references to the Spirit.

such as tongues and prophecy are available today, and whether there is more than one Spirit-reception to be experienced subsequent to conversion. Also examined are the increasing claims that theology now needs to start from the third article of the creed: namely, the person and work of the Spirit. In so doing some maintain that whatever is good, true, and beautiful in the religions of the world can be cited as the Holy Spirit's present manifestation. Such controversial issues raise urgent criteriological questions concerning spiritual discernment.

At the end of each chapter in each part there will be a section dealing with implications for belief and behavior arising from the immediately preceding discussion and in some instances an excursus dealing at more length with one of the debated questions mentioned previously. Theology must not be left unapplied. There is always the temptation in formal theology merely to lay out the conceptual geography of the key ideas with the appropriate definitions and logical linkages shown. However, as Karl Barth (1886–1968) wisely wrote, ". . . we must not present the being and work, Word and Spirit of God as an hypothesis which, even with great majesty and glory, simply hovers over the mind and heart and life of man like a radiant ball of glass or soap-bubble, but never leads to the result that something happens."[35] The Spirit is real and no mere idea. His reality calls for the appropriate understanding, attitudes, and actions on our part.

Drawing out theological implications from the scriptural testimony must be done in a responsible way. Bernard Ramm helpfully argues that, "Theological exegesis extends grammatical exegesis in that theological exegesis is interested in the largest implications of the text."[36] And yet a caveat is needed:

> Propositions imply other propositions. In formal systems (logic, mathematics, geometry), the process of drawing propositions from other propositions is strictly controlled. In material systems (science, history, psychology, etc.), the implications of a proposition are not always obvious and the verification of a proposition may be very difficult. The Bible as a literary and historical document does not belong to the formal but to the material. Therefore deducing propositions from Scripture faces all of the problems typical of deducing propositions in a material system.[37]

As we endeavor to draw out the implications of the scriptural text we will keep Ramm's caveat in mind.

35. Karl Barth, CD, IV, 3, 498.
36. Bernard Ramm, "Biblical Interpretation," in Bernard Ramm et al., Hermeneutics (Grand Rapids, Mich.: Baker, 1974), 28.
37. Ibid. Ramm's point is easily illustrated. In a formal system, if A is greater than B, and if B is greater than C, then it follows indubitably that A is greater than C. But, materially speaking, if X is Y's husband, then X is male by definition, but it is only highly probable that X is over eighteen years of age. It is possible that the husband had parental permission to marry earlier than the customary age.

Finally, the whole argument of the study under the broad heads of the mystery and ministry of the Spirit will be summarized by way of conclusion. In the conclusion the magnificence of the self-effacing Spirit comes into prominence. In particular the Spirit as the searcher of the depths of God, as the bond within the Godhead, as the executor of the divine purposes, and as the perfecter of those purposes will come to the fore. The Holy Spirit of God is the glorifier of others. A glossary rounds out the work to help the reader to navigate some of the technical language of the discussion.

How to Use This Study

Since the study falls into four parts, several reading strategies are possible for a work of this kind. One might read from beginning to end. The logic of the work is more easily seen this way: first the person of the Spirit theologically considered and then the work of the Spirit biblically revealed. The questions and issues in contemporary Christian thought and practice, that arise from the NT's presentation of the work of the Spirit, will figure prominently. Or one may turn first to the discussion of the biblical evidence concerning the Spirit in either OT or NT. Again, the contemporary scene may be the driver and so the last part of each chapter on the person or the work of the Spirit in either Old or New Testament perspective which deals, by way of application, with contemporary matters, may be the place to go. Or the reader might turn first to the debated questions and controversial issues found in the excurses, before exploring other parts. Or one might start at the end with the conclusion and then read the rest to explore in detail the path that led there.

Whichever reading strategy is adopted, the witness of Christian song also needs to be heard at the start of this venture. For the best of our songs arise from the life of God's people with their God. Bianco da Siena's (d. A.D. 1434) great pneumatological hymn is no exception. It is redolent with biblical allusions and expresses a desire that any serious reader of Scripture needs to foster:

> Come down, O Love divine,
> Seek Thou this soul of mine,
> And visit it with Thine own ardor glowing.
> O Comforter, draw near,
> Within my heart appear,
> And kindle it, Thy Holy flame bestowing.
>
> O let it freely burn,
> Till earthly passions turn
> To dust and ashes in its heat consuming;
> And let Thy glorious light
> Shine ever on my sight,
> And clothe me round, the while my path illuming.

Let holy charity
Mine outward vesture be,
And lowliness become mine inner clothing;
True lowliness of heart,
Which takes the humbler part,
And o'er its own shortcomings weeps with loathing.

And so the yearning strong,
With which the soul will long,
Shall far outpass the power of human telling;
For none shall guess its grace,
Till he become the place
Wherein the Holy Spirit makes His dwelling.[38]

May this become our prayer in the course of this study.

38. Bianco da Siena, *Anglican Hymn Book,* trans. R. F. Littledale (London: Church Book Room Press, 1965), Hymn 214.

I

THE MYSTERY

OF THE SPIRIT

TWO

THE ELUSIVENESS OF THE SPIRIT

In his celebrated encounter with Nicodemus, Jesus makes a crucial point about the elusiveness of the Spirit (John 3:3–8).[1] Jesus said that the Spirit's action is like that of the wind. The movements of the wind have a *mystery* to them. You can't tell where the wind comes from or where it is going.[2] Likewise the Spirit. Indeed the Spirit blows where he wills. No one is master of the Spirit. As John Goldingay points out with regard to both Old and New Testaments, "Wind suggests something of the mysterious, invisible, dynamic power of God."[3] Nicodemus should have known such things, according to Jesus (John 3:10). After all he was a teacher of Israel, a learned Pharisee and community leader. He presumably knew his Scriptures. Perhaps Jesus had in mind that scene in Ezekiel where the valley of dry bones comes alive through the mighty wind of God blowing through it (Ezekiel 37). A whole people needed to be born again. But all Jesus' talk of being born from above or again had passed Nicodemus by. He simply did not get the thrust of the metaphor and was thinking in crass, all too

---

1. An evangelical—albeit controversially so—theologian who has recognized the elusiveness of the Spirit is Clark H. Pinnock in his *Flame of Love: A Theology of the Holy Spirit* (Downers Grove, Ill.: InterVarsity Press, 1996), 9. Michael Welker also acknowledges the elusive nature of the Spirit's identity in "The Holy Spirit," *Theology Today* 46 no. 1 (April 1989): 5.

2. Michael Welker describes the Holy Spirit as a "public person" in his *God the Spirit*, trans. John F. Hoffmeyer (Minneapolis: Fortress, 1994), esp. 312–315. How this characterization squares with Jesus' words about the Spirit's mysterious wind-like movements and whom the world neither receives (*labein*) nor sees (*theōrei*) nor knows (*ginōskei*) is not clear (cf. John 3:8 and 14:17).

3. John Goldingay, "Was the Holy Spirit Active in Old Testament Times? What Was New about the Christian Experience of God?" *Ex Auditu* 12 (1996): 15. He cites John 3:8 as evidence for the way in which the term "wind" can be used to "safeguard God's mystery" (18).

literal categories. How could man enter his mother's womb and be born a second time (John 3:4)? It made no sense.

Jesus' words are salutary. Anyone writing about God in general and the Spirit of God in particular needs to reckon with mystery.[4] As George S. Hendry suggests, "The true doctrine of the Holy Spirit will always be one that recognizes the inherent subtlety and complexity of the subject and is most conscious of its inadequacy to grasp the mystery after which it gropes."[5] Back in the nineteenth century Sir Leslie Stephen was able to criticize some of the theologians of his day for discussing God as Trinity as though they could define ". . . the nature of God Almighty with an accuracy from which modest naturalists would shrink in describing the genesis of a black beetle."[6] Of course, the hopefully dead beetle was a mere object and therefore legitimately subject to human manipulation and control. However, the living God—and the Spirit of the living God—is always subject, never object in the sense that we can manipulate or control deity. God is God, and we are not. Christians don't practice magic.

Bernard Ramm was aware of the difficulty of writing about the Spirit when he commented,

> To profess to know a great deal about the Spirit of God is contrary to the nature of the Spirit of God. There is a hiddenness to the Spirit that cannot be uncovered. There is an immediacy of the Spirit that cannot be shoved into vision. There is an invisibility of the Spirit that cannot be forced into visibility. There is a reticence of the Spirit that cannot be converted into openness. For these reasons one feels helpless, inadequate, and unworthy to write a line about the Spirit.[7]

Bernard Ramm is one evangelical theologian to whom Sir Leslie Stephen's strictures don't apply.

This work will be filled with analyses and syntheses, but the mystery will remain. But just what is *mystery* as a theological category, and is it a valid one?

4. The classic work on the mysterious nature of God or the sacred in general is that of Rudolf Otto, *The Idea of the Holy: An Inquiry into the Non-Rational Factor in the Idea of the Divine and Its Relation to the Rational,* trans. John W. Harvey, 2nd ed. (London, Oxford, and New York: Oxford University Press, 1981). Otto famously wrote of the sacred as the *mysterium tremendum et fascinans.*

5. George S. Hendry, *The Holy Spirit in Christian Theology* (Philadelphia: Westminster, 1956), 11–12.

6. See Leslie Stephen, *An Agnostic's Apology and Other Essays* (New York and London: G. P. Putnam's Sons and Smith, Elder, 1893), 5.

7. Bernard Ramm, *Rapping about the Spirit* (Waco, Tex.: Word, 1974), 7. On the matter of the difficulties in studying the Holy Spirit see also Millard J. Erickson, *Christian Theology,* unabridged, one-volume ed. (Grand Rapids, Mich.: Baker, 1993), 846–848.

Mysteries, Puzzles, Riddles, and Problems

To begin with, some conceptual brush clearing is in order. A *mystery* is not a puzzle.[8] A jigsaw puzzle may be solved by putting the various pieces together in a way that a coherent picture appears and no piece is left over or is out of place. At last, Mount Rushmore comes clearly into view. Puzzles can be solved. Once the solution is found, we move on. Detective *mysteries* are really detective puzzles. The reader of the novel would be desperately disappointed if at the end of the book the murderer's identity were still unknown—if it wasn't the butler, then who?—or if there had not been sufficient clues along the way—the footprint with the distinctive sole and the bloodstained scarf, don't they mean something?—to make the final identification of the murderer plausible. In other words, as with a jigsaw puzzle, all the pieces (clues) have been put together in a coherent way and the murderer comes clearly into view. A mystery is not a riddle either. Riddles may find an answer. Riddles are usually found expressed in words that require some lateral thinking and knowledge to unravel. Samson's riddle about the honey and lion is a biblical example (Judg. 14:10–18). Nor is a mystery a problem. There are problems in math. Fermat's last theorem was eventually solved by British mathematician Andrew Wiles after some four hundred years.[9] However, when I employ the category of mystery it is not to be confused with either puzzles, problems, or riddles. One final clarification: nor am I using mystery in that NT sense of an open secret (Gk. *mustērion*). In that sense, what was formerly unrevealed now stands on display. A prominent Pauline example is the mystery that Jews and Gentiles are joint heirs of the promises of God, as the gospel now reveals.[10]

Mystery as I am using the term is an epistemological claim about an ontological reality. It is an expression of epistemic humility rather than of epistemic arrogance. God has spoken. God has made his name known—that is, his very nature, truly if not exhaustively. But the more one considers the revelation of God, the more there is to know and the more one knows how little one knows, and yet what is increasingly known throws light on other realities (nature, history, and humankind). British Anglo-Catholic theologian E. L. Mascall put it so well that an extensive quote is appropriate:

---

8. Many philosophers, theologians, and apologists have pointed out the conceptual differences between mysteries, puzzles, problems, and riddles, including Gabriel Marcel, Eric L. Mascall, Michael Foster, and Norman Geisler. The classic work on mystery is Gabriel Marcel's Gifford Lectures, *The Mystery of Being, I: Reflection and Mystery* (London: Harvill, 1950), 204–219.

9. Peter Tallack, ed., *The Science Book* (London: Weidenfeld & Nicolson, 2001), 506.

10. William J. Dumbrell, *The Search for Order: Biblical Eschatology in Focus* (Eugene, Ore.: Wipf & Stock, 2001), 297–298. See also H. H. D. Williams III, "Mystery," *NDBT*, 674–675.

> There are in fact three features which belong to a mystery. . . [i]n the first place, on being confronted with a mystery we are conscious that the small central area of which we have a relatively clear vision shades off into a vast background which is obscure and as yet unpenetrated. Secondly, we find, as we attempt to penetrate this background . . . that the range and clarity of our vision progressively increase but at the same time the background which is obscure and unpenetrated is seen to be far greater than we had recognised before. . . . The third feature of a mystery to which I want to draw attention is the fact that a mystery, while it remains obscure in itself, has a remarkable capacity of illuminating other things.[11]

Descartes in his *Meditations* may have pursued clear and distinct ideas as the key to philosophical rigor. But the theologian knows that the living God of biblical attestation is no mere idea, and even some philosophers have recognized the legitimate place of mystery in human thought.[12]

Biblical Perspectives

More to the point, to fail to reckon with *mystery* is a failure to reckon with the actual content of biblical revelation. In the Torah the climactic scene in Exodus 33–34 is instructive here. Moses wanted to see God's glory (*kābōd*). He wanted to view the divine splendor (Ex. 33:18). But to do so God put him in the cleft of the rock (v. 22). God had to cover him, and what Moses saw on that occasion was the back, not the face, of God (v. 23). The glory of God consisted of his goodness, and that goodness was clustered in a number of properties, or as the rabbis termed it, "measures" (the *middoth*). And so Moses heard the proclamation of God's mercy, grace, slowness to get angry, steadfast love and faithfulness, and yet this God was not a God who would condone evil (34:6–7). The gracious and merciful God is also the judge of his people. Forgiveness, yes, but also judgment. In fact God's dealings with his people in the Torah from this point on—and also before—exhibit in story after story each of these characteristics (for example, see Num. 21:4–9 and the bronze serpent incident as representative).

The last book of the Torah gives us Moses' rehearsal of the Torah a second time as Israel stood gathered on the plains of Moab. His address climaxes with the claim that the secret things belong to the Lord but the things that have been revealed have been revealed with a practical purpose in mind: namely, the doing of all the works of the Law (Deut. 29:29). The

---

11. E. L. Mascall, *Words and Images: A Study in Theological Discourse* (London, New York, Toronto: Longman, Green, 1957), 79. Mascall also notes the "peculiar elusiveness about the Spirit" in his *The Triune God: An Ecumenical Study* (Eugene, Ore.: Pickwick, 1986), 34.

12. Michael Foster, *Mystery and Philosophy* (London: SCM, 1957), 13–28. Likewise an apologist such as Norman Geisler: see his article on "mystery" in his *Baker Encyclopedia of Christian Apologetics* (Grand Rapids, Mich.: Baker, 2000), 515.

great desideratum in biblical religion as positively presented in the OT is not contemplation, as though reason were the essence of humanity. Rather the great accent falls on praxis. God is to be believed and obeyed. Moses is not Plato with a Hebrew voice.

The Prophets likewise contribute to the epistemic picture. Isaiah tells of God whose thoughts are not our thoughts and whose ways are not our ways. A spatial image is employed to reinforce the point. The phenomenology is clear. As any one of us may observe, the heavens are higher than the earth; likewise are God's ways and thoughts when compared to our own (Isa. 55:8–9). Indeed earlier in the book when Yahweh makes his glory present in the temple, the prophet is completely undone (Isa. 6:5). Outside of Eden, the revelation of the glory of God overwhelms. Moses was protected in the cleft of the rock. Isaiah was undone by the experience and needed divine restoration—the live coal to his lips (v. 6).

In the Writings—the last great division of the Hebrew Bible—the mystery of God is also affirmed. Psalm 97 presents the Lord as king. He reigns (v. 1). He is surrounded by thick clouds and darkness (v. 2). These metaphors speak of the incomprehensibility of God. He stands in marked contrast to idols (v. 7). The real God is the exalted one in whom Israel can rejoice (vv. 9–12). J. I. Packer wisely comments,

> Theology states this [the greatness of God] by describing him as incomprehensible—not in the sense that logic is somehow different from what it is for us, so that we cannot follow the working of his mind at all, but in the sense that we can never understand him fully, just because he is infinite and we are finite.[13]

As Packer helpfully goes on to point out, John Calvin knew this important truth about the incomprehensibility of God when he famously used the idea of God's stooping down to accommodate his revelation to our epistemic needs as finite creatures.[14]

Upholding the mystery of God or the incomprehensibility of God should keep idolatry at bay. As Calvin in his classic *Institutes of the Christian Religion* averred, "man's nature, so to speak, is a perpetual factory of idols."[15] Fallen humankind is drawn to gods made with our own hands

13. J. I. Packer, *Concise Theology: A Guide to Historic Christian Beliefs* (Australia, Singapore, and England: Anzea, Campus Crusade Asia, and Inter-Varsity, 1993), 51. Elsewhere Packer writes: ". . . it needs to be stated that a dimension of *mystery* is inescapable and must be acknowledged whenever we set ourselves to think about God" ("Is Systematic Theology a Mirage? An Introductory Discussion," in John D. Woodbridge and Thomas Edward McComiskey, eds., *Doing Theology in Today's World: Essays in Honor of Kenneth S. Kantzer* [Grand Rapids, Mich.: Zondervan, 1991], 29–30, emphasis original).

14. Packer, *Concise Theology,* 52.

15. John Calvin, *Institutes of the Christian Religion,* ed. John T. McNeill, trans. Ford Lewis Battles, vol. 1 (Philadelphia: Westminster, 1977), I.11.8 (108).

and which we control. But such idols are impotent, as both the Prophets and the Writings assert (see, for example, Jer. 10:1–16 and Ps. 115:4–8, respectively). The God of biblical depiction is untamable. There is no one like him (e.g., Ex. 15:11).[16]

The NT Scriptures do not change the picture. Jesus walked the earth in what theologians describe as the state of humiliation rather than glory. In terms of the Isaianic prophecy of the servant of the Lord, "he had no form or majesty that we should look at him, and no beauty that we should desire him" (Isa. 53:2). Jesus spoke with authority and acted with authority (Matt. 7:28–29 and Mark 2:12, respectively). But in appearance—phenomenologically speaking—he was another one of us. However, when the incarnate Son of God was transfigured on the mountain, the disciples were overwhelmed by the glory so revealed (Mark 9:1–13). The experience made them afraid in his presence. After the resurrection, when Jesus returned to his glory, he marvelously took our humanity with him (cf. John 17:5; Phil. 2:8–11; and Heb. 2:10–18). Of course, at one level, so much more now is revealed about God's will and ways (Heb. 1:1–2). We do have "the light of the knowledge of the glory of God in the face of Jesus Christ" (2 Cor. 4:6). Even so, the apostle Paul maintains that God's ways are inscrutable and his judgments are unsearchable (Rom. 11:33). He argues that we "know in part" and "we see in a mirror dimly" (1 Cor. 13:12). In fact, he tells the Galatians that it is not so much that we know God as it is that God knows us (Gal. 4:9). Seeing God face-to-face is the great eschatological prospect. It is the substance of the Christian's hope (cf. 1 Cor. 13:12 and 1 John 3:1–3). But to do so requires nothing less than the ontological transformation of the believer. As for the Holy Spirit, we have already noted at the outset of this chapter how Jesus compared the movement of the Spirit to the mysterious movement of the wind (John 3:8).

In sum: the mystery of God stems from his transcendence as the Creator, his invisibility, his hiddenness, and his incomprehensibility.[17] The glory of the gospel is that this God—the only God there is—has chosen to make himself known. *Deus absconditus* has chosen to become *Deus revelatus*.[18]

16. A recent major theological contribution (which is part of this series) that takes the biblical theme of the uniqueness of God as its identifying motif is John S. Feinberg, *No One Like Him: The Doctrine of God* (Wheaton, Ill.: Crossway, 2001).

17. Pascal maintained, "God being thus hidden, any religion that does not say that God is hidden is not true, and any religion which does not explain why does not instruct. Ours [i.e., the Christian religion] does all this. *Verily thou art God who hidest thyself*" (emphasis original). From the last sentence it is clear that Pascal's insight was biblically based (Isa. 45:15) (see Blaise Pascal, *Pensées*, trans. A. J. Krailsheimer [Harmondsworth, Middlesex: Penguin, 1972], 103).

18. For this distinction—so important in Luther's theology—see Richard A. Muller, *Dictionary of Latin and Greek Theological Terms: Drawn Principally from Protestant Scholastic Theology* (Grand Rapids, Mich.: Baker, 1985), 90.

Some Traditional Perspectives

It is a fundamental given in the Orthodox tradition that the triune God is *mystery*. The very first chapter in Orthodox theologian Kallistos Ware's classic book *The Orthodox Way* is entitled "God as Mystery."[19] In that chapter, he uses Rudolf Otto's celebrated expression that God is *mysterium tremendum*.[20] Ware suggests that the archetypal symbols of the spiritual way for Orthodoxy are Abraham and Moses. He writes, "Abraham journeys from his familiar home into an unknown country; Moses progresses from light into darkness."[21] He maintains that Moses had multiple successive visions of God in the book of Exodus which show the interplay of images of light and darkness:

> Moses receives three successive visions of God: first he sees God in a vision of light at the burning bush (Ex. 3:2); next God is revealed to him through mingled light and darkness, in the 'pillar of cloud and fire' which accompanies the people of Israel through the desert (Ex. 13:21); and then finally he meets God in a 'non-vision', when he speaks with him in the 'thick darkness' at the summit of Mount Sinai (Ex. 20:21).[22]

The essence of God's being is unknowably mysterious—hence the darkness motif—but his energies manifest the grace, life, and power which we may experience, and hence the motif of light.[23] According to Ware, our access to God is through his energies, as St. Athanasius and St. Basil taught.[24] Vladimir Lossky (1903–1958), perhaps the greatest Orthodox theologian of the twentieth century, writes:

> The distinction is between the essence of God, or His nature, properly so-called, which is inaccessible, unknowable and incommunicable; and the energies of divine operations, forces proper to and inseparable from God's essence, in which He goes forth from Himself, manifests, communicates, and gives Himself.[25]

19. Kallistos Ware, *The Orthodox Way* (London and Oxford: Mowbray, 1981), 12.

20. Ibid., 16; cf. Otto, *Idea of the Holy.*

21. Ibid., 15–16.

22. Ibid.

23. Ware's theological use of mystery is to be distinguished from the Orthodox use of mysteries to designate the sacraments, which he would also endorse. On the sacraments as mysteries in Orthodoxy see Demetrios J. Constantelos, *Understanding the Greek Orthodox Church: Its Faith, History, and Practice* (New York: Seabury, 1882), 35–36.

24. Ware, *Orthodox Way,* 27.

25. Vladimir Lossky, *The Mystical Theology of the Eastern Church* (Cambridge: Clark, 1944), quoted in Winfried Corduan, *Mysticism: An Evangelical Option?* (Grand Rapids, Mich.: Zondervan, 1991), 98–99. Corduan gives no page number for Lossky.

Untangling the skein of Platonic and biblical elements in the Orthodox approach to the mystery of God need not detain us at this point.[26]

God as mystery is fundamental to the Roman Catholic construal of the triune God. As the *Catechism of the Catholic Church* has it, "The mystery of the Most High Trinity is the central mystery of Christian Faith and Life. It is the mystery of God in himself."[27] The *Catechism* is also aware that, "Our human words always fall short of the mystery of God."[28] To give this theology a human face, let us consider Karl Rahner (1904–1984), a giant of Roman Catholic theology in the twentieth century. He was a key theological figure in the shaping of Vatican II in the 1960s.[29] Mystery plays an important role in his theology too. Indeed, one student of Rahner's thought, Bernard McCool, argues that mystery "is one of the principal structural elements in his [Rahner's] system."[30] According to Rahner the scholastic tradition, as quintessentially expressed in the theology of Vatican I, had an inadequate concept of mystery. In that tradition mystery has to do with those truths that are divinely revealed and which for us as pilgrims in this life are therefore accessible only to faith and not to reason (*ratio*).[31] That tradition maintained that in the beatific vision such mysteries (truths) as the Trinity, incarnation, and grace will be understood. But Rahner, in contradistinction, contends that even in the beatific vision as experienced by the believers in heaven God will remain the "primordial" mystery because of his intrinsic incomprehensibility as the infinite God and because of our creaturely limitations as finite beings.[32] For him, God is "absolute mystery" and "holy mystery."[33]

26. For an Orthodox attempt at such an untangling see Vladimir Lossky, *Orthodox Theology: An Introduction*, trans. Ian and Ihita Kesarcodi-Watson (Crestwood, N.Y.: St. Vladimir Seminary Press, 1978), prologue and chapter 1. See also Corduan's critique in *Mysticism*, 98–102, chapter 6.

27. CCC, part 1, section 2, chapter 1, paragraph 2, I, 234 (62). The eminent Roman Catholic theologian Avery Cardinal Dulles says of the *Catechism*: "As a reliable source of Catholic doctrine, the Catechism brings together the wisdom of the centuries in an appealing synthesis. By virtue of its consistency, beauty, and spiritual power it offers a veritable feast of faith" (in "The Challenge of the Catechism," *First Things* [January 1995]: 53). Given its official status, I will especially appeal to the *Catechism* for the Roman Catholic position on matters of doctrine.

28. Ibid., part 1, section 1, chapter 1, IV, 42 (17).

29. See Karen Kilby, "Rahner, Karl," in Adrian Hastings, Alister Mason, and Hugh Pyper, eds., *The Oxford Companion to Christian Thought* (Oxford: Oxford University Press, 2000), 591.

30. Bernard McCool, ed., *A Rahner Reader* (London: Darton, Longman & Todd, 1975), 118.

31. Karl Rahner, "Theological Investigations, Vol. 4," in McCool, ed., *Rahner Reader,* 109–120.

32. Ibid., 112.

33. Ibid., 119. Like Ware, Rahner understands that there is another historic use of "mystery" in theology, which is to refer to the specific mysteries of God as Trinity, the incarnation, and grace.

If Rahner was a towering figure in twentieth-century Roman Catholic thought, then Karl Barth was the towering figure in Protestant thought.[34] In Barth's early writings there was an "infinite qualitative distinction"—as Kierkegaard (1813–1855) had argued before him—between eternity and time, between God and humanity. God is "wholly other." Barth argued that, "The Gospel proclaims a God utterly distinct from humanity."[35] Only God can make God known, and he does so in Jesus Christ. George Hunsinger, in his rich discussion of Barth's theology entitled *How to Read Karl Barth,* maintains that Barth in contrast to other theologies, instead of adopting the language of experience and reason, embraced the language of mystery.[36] God's own freedom as God and his singularity are at the heart of the mystery. In fact Hunsinger argues that "[a] high tolerance for mystery is a hallmark of Barth's theology."[37] So Barth too held firmly to the mystery of God—albeit in his own distinctive way—from his early commentary on Romans of 1918 to his *The Humanity of God*. Although in the latter work, he signals a *"change of direction."*[38] Barth had come to recognize the need to balance the accent on the "wholly other" God with a concomitant one on God's *"togetherness with man."*[39]

The foregoing sampling of views should not be taken to suggest that there is universal agreement on the exact nature of the mysteriousness of God. Orthodoxy has its criticisms of Western theology, especially in its Roman Catholic expression. Barth had serious issues with Roman Catholicism. What is significant is the widespread sense, both past and present, that God cannot be domesticated and that there are limits to our conceptualizing God.

EVANGELICAL PERSPECTIVES

Evangelical theologians too have found the category of mystery an important one for preserving the sense of the otherness or transcendence of triune God. With regard to the Trinity, Bruce Milne comments, "Indeed if we did not encounter deep mystery in God's nature there would be every reason for suspicion concerning the Bible's claims."[40] Donald Bloesch likewise recog-

34. See Bruce L. McCormack, "Barth, Karl" in Hastings, Mason and Pyper, *Companion,* 64–67.

35. Karl Barth, *The Epistle to the Romans* (Oxford: Oxford University Press, 1933), 28–29, quoted in Alister McGrath, ed., *The Christian Theology Reader* (Oxford, and Cambridge, Mass.: Blackwell, 1995), 117.

36. George Hunsinger, *How to Read Karl Barth: The Shape of His Theology* (New York and Oxford: Oxford University Press, 1991), ix.

37. Ibid., 34.

38. Karl Barth, *The Humanity of God* (London: Collins, 1961), 37, emphasis original.

39. Ibid., 45, emphasis original.

40. Bruce Milne, *Know the Truth: A Handbook of Christian Belief* (London and Singapore: Inter-Varsity and S+U, 1983), 63.

nizes that the Trinity is a mystery: "The Trinity can be stated in paradoxical and symbolic language, but it cannot be resolved into a rational system."[41] Roger E. Olson adds his voice to this chorus with a caution, when he writes of the Trinity, ". . . we must know where to draw the line of peering into God's mysterious being."[42] Lastly, Carl F. H. Henry—so often accused of theological rationalism—could write of God, "Divine revelation does not completely erase God's transcendent mystery, inasmuch as God the Revealer transcends his own revelation."[43]

This recognition of mystery with regard to the Trinity per se is also in view when evangelical theologians have written about the Holy Spirit, as a brief history of some of their contributions will show.

In the seventeenth century, the great Puritan divine John Owen wrote in the preface to his magisterial work on "The Holy Spirit of God, and His Operations," "the things here treated of are in themselves mysterious and abstruse."[44] In the course of the Preface he refers to "the whole mystery of the Gospel" and "the mysteries of our religion."[45] But he allows no place for mindless religious enthusiasm nor for arid rationalism in the pursuit of theological understanding. Instead he relies on "the plain testimony of Scripture, the suffrage of the ancient Church, and the experience of believers."[46]

Dutch theologian and statesman Abraham Kuyper's (1837–1920) massive work on the Holy Spirit, published toward the end of the nineteenth century, strikes the note of mystery from the start. In the first chapter, entitled "Careful Treatment Required," he cautions concerning the Spirit,

> Of Him nothing appears in visible form; He never steps out from the intangible void. Hovering, undefined, incomprehensible, He remains a mystery. He is as the wind! We hear its sound, but can not tell whence it cometh and whither it goeth. Eye can not see Him, ear can not hear Him, much less the hand handle Him.[47]

41. Donald G. Bloesch, *God the Almighty: Power, Wisdom, Holiness, Love* (Downers Grove, Ill.: InterVarsity Press, 1995), 167. Bloesch entitles his chapter on the Trinity "The *Mystery* of the Trinity" (emphasis mine).

42. Roger E. Olson, *The Mosaic of Christian Belief: Twenty Centuries of Unity and Diversity* (Downers Grove, Ill., and Leicester, England: InterVarsity Press and Apollos, 2002), 151.

43. Carl F. H. Henry, *God, Revelation, and Authority,* 6 vols. (reprint Wheaton, Ill.: Crossway, 1999), 2:9. For a useful discussion of whether Henry was a rationalist or not, see Chad Owen Brand, "Is Carl Henry a Modernist? Rationalism and Foundationalism in Post-War Evangelical Theology," *The Southern Baptist Journal of Theology* 8 no. 4 (Winter 2004): 44–60.

44. John Owen, *The Holy Spirit, His Gifts and Power: Exposition of the Spirit's Name, Nature, Personality, Operations and Effects* (reprint, abridged, Grand Rapids, Mich.: Kregel, 1967), 9.

45. Ibid., 14, 15.

46. Ibid., 12.

47. Abraham Kuyper, *The Work of the Holy Spirit,* trans. Henri De Vries (Grand Rapids, Mich.: Eerdmans, 1975), 6.

Kuyper sees a great contrast between Christology and pneumatology on the question of visibility. The incarnate Son as human was visible like us. He could be seen, heard, and touched. A text like 1 John 1:1–3 backs Kuyper up on this point. But not so the Spirit, because "nothing lingers behind, not even the trace of a footprint."[48]

More recent evangelical theologians argue similarly. Bernard Ramm, who in his own work was heavily influenced by Kuyper's work on the Spirit, writes of the "mystery of the Spirit." No biological experiment will ever reveal the presence of the Spirit nor any psychological one detect the Spirit's "unequivocal action" on men and women.[49]

THE MYSTERY OF OURSELVES

Let's approach the question of mystery another way. Reflect for a moment on your own knowledge of yourself. How much do you really understand of your own nature? Philosophers have wrestled with the question of human nature for millennia and still there is no consensus—although these days the majority of Western philosophers favor some kind of materialist account. However, philosopher Colin McGinn represents a new, humbler position on the question of body and mind. He argues that as finite beings there are some questions that we will never know the answers to. The exact relation of body to mind is one of them. Hence his position has been described as "mysterian."[50] What makes his position a philosophical one rather than an expression of despair is that he has a theory about the limitations of reason to give it plausibility. He argues,

> Just as a dog cannot be expected to solve the problems about space and time and the speed of light that took a brain like Einstein to solve, so maybe the human species cannot be expected to understand how the universe contains matter and mind in combination. Isn't it really a preposterous overconfidence on our part to think that our species—so recent, so contingent, so limited in many ways—can nevertheless unlock every secret of the natural world?[51]

McGinn, writing as a secularist, shows a refreshing epistemic humility.[52] I would expand his last sentence to include "and every secret of the supernatural world." The secret things do indeed belong to the Lord.

48. Ibid.
49. Ramm, *Rapping about the Spirit*, 24.
50. Colin McGinn, *The Making of a Philosopher* (New York: Harper Collins, 2003), 183.
51. Ibid., 182.
52. For another philosopher who recognizes the challenge of accounting for consciousness on materialist premises see Jonathan Shear, "Mysticism and Scientific Naturalism," *Sophia* 43 no. 1 (May 2004): 85. Shear describes the challenge as "the hard problem."

If we are a mystery to ourselves and yet as research is done on body and brain more light is shed on ourselves, how much more should we be "mysterians" when it comes to the living God, maker of heaven and earth, the Holy Trinity? What God has made known concerning the divine name, will, and ways we know truly but not exhaustively. As for the Spirit, the mystery deepens. For as will be argued at a later stage, the Spirit points away from himself to another. Thus there is an elusiveness about the Spirit when thematized as the object of inquiry. The Spirit blows where he wills. He is a person in his own right. But what kind of person? We are persons, but just as the heavens are higher than the earth, is the Spirit's person-hood higher than our personhood? If so, how does the Spirit's personhood comport with that of the Father and the Son, or for that matter with God conceived of as a person? These are weighty questions to which we must turn in the next chapter. But before we do, two questions need to be faced and some practical implications of our study explored.

Some Important Questions

Does the Idea of God as Mysterious Demand a Christian Agnosticism?

The notions that we are fallen and finite and that God is exalted and infinite might suggest that the only appropriate epistemic attitude to the divine is a reverent agnosticism. We simply don't know what God is like. Moreover it may be argued that, when it comes to talking about God, our finite language is a broken instrument. The only possible way forward theologically is the negative way (*via negativa*). We can say what God is not rather than what God is. Even some who have entertained the idea of a special revelation from God have adopted such a stance. In the nineteenth century Dean Henry Mansel (1820–1871)—albeit with considerable debts to William Hamilton and Immanuel Kant—maintained that we cannot know God as he is.[53] Rather, what God has given us in special revelation is the least misleading way of speaking about him.[54] At first glance, this seems suitably humble. But the biblical accent on worshiping God both in Spirit—i.e., in keeping with his nature as Spirit, a subject that we shall return to at a later stage—and truth prohibits such pessimism (John 4:24). To affirm the incomprehensibility of God or God as mystery is not to claim that we cannot know what God is really like in character and ways. Instead it is a claim that God has made only so much known about himself but

53. Ninian Smart, *Historical Selections in the Philosophy of Religion* (London: SCM, 1962), 361.
54. Mansel's classic work is "The Limits of Religious Thought" (1858). See Smart, *Historical Selections in the Philosophy of Religion,* 362–377.

that what has been made known is really true in that it does correspond to who God is. Moreover even if the language we use to talk about God is finite, finite does not necessarily mean inadequate. After all, who made humanity's mouth (Ex. 4:10–12)?[55]

Diogenes Allen appreciates both the importance of epistemic humility and yet confidence in God's revelation. He writes,

> One need not feel threatened by the necessary limitations in our knowledge of God. It does not mean that we are totally in the dark. For even with created things, we can understand a great deal without full comprehension of them. We can see a lot by means of light and know many of its properties without being able fully to comprehend *what* light is. It has both particle and wave properties, and yet nothing can be both a wave and a particle. And so we do not know precisely what it is, and yet we are not without reliable knowledge about some of its paradoxical properties. So too with God, who is in principle beyond a creature's full comprehension. We may see by the "light" God has given us and have quite reliable knowledge about God, without a full comprehension of the divine nature.[56]

What Allen argues with regard to God he also argues with regard to creatures other than ourselves. As Thomas Nagel famously argued, we can know a great deal about bats but not what it is to be a bat.[57] Likewise we can know a great deal about God, if God chooses to make himself known, but we will never know what it is like to be God. Wonderfully, however, given the incarnation, God knows what it is to be human.

Be that as it may, a caveat is in order. In his critique of Stephen Davis's treatment of the Trinity, Millard Erickson outlines Davis's use of the category of mystery in his discussion of the nature of God, then adds a reservation. Has Davis opted too prematurely for the category of mystery? Erickson asks of Davis, "Even if we cannot understand God fully, have we yet understood

---

55. My own view, which we will revisit in the next chapter when discussing the Trinity, is that given the doctrine of *imago dei,* and therefore our theomorphic character, there is nothing necessarily alien in human creaturely language when used of the Creator. In Christology, human personhood inheres in the divine personhood of the Son enhypostatically—as Leontius of Byzantium (d. A.D. 543) suggested—so there is only one Person and not two. On analogy, there may be nothing alien to the divine, in principle, with human language when used of its maker (e.g., Jesus' own prayer life). This is an enhypostatic understanding of religious language. For the concept of *enhypostasia* see Van A. Harvey, *A Handbook of Theological Terms* (New York: Simon & Schuster, 1997), 79. The Roman playwright Terence said famously: *"homo sum: humani nil a me alienum puto"* ("I am human, and nothing human is alien to me"). Given the doctrine of *imago dei* we might say *"imago dei sum. humani divinique nil alienum puto"* ("I am the image of God. Nothing divine is alien to me."). See Stanley L. Jaki, *A Mind's Matter: An Intellectual Autobiography* (Grand Rapids, Mich., and Cambridge: Eerdmans, 2002), viii-ix.

56. Diogenes Allen, *Philosophy for Understanding Theology* (London: SCM, 1985), 13, emphasis original.

57. See Rick Lewis, "A Ridiculously Brief Overview of Consciousness," *Philosophy Now* 48 (October/November 2004): 9; see also McGinn, *Making of a Philosopher,* 178–179.

all that might be understood?"[58] Those of us comfortable with employing the language of mystery with regard to the triune God in general and the Holy Spirit in particular need to hear that reservation lest we do less than justice to what God has actually made known in the biblical revelation.

Does the Idea of God as Mysterious Demand Mysticism?

Fundamental to mysticism is the idea of a direct knowledge of the One or God or the Holy or the Abyss. Characteristics of mystical experience include ineffability. The ultimately Real is beyond words. Such is its mysteriousness. We have seen that many traditions of Christianity conceive of God as a mysterious being. Historically some of those traditions have included numbers of mystics in their ranks. Examples abound, from Augustine to Evelyn Underhill. Does the idea of the God of biblical revelation as a mysterious deity demand a Christian mysticism?

Here definitions are crucial. If by mysticism is meant a monistic experience of oneness that abolishes the ontological distance between the human and the divine, then the biblical doctrine of creation is against it.[59] The Creator is never to be confused with the creature. Hence idolatry is foolishness to the biblical writers and subject to prophetic ridicule (Isaiah 44; 46; and Jeremiah 10). However, if mysticism is being used loosely to refer to extraordinary experiences of God's presence, then that is another matter. Such a claim acknowledges the ontological distance between God and what God has made. Strictly speaking such a claim is really a claim to numinous experience (i.e., an experience in which the subject-object distinction is preserved).

The biblical witness contains much of the numinous but little of the mystical in the technical sense of an ineffable experience. Isaiah 6 and the prophet's encounter with Yahweh in the temple is a numinous one. And the apostle Paul's being caught up into the third heaven, narrated in 2 Corinthians 12, allows no suggestion that the Creator-creature distinction was ever under threat of dissolution. But both experiences of God were extraordinary.

Are there versions of Christian mysticism that are consistent with evangelical faithfulness to the biblical revelatory deposit? Winfried Corduan argues so. He contends that there are many forms of mysticism that are incompatible with the biblical witness: pantheistic, world-denying dualisms, experience-displacing revelation, those that minimize sin and/or grace, and those that make mystical experience central.[60] On these grounds

---

58. Millard Erickson, *God in Three Persons* (Grand Rapids, Mich.: Baker, 1995), 258.

59. With regard to the Spirit and "mysticism of the classic type," see Hendry, *Holy Spirit in Christian Theology*, 41. He argues that there is no place in Christian spirituality for a mysticism "in which the frontiers of personal distinctness are blurred."

60. Corduan, *Mysticism*, 114–115.

he is critical of much that passes for putative Christian mysticism both in Orthodoxy and in Roman Catholicism. Even so he advocates a form of mysticism as an evangelical option because he maintains that it is in keeping with the NT. He concludes that, "There is mystical reality in the believer's relationship to the divine Trinity through adoption as God's child, a position 'in Christ,' and the indwelling of the Holy Spirit."[61] However, mystical experiences per se are not to be sought, nor does the NT present a "plan of asceticism or meditation to actualize this mystical reality."[62] Bruce Demarest writes that those in union with Christ practice "a true mysticism."[63] Such a mysticism has relational, moral, and epistemological elements. But he also contends that "Biblical Christians, however, never posit a *metaphysical* mysticism, where the individual allegedly melts into the Divine as a drop of water is absorbed into the ocean."[64] I would contend that the Scriptures don't demand the language of mysticism in any technical sense to do descriptive justice to its stories, whether of prophet or apostle, nor for us to understand its normative expectations of the godly life.

Does the Idea of Mystery Exclude Problem Solving?

Thomas Weinandy argues that there are two kinds of theology. There are theologies that articulate mystery. In contrast, however, there are theologies that attempt to solve problems. Older theologies had a proper sense of the mystery of the Creator. But new theologies, shaped by the eighteenth-century Enlightenment and the growing success of scientific problem solving, disastrously treat theology as a problem solving discipline. He contends, "However, the true goal of theological inquiry is not the resolution of theological *problems,* but the discernment of what the *mystery* of faith is."[65] In his view, ". . . theology by its nature is not a problem solving enterprise, but rather a mystery discerning enterprise."[66] Controversially he claims that history shows examples of how the problem solving approach generates heresy (e.g., Arianism).[67] But is this a genuine either/or? Marcel Sarot rightly judges that Weinandy's distinction is "overly

61. Ibid., 138.

62. Ibid.

63. Bruce Demarest, *The Cross and Salvation: The Doctrine of Salvation* (Wheaton, Ill.: Crossway, 1997), 340.

64. Ibid., 341, emphasis original.

65. Thomas Weinandy, *Does God Suffer?* (Notre Dame, Ind.: University of Notre Dame Press, 2000), 32, emphasis original.

66. Ibid.

67. Ibid., 33–35. Interestingly, although he sees the rise of science and the Enlightenment as the key factors in the rise of the problem solving approach, his example comes from the fourth century.

simplistic."[68] God is mysterious. But there are genuine problems thrown up by revelation that require clarification, and those clarifications need to be argued and therefore justified. For example, how can Scripture be the words of both David and the Holy Spirit, as in Hebrews (cf. Heb. 3:7 and 4:7)? Do we simply say "Mystery!" and be done with it? Or do we attempt to offer a plausible account of how such a joint action (double-agency) may be possible? The notion of faith seeking understanding, so important to Weinandy (and to the present writer), does not exclude either the appeal to mystery or the recognition of the problematic.[69] Of course, an appropriate epistemic humility is in order when the revelatory data run out and the speculative takes over. The secret things still belong to the Lord (Deut. 29:29).

Implications for Belief and Practice

Believing that God is mysterious in the sense of incomprehensible has a number of practical corollaries.

At the attitudinal level, humility is the appropriate virtue. In Pauline terms, we should not think more highly of ourselves than we ought to think (Rom. 12:3). Humility appreciates both the grandeur of God and our own contrasting limitations. We are finite creatures, limited in ways that God is not. We are also fallen creatures and as Christians are in the process of re-creation. As we shall see, the Spirit is integral to that re-creation. Mascall puts it well when he writes, ". . . a mystery is not itself a question demanding an answer, but an object inviting contemplation."[70] Such an object, he argues, requires ". . . an attitude of humble and wondering contemplation."[71] Anselm (1033–1109) exhibited that humility when he prayed, "I do not endeavour, O Lord, to penetrate thy sublimity, for in no wise do I compare my understanding with that; but I long to understand in some degree thy truth, which my heart believes and loves."[72]

68. Michael Sarot, "Does God Suffer? A Critical Discussion of Weinandy's *Does God Suffer?*" http://www.arsdisputandi.org/publish/articles/000018/article.htm, 3, accessed October 11, 2005.

69. A theologian who acknowledged the importance of addressing "quite fundamental problems," especially methodological ones, was Donald M. MacKinnon, *Themes in Theology: The Three-Fold Cord: Essays in Philosophy, Politics, and Theology* (Edinburgh: T. & T. Clark, 1987), 208.

70. Mascall, *Words and Images,* 78.

71. Ibid., 78. Evangelical theologian Norman Geisler contributes a slightly different nuance: "A problem has a *solution;* a mystery is the object of *meditation"* (*Baker Encyclopedia of Christian Apologetics,* 515, emphasis original).

72. Quoted in Nicholas Wolterstorff, "Analytical Philosophy of Religion: Retrospect and Prospect," in Tommi Lehtonen and Timo Koistinen, eds., *Perspectives in Contemporary Philosophy of Religion* (Helsinki: Luther-Agricola Society, 2000), 166. Wolterstorff does not supply

Again, if we take seriously Jesus' comparison of the Spirit's activity to that of the wind, then our expectations of definitive answers to some of our pneumatological questions need to be disciplined by that reality. Accordingly this work will at times point out the dogmatic rank of some of its claims concerning the Spirit. For example, as we shall see, there is ample biblical evidence for the Spirit's personhood. The personhood of the Spirit ought to be a nonnegotiable Christian conviction. However, the precise relation of the Spirit to the Father and the Son—which we shall also go on to explore anon—will take us into the area of Christian opinion (or more technically, *theologoumena*). Historically, some Christian traditions have disagreed strongly on this matter—especially Orthodoxy and Roman Catholicism. And theological reflection upon the role of the Spirit in the atonement will lead us into Christian speculation—not that much hangs on a theological speculation as long as it is clearly identified as such. There should be room in the house of evangelicalism for theological kites to fly and crash if need be. Theological opinion is more serious in that Christians may so strongly disagree that it may affect one's membership in a church. Denying the doctrine of consubstantiation and wanting full membership in a Lutheran church would be problematical. Christian convictions, however, are part of Christian identity, not merely Lutheran identity. To deny the goodness of God and to claim Christian identity is an oxymoron.

God is God and we are not. The primeval temptation—"you will be like God"—may remain in us in subtle ways, however. We can write of the Spirit of God as though we were in glory beholding God's face rather than living as we do outside of Eden in the groaning creation and as those "on whom the end of the ages has come" (cf. Genesis 3; Rom. 8:18–25; and 1 Cor. 10:11). To forget that we are to live in the light of the cross in a particular eschatological frame of reference is to risk indulging in what Luther called a theology of glory (*theologia gloriae*) as opposed to a theology of the cross (*theologia crucis*).[73] We can forget all too readily who we are, where we are, and when we are.

Various traditions of the Christian faith have recognized the *mystery* of God: Orthodoxy (e.g., Lossky and Ware), Roman Catholicism (e.g., Rahner and von Balthasar), and Protestantism (e.g., Barth). A similar recognition is featured in the evangelical tradition too (e.g., Kuyper, Ramm, Milne, Erickson, Packer, Pinnock, Ferguson, Feinberg, and Corduan). But tradition ought not to determine normative theology: namely, what we ought to believe and obey. The fact that the mystery of God—understood as the incomprehensibility of God—has firm biblical anchorage is the key.

---

the source. However, it is found in the last paragraph of Anselm's *Proslogion*, chapter 1. See http://www.ccel.org/ccel/anselm/basic_works.txt, accessed May 1, 2007.

73. On these important terms see Muller, *Dictionary of Latin and Greek Theological Terms*, 300 and 302.

EXCURSUS: THE ELUSIVE REFERENT

One of the challenges confronting the theologian who uses scriptural evidence to construct the doctrine of the Holy Spirit is the fluidity of meanings that attaches to the Hebrew term *rûach* and the Greek term *pneuma*. For example, it is one thing to learn that "The GK. root *pneu-*, from which the NT word for s/Spirit is derived, denotes dynamic movement of the air."[74] It is quite another to know at times precisely what the referent for *pneuma* is. A similar problem pertains to the use of *rûach* in the Hebrew Bible. The semantic field of possibilities includes, at the very least, the following: breath, wind, attitude, spirit (human), spirit (angelic or demonic), Spirit (divine), Spirit (Holy Spirit).

C. F. D. Moule presents the issue of translation in a most helpful way in his discussion of Psalm 51.[75] Psalm 51 has four references to *rûach*. Three of them are unproblematic: Psalm 51:10, 12 and 17. With regard to these verses, the ESV, NIV, NRSV, and JSB use lower case in translating "spirit." The human spirit is in view. But Psalm 51:11 is the challenge. Is this text referring to "your holy spirit" or "your Holy Spirit"? As Moule points out, neither the ancient Hebrews nor the Greeks used capitals the way English or German writers do. The NRSV and JSB employ lower case ("holy spirit") but the ESV and NIV use upper case ("Holy Spirit").[76] So in Psalm 51:11 is the text referring merely to the vigor and power of God, and thus the psalmist is praying to God that divine power and vigor may not be withdrawn? Or is the text speaking of God the Holy Spirit, and hence the need for capitals? The answer is not immediately obvious, and a theological judgment is called for which places the text in its context, in its epoch, and in the canon.[77]

The purpose of this excursus is not to decide the question but to highlight the challenge. If in the course of subsequent discussion a biblical text is appealed to that contains such an ambiguity, I will address the translation issue *in situ*.

---

74. E. Kamlah, "Pneuma," in *NIDNTT.*

75. C. F. D. Moule, *The Holy Spirit* (London and Oxford: Mowbrays, 1978), 7–21. Also helpful is Charles Sherlock, *God on the Inside: Trinitarian Spirituality* (Canberra: Acorn, 1991), 88–89. With regard to the difficulties of translating *pneuma* in the NT see the discussion of the Paulines in Gordon D. Fee, *God's Empowering Presence: The Holy Spirit in the Letters of Paul* (Peabody, Mass.: Hendrickson, 2005), 14–36. At times Fee adopts as a convention "s/Spirit" in discussing some of the specific texts (e.g., Rom. 8:11).

76. Ibid., 7.

77. Richard Lints, *The Fabric of Theology: A Prolegomenon to Evangelical Theology* (Grand Rapids, Mich.: Eerdmans, 1993), 290–311.

THE SPIRIT AND THE TRIUNE GOD

Debate over doctrine was a feature of Christianity from its very beginnings. Paul debated those who would add Moses to Jesus (the Judaizers dealt with in Galatians). John argued against those who claimed that Jesus had not come in the flesh (the docetists of 1 John). By A.D. 381 the question of the deity of Christ had largely been resolved. The Arians and semi-Arians had lost the theological and political battles. Jesus is of the same substance (*homoousios*) as the Father, yet distinct from him. In other words, Jesus is as much God as the Father is God. Jesus was not merely of a like substance (*homoiousios*) with the Father. Athanasius had prevailed. But what about the Holy Spirit? Some were arguing, most notably the *pneumatomachoi* ("fighters against the Spirit"), that the Spirit stood on a lesser ontological plane than the Father and the Son (e.g., Eustathius of Sebaste).[1] At Constantinople, the Fathers agreed that the Spirit is as much God as the Father is God and as the Son is God. Athanasius, earlier in the fourth century, and then later in the same century the Cappadocian fathers—Basil of Caesarea, Gregory of Nazianzen, and Gregory of Nyssa—had much to do with this outcome.[2] But were they on good biblical grounds? Just what does the Holy Spirit have to do with the triune God of historic Christian belief?[3]

1. Alister McGrath, *Christian Theology: An Introduction,* 3rd ed. (Oxford, and Malden, Mass.: Blackwell, 2001), 310.

2. See Henry Bettenson, ed. and trans., *The Later Christian Fathers* (Oxford: Oxford University Press, 1977), 294–298, for Athanasius on the Holy Spirit, and esp. 294, fn 1, for Athanasius and the *Pneumatomachoi.* For Athanasius and the Cappadocians in relation to the debates see Geoffrey Wainwright, "The Holy Spirit," in Colin E. Gunton, ed., *The Cambridge Companion to Christian Doctrine* (Cambridge: Cambridge University Press, 1997), 279. For an excellent survey of early church theology including the Cappadocians, see Frances Young, *The Making of the Creeds,* new ed. (London: SCM, 2002), esp. chapter 4.

3. For all their strengths, recent evangelical contributions to pneumatology have somewhat neglected the question of the Holy Spirit and the Trinity, e.g., J. I. Packer, *Keep in Step with the*

In this chapter we shall first note the revival of theological interest in the doctrine of the Trinity. Then we shall explore the doctrine's biblical anchorage in general before examining the biblical evidence for the deity of the Holy Spirit in particular.[4] Next we shall consider the seminal contributions of those early church theologians, Basil of Caesarea and Augustine, to our understanding of the Spirit, first in Basil's idea of the Spirit as "the perfecting cause" and then second in Augustine's idea of the Spirit as the "bond" (*vinculum*) within the triune Godhead. Third, we shall consider the social Trinitarianism of the medieval theologian Richard of St. Victor. Lastly we shall attend to some of the practical implications that flow from the discussion.

THE REVIVAL OF INTEREST

Immanuel Kant (1724–1804) had little good to say about the concept of the Trinity. Writing at the height of the eighteenth-century Enlightenment, he argued: "The doctrine of the Trinity, taken literally, has *no practical relevance at all*, even if we think we understand it; and it is even more clearly irrelevant if we realize that it transcends all our concepts."[5] Famously, Friedrich Schleiermacher (1768–1834)—the founder of modern liberal theology—in his groundbreaking *The Christian Faith* thought the proper place to discuss the Trinity was in an appendix-like conclusion.[6]

However, starting with Karl Barth in particular, the doctrine of the Trinity has come back as central to the Christian construal of God. Indeed in

---

Spirit (Leicester, England: Inter-Varsity, 1984); and Sinclair Ferguson, *The Holy Spirit* (Leicester, England: Inter-Varsity, 1996). In contrast, the older work of Abraham Kuyper's *The Work of the Holy Spirit* (trans. Henri De Vries [Grand Rapids, Mich.: Eerdmans, 1975]) explicitly considers the Spirit in relation to the Trinity right from the start; see chapter 1, sections 3–4. Clark H. Pinnock's *Flame of Love* (Downers Grove, Ill.: InterVarsity Press, 1996) is a recent exception to the neglect. Some other theologians, who work in a different theological tradition, have also neglected discussing the Holy Spirit in a clear Trinitarian frame of reference, which weakens their discussion. See, for example, Michael Welker, *God the Spirit,* trans. John F. Hoffmeyer (Minneapolis: Fortress, 1994), esp. the important footnote on 240 (n. 25), where a reference is made to the doctrine of the Trinity.

4. Since this study is exploring the relation of the Holy Spirit to the Trinity, it is an example of a pneumatology "from above" rather than "from below." For some theologians, the place to start the exploration of the doctrine of the Holy Spirit is from below, namely, from our experiences of the Holy Spirit in this life, before any move is made toward Trinitarian theology per se. See, for example, Philip J. Rosato, *The Spirit as Lord: The Pneumatology of Karl Barth* (Edinburgh: T. & T. Clark, 1981). For a discussion of the different approaches see Donald G. Bloesch, *The Holy Spirit: Works and Gifts* (Downers Grove, Ill.: InterVarsity Press, 2000), 50–52.

5. Quoted in Thomas R. Thompson, "Trinitarianism Today: Doctrinal Renaissance, Ethical Relevance, Social Redolence," *Calvin Theological Journal* 32 no. 1 (April 1997): 9, emphasis original.

6. See Friedrich Schleiermacher, *The Christian Faith,* trans. of 2nd German ed., various translators (Edinburgh: T. & T. Clark, 1948), 738–751. The amount of space given to the discussion of the Trinity and its place in the work is indicative of its lack of importance for Schleiermacher.

contradistinction to the Schleiermachian tradition, for Barth the only God who meets us in Jesus Christ is the Holy Trinity.[7]

The term "Trinity" is the right theological descriptor for the Christian God over against secularism's atheolgical denials and the alternatives proffered by the other religions of the world. Indeed, Brevard S. Childs strongly argues that: ". . . it is the doctrine of the Trinity which makes the doctrine of God actually Christian."[8] Childs is right. For example, the doctrine of the Trinity distinguishes historic Christianity from Islam. To affirm the Trinity in Islam is to commit the gravest of sins: namely, the sin of *shirk,* which is to associate another with Allah. Interestingly, in the Qur'an the Trinity appears to consist of the Father, the Son, and the Virgin Mary, which is eloquent evidence about the kind of Christianity Muhammad encountered in Arabia.

Moreover, theologians have found in the doctrine of the Trinity solutions to the "one and the many" problem of classic philosophic thought, a key to the value of persons and their relations in community, and a paradigm for human relations in marriage, the church, and even society—although with regard to the latter, some renderings of the doctrine have been used to justify hierarchies in society and others to justify egalitarian socialism. (See excursus.)

So important is the doctrine for Australian theologian D. Broughton Knox that he argues, "The doctrine of the Trinity is the foundation of the Christian religion. Unless this doctrine is held to firmly and truly, it is not possible to be a Christian."[9] However, Dutch theologian Hendrikus Berkhof has a very different view: ". . . this doctrine [the doctrine of the Trinity] has saddled us with problems that are foreign to Scripture and indigestible to the believing mind."[10] Emil Brunner offers a mediating view. He argues that the doctrine of the Trinity, while not formally part of the gospel proclamation of the church, nonetheless is protective of the gospel. He maintains,

> The Ecclesiastical doctrine of the Trinity, established by the dogma of the ancient Church, is not a Biblical *kerygma,* therefore it is not the *kerygma* of the Church, but it is a theological doctrine which defends the central faith of the Bible and of the Church. Hence it does

7. For a useful survey of recent Trinitarian theologies see Donald K. McKim, "The Stirring of the Spirit among Contemporary Theologians," *Perspectives,* May 1998, 15–19. For a more extensive survey covering the recent past and present see T. R. Thompson, "Trinitarianism Today"; and Robert Letham, "The Trinity—Yesterday, Today, and the Future," *Themelios* 28 no. 1 (Autumn 2002): 26–36. See also the survey in Ted S. Peters, *God as Trinity: Relationality and Temporality in Divine Life* (Louisville: Westminster/John Knox, 1993), chapter 3, in which he competently covers Barth through to Pannenberg.

8. Brevard S. Childs, *Biblical Theology of the Old and New Testaments: Theological Reflection on the Christian Bible* (Minneapolis: Fortress, 1993), 375.

9. D. Broughton Knox, *The Everlasting God* (Hertfordshire: Evangelical Press, 1982), 49.

10. Hendrikus Berkhof, *Christian Faith: An Introduction to the Study of Faith* (Grand Rapids, Mich.: Eerdmans, 1979), 330.

not belong to the sphere of the Church's message, but it belongs to the sphere of theology; in this sphere it is the work of the Church to test and examine its message, in the light of the Word of God given to the Church. Certainly in this process of theological reflection the doctrine of the Trinity is central.[11]

By this he appears to mean that when questions are asked of the gospel then the doctrine of the Trinity is the way forward in explanation. One can think of examples, such as the question as to whom Jesus was praying in the garden of Gethsemane, if he was God (Mark 14:32–43).

So then what do the Scriptures say? Is the doctrine of the Trinity so well-grounded in Scripture that its denial is to risk one's salvation? In other words, is the doctrine pivotal? Does our salvation turn on it? Or is the doctrine problematical? In fact, would Christianity be better off without it?

Biblical Perspectives

Right from the start of the OT witness it is clear that the Creator of the heavens and the earth is without rival. God speaks the creation into existence, and those elements in creation which in the Ancient Near East were gods are mere creatures—for example, the sun, the moon, and the stars (Gen. 1:1–2:3). The only image that God allows is the one he creates. This creature is alive as he is and is given the God-like task of exercising dominion over the creatures (1:26–28)—although by the time one has read the second chapter of Genesis it is apparent that such dominion is as much about care as it is about control. Adam is given a mandate to care for the garden as well as that of naming other creatures (2:4–24).

After the wilderness years, Israel needed to hear afresh that the only God who exists is the Lord (Deut. 6:4). On the plains of Moab, Moses calls upon Israel to hear that "the Lord is one" (*echad*). This assertion claims either that the Lord is unique or that he is without rival (contra idols).[12] This Lord is to be loved with all that Israel has (v. 5). So important is this claim that Israel is to teach its young this "creed" (v. 7). What a culture teaches its young is the true index of what it values. This passage of the Torah remains central to the various forms of observant Judaism to this day. One is not surprised then by the later prophetic critiques of the folly of idolatry. Idolatry suggests the Lord is not unique and has rivals like the Baals (see Isa. 44:6–20, 46; and Jer. 10:1–16).

11. Emil Brunner, *The Christian Doctrine of God,* vol. 1 of *Dogmatics,* trans. Olive Wyon (London: Lutterworth, 1970), 206, emphasis original.

12. The Hebrew is capable of several possible renderings, including: "The Lord our God is one Lord"; "The Lord is our God, the Lord is one"; and "The Lord is our God, the Lord alone." With any of these views in the context of the argument of Deuteronomy, the anti-idolatry thrust is plain.

In the NT, the claim of the oneness of God is reaffirmed by Jesus. In Mark's account Jesus is asked by a scribe, "Which commandment is the most important of all?" Jesus' answer is classic OT 101 (Mark 12:28–34). He reminds the scribe of the *shema* ("hear"): that is, "Hear, O Israel, the Lord our God, the Lord is one"; and that the Lord is to be loved with all that one is, and so too is one's neighbor (Mark 12:29–30). Similarly the apostle Paul asserts, in relation to the problem of food offered to idols at Corinth, that there is only one God (1 Cor. 8:6). In fact, over against the real God, idols have no real existence (v. 4). Other NT writers add their witness. James famously discusses the relationship of faith and works and the problem of dead faith: namely, a faith that is mere talk (James 2:14–26). In the course of his presentation he points out that the demons believe in the oneness of God. They believe and shudder, but, the implication is, that belief does them no saving good (v. 19). Likewise James's readers may claim to have faith but like the demons have a belief that does no saving good.

However, the NT presentation of God does move to a higher key. The oneness of God is nuanced in the light of Christ's coming and the outpouring of the Holy Spirit. Christmas, Good Friday, Easter, and Pentecost make a difference. The risen Christ in Matthew's Gospel commissions his disciples to baptize followers in the name (singular) of the Father, Son, and Holy Spirit (Matt. 28:18–20). There is a complexity to the oneness of God. The same Jesus who reaffirms the *shema* of Israel about the oneness of God is the Christ who expands the name to include Father, Son, and Holy Spirit, and does so without any hint of contradiction. This is remarkable whether one believes that one hears in the Gospels the authentic voice (*ipsissima vox*) of Jesus, as I do, or that of the early church. The name of God is sacred to the Jew. Indeed what makes Israel unique is that God gave Israel his name, which in the Ancient Near Eastern world was as close to making a claim about one's essential reality as one could get (Ex. 3:13–15; 33:17–34:9; Lev. 21:6; Ps. 76:1). As Donald G. Bloesch suggests, "A name in the Bible reveals the character and personality of the subject."[13] Therefore, Jesus' elaboration of the name of God is extraordinary. The apostle Paul similarly displays this nuanced understanding of the reality of God. The same apostle who affirmed the *shema* in 1 Corinthians 8:6 concludes 2 Corinthians with a famous benediction: "The grace of the Lord Jesus Christ and the love of God and the fellowship of the Holy Spirit be with you all" (2 Cor. 13:14).

But are such evidences as presented above sufficient to warrant a Trinitarian understanding of God? After all, our English word "trinity" comes ultimately from Tertullian's (c. 160–c. 225) Latin coinage during the early

---

13. Donald G. Bloesch, *A Theology of Word and Spirit: Authority and Method in Theology* (Downers Grove, Ill.: InterVarsity Press, 1992), 81.

church period (*trinitas,* ca. 220). The word "trinity" is not an NT term. How then can a theology of the Trinity be biblical?

TRINITY A BIBLICAL DOCTRINE?

Although the term "trinity" does not appear in Scripture—How could it, as an English word with a Latin background?—the question to ask is whether the idea of the Trinity is to be found in Scripture. On this point B. B. Warfield, the great systematician of Princeton fame, has some wise words to offer, and I quote *in extenso:*

> The term "Trinity" is not a Biblical term, and we are not using Biblical language when we define what is expressed by it as the doctrine that there is one only and true God, but in the unity of the Godhead there are three coeternal and coequal Persons, the same in substance but distinct in subsistence. A doctrine so defined can be spoken of as a Biblical doctrine only on the principle that the sense of Scripture is Scripture. And the definition of a Biblical doctrine in such un-Biblical language [better, "non-biblical"] can be justified only on the principle that it is better to preserve the truth of Scripture than the words of Scripture. The doctrine of the Trinity lies in Scripture in solution; when it is crystallized from its solvent it does not cease to be Scriptural, but only comes into clearer view. Or, to speak without a figure, the doctrine of the Trinity is given to us in Scripture, not in formulated definition, but in fragmentary allusions; when we assemble the *disjecta membra* into their organic unity, we are not passing from Scripture, but entering more thoroughly into the meaning of Scripture. We may state the doctrine in technical terms, supplied by philosophical reflection; but the doctrine stated is a genuinely Scriptural doctrine.[14]

Warfield's fine words are not only an admirable statement of the doctrine of the Trinity with reference to the nature of its biblical support but also an excellent articulation of the rationale for the development of extrabiblical technical language for doing theology responsibly.

Put another way, the term "Trinity" stands for a master concept as well as referring to the only God there is. As a master concept it catches up several strands of biblical evidence. For example, one strand, as we saw, is the *shema* one which accents the oneness of God as the maker of heaven and earth and as the maker of Israel. Another strand points out the complexity of the one God's name as understood in the NT: Father, Son, and

14. B. B. Warfield, *Biblical Foundations* (London: The Tyndale Press, 1958), 79, emphasis original.

Holy Spirit. Yet another strand highlights the distinction between Father, Son, and Holy Spirit.[15]

Hopefully enough argument has been given—albeit in outline since other works in this series deal more extensively with the subject—to justify our confidence that the only God is the Holy Trinity and to provide a sufficient theological context for our discussion of the deity and personal nature of the Holy Spirit as a member of the triune Godhead, before dealing with some of the practical questions that arise from affirming the deity of the Spirit.

THE SPIRIT AND THE TRINITY: SOME SPECIFICS

In this section of our study of pneumatology we shall look at the question of the Holy Spirit's personhood and the Holy Spirit's deity.

The Spirit as a Person

In Jürgen Moltmann's judgment, to "discern" with precision "the person-hood of the Spirit is the most difficult problem in pneumatology."[16] He explains further that, "If we take the experience of faith as our starting point, then even in the New Testament it is already an open question whether God's Spirit was thought of as a person or a force."[17] One can understand his point. The NT in places—but as we shall see this is not the whole story—presents the Spirit using impersonal categories. And so on the day of Pentecost, the Spirit's activity is "a sound like a mighty rushing wind" and "tongues as of fire" (Acts 2:2–3). The Spirit fills the disciples like a liquid (e.g., v. 4) and is poured out by the risen Christ like a liquid

15. For a brief but helpful coverage of the biblical evidence for the doctrine of the Trinity see Wayne Grudem, *Systematic Theology: An Introduction to Biblical Doctrine* (Leicester, England, and Grand Rapids, Mich.: Inter-Varsity and Zondervan, 1994), 231–241. Grudem argues that there are three claims that are biblically defensible: "1. God is three persons"; "2. Each person is fully God"; and "3. There is one God" (231, 239, and 241). For more specialized studies from an evangelical perspective see John S. Feinberg, *No One Like Him: The Doctrine of God* (Wheaton, Ill.: Crossway, 2001), chapter 10; and Millard Erickson, *God in Three Persons* (Grand Rapids, Mich.: Baker, 1995), chapters 4, 7, 8 and 9.

16. Jürgen Moltmann, *The Spirit of Life: A Universal Affirmation,* trans. Margaret Kohl (Minneapolis: Fortress, 1994), 268. For his more recent discussion of the personhood of the Spirit see his "The Trinitarian Personhood of the Holy Spirit," in Bradford E. Hinze and D. Lyle Dabney, eds., *Advents of the Spirit: An Introduction to the Current Critical Study of Pneumatology* (Milwaukee: Marquette University Press, 2001), 302–314.

17. Ibid. Perhaps Moltmann's view here is too much driven by the strange mix of metaphors by which he seeks to understand the personhood of the Spirit (see esp. 269–285). Only some of them are clearly grounded in the biblical testimony (e.g., "Lord," "tempest," "fire," "water"). Others come from a variety of places in the history of theology (e.g., Mechtild of Magdeburg and Hildegard of Bingen) and from inferences drawn—somewhat optimistically—from biblical texts (e.g., the Spirit as space, based on Ps. 139:5). However, he is right to point out that the biblical metaphors consist of both personal ("Lord") and impersonal ones ("fire").

(v. 33). In the Paulines, the Spirit is likened to the firstfruits of a harvest (Rom. 8:23), a seal (Eph. 1:13), and a guarantee or down payment on a block of land (v. 14). So is the Holy Spirit of God personal or an impersonal force from God?

Minimally a person is a being who can say "I" with self-reflexivity or, put another way, with self-awareness.[18] In the biblical presentation God can say "I" (Ex. 3:14), an angel can say "I" (Rev. 22:8–9), and a human being can say "I" (Gal. 5:2).[19] With regard to the Trinity we find that the Father says "I" and "my" at Jesus' baptism (Matt. 3:17). Jesus says an emphatic "I" before the High Priest at his trial (Mark 14:62). The Holy Spirit says "I" and "for me" in the course of the church's choosing of the apostle Paul and Barnabas for mission work (Acts 13:2). In philosophical terms, the Acts 13:2 text concerning the Holy Spirit exhibits "first-person perspective," which is a sufficient condition for personhood.[20] If the Spirit were a mere force or simply the energy of God in action, such a reference would be exceedingly strange.[21] But it is not strange if the Holy Spirit is a person. Of course, a single reference in Acts is a very slim base to build a doctrine of the personhood of the Spirit upon. Perhaps it is only a *façon de parler*. However, in the NT there are evidences aplenty that the Holy Spirit is construed by the biblical writers as a person. Let's consider some of that evidence. But before we do, a caveat is in order.

18. Feinberg in *No One Like Him*, 225, rightly points out that, "Though it is important to attribute personhood to God, this is a very thorny issue. It is so for various reasons, not least of which is the matter of what it means to be a person." See his valuable discussion on 225–231.

19. The personhood of angels raises interesting questions. Some argue that human beings are in the image of God (*imago dei*) because of certain properties which make human beings substantially different from other creatures (e.g., rationality, self-awareness, and moral sense). However, in the biblical presentation angels display these properties. But nowhere does Scripture suggest that angels are in the image of God and, in fact, according to the apostle Paul, believers (human beings) will judge the angelic order (1 Cor. 6:3). Having these properties may be part of the story of the *imago dei*, but not sufficiently so. The task of exercising Godlike dominion and the relationality of male and female also need to be incorporated into a full theological account of the image (Gen. 1:26–31).

20. See Lynne Rudder Baker, "Materialism with a Human Face," in Kevin Corcoran, ed., *Soul, Body, and Survival* (Ithaca, N.Y.: Cornell University Press, 2001), 160–161. This writer, however, does not subscribe to Baker's nonreductive materialism. See the critique of this position in C. Stephen Evans, "Separable Souls: Dualism, Selfhood, and the Possibility of Life after Death," *CSR* 34 no. 3 (Spring 2005): 327–340.

21. A theologian who is particularly partial to the idea of the Spirit as God in action or even Christian action in the world is Hendrikus Berkhof, *The Doctrine of the Holy Spirit* (Atlanta: John Knox, 1977), 94. Berkhof's theology is a modified modalistic monarchianism with regard to the Trinity. Geoffrey Lampe takes a similar view. He contends that the expression "the Spirit of God" is "not . . . referring to a divine hypostasis" (*God as Spirit* [Oxford: Clarendon, 1977], 11). Raymond E. Brown suggests that, "The author [of Acts] is not clear whether he thinks of the Spirit as a person" (*The Churches the Apostles Left Behind* [New York: Paulist, 1984], 67). This is surprising because on the very next page he describes the Spirit as directing, guiding, etc., in the presentation of Acts (ibid., 68).

The line of thought that highlights the distinctiveness of the persons of the triune Godhead needs to be balanced by the Old and New Testaments' accent on the oneness of God, lest the accent be pushed too far and distinctiveness becomes tritheism. And yet in my view social Trinitarianism is more grounded in the biblical evidence than are the "neomodalistic" expositions of the Trinity found in both Barth and Rahner.[22] We need to go beyond Boethius's (c. 475/80–524) famous definition of a person as "an individual substance of rational nature" and embrace Richard of St. Victor's (d. 1173) Trinitarian starting point for understanding persons as constituted through their relations with other persons. Donald Bloesch is one theologian not locked into Boethian categories. He writes of "the three subjectivities that compose the Godhead."[23] As a philosophical and theological personalist, Pope John Paul II sums up human personhood in these terms: ". . . a person is constructed on the 'metaphysical site' of substance, but the process of construction involves the dynamics of relationships."[24] Unlike the persons of the Trinity, who are eternal, human personhood has a diachronic dimension to its full emergence. However, "the dynamic of relationships" is true of God and always has been.

Turning to the NT, we find in John's account that Jesus shared with his disciples that his leaving to return to the Father would be to their advantage (John 16:7) because, in his so leaving, the Spirit would come as the "Comforter" (*paraklētos*). As such he would be another of the same kind as Jesus (John 14:16, *allon paraklēton*). Thus his predicted activities are clearly those of a personal agent. He will teach the disciples (v. 26). He will bear witness to Christ, as will the disciples (15:26–27). He will convict the world, guide disciples into all the truth, hear and speak, glorify and declare (16:8–15). In the early church period John's Gospel played a crucial role in the development of a high Christology, which culminated in the famous Chalcedonian Definition of A.D. 451. Likewise this account of Jesus is vital for understanding the personhood of the Spirit and for developing a "high" pneumatology which does not reduce the Spirit to simply God in action or an impersonal force from God.

The value of John's account for our purposes cannot be gainsaid. However, we should also note one argument for the personhood of the Spirit—common in evangelical circles—which must not be embraced too facilely. The argument contends that in John's account of Jesus' teaching about the

22. See Pinnock, *Flame of Love*, 34.

23. Donald G. Bloesch, *God the Almighty: Power, Wisdom, Holiness, Love* (Downers Grove, Ill.: InterVarsity Press, 1995), 169. See also Paul C. Vitz, "A Christian Theory of Personality: Interpersonal and Transmodern," in James M. Dubois, ed., *The Nature and Tasks of a Personalist Psychology* (Lanham, Md., New York, and London: University Press of America, 1995), 24.

24. Quoted in Vitz, "Christian Theory of Personality," 31. A personalist argues that the category of person is the most important one in ontology (theory of being), epistemology (theory of knowledge), and axiology (theory of value).

Holy Spirit, although "Spirit" (*pneuma*) is neuter, the masculine pronoun *ekeinos* (translated "he" e.g., ESV) rather than the neuter one *ekeino* (which would be translated "it") is used repeatedly (John 14:26; 15:26; 16:8, 13–14). For example, J. I. Packer says,

> This masculine pronoun [*ekeinos*] . . . is the more striking because in 14:17, where the Spirit is first introduced, John uses the grammatically correct neuter pronouns (*ho* and *auto*), thus ensuring that the subsequent shift to the masculine would be perceived not as incompetent Greek, but as magisterial theology.[25]

However, Daniel B. Wallace argues in his *Greek Grammar Beyond the Basics* that the antecedent of the masculine pronoun in the key passages is not the neuter "Spirit" (*to pneuma*) but the masculine "the Paraclete" (*ho paraklētos*) and thus the pronominal argument is a fallacious one in this instance.[26] If Wallace is right, then the pronominal argument for the personhood of the Spirit is far less compelling than Packer and many others seem to think.

The Pauline witness evidences the same high regard for the personal nature of the Holy Spirit. In Romans 8, Paul writes of the leading of the Spirit (Rom. 8:14), the witness of the Spirit (v. 16) and the help of the Spirit (v. 26). In this same chapter Paul does personify the created order when he writes of the creation itself longing for its own redemption and groaning like a woman in childbirth awaiting the delivery of the child (vv. 18–25). So perhaps it could be argued that Paul is personifying an impersonal energy from God at work in believers—albeit to their saving benefit—in ascribing the personal activities mentioned above to the Spirit. However, Paul goes on to write of the Spirit's intercessory activity on behalf of believers who struggle to know how and what to pray (vv. 26–27). Prayer is a most personal of activities. Moreover in verse 27 Paul writes of the "mind of the Spirit" (*to phronēma tou pneumatos*).[27] Such a descriptor would be puzzling indeed if the Spirit were simply divine energy. Still further, according to the apostle Paul the Holy Spirit may be grieved (Eph. 4:30; see also Isa.

---

25. Packer, *Keep in Step with the Spirit*, 61.

26. I thank my former student Andrew Malone for drawing this to my attention. See his "Essential Theology: The Personhood of the Holy Spirit and Masculine Pronouns in John's Gospel," *Essentials* (Autumn 2005): 7–8.

27. With reference to this text, Wolfhart Pannenberg argues, "The leading of the Spirit is not, however, the leading of a blind force of nature, but is of a personal sort. In this sense, Paul can speak of a 'mind' of the Spirit (Rom. 8:6, 27, *phronēma*)" (*Jesus—God and Man*, trans. Lewis L. Wilkins and Duane A. Priebe [London: SCM, 1976], 176–177). Paul also writes of the mind (*vous*) of the Lord—presumably the Father—in distinction from the mind (*vous*) of Christ (1 Cor. 2:16). These references have strong social Trinitarian implications.

63:10).[28] As Bruce Milne suggests, ". . . one can resist a power, but grieve only a person."[29]

A further NT line of evidence is provided by the writer to the Hebrews when speaking of the great salvation provided by God and the danger of neglecting it (Heb. 2:3). In this section of his argument he writes of the Holy Spirit's distribution of gifts to God's people, which the Spirit apportions according to the Spirit's own will (*kata tēn autou thelēsin*). It is hard to conceive of an impersonal force possessing a will.

But could the Spirit be merely angelic? Islam thinks so. In Islam, the Holy Spirit is the angel Gabriel. To this important question of the deity of the Holy Spirit we now turn our focus.

The Spirit as God

A good question to ask of any theological proposal is, What would be lost if the proposal were untrue? For example, What would be lost if Christ were not human? For a start, the argument of Hebrews about Jesus' sympathetic priesthood would dissolve (e.g., Heb. 2:14–18). Moreover, the docetists would have been right all along. Christ only appeared to be human (*dokein*). The argument of 1 John about Christ's coming in the flesh (e.g., 1 John 4:1–6) would fall to the ground. Furthermore the Pauline argument that there is one mediator between God and ourselves, who himself is human (e.g., 1 Tim. 2:5), would fail. We would be left without our great High Priest, without a mediator, and with only a deceptive appearance of humanity in Christ.

With regard to the Holy Spirit, John Feinberg aptly writes,

> As to the Holy Spirit, if he is not fully God, the implications for salvation are again serious. Scripture teaches that the Holy Spirit regenerates believers and indwells and fills them, but if the Holy Spirit is a lesser God or no God at all, how can we be sure that he can do any of these things? Moreover, unless he is coequal in being and purpose with the Father and the Son, what guarantees that even if he tried to do such things, the Father and the Son would recognize his actions as appropriate and relate to us accordingly?[30]

Feinberg rightly sees that the stakes are certainly high. But the question remains to be answered as to how well-grounded is the claim of the Spirit's deity in the Scripture.

---

28. The Isaiah 63:10 reference is intriguing and one that we shall return to when examining Ephesians 4:30 in part 3 of the study.

29. Bruce Milne, *Know the Truth: A Handbook of Christian Belief* (London and Singapore: Inter-Varsity and S+U, 1983), 177. For a contemporary religious group that reduces the Holy Spirit to divine power or energy see the Jehovah's Witnesses' *Should You Believe in the Trinity?* (Brooklyn, N.Y.: Watch Tower Bible and Tract Society, 1989).

30. Feinberg, *No One Like Him*, 440.

There are some important lines of evidence that are relevant to our question: the Spirit's relationship to the name of God, the Spirit's attributes and activities according to biblical testimony, and possibly the worship of the Holy Spirit.

The first line of evidence has to do with the name of God. In my Western culture, my name simply identifies me. If someone calls out "Graham Cole" in a crowd, I pay attention. My name identifies me. But it does not tell a story about my nature. In Scripture, God's name is about identification. "Yahweh" identifies only one God. But God's name (*šēm*) also says something about God's very identity. Brevard S. Childs comments, "God's identity has been made known through his name."[31] The name of God says something about his very nature. Charles H. H. Scobie goes so far as to argue that, "*. . . God's name is an expression of his essential nature.*"[32] God's name is to be venerated and never abused. The Third Commandment makes this plain (Ex. 20:7). As we observed, Jesus tells his disciples that the singular name (*to onoma*) to be baptized in includes Father, Son, and Holy Spirit. If we apply the philosophical technique of substitution we shall see the significance of Jesus' words.[33] Imagine *par impossible* if the Son were a merely human prophet and the Spirit were an impersonal force, then Christian baptism would be in the one name of God, a human prophet, and a force. Jesus' climactic commission reduces to incoherence of the highest disorder. In the light of Jesus' words, the biblical reality is that to name the Holy Spirit is to name God truly but not exhaustively. The Holy Spirit is as much deity as is the Father as is the Son, but distinct as a person from both. So it is not surprising that in the Acts narrative when Ananias and Sapphira lie to the Holy Spirit they are, in fact, lying to God, as the text makes clear with its parallelism (Acts 5:1–11). Nor is it surprising then that the Holy Spirit may be blasphemed against (Matt. 12:28–31).[34]

A second line of evidence consists of the biblical presentation of those attributes of the Holy Spirit which are traditionally the attributes of deity and the divine activities which flow from them. Psalm 139 is a magnificent statement of the inescapable presence of God.[35] Traditionally, systematic theologians have appealed to this psalm as one reason for asserting the

---

31. Childs, *Biblical Theology*, 371. For an excellent theological—rather than narrowly biblical—discussion of the divine names and their significance, see Bloesch, *Word and Spirit*, 81–85.

32. Charles H. H. Scobie, *The Ways of Our God: An Approach to Biblical Theology* (Grand Rapids, Mich., and Cambridge: Eerdmans, 2003), 108, emphasis original.

33. Julian Baggini and Peter S. Fosl, *The Philosopher's Toolkit: A Compendium of Philosophical Concepts and Methods* (Malden, Mass., and Oxford: Blackwell, 2003), 16–17.

34. What precisely is the blasphemy against the Holy Spirit will be explored in its own right at length in another place.

35. In the NT the nearest analog is the inescapable love of Christ (Rom. 8:38–39).

omnipresence of God, which is one of his incommunicable attributes.[36] The psalmist sings, "Where shall I go from your Spirit [*rûach*]? Or where shall I flee from your presence [*pānîm*]?" (Ps. 139:7). Whether heaven or Sheol or the farthest parts of the sea is in view, the Spirit is there (vv. 8–10).

The Holy Spirit, according to the apostle Paul, is the one who searches the depths (*ta bathē*) of God (1 Cor. 2:10). Therefore (*gar*) in Pauline thought the Spirit is the one who can reveal the mind of God to others. Paul draws an analogy between ourselves and God. Our spirit enables us to know our own thoughts (lit. *ta,* the things). (What Paul means by "spirit" [*pneuma*] need not detain us at this point.) Likewise with God, only the Spirit of God knows the thoughts (lit. *ta,* the things) of God (2:11). Only God can know God in this way. Otherwise there would be two omniscient beings.[37] Scripture allows no such metaphysical dualism. Both the Holy Spirit's knowledge of God's thoughts and his activity as the searcher of the depths are evidences of his deity.[38]

Furthermore both in the apostle Paul's theology and in that of the writer to the Hebrews, the Holy Spirit is the one who sovereignly distributes the gifts of God. In Paul's discussion of spiritual gifts (*charismata*) in 1 Corinthians 12, which we shall explore at greater length in a later part of our study, he lists a great variety of them: the word of wisdom, the word of knowledge, faith, gifts of healing, miracle working, prophecy, discernment of spirits, tongues, and the interpretation of tongues (1 Cor. 12:7–10). Then in verse 11 he asserts that such gifts are apportioned by the Spirit "to each one individually as he wills" (*kathōs bouletai*). Who but God can distribute the gifts of God as he wills?

The same question may be asked of Hebrews 2:4, which speaks of the gifts of the Spirit. In the previous verse, the writer asks, ". . . how shall we escape if we neglect such a great salvation?" The writer then goes on to argue in the same verse that this salvation had been declared by the Lord, attested by witnesses, and borne witness to by God himself. The divine witness falls into two categories. There are signs, wonders, and miracles, which we shall explore at greater length in a later part of our study, and there are the gifts (lit. "distributions," *merismois*) of the Spirit. These gifts are sovereignly distributed by the Holy Spirit, according to his will (*kata*

---

36. For example, Fred H. Klooster, "The Attributes of God: The Incommunicable Attributes," in Carl F. H. Henry, ed., *Basic Christian Doctrines* (New York, Chicago, and San Francisco: Holt, Rinehart & Winston, 1962), 25, fn 19.

37. By omniscience I mean God knows the past, present, and future. He knows all necessity, actuality, and possibility. He knows all true propositions and that they are true, and he knows all false propositions and that they are false. For this God the future is no guesswork.

38. Thomas Aquinas made the same point (*Summa Contra Gentiles of Saint Thomas Aquinas,* trans. Joseph Rickaby [London: Burns & Oates, 1905], 4.17.7). Indeed Thomas's discussion of the Holy Spirit ("17. That the Holy Ghost Is True God," and "18. That the Holy Ghost Is a Subsistent Person") is very instructive and still useful.

tēn autou thelēsin). Again, who but God can distribute the gifts of God as he wills?

A third line of possible evidence was widely recognized in the early church. For example, with Philippians 3:3 in mind Augustine argues,

> The Spirit is certainly not a creature, for worship is offered to him by all the saints; as the Apostle [Paul] says, 'We are the circumcision, serving the Spirit [*pneumati*] of God', where the Greek word *latreuontes* means 'worshipping'. . . . If then the 'members of Christ' are the 'temple of the Holy Spirit', the Holy Spirit is not a creature . . . we must owe him the service which is due God alone, which in Greek is called *latreia*.[39]

If Augustine is to be followed, which is debatable, then the Nicene Creed has biblical support in Philippians 3:3 for declaring that the Holy Spirit is the One "who with the Father and the Son together is worshiped and glorified."[40] To worship any other than God is in biblical categories nothing less than idolatry (Ex. 20:3–6; Rom. 1:18–32).

However, the Pauline argument in Philippians at this juncture, which contrasts external and internal religion, may be affirming only that it is by the instrumentality of the Spirit that God is to be worshiped. Even so, divinity of the Spirit may still be in view in a more subtle way. As Gerald F. Hawthorne comments,

> The apostle's choice of the verb λατρεύειν, "to worship," modified as it is by πνεύματι θεοῦ, "by the Spirit of God," stresses that the Spirit of God is the *divine initiator* at work in the depths of human nature, profoundly transforming a person's life so as to promote a life of love and service, and generate a life for others; for "such a life is the only worship ("latreuō") acceptable to God."[41]

FOUR SEMINAL THEOLOGICAL IDEAS OF HEURISTIC WORTH

Doing theology is not simply a matter of reading the Scriptures and drawing some conclusion in an individualistic fashion as though nothing much has been thought about these things by the people of God down the ages. Now, of course, ideas generated by Christian reflection on Scripture, further reflections on the logic of such reflections, so often forged in debate, do not have the status of special revelation. But they may serve as heuristic devices

---

39. Augustine, *De Trinitate* 1.13, in Bettenson, ed., *Later Christian Fathers*, 233.

40. Quoted in Grudem, *Systematic Theology,* 1169.

41. Gerald F. Hawthorne, *Philippians,* rev. and expanded by Ralph P. Martin, WBC, comment on Phil. 3:3, emphasis mine. Interestingly, Augustine was aware that some Latin versions had "serving God by the Spirit" (*De Trinitate* 1.13, in Bettenson, ed., *Later Christian Fathers*, 233). The key question is whether the dative is one of personal interest or of instrument.

that aid our reading of Scripture insofar as they illuminate them and are consistent with them. Let us explore four such ideas.

Basil of Caesarea and the Ideas of Perfecting Cause and Appropriation

Basil of Caesarea (c. 330–379), one of the Cappadocian Fathers, was one of the architects of the mature doctrine of the Trinity that is enshrined in the Niceno-Constantinopolitan Creed of A.D. 381. His reflections on the person and work of the Holy Spirit still repay careful attention. He saw the significance of the practice of Christian baptism in the threefold name of Father, Son, and Holy Spirit as taught by Jesus as important evidence for the Spirit's deity.[42] He also assigned particular divine operations to different Persons of the Trinity. The Father is "the original cause of all things made." The Son is "the creative cause." And the Spirit is "the perfecting cause."[43] Colin Gunton comments, "The Spirit as the perfecting cause of the creation is one who enables things to become what they are created to be; to fulfill their created purpose of giving glory to God in their perfecting."[44] We shall return to Basil's fecund idea at a later stage of our study. Suffice it to say at this juncture that the Spirit's role in eschatology—broadly conceived as the realization of God's purposes for creation, rather than more narrowly conceived as the traditional Four Last Things of death, judgment, heaven, and hell—will throw much light on the theological coherence of the biblical drama of salvation.

Basil's construal of the Holy Spirit also shows an early use of what is known traditionally as the concept of appropriations.[45] Alister McGrath

---

42. Basil of Caesarea, *"De Spiritu Sancto"* in Bettenson, ed., *Later Christian Fathers,* 72.

43. Basil of Caesarea, "On the Holy Spirit," XV. 38, quoted in Colin Gunton, "The Spirit Moved over the Face of the Waters: The Holy Spirit and the Created Order," *International Journal of Systematic Theology* 4 no. 2 (July 2002): 191. See also Colin Gunton, "The Doctrine of Creation," in Gunton, ed., *Cambridge Companion to Christian Doctrine*, 142.

44. Ibid., 203. Kuyper argues similarly: "Thus to lead the creature to its destiny, to cause it to develop according to its nature, to make it perfect, is the proper work of the Holy Spirit" (*Work of the Holy Spirit,* 21).

45. For this important theological concept see Van A. Harvey, *A Handbook of Theological Terms* (New York: Simon & Schuster, 1997), 27. Harvey sees the doctrine as arising from the needs of piety "to ascribe some property or character to one of the persons [of the Trinity] that really belongs to all three." This is too dismissive and does not deal with the fittingness of the doctrine when at issue is not a property per se but a particular role in the created and redemptive orders. See McGrath, *Christian Theology: An Introduction,* 326–327 for a wise and careful explanation of the concept. See also Daniel L. Migliore, *Faith Seeking Understanding: An Introduction to Christian Theology,* 2nd ed. (Grand Rapids, Mich. and Cambridge: Eerdmans, 2004), 404. The concept has not gone uncriticized in theological discussion. Although the idea of appropriation can be found in theologians of the past such as Augustine and Aquinas, more recently both Karl Rahner and Catherine Mowry LaCugna have expressed their doubts about it. According to Frederick Christian Bauerschmidt, Rahner and LaCugna maintain that the idea represents something of a rescue operation to uphold the distinctiveness of the Persons of

explains "appropriation" in the following helpful way: "A term relating to the doctrine of the Trinity, which affirms that while all three persons of the Trinity are active in all the outward actions of the Trinity, it is appropriate to think of those actions as being the particular work of one of the persons."[46] For example, all the Persons of the Trinity are involved in creation, revelation, and redemption according to Scripture. There is a theological appropriateness, because of biblical emphasis and logic, to assign particular roles to one Person especially rather than to another Person of the Trinity.[47] Hence, the Father is particularly associated with creation, the Son with redemption, and the Spirit with sanctification. The doctrine of appropriations helps explain why, if the Spirit is God, so little of the Scripture deals with the Spirit's role in creation and so much of it with the Spirit's role in forming a people for God even though the works of the Trinity are undivided.[48]

In discussing some ideas from Basil of Caesarea we have been retrieving ideas from a theologian especially beloved in the Eastern church. Now we turn our attention to the towering figure of Augustine, so crucial for understanding Western theology. In particular we shall consider Augustine's idea that the Holy Spirit is the bond of love (*vinculum caritas*) in the Trinity.

Augustine and the Idea That the Spirit Is the Bond

Any theologian considering the immanent Trinity is challenged to articulate how the Persons of the Godhead are to be distinguished. For Augustine the Father is unbegotten, the Son timelessly begotten, and the Spirit timelessly proceeds from both the Father and the Son.[49] He justifies the latter idea with an argument based on the text of John's Gospel, where Jesus is said to send the Spirit and where the risen Jesus is described as bestowing the Holy Spirit on the disciples in an insufflation (cf. John 15:26 and 20:22). In Augustine's thinking these texts show that the Spirit is a gift of the Son and therefore proceeds from him.[50] Likewise the Spirit is a gift of the Father. A gift has a source, and in the case of the Holy Spirit the source is twofold:

---

the Trinity in theologies that threaten the distinctiveness. See the lengthy footnote in Frederick Christian Bauerschmidt, *Holy Teaching: Introducing the Summa Theologiae of St. Thomas Aquinas* (Grand Rapids, Mich.: Baker, 2005), 89–90, fn 13.

46. McGrath, *Christian Theology: An Introduction*, 579.

47. Unlike McGrath, I prefer to use a capital "P" when referring to the triune Godhead.

48. In Augustine's celebrated words, *"opera Trinitatis ad extra sunt indivisa,"* or, "The Trinity's works on the outside are undivided" (author's translation). See Richard A. Muller, *Dictionary of Latin and Greek Theological Terms: Drawn Principally from Protestant Scholastic Theology* (Grand Rapids, Mich.: Baker, 1985), 212.

49. Augustine, *De Trinitate* 15.47, in Bettenson, ed., *Later Christian Fathers*, 228.

50. Ibid., 4.29, 227.

the Father and the Son.[51] Indeed, the Spirit can be described as both "the Spirit of the Father and the Son."[52] According to Augustine the way to understand the Spirit's place in the triune Godhead is as the bond that binds Father and Son together.[53] That bond is love, which is the very substance of God, and therefore "Love" could serve as "the title of the Holy Spirit."[54] The Spirit is the key to understanding "the inexpressible communion, as it were, of Father and Son."[55]

As we have seen, Augustine saw the role of the Holy Spirit within the Godhead as that of a bond of love. So what, one may ask? What heuristic value lies in that idea? To anticipate a later discussion of the atonement and the Spirit, if the Holy Spirit is the bond of love within the Trinity, then light may be thrown on how the triune God could absorb the Father's turning his face away from the Son on the cross. The Spirit maintained the bond of relationship even when the fellowship of Father and Son entered that thick darkness of chaos returned that was the cross.

However, a possible weakness in the Augustinian idea of the Spirit as the bond of love must be noted. The idea of bond may suggest that the Spirit is somewhat impersonal. The Spirit "reduces" to a mere mode of divine being. Clark H. Pinnock is sensitive to this danger when he writes, "Even this image, 'bond of love,' falls short of attributing personality to Spirit, leaving the possible impression of a binity—Father and Son plus a bond—rather than Trinity."[56]

Richard of St. Victor and the Idea That Love Needs a Third Person

In my view, the Augustinian account of the Trinity needs to be balanced by the Trinitarian theology of Richard of St. Victor. In the later medieval period, Richard, although indebted to Augustine in many ways, analyzed the idea of love in a triadic fashion. Love may characterize a pair as in a marriage of a man and a woman, but the fullest love requires a third. The perfection of love requires sharing with a third. Within the Trinity the Holy

51. Ibid., 5.15, 231. In fact it is the Father's gift to the Son, according to Augustine, that the Son gives the Spirit too: ". . . it is by the Father's gift that he proceeds from the Son also, as from the Father himself" (ibid., 15:48, 228). Note that Bettenson's extracts do not follow Augustine's own order of discussion but are arranged thematically.

52. Ibid., 5.12, 231.

53. Ibid., 15.29, 229. For a modern advocate of the mutual love theory see David Coffey, "The Holy Spirit as the Mutual Love of the Father and the Son," *TS* 51 (1990): 193–229; and his *Deus Trinitatis: The Doctrine of the Triune God* (New York: Oxford University Press, 1999).

54. Augustine, ibid.

55. Ibid., 5.12, 231.

56. Pinnock, *Flame of Love,* 40. Michael Welker is aware of this same danger when the Spirit is described as bond or relation within the Godhead ("The Holy Spirit," *Theology Today* 46 no. 1 [April 1989]: 5).

Spirit is that third one.[57] He thought up abstract and elaborate ways of arguing his point. In fact he thought—too ambitiously, to my mind—that he could show that "a Trinity of divine persons *must* exist."[58] In his pioneering work of social Trinitarianism, he reflected on the origins of the three Persons of the Trinity in relation to one another. The Father is from himself, the Son is from the Father, and the Holy Spirit is from the Father and the Son. Richard, very much a Western rather than an Eastern Trinitarian thinker, staunchly maintained the *filioque* ("and from the Son") of the creeds. The Holy Spirit proceeds from the Father and the Son. But how so?

The above question brings us to one of the greatest controversies in Christian history, which is still unresolved and which still divides Eastern churches from many Western ones. Importantly it is a controversy that brings us to the heart of our Trinitarian understanding of God and the Holy Spirit's place in the Godhead. As we shall see, one's theological decisions with regard to the issues raised may have a huge bearing on how Christians are to relate to those of other faiths, an issue that we shall raise in this chapter but examine at length in a later one.

THE SPIRIT AND *FILIOQUE*

In A.D. 589, King Reccared of the Goths—and therefore his tribe—converted from Arianism to the Catholic faith.[59] But how could the reality of the conversion be established? No Arian would say that the Holy Spirit proceeded from the Father and the Son (*filioque*) because of the high Christology

57. In the Spring semester of 1987 at the University of Cambridge, at a D Society meeting in the Lightfoot Room of the old Divinity School, the writer heard Richard Swinburne, the eminent philosopher of religion, give a spirited defense of a Victorine-like understanding of the Trinity based on a phenomenology of love. He argued that the love between the three Persons of the Trinity instantiated the perfection of love. That perfection required of necessity three. See Richard Swinburne, *The Christian God* (Oxford: Clarendon Press, 1994), 190–191 and 250, fn 11, for his presentation of Richard of St. Victor's Trinitarianism, and some criticism of the Victorine's argumentation. Like Richard of St. Victor, however, Richard Swinburne believes goodness of necessity diffuses itself, which is why "a divine individual *must* give rise to another and hence a third" (190, emphasis mine). I wondered in 1987, and still today, Why not two or four or five? One presumably could maintain that love between two may become obsessive and exclusive in an unhealthy way and therefore run the risk of imperfection, whereas love between three may not. The application of Ockham's Razor would dictate that we stop at three. All this is, of course, highly speculative and in terms of dogmatic rank needs to be seen as such.

58. Richard of St. Victor, "*De Trinitate*" III.14, quoted in Alister McGrath, ed., *The Christian Theology Reader* (Oxford, and Cambridge, Mass.: Blackwell, 1995), 110, emphasis mine. For the full text of *De Trinitate*—albeit with a French translation on the opposite page—see Gaston Salet, ed. and trans., *La Trinité: Texte Latin, Introduction, Traduction et Notes, No. 63 Sources Chrétiennes* (Paris: Les Éditions du Cerf, 1959).

59. For an excellent presentation of the history of the controversy from a largely Western perspective see Alasdair Heron, "The *Filioque* Clause," in Peter Toon and James D. Spiceland, eds., *One God in Trinity: An Analysis of the Primary Dogma of Christianity* (Westchester, Ill.: Cornerstone, 1980), 62–73.

such a confession assumes. Consequently the creed that Reccared was to affirm had the *filioque* addition. Eastern Christians were offended by such a unilateral move. Alasdair Heron argues that,

> It is unlikely that this council [the Third Council of Toledo] actually altered the wording of the Nicene Creed itself; but in the following centuries, versions of the Creed including the *filioque* clause came to be used quite widely in the West, especially in Spain and France.[60]

But who had the authority to expand the Niceno-Constantinopolitan Creed, apart from an ecumenical council of the churches involving both Greek- and Latin-speaking leaders? Tensions, both theological and political, grew over the succeeding centuries. In A.D. 1014 in the West, Pope Benedict VIII "finally approved the expansion of the creed."[61] Some forty years later, East and West went their separate ways.[62]

The differences between Eastern and Western Trinitarianism may be summed up in the following way. In the East, the Irenaean "two hands of God" theology prevailed. The Father is the fount of Deity and the Son and the Spirit are likened to his two hands.[63] The Son is distinguished from the Spirit as the one eternally begotten of the Father, while the Spirit is the one eternally breathed out by the Father. With regard to the Spirit there is a single, timeless breathing. In the West, however, which followed the Augustinian path, the Father indeed eternally begets the Son but the Spirit is jointly and eternally breathed out by them. With regard to the Spirit on this model there is a double breathing.[64]

60. Ibid., 64–65, emphasis original. Robert G. Gromacki, in contradistinction, writes that the *"filoque"* (*sic*) was added to the Constantinople Creed ("The Holy Spirit: Who He Is, What He Does," in Charles R. Swindoll and Roy B. Zuck, eds., *Understanding Christian Theology* [Nashville: Thomas Nelson, 2003], 419). Feinberg adopts a similar view to Gromacki (*No One Like Him*, 486). See also the comment in Henry Bettenson and Chris Maunder, eds., *Documents of the Christian Church*, 3rd ed. (Oxford: Oxford University Press, 1999), 28, fn 3.

61. Ibid., 65.

62. For a discussion of the history of the controversy from an Eastern perspective see John Meyendorff, *Byzantine Theology: Historical Trends and Doctrinal Themes* (London and Oxford: Mowbrays, 1974), 91–102. Interestingly, Meyendorff does not refer to the Council of Toledo of A.D. 589 in his presentation. Nor does Jaroslav Pelikan in his discussion of the controversy (*The Spirit of Eastern Christendom [600–1700]*, vol. 2 of *The Christian Tradition: A History of the Development of Doctrine* [Chicago and London: University of Chicago Press, 1975], 183–198). Now that Richard Swinburne has converted to Orthodoxy it would be interesting to know how that has affected his debt to Richard of St. Victor, who was very much a Western Trinitarian.

63. Kallistos Ware, *The Orthodox Way* (London and Oxford: Mowbray, 1981), 44 and 122.

64. See McGrath, *Christian Theology: An Introduction*, for a helpful discussion with diagrams of both the Eastern and Western approaches (322–325). Bloesch offers some seven models with diagrams of the *taxis* (order) within the Trinity (*God the Almighty*, 199–204). Of course, any such diagramming must be taken as suggestive rather than definitive, given the mystery of the triune God.

The tensions that have emerged historically over the competing models of the Godhead have not yet been resolved. Theologian Alasdair Heron suggests four possibilities for a resolution, each of which has its advocates. The *filioque* might be maintained with full rigor (Karl Barth). *Filioque* might be dropped with no alteration to the original creed allowed (Vladimir Lossky). These are the polar opposite positions. Mediating positions would argue that the Spirit might be characterized as proceeding from the Father through the Son (V. V. Bolotov) or might be redescribed in creedal terms as the Spirit of the Son who proceeds from the Father (Heron).[65]

Not all Christian churches find the debate of gripping interest, especially if they are nonliturgical and therefore don't have the affirmation of one of the classic creeds as part of the warp and woof of their corporate life.[66] But what is at issue here is not simply how Christology and pneumatology are to be related in a robust Trinitarianism. Increasingly there are contemporary voices advocating the dropping of *filioque* theology with the world of other religions in mind. The issue becomes: If the Spirit of God proceeds from the Father only, then there may be a theological argument that this same Spirit may relate adherents of other faiths to the Father without the need of Christology. Put another way, how needful is the mediatorship of Christ? In fact some are now arguing that it is time to reconceptualize the theological task by starting neither from the first article of the Apostles' Creed ("the Father Almighty, maker of heaven and earth") nor from the second ("his only Son our Lord") but from the third ("I believe in the Holy Spirit").[67] Starting with a pneumatology freed from *filioque* opens further the possibilities of a way to God without the mediation of Christ. This crucial issue is one to which we shall return in the final part of the study, where contemporary questions arising from debates in pneumatology will be considered. Suffice it to say at this point that what at first hearing to an evangelical might seem an arcane theological debate has ramifications that affect the very fabric of the Christian's engagement with those of other faiths in a pluralist context.

---

65. For the substance of this paragraph the writer is indebted to the excellent discussion of the issues in Heron, *"Filioque* Clause," 73–75. Bloesch's view is consistent with that of Bolotov and the writer's own. See Bloesch, *God the Almighty,* 202–203 and 300, fn 94.

66. Roger E. Olson points out that, "Free church Protestants such as Baptists, who generally do not recite the Nicene Creed, have tended to sit out this controversy" (Roger E. Olson, *The Mosaic of Christian Belief: Twenty Centuries of Unity and Diversity* [Downers Grove, Ill., and Leicester, England: InterVarsity Press and Apollos, 2002], 151).

67. An example of an advocate for starting theology from the third article of the Creed is D. Lyle Dabney. See his "Why Should the Last Be First? The Priority of Pneumatology in Recent Theological Discussion," in Hinze and Dabney, eds., *Advents of the Spirit,* 240–261; and his "Starting with the Spirit: Why the Last Should Now Be First," in Stephen Pickard and Gordon Preece, eds., *Starting with the Spirit* (Hindmarsh, South Australia: ATF, 2001), 3–27. Bloesch comments, ". . . a radical shift is taking place among theologians on this subject [the person and work of the Spirit]. For a growing number of scholars the Spirit is no longer the third person of the Trinity but the first person, in some cases the only person" (*Holy Spirit,* 265).

THE SPIRIT AND GENDER LANGUAGE

The word spirit in Hebrew (*rûach*) is feminine, in Greek (*pneuma*) it is neuter, and in Latin (*spiritus*) it is masculine.[68] One does not build a doctrine of God on grammar per se. How words are used is the key to their import, as Wittgenstein has taught us. "The meaning of a word is its use in the language," he famously argued.[69] On the basis of how John 3 describes the Spirit's work in new birth, Moltmann maintains that the Spirit is to be understood in feminine terms as the one who births the believer like a mother. He argues that tradition is on his side. At least some of it is. He points out how the early Pietists—in particular the founder of the Moravian Brethren, Count Zinzendorf (d. 1760)—made reference to the Spirit's "motherly ministry." Indeed the Count understood the Trinity in familial categories: the Father as "our true Father," the Spirit as "our true Mother," and the Son as "our true Brother."[70] Feminist theologian Elizabeth Johnson similarly has advocated that feminine designations and descriptors be used of the Holy Spirit and indeed of the other persons of the Godhead. She contends, "Introducing female symbols has the effect of purifying God-talk of its direct, even if unintentional, masculine literalism."[71] She points to the doctrine of the Trinity as a case in point of the need for reform:

> To wit: the Spirit is virtually forgotten in the West, being faceless, with no proper name; the Christ is distorted through assimilation to the framework of male dominance; and God's maternal relation to the world is eclipsed through concentrating on the paternal metaphor: "You forgot the God who gave you birth" (Deut. 32:18).[72]

She argues that retrieving feminine imagery of the Spirit from Scripture will help us see with regard to the Spirit that "She is the giver of life."[73] In fact the Trinity might be redescribed as "a community in diversity . . . unoriginate Mother, her beloved Child, and the Spirit of their mutual love."[74] Some theologians go so far as to maintain that the Spirit is the feminine counterpart to Jesus. Irenaeus's idea of the Word and the Spirit as the two

68. See Migliore, *Faith Seeking Understanding*, 233.

69. L. Wittgenstein, *Philosophical Investigations* (New York: Macmillan, 1968), sec 43, 20e. See also Bloesch, *Word and Spirit*, 103.

70. Jürgen Moltmann, *The Source: The Holy Spirit and the Theology of Life*, trans. Margaret Kohl (Minneapolis: Fortress, 1997), 35–37.

71. Elizabeth A. Johnson, "A Theological Case for God-She: Expanding the Treasury of Metaphor," *Commonweal*, January 29, 1993, 11. For her major work on the doctrine of God see *She Who Is: The Mystery of God in Feminist Theological Discourse* (New York: Crossroad, 1992). For a sensitive critique of her book from an evangelical position see Feinberg, *No One Like Him*, 134–138.

72. Johnson, "Theological Case for God-She," 12.

73. Ibid.

74. Ibid., 13.

hands of God becomes Jesus and the Spirit as the Son and Daughter of God.[75] Some evangelical theologians are also comfortable in using feminine pronouns with regard to the Spirit. Evangelical theologian—some say "evangelical maverick"—Clark H. Pinnock maintains that, "Speaking of Spirit in feminine ways might be a way for evangelicals who respect the Bible and trinitarian language to make a contribution to this debate [about gender, language, and God]."[76] He himself uses "her" and "she" of the Spirit.[77]

The question must be asked, however, as to the legitimacy of moving in this direction. Is it appropriate to name the Spirit as Mother? Is it legitimate to talk of the Spirit using similes such as, the Spirit is like a mother in giving us new life? Are we justified in employing feminine imagery of the Spirit, as Count Zinzendorf did, when speaking of the Spirit's "motherly ministry"? And what of Elizabeth Johnson's designation of the Holy Spirit as "She"? These questions raise the broader one of how our finite language may be used of the infinite God. To this general subject we now turn before returning to the specific question of the Spirit and the feminine.

How our ordinary language can be stretched to apply to God has challenged theologians and philosophers for centuries. The classic discussion is found in Aquinas, who argued that our terms when used of God may be either equivocal, univocal, or analogical in meaning.[78] We are using our words equivocally when they have the same form but different meanings and referents. Consider the word "bat" as used in the following two sentences: "The bat flew over her head, flapping its wings quietly." "The baseball player swung the bat so well he scored a home run." This is not cruelty to animals. There is no overlap in meaning. I have used the term "bat" equivocally. Likewise, if I regard language about God and us as equivocal and say "God is kind" and "King David is kind," there is no overlap of meaning. Aquinas rejected this approach. He was right, because it leaves us in deep agnosticism about the nature and character of God. If, as a second option, I say "God is kind" and "King David is kind" in an identical sense then I am using the term "kind" univocally—that is to say, with the exact same meaning but with different referents. Aquinas had problems with this approach too. God is of a different genus than us, and our understanding of language needs to reflect this lest we anthropomorphize God, bringing

75. See Migliore, *Faith Seeking Understanding*, 233–234, for a presentation and critique of this view.

76. Clark H. Pinnock, "The Role of the Spirit in Creation," *AsTJ* 52 no. 1 (Spring 1997): 48. See also Daniel Strange, "Clark H. Pinnock: The Evolution of an Evangelical Maverick," *Evangelical Quarterly* 71 no. 4 (October 1999): 311–326.

77. Pinnock, ibid., 50 for "her universal activity," 53 for "to her" and "She calls . . ." In his article, Pinnock abandons the caution on the issue to be seen in his *Flame of Love*, 17, which caution he makes clear was not his choice (48).

78. Thomas Aquinas, *Summa Theologica*, I, 13, 5–6, in Peter Kreeft, ed. and annotator, *Summa of the Summa: The Essential Philosophical Passages of St. Thomas Aquinas' Summa Theologica Edited and Explained for Beginners* (San Francisco: Ignatius, 1990), 126–128.

THE SPIRIT AND THE TRIUNE GOD □ *81*

God down to our level.[79] Lastly, if I say "God is kind" and "King David is kind" and there is some overlap of meaning but not strict identity in meaning, I have used the term "kind" analogically. Aquinas argues that our ordinary terms when used of God are used analogically because God is perfect and infinite whereas we are imperfect and finite. Analogy preserves the "Godness" of God. So the terms when used of God and ourselves are neither equivocal nor univocal. This was Aquinas's favored approach, and mine too in this work.

John Feinberg, in a useful discussion of the nature of religious language, canvasses the various possibilities and recognizes the merit in the Thomistic proposal.[80] He also draws attention to the recent work of analytical philosopher W. P. Alston on religious language. Language when used of God and ourselves, according to this view, functions in similar ways. We say that God acts and we mean thereby that God brings about certain effects in the world, as do we. But how God brings about such effects and how we do, *ex hypothesi*, will presumably be very different. For example, we use our bodies. God has none. So we cannot know *how* God so acts even though we may meaningfully assert that he acts. One of the strengths of Alston's proposal and Feinberg's discussion is that the mystery of God is preserved and yet we are not left bereft of anything meaningful to say about the divine nature.[81]

It seems to me that Alston's helpful proposal requires some notion of analogy to work. When we use the same term—for example, "good"—of God and ourselves, there needs to be some element of the univocal within the analogical predication; otherwise we are left in agnosticism about the divine nature, even if only function is at issue.

With regard to religious language and gender, Scripture does use feminine imagery of God both in the Old Testament and the New. In the OT, for example, Yahweh gives birth to his people (Deut. 32:18). God also acts like a midwife (Ps. 22:9–10). Again, God acts like a mother giving comfort (Isa. 66:13). But importantly there are no examples of God being designated in feminine terms in worship. As J. W. Miller points out, ". . . not once in the Bible is God addressed as mother, said to be mother, or referred to with feminine pronouns."[82]

A similar story pertains to the NT presentation. Jesus likens God to a woman searching for a coin and himself to a hen wanting to gather her chicks when they are in danger (cf. Luke 15:8–10 and 13:31–35). But he

79. Ibid. I am following Kreeft here in his reading of the *Summa*, 126, fn 95.
80. See Feinberg, *No One Like Him*, 75–80. I am much indebted to Feinberg's discussion for this paragraph.
81. Ibid., 76. As Feinberg says, "There are undoubtedly mysteries about him which none of us understands. But we must recognize that this doesn't mean we know nothing about him whatsoever or that none of our claims, whether literal or figurative, are true."
82. Quoted in Scobie, *Ways of Our God*, 119.

teaches disciples to pray "Our Father" and prays himself to God as "Father" (cf. Matt. 6:9 and John 17:1). But the qualifier "heavenly Father" (e.g., Matt. 5:48, *ho patēr humōn ho ouranios*) should keep disciples from confusing God the Father and earthly fathers, who may fail their children dramatically. So too should his *a fortiori* argument contrasting the generosity and good will of earthly fathers to their children and that of God as Father (Luke 11:11–13).

British philosopher of religion Basil Mitchell has some wise remarks concerning the use of analogy. He recognizes that there is a problem ". . . about the meaning of predicates as applied to God."[83] The problem concerns ". . . the possibility of giving a determinate meaning to expressions like 'father', 'loving', 'wise' when they are used of God, given that these words and others like them are normally used of human beings who are finite."[84] He acknowledges that the custom is to argue that these terms are being used analogically. However, the question, he rightly notes, becomes how much of the ordinary meaning still applies. What then is Mitchell's recommendation as far as a way forward is concerned? He suggests,

> The answer would seem to be that a word should presume to carry with it as many of the original entailments as the new context allows, and this is determined by their compatibility with other descriptions which there is reason to believe also apply to God. That God is incorporeal [without a body] dictates that 'father' does not mean 'physical progenitor', but the word continues to bear the connotation of tender protective care.[85]

If Mitchell is right then some feminine imagery may indeed be used of the Holy Spirit but not all feminine imagery may be so used. For example, to speak of the Spirit's motherly role in the new birth has good biblical grounding in the light of John 3. But to address the Holy Spirit as "Our Mother"—or "She" for that matter—is a different story.[86] Not only may it lead in an "earth mother" direction that compromises the divine transcen-

---

83. Basil Mitchell, *The Justification of Religious Belief* (New York: Oxford University Press, 1981), 19.

84. Ibid.

85. Ibid.

86. Contra Elizabeth A. Johnson, "Theological Case for God-She," 11–14. The whole article is an excellent presentation of a feminist view of traditional descriptions of God and the problems they pose for feminist theologians like Johnson. Her suggested ways forward, however, need to be sifted critically, as Scripture does not exercise sufficient control over the theologizing and an inadequately nuanced use of the doctrine of analogical religious language is in play. Basil Mitchell's more nuanced understanding of how analogous religious language is to be disciplined by Scripture is the needed corrective.

dence but *prima facie* it clashes with the way of address that Jesus taught his disciples, his own prayer practice, and that of the apostolic church.[87]

The God of scriptural revelation desires to be worshiped in both spirit (*pneuma*), which is to say in keeping with his nature, and truth (*alētheia*), which is to say, in keeping with reality. From our brief survey of Scripture, suffice it to say that a case can be made for using feminine imagery of God the Holy Spirit at both the adjectival and adverbial levels. But the onus is firmly on those who want to argue that God the Holy Spirit should be addressed and designated as feminine. And so in this study of the Holy Spirit's person and work, although feminine imagery might appear from time to time, the Holy Spirit, following scriptural precedent, will be designated "he" rather than "she" or "it."

IMPLICATIONS FOR BELIEF AND PRACTICE

We now turn to three practical matters of Christian thought, practice, and mission. If God is Spirit, how are we also able to speak of God the Spirit? And may we pray to the Holy Spirit? Lastly, how are we to engage with Islam in relation to the Holy Spirit?

If God Is Spirit, How Are We Also Able to Speak of God the Spirit?

The Johannine account of Jesus' baptism tells us that John the Baptist saw the Spirit (*pneuma*) descend from heaven like a dove (John 1:32). But a few chapters later, in John 4:24, Jesus informs the Samaritan woman at the well that God is spirit (*pneuma*). How can both claims be true if spirit has the same sense and referent in both cases?

Perhaps a parallel case may help. Scripture speaks of God as Father (Deut. 32:6) and also of Jesus' praying to the Father (John 17:1). Theologians have already turned their attention to this case and have drawn a distinction. If we call God "Father" when we are speaking of the Godhead in relation to us, we are speaking of God *essentialiter*. But when, for example, Jesus commands disciples to pray to the Father, at issue is the First Person of the Trinity. In this latter case we are thinking of God *personaliter*. According to the Protestant Scholastics, whether Lutheran or Reformed, we may predicate "Father" of God either *essentialiter* or *personaliter* depending on whether in mind is the whole triune Godhead or only the First Person of the Trinity, respectively.[88]

With regard to "spirit," when predicated of the Godhead as Jesus does in this encounter with the woman at the well, theologically considered, he

---

87. See Scobie, *Ways of Our God*, 146–147. For a careful theological treatment of the gender issue from an explicitly evangelical perspective see Bloesch, *God the Almighty*, 25–27.

88. See Muller, *Dictionary of Latin and Greek Theological Terms*, 106.

is speaking *essentialiter.* God is by nature spirit and therefore not limited to geographical location, which the woman was attempting to argue. Put more philosophically, God is not a material being located in space or constricted by space. Spirit is not matter (cf. Isa. 31:3 and John 4:24).[89] But theologically considered, when the Baptist speaks of the Spirit descending, he is speaking *personaliter.* The Third Person of the Trinity is in view. Such distinctions are the lifeblood of theological thought.

May We Pray to the Holy Spirit?

The Orthodox answer to the question is simply, "Of course!" In fact, the Orthodox prayer book opens with a prayer which invokes the Holy Spirit. Each morning the faithful of this church pray as they were taught to do as small children:

> Heavenly King, Paraclete, Spirit of truth, who art present everywhere and fillest all things, Treasury of goodness and Giver of life, come, dwell in us and cleanse us from all stain, and, of thy mercy, save our souls. Amen.[90]

Likewise in the Western church there are invocations addressed to the Holy Spirit, as in Bianco da Siena's hymn quoted in the opening chapter: "Come down, O Love divine." There are also prayers. For example, here is the beginning of one from William of St. Thierry of the twelfth century: "O God, Love, Holy Spirit, Love of the Father and the Son and their substantial will."[91] In addition, in both East and West, the Niceno-Constantinopolitan Creed affirms that the Spirit along with the Father and the Son ". . . is worshipped together and glorified together."[92] John Owen, perhaps the greatest Puritan theologian, argued that prayer to the Spirit could be justified on the basis of Revelation 1:4.[93] However, despite such examples, the question needs to be raised, is it appropriate to pray to the Spirit? For as John Macquarrie rightly says, "Most of the Church's prayers are in fact directed to the Father through the Son."[94]

89. See the helpful discussion on the metaphysics of the immaterial in contradistinction to the material in Feinberg, *No One Like Him,* 214–224.

90. Quoted in Parthenios, Patriarch of Alexandria and All Africa, "The Holy Spirit," in Michael Kinnamon, ed., *Signs of the Spirit: Official Report of the Seventh Assembly* (Geneva: WCC, 1991), 32.

91. Quoted in Bernard McGinn and Patricia Ferris McGinn, *Early Christian Mystics: The Divine Vision of the Spiritual Masters* (New York: Crossroad, 2003), 255.

92. Quoted in Bettenson and Maunder, eds., *Documents of the Christian Church,* 26.

93. See J. I. Packer, *A Quest for Holiness: The Puritan Vision of the Christian Life* (Wheaton, Ill.: Crossway, 1990), 207. Owen's exegetical warrant for such a claim is not easy to see.

94. John Macquarrie, *Two Worlds Are Ours: An Introduction to Christian Mysticism* (Minneapolis: Fortress, 2005), 72.

Questioning prayer to the Holy Spirit may seem inappropriate both on theological and logical grounds. After all, the Trinitarian Christian is praying to one God in three divine Persons: Father, Son, and Holy Spirit. Therefore, it may be argued, we quite properly may pray to the Spirit because the Spirit is God. Our Trinitarian theology would legitimate such a practice. Indeed if we only prayed to the Father then would our prayer life be in effect unitarian? J. I. Packer believes there is a case for praying to the Holy Spirit based on the deity of the Spirit and the Spirit's role in Christian experience.[95]

However, there is a problem. Scripture furnishes no examples of prayers to the Holy Spirit. Nor are there any examples in the text, either in the OT or in the NT, of characters offering prayer to the Holy Spirit.[96] Indeed, according to Max Turner the earliest example of worship which invokes the Holy Spirit is not found until the second century *Martyrdom and Ascension of Isaiah* (9:33–36).[97] In the Sermon on the Mount, Jesus taught his followers to invoke their heavenly Father. They are to pray, "Our Father in heaven" (Matt. 6:9). Moreover, he practiced himself what he taught his disciples to do, as can be seen in his so-called high priestly prayer. He prayed: "Father, the hour has come" (John 17:1). John's Gospel, it must be noted, appears to recognize a qualitative difference between Christ's natural sonship and the disciples' adoptive one, as John 20:17 implies.

What of prayer to Jesus? There are a few biblical texts that invoke Jesus himself as the addressee of NT prayers. Stephen, the early Christian martyr, provides one example. As the angry crowd stones him, Stephen prays, "Lord Jesus, receive my Spirit," and again, "Lord, do not hold this sin against them" (Acts 7:59–60). Another example is that of Paul. Paul prayed to Jesus his Lord with regard to the thorn in the flesh that he experienced, and did so repeatedly (2 Cor. 12:8–10). Regular prayer to Jesus also seems to have been a practice in the churches (1 Cor. 1:2). The letter to the Hebrews presents Jesus as our great High Priest. In this role he is ready to receive our pleas for help as we "draw near to the throne of grace" (Heb. 4:14–16). Even granted that there are NT examples of praying to Jesus, the great bulk of biblical evidence is that prayer is addressed to the Father. What's the explanation?

The reason is twofold: Jesus is our great High Priest, and the believer is adopted into the family of God. In his role as our great High Priest, Christ represents us to God and God to us. The Levitical priesthood pointed to him, as did the mysterious figure of Melchizedek. What was temporary and provisional is superseded by the permanent. But more than that, the

95. Packer, *Keep in Step,* 261.
96. Ibid. Packer acknowledges the absence.
97. Max Turner, "'Trinitarian' Pneumatology in the New Testament?—Towards an Explanation of the Worship of Jesus," *AsTJ* 57/58 no. 2/1 (Fall 2002/Spring 2003): 168.

preeminent blessing of the gospel, as Packer so helpfully has pointed out, is sonship (*huiothesia*).[98] Through the grace of God—not through any merit of our own—we are adopted into the family of God. The source of the believer's new life is the indwelling Spirit, who is the Spirit of the Son (Rom. 8:9). Consequently, when the believer prays in Christ (*en tō Christō*), the prayer language of Jesus—*abba*—becomes his or her own in effect (Rom. 8:15 and Gal. 4:6). For the same Spirit who energized Christ's humanity energizes our own. Thus it is fitting that we pray in Christ's name, not our own. His Spirit impels Christian prayer (John 14–16).

Scottish theologian James B. Torrance has paid particular attention to the theological implications of Christ's mediatorial role and that of the Spirit in relation to it. Torrance maintains,

> The Holy Spirit, through whom we participate in the person and work of Christ, exercises a twofold ministry which in a further way corresponds to the twofold ministry of Christ—namely—of *representing God to humanity* and of *representing humanity to God*.[99]

Christ in his humanity is our leader in worship, according to Torrance. Christ catches up our worship in his own as our great High Priest set over the household of God. This he does through the Holy Spirit. Torrance contends, "So in and through the mediatorial ministry of the Spirit, we worship the Father in the name of Christ."[100] In a somewhat speculative fashion, he asks whether the wording of Galatians 2:20 might be adapted. Thus, when we pray it is not we who pray but Christ who prays for us, and our prayers offered in the flesh (our creatureliness) are grounded on the faithfulness of the Christ who loved us and sacrificed himself for us. How is this possible? And how can this be? Through the dual mediatorial work of Christ and the Spirit, is Torrance's answer.[101]

In my view, it is not theologically wrong to pray to the Holy Spirit on occasion. However, if that practice becomes the norm then the problem of disproportion emerges. The gospel may be spoiled in many different ways. Christ may be "added to," as though his work were not enough to secure our reconciliation to God. For example, the teachers troubling the Galatians appear to have added the requirement of circumcision to that of trust in Jesus. In Paul's view, requiring such an addition of Gentiles nullified Christ's finished achievement on the cross (Gal. 2:21). The gospel may also be degraded by subtraction. Some in the early church period affirmed the

98. J. I. Packer, *Concise Theology: A Guide to Historic Christian Beliefs* (Wheaton, Ill.: Tyndale, 1993), 167.

99. James B. Torrance, *Worship, Community, and the Triune God of Grace* (Carlisle, England: Paternoster, 1996), 77, emphasis original.

100. Ibid.

101. Ibid., 78.

divinity of Christ but denied his humanity. Jesus only seemed to be human. This docetic error, as we have noted previously, confronted the original readers of John's first letter (1 John 4:1–3). The gospel may also be spoiled by giving part of the story more emphasis than Scripture warrants. Some present-day gospel preaching presents exceptionally elaborate and detailed eschatological schemes, whereas the apostles majored on the judgment to come, as the book of Acts makes plain (e.g., cf. Acts 10:42 and 17:31). Making prayer to the Holy Spirit the chief practice in Christian praying would be to fall into such an error. The Holy Spirit may be prayed to. The Spirit, after all, is God. And yet, the Holy Spirit is not to be prayed to in such a way as to displace the mediatorship of Christ as our great High Priest. In fact, if our regular prayer practice is to pray to the Father in the name of the Son in dependence upon the Spirit, then such praying exhibits the very structure of the gospel: the Father's sending of the Son, the Father's and the Son's sending of the Spirit of the Son, and our response through the one mediator between God and humankind.

How Are We to Understand Islam in Relation to the Holy Spirit?

From an Islamic point of view, belief in the Trinity, and with it belief in the deity of the Holy Spirit as the Third Person of the Godhead, are grave theological errors. The true religion is monotheism as taught in the Qur'an and by the Prophet. According to this view, Trinitarianism is an amalgam of pagan polytheistic ideas and the Pauline deification of Christ. In fact it is the invention of Athanasius in the fourth century.[102] Indeed, the Christian Trinity according to the Qur'an consists of Allah, Jesus, and Mary, as the Sura (chapter) on Women suggests:

> People of the Book [Christians], do not transgress the bounds of your religion. Speak nothing but the truth about Allah. The Messiah, Jesus the son of Mary, was no more than Allah's apostle and His Word which he cast to Mary: a spirit from Him. So believe in Allah and His apostles and do not say: 'Three.' . . . Allah is but one God. Allah forbids that He should have a son![103]

The last sentence above describes what is the sin of *shirk* (association), claiming as it does that Allah has a son. Hence anyone who abandons Trinitarianism and returns to the Islamic path is a revert, not a convert. He or she has reverted to the true religion of Abraham, Moses, and Jesus.

102. See the argument in "Ask About Islam," at http://www.islamonline.net/askaboutislam/display.asp?hquestionID=4987, accessed February 2, 2005.
103. *The Koran*, 4th rev. ed., trans. N. J. Dawood (Harmondsworth, Middlesex: Penguin, 1980), Sura 4:171, 383–384.

If there is no divine Trinity in Islam, who or what is the Holy Spirit for that religion?

A widely held view in Islam is that the Holy Spirit (Arabic, *Ruh Al-Qudus*) is definitely a "who."[104] The Holy Spirit is none other than the angel Gabriel, as in the Sura 19:17–19: "We sent to her [Mary] Our *ruuh* [angel Gabriel], and he appeared before her in the form of a man . . ."[105] But what of the Johannine teaching about the Paraclete (John 14–16)? In the Islamic view Jesus was predicting not the coming of the Holy Spirit but Muhammad as the prophet greater than he.

Islam joins a number of other first-millennium false trails in misunderstanding the Holy Spirit, all of which try to secure the sole rule of God (monarchy). Some in that period reduced the Holy Spirit to a force from God who indwells the man Jesus to a greater degree than in any other (technically, dynamic monarchianism).[106] Others argued that the Holy Spirit was one of the temporary modes of God's self-presentation in the history of salvation. The Father face of God gave way to the Son face and then finally to the Spirit face (technically, modalistic monarchianism).[107] Islam seeks to preserve the sole rule of God by reducing Jesus to the second greatest prophet and the Holy Spirit to merely an angel.

As in all such "unitarianisms," we are left with a deity who logically seems bereft without a creation, and we are left wondering how love can be (and has always been) the center of reality. Love is a relational value, and if God is the eternal Trinity then there has always been an object of love intra-deically: The Father loves the Son and the Spirit, the Son loves the Father and the Spirit, and the Spirit loves the Father and the Son. But not so if God is a simple monad.

In Islam, the awesomely transcendent Allah is merciful and is to be submitted to by all. After all, a Muslim is one who submits to the will of Allah. For in such submission, the argument runs, there is peace. How very different from the God who is the Holy Trinity and in whose divine dance

104. See the excellent discussion of the Holy Spirit in the Qur'an by Mark Durie, *Revelation? Guidance for the Perplexed* (Upper Mt. Gravatt, Queensland, Australia: CityHarvest, 2006), 55–61, esp. 57.

105. Quoted in the discussion of the Holy Spirit as Gabriel the angel in "Ask about Islam," in http://www.islamonline.net/askaboutislam/display.asp?hquestionID=4987, accessed February 2, 2005. The online article is a response to the question, "What Is the Holy Spirit?" The identification of Gabriel with the Holy Spirit is established by linking Matthew 1:18; Luke 1:26–27; and Sura 19:17–19.

106. Geoffrey Wainwright, "The Holy Spirit," 279. See also Pannenberg, *Jesus—God and Man,* 120–121, who argues, "Concepts very similar to patristic adoptionism have appeared in the eighteenth and nineteenth centuries in Kant, Schleiermacher, Ritschl, Adolf von Harnack, and others." Since he refers to Theodotus the tanner of the second century as a Patristic era adoptionist, it is clear that what others term "dynamic monarchianism" is in mind (ibid., 120).

107. Ibid. A contemporary manifestation of modalistic monarchian theology can be found in Oneness Pentecostalism. See David A. Reed, "Origins and Development of the Theology of Oneness Pentecostalism in the United States," *Pneuma* 1 (Spring 1979): 31–37.

of love we may participate through the Spirit! For in that holy fellowship lies our eternal life (John 17:3). This God is love and is to be loved.

EXCURSUS: How PARADIGMATIC IS THE TRINITY?

As noted in the previous chapter, as an expression of the Trinitarian revival, some Christian theologians see in the doctrine of the Trinity a social program for today. Brian Edgar, for example, writes, "The Trinity is also the Christian's paradigm for *social and political life.*"[108] The question may be raised as to whether, generally speaking, such an approach fails to be evangelical enough in the classic sense of the word. Donald Bloesch puts that classical sense well when he writes that he uses ". . . the term 'evangelical' in the sense of 'centered in the gospel' rather than in any ideological sense."[109]

My observation is that when the NT writers want to inform the consciences of their readers, they move from some aspect of the narrative of the gospel to do so. For example, if Paul wants to see an other-person-centered humility at Philippi, he does not describe an eternal humility of the Son toward the Father in the Godhead. Instead he draws his readers' attention to the Christ who humbled himself and became obedient even to the point of death (Phil. 2:5–11). Similarly when Paul calls upon readers to imitate God, they are to imitate how God in the gospel of Christ forgave them (Eph. 4:32–5:2).

Paul's imperatives are grounded on the indicatives of the gospel, likewise with Jesus. For example, when Jesus commands his disciples to love one another, he does not base the new commandment on his relationship of love with the Father. Instead the disciples are to love each other as Christ has loved them (John 13:34). The context of the issuing of the new commandment is the famous footwashing episode in which Jesus washes his disciples' feet (John 13). As is the case so often in John's account, the narrative has many layers of meaning. The need to wash feet points to a more ultimate need: the washing that the cross would provide (John 13:1–20). NT writers emphasize imitating the historic Christ in his post-incarnation ministry, not in the inner life of the essential Trinity (e.g., Rom. 15:1–3; 1 Cor. 11:1; 1 Pet. 2:21–23; 1 John 2:6).[110]

---

108. Brian Edgar, *The Message of the Trinity* (Leicester, England: Inter-Varsity, 2004), 29, emphasis original. Edgar, though, is aware of the difficulty of "connecting fundamental theological principles to large-scale social outcomes" (277). The *Catechism of the Catholic Church* appears to appreciate this difficulty when it states vaguely, "There is a certain semblance between the union of the divine persons and the fraternity that men are to establish among themselves in truth and love" (CCC, part 3, section 1, chapter 2, article 1, I, 1878 [459]). In fact, in this massive work of some 800 pages and 2,865 numbered paragraphs, the Trinity per se is hardly ever appealed to as an ethical paradigm.

109. Bloesch, *Holy Spirit*, 268.

110. Interestingly the Scriptures call upon believers to imitate the action of the God who forgives (e.g., Eph. 4:32–5:1), the Father who shows mercy (e.g., Luke 6:32–36), and the Son who humbled himself for us (e.g., Phil. 2:4–11), but nowhere does Scripture call on believers

The other approach, however, which is optimistic about the value of using a Trinitarian model for shaping our social life, needs some comment because of its increasing popularity. The works of D. Broughton Knox and the much more famous Jürgen Moltmann illustrate the point. Knox argues that Paul's words in 1 Corinthians 11:3 ("the head of Christ is God") provide us with a window into the very Trinitarian nature of God. He sees in this language a pattern of headship and response which the Christian and the church are to emulate. The Father is the eternal head of the Son. It is important to observe, though, that the headship he recommends is defined in terms of taking the initiative in service. This order is based in the first instance in the very nature of God and subsequently in the creation of male and female as images of God. Thus this style of headship ought to be reflected in the way men and women ought to relate to one another in a pattern of headship and response in the home and in the church.

Knox's position is a species of complementarianism. Complementarians argue that in the divine plan men and women are equal in value but differ in function. They are equal but different. Knox believed that this order with its pattern of headship and response ought to be seen not only in the family and the church but also in wider society.[111] Indeed, if this order is in the very nature of God and we are created as images of God, then it would appear to follow that this view should apply to the public square and not only to the home and the church. The logic of his view is hierarchical. For example, he is very comfortable with the language of the eternal subordination of the Son to the Father within the Trinity *ad intra*.[112] However, it is important to note that he did not subscribe to any kind of domineering of men over women.[113]

Other social Trinitarians take a very different course to the one described above. Jürgen Moltmann also sees the Trinity as our social program. But

---

to imitate the activity of the Spirit. The Spirit points away to the actions of another, as we shall see when at a later stage we turn to the ministry of the Spirit in NT perspective.

111. Complementarian Wayne Grudem pushes the envelope a tad too far when he seeks to establish an analogy between the Father and the Son in the Godhead, and the husband and wife in their marriage, with the children of the marriage as analogues of the Holy Spirit within the Godhead. See Grudem, *Systematic Theology*, 257.

112. Although taught by Charles Hodge, Augustus H. Strong, and Wayne Grudem inter alios, Kevin Giles has recently critiqued the notion of an "eternal subordination" as unorthodox. See his *The Trinity and Subordinationism: The Doctrine of God and the Contemporary Gender Debate* (Downers Grove, Ill.: InterVarsity Press, 2002); and the spirited reply by Mark Baddley, "The Trinity and Subordinationism: A Response to Kevin Giles," *RTR* 63 no. 1 (April 2004): 29–42. Giles scores some good points but overstates the case. Moreover his use of sources is questionable. The debate is not between orthodoxy and heterodoxy but an intramural one about order (*taxis*) within the essential Trinity and its implications.

113. For the substance of this paragraph see D. Broughton Knox, *The Everlasting God* (Homebush, N.S.W., Australia: Lancer, 1988), 69–75 and 129–146. In other places, Knox seems to restrict the pattern to family and church life but to exclude wider social life. See D. Broughton Knox, *Sent by Jesus* (Edinburgh, and Carlisle, Pa.: Banner of Truth, 1992), 46–47.

unlike Knox, for Moltmann the Trinity is the model of egalitarianism rather than complementarianism. Given the divine nature with its eternal, internal freedom and equality, the God who is Father, Son, and Holy Spirit stands opposed to all hierarchical uses of power whether in the church or the wider world. Moreover, simple non-Trinitarian monotheisms can be and have been historically agents of oppression. So he argues. On Moltmann's more radical proposal, the social program that Trinitarian theology ought logically to underwrite is one of "social personalism or personalistic socialism."[114] Men and women, according to this view, are equal in value and, excepting functions tied to biology, there is no necessary difference in function between them whether in the family or church or wider society. In Moltmann's theology the equality of the sexes flows from his model of the Trinity.

What are we to make of these very divergent applications of Trinitarian theology? At the very least the divergence of opinion between a Knox and a Moltmann underlines the difficulty of moving from describing a model of the Trinity to prescribing the shape of our social life. Precisely which model is to be followed is the issue.[115]

My own view is that Trinitarian theology helps us see that, in the Christian frame of reference, the one tri-personal God, who is relational on the inside, is ultimate in reality and value. In addition, our Trinitarian theology helps us see that human persons and their relations as divine image-bearers (more anon) are next to ultimate in reality and value—albeit as creatures. Such a frame of reference, in general terms, enables the Christian to be humanistic but not a humanist per se. Human persons and their relationships really do matter in the scheme of things. Human beings are not simply thrown up by a blind evolutionary process to become flotsam and jetsam in an impersonal universe that is at the mercy of time and chance. One would expect and hope then that Christians would be the great defenders of the human in a world where the value of humans and their relations are at risk, not only from the traditional threats of war, disease, poverty, and famine but also from those who would seek to see the human replaced through technology by the post-human in some kind of techno-utopia.[116] However, I am not convinced that we can be much more specific and erect social models for marriage, church, and society based on speculative reconstructions of the inner life of the Trinity.

114. See Jürgen Moltmann, *The Trinity and the Kingdom of God* (London: SCM, 1981), 199. See also his *Experiences in Theology* (London: SCM, 2000), 332, where the heading is "The Trinity is our social programme."

115. Which model to follow gets even more complicated if the *filioque* dispute is factored into the discussion. Is the Eastern *taxis* to be followed or the Western one?

116. See the brilliant but chilling article by Ellen Ullman, "Programming the Post-Human," in *Harper's Magazine*, October, 2002, 60–70.

II

THE MINISTRY OF THE SPIRIT—
OLD TESTAMENT PERSPECTIVES

CHAPTER

FOUR

THE SPIRIT AND CREATION

In the previous part we considered the Spirit's person and thus the question, Who is the Spirit? We now turn our attention to the Holy Spirit's role in creation and its preservation. Or in classical terms, we now begin to explore the Spirit's work.[1] With regard to this aspect of the Spirit's work there are important perspectives on the Spirit and creation to be found in the Torah (esp. Genesis) and the Writings (esp. Job and the Psalms).[2] However, tricky questions of translation of the key texts and therefore of theological interpretation will be unavoidable. One of the theological questions that will be raised is whether the Spirit's ongoing work in creation should be understood as continuous creation (*creatio continuata*) or as providentially preserving the created order in its existence (*conservatio*), or as the perfecting cause that leads creatures to their destinies. Questions of the translation of terms and the interpretation of the texts, as well as the diversity of scholarly opinion, bring to the fore a critical hermeneutical consideration: How is the OT testimony to be understood as part of

1. According to George S. Hendry there are two possible methodological approaches to pneumatology. The first is what he terms "the canonical." This method follows the flow of redemptive history. He himself prefers the second, "the chronological," which follows the order of theological debate in the course of subsequent church history. This latter approach focuses on problems such as the Spirit's relation to the Trinity. See George S. Hendry, *The Holy Spirit in Christian Theology* (Philadelphia: Westminster, 1956), 15–16. The present writer has begun this study with the chronological—to use Hendry's categories—but continues with the canonical. In so doing, topics such as the Spirit's relation to creation won't fall out of view, which is the danger of the Hendry preference *simpliciter* (see esp. ibid., 27–29).

2. In this part of our study it is a moot point as to whether the key story of the Spirit at work in the re-creation of God's people in the valley of dry bones (Ezekiel 37) should have been included. The Spirit is not only *spiritus creator* but also *spiritus recreator*. However, I have elected to discuss the re-creation of Israel in the chapter dealing with the Spirit and messianic expectations.

Christian Scripture? Next we shall look at the stimulating contribution of Calvin to our theme. Lastly we shall examine some practical implications of our study of the Spirit's work in creation. In particular we shall discuss the appreciation we should have of the Spirit's role in creation and the modesty with which we should make claims about how much we exactly know of that work in its detailed execution.

However, as alluded to earlier, before we turn to the biblical testimony per se it is important to note a fundamental challenge to any who attempt to reflect theologically on the subject of the Holy Spirit, whether in terms of the Old or the New Testament. Charles H. H. Scobie describes the problem concisely:

> The Hebrew *rûach* (feminine; LXX predominantly *pneuma*, neuter) can mean, depending on context, "wind," "breath," or "spirit." . . . In the NT the Greek *pneuma* carries the same three basic connotations.[3]

Each one of the texts that we shall examine in this chapter will raise the question of how best to render the Hebrew *"rûach."* Contextual considerations will be paramount in addressing the question.

THE CHALLENGES OF TRANSLATION

Traditionally, Christian theology has seen in the opening chapter of the Bible a reference to both the Trinity and to the Holy Spirit. God creates (*bārā'*) the heavens and the earth, and it is his Spirit (*rûach*) who hovers over the chaotic deep (Gen. 1:1–2). This same God creates male and female in his image and prefaces this creative act by saying, "Let us make man in our image" (v. 26). God acts like a great king. What he says happens. His will is done. The creative process is achieved by the divine Word, which by implication is carried by the divine breath.[4] This is very much like our own human words, which are also carried by our breath if they are to be known. All this is redolent with suggestiveness for later Trinitarian thinking, as can be seen in the theological labors of theologians as separated in time as Irenaeus of the second and third centuries and Karl Barth of

---

3. Charles H. H. Scobie, *The Ways of Our God: An Approach to Biblical Theology* (Grand Rapids, Mich., and Cambridge: Eerdmans, 2003), 269. See also on this point Max Turner, *The Holy Spirit and Spiritual Gifts: Then and Now*, rev. ed. (Carlisle, England: Paternoster, 1999), 4, esp. fn 2.

4. There is a helpful treatment of the relation between Word and Spirit in Genesis 1 and in other OT texts in George T. Montague, *The Holy Spirit: Growth of a Biblical Tradition: A Commentary on the Principal Texts of the Old and New Testaments* (New York and Toronto: Paulist, 1976), 66. Montague's critical commitments need to be noted, though, and also his use of the Apocrypha, which for him as a Catholic is the Word of God.

the twentieth.[5] And it is also redolent with suggestiveness as to how God works his purposes out by both Word and Spirit. But is the Scripture able to bear this dogmatic weight with regard to the Trinity in general and the Holy Spirit in particular?

With regard to the Spirit's role in creation, some recent translations illustrate the issue. The English Standard Version of Genesis 1:2b reads,

> And the *Spirit* of God was hovering over the face of the waters.

And the New International Version,

> . . . and the *Spirit* of God was hovering over the waters.

But the New Revised Standard Version translates the Hebrew,

> . . . a *wind* from God swept over the face of the waters.

And the Jewish Study Bible,

> . . . and a *wind* from God sweeping over the water . . .

Both the NRSV and JSB have alternatives in the margins. The NRSV offers two of them: "the spirit of God" and "a mighty wind." The JSB offers one alternative: "the spirit of." In both of these translations "spirit"—albeit in the margin—is lower case. In contrast, both the ESV and NIV offer no alternatives and both have assumed that there is an implied metaphor at work in the text, which is that of the Spirit's (capital "S") acting like a bird that hovers.

Such differences show the challenge of translation.[6] Are the ESV and NIV theological maximizers on dogmatic grounds? Hence the Spirit is clearly God the Spirit as the capital "S" suggests, and "hovering" brings with it the implied metaphor of bird-like behavior, which links with the NT symbol

---

5. For Irenaeus see Sinclair Ferguson, *The Holy Spirit* (Leicester, England: Inter-Varsity, 1996), 258, endnote 7. Ferguson describes this use of "the opening words of Genesis" as "a misplaced hermeneutical desire" (18). See also Augustine's "The Literal Meaning of Genesis," in *Saint Augustine on Genesis*, trans. Edmund Hill (Hyde Park, N.Y.: New City, 2002), 234, for his Trinitarian reading of Genesis 1:26. Calvin is much more cautious in his commentary on Genesis 1:26. Even so he argues that the text provides a testimony to the plurality of Persons in the Godhead (*Commentary on Genesis*, trans. and ed. John King [Albany, Ore.: 1998]). For Barth see Karl Barth, *CD*, III, 1, 191–192, quoted in John McTavish and Harold Wells, *Karl Barth: Preaching through the Christian Year* (Edinburgh: T. & T. Clark, 1978), 70–75, esp. 71.

6. The challenge is a long-standing one. For example, according to Max Turner, "one of the oldest translations of the OT, the Aramaic targum," renders *rûach* as "wind" (*Holy Spirit and Spiritual Gifts*, 4). But as C. F. D. Moule points out, *The Odes and Psalms of Solomon* renders *rûach* along what became the traditional line (*The Holy Spirit* [London and Oxford: Mowbray, 1978], 106, endnote 10).

of the Spirit as a dove.[7] In contradistinction, the NRSV and JSB seem to be theological minimizers.[8] The Spirit becomes an inanimate wind from God that sweeps rather than hovers. These differences show that translation of Scripture is not theologically neutral. The question, which applies to any of the translations, is whether it exhibits academic integrity. In my view each of the translations is academically respectable, which is to say that a linguistic argument may be made for each. None is arbitrary. However, some arguments are more convincing than others.[9]

Any responsible commentator on Genesis has to wrestle with this question.[10] The problem is long-standing. In the sixteenth century Calvin commented: "Interpreters have wrested this passage in various ways. The opinion of some that it means the wind, is too frigid to require refutation."[11] His own exegetical assessment was that, "They who understand by it the Eternal Spirit of God, do rightly."[12] Recently evangelical commentator Gordon J. Wenham acknowledges the "deep disagreement among modern commentators as to the correct interpretation" of the phrase "And the Wind of God hovered over the waters."[13] His own view is to translate the phrase as "the Wind of God," taking wind "as a concrete and vivid image of the Spirit of God."[14] Presumably this is the reason that he uses a capital "W." He suggests that "hovered" fits better with "wind" than either "breath" or

7. This would constitute the first symbol of the Spirit in the canon. Such symbols are either implicit as in Genesis 1:2 or explicit as in Mark 1:10 (the dove). According to Edwin H. Palmer (*The Holy Spirit,* rev. ed. [Philadelphia: Presbyterian & Reformed, 1971], 153–163), other symbols of the Spirit include water (an implied symbol, e.g., Titus 3:5); wind (implied, e.g., John 3:8); breath (implied, e.g., Ps. 104:29); fire (implied, e.g., Acts 2:3); oil (implied, e.g., Luke 4:18); and fruit tree (implied, Gal. 5:22). The theologian needs care in reflecting on such symbols lest he or she go well beyond what is warranted by the text into the realm of fantasy. Hence there is no separate treatment of such symbols in the present work.

8. Theological reflection on Genesis 1:2 also falls in either a maximizing or minimizing direction. For example, Abraham Kuyper is a maximizer, while C. F. D. Moule adopts a "minimizing position." See Abraham Kuyper, *The Work of the Holy Spirit,* trans. Henri De Vries (Grand Rapids, Mich.: Eerdmans, 1975), 27; and Moule, *Holy Spirit,* 19 and 106, endnote 12, respectively.

9. These remarks apply *mutatis mutandis* to the translation challenge of the very first statement in Scripture. Does Genesis 1:1 speak of "In the beginning God . . ." (ESV and NIV) or "In the beginning when God . . ." (NRSV) or "When God began to create . . ." (JSB)?

10. Back in the Patristic era, Augustine saw the difficulty and canvassed the three common interpretations of his day: "the Holy Spirit," "a created vitality," and "the element air" (*Saint Augustine,* 122–123). He wisely observed, "But whichever of these opinions is true, we are bound to believe that God is the author and founder of all things that have originated, both those that are seen and those that are not seen" (ibid., 123).

11. John Calvin, "Genesis," *CJCC,* comment on Gen. 1:2.

12. Ibid.

13. See Gordon J. Wenham, *Genesis 1–15,* WBC, comment on Gen. 1:2.

14. Ibid. Wolfhart Pannenberg takes a similar view (*The Apostles' Creed: In the Light of Today's Questions,* trans. Margaret Kohl [London: SCM, 1972], 133). He prefers "stormy wind."

"spirit" does.[15] John H. Sailhamer, also commenting from an evangelical stance, has a different view.[16] Like Wenham he acknowledges the diversity of scholarly opinion. However, in contradistinction to Wenham and others he maintains that the notion of hover (*mĕrahepeth*) fits better with "Spirit" than does "wind." His reason is as follows. In the last book of the Torah occurs the only other reference to "hover." In this text God is compared to an eagle hovering (*yĕrahēp*) over its nest of young (Deut. 32:11).[17] There are deliberate parallels, he argues, between the creation of the world and the creation of Israel. He also sees a parallel between the Spirit of God's (*rûach 'elohim*) work in creation (Gen. 2:2, does he mean 1:2?) and the Spirit of God's (*rûach 'elohim*) work in the creation of the tabernacle (Ex. 31:3).[18]

What then is the pastor to do, when even evangelical commentators divide on detail? In addressing the question, it is important to note that both Wenham and Sailhamer understand Genesis 1:2 as a reference to the Holy Spirit of God. Philosopher D. Elton Trueblood offers a useful tool for thought, which may be applied to our problem. He calls it "the method of comparative difficulties."[19] Whose argumentation in general, and use of evidence in particular, has the fewer and/or less weighty difficulties? In my view, Sailhamer has the better of the argument. For example, Wenham thinks that "the verb" "hovering" fits best with the metaphor of wind, while Sailhamer argues for "Spirit" as a better fit, especially in the light of the reference in Deuteronomy 32:11 to the eagle's hovering. I find it hard to imagine a wind that hovers (or a breath that hovers, for that matter). But I can imagine a hovering eagle and such a metaphor used of a living reality such as the Spirit of God.[20]

15. Ibid. See Wenham, *Genesis 1–15*, WBC, comment on Gen. 1:2.

16. John H. Sailhamer, "Genesis," *EBC*, comment on Gen. 1:2.

17. George T. Montague has an excellent treatment of the translation options and decides against "wind" and for "spirit" on the basis of Deuteronomy 32:11 and the relation of the Hebrew to the Ugaritic *rhp* as used in the *Tales of Aqhat* ("The Fire in the Wind: The Holy Spirit in Scripture," in Bradford E. Hinze and D. Lyle Dabney, eds., *Advents of the Spirit: An Introduction to the Current Critical Study of Pneumatology* [Milwaukee: Marquette University Press, 2001], 37–40).

18. Sailhamer, "Genesis," *EBC*. Evangelical commentator William J. Dumbrell favors the traditional translation of "Spirit" rather than "wind." He points out that: ". . . if the adversarial role of the Spirit is accepted (indicated by the translation of the conjunction at the beginning of the clause as 'but' rather than 'and'), then the verse paints a picture of order imposed upon an unruly element in creation in a way that is completely congruent with the notion of creation emerging as a result of conflict, which is found in later biblical poetry" (*The Search for Order: Biblical Eschatology in Focus* [Eugene, Ore.: Wipf & Stock, 2001], 17). However, he maintains that the Spirit in view in this particular text is God in action rather than the Third Person of the Trinity (18).

19. D. Elton Trueblood, *General Philosophy* (Grand Rapids, Mich.: Baker, 1976), 73–75.

20. In terms of symbols of the Spirit, the association of the Spirit with a bird, based on Genesis 1:2, began early in Christian commentary. See, for example, Ephrem the Syrian (fl. 363–373) , "Commentary on Genesis," in Andrew Louth, ed., *Ancient Christian Commentary on Scripture, Old Testament I: Genesis 1–11* (Downers Grove, Ill.: InterVarsity Press, 2001), 6.

The challenge of translating *rûach* will arise at many other points in this work—indeed, later in this chapter—and will be addressed in situ as necessary.

THE SPIRIT AND THE PRIMORDIAL CREATION

So what then is the opening chapter of Scripture telling us about the Holy Spirit's role in the primordial creation? According to Calvin, the Spirit renders the "undigested mass" of the initial creation ("without form and void") into a stable platform for the subsequent acts of divine creating.[21] The Holy Spirit exercises chaos management.[22] The creation week then unfolds, climaxing in the seventh day of rest. The Hebrew working week provides the literary framework for understanding the divine activity.[23] Whether the divine days of creating correspond to our twenty-four-hour day or to whole geological ages is beyond the scope of our discussion. Suffice it to say that Scripture presents the work of God in a readily comprehensible way using ordinary language with the profoundest content. Interestingly, apart from the initial reference to the Spirit in Genesis 1:2, there is no subsequent explicit reference in the rest of the rhetorical unit (Gen. 1:3–2:3). However, as we shall see next, the Writings amplify the Genesis story.

In the Psalms we find some important references to *rûach* that display their indebtedness to the Genesis creation narratives or a similar tradition.[24] In Psalm 33:6 we find that, "By the word of the LORD the heavens were made, and by the breath [*rûach*] of his mouth all their host" (ESV). The New International Version, the New Revised Standard Version, and the Jewish Study Bible also translate *rûach* as "breath." Creation is by God's

---

This association will also figure at a later stage in our discussion of the NT evidence concerning the Spirit, especially that provided by the account of Jesus' baptism and the role of the dove. In an earlier footnote I cautioned against letting symbols take on a life of their own beyond the warrant of the text. Ephrem provides a case in point. He maintained that, "[The Holy Spirit] warmed the waters with a kind of vital warmth, even bringing them to the boil [How does he know this?] through intense heat in order to make them fertile. The action of a hen is similar. It sits on its eggs, making them fertile through the warmth of incubation."

21. Calvin, "Genesis," *CJCC*, comment on Gen. 1:2.

22. Kuyper contends, ". . . the material forces of the universe do not proceed from the Holy Spirit [per se], nor did He deposit in matter the dormant seeds and germs of life. His special task begins only *after* the creation of matter with the germs of life in it" (*Work of the Holy Spirit*, 29, emphasis original). This appears to be Kuyper's application of the idea of appropriation. Montague argues in *Holy Spirit*, 67, "The *spirit* of God thus disposes the chaos to hear in obedience the *word* of God" (emphasis original).

23. The precise nature of the genre of Genesis 1:1–2:3 is much debated, even in evangelical circles. For a good coverage of the approaches—and with a view different than this writer's—see John Feinberg, *No One Like Him: The Doctrine of God* (Wheaton, Ill.: Crossway, 2001), 574–624. Feinberg holds to a modified twenty-four-hour-day theory.

24. For example see the comments by Peter C. Craigie on the background to Psalm 33:6 (*Psalms 1–50*, WBC, comment on Ps. 33:6).

word and God's breath.[25] But is this more than synonymous parallelism? C. F. D Moule thinks not. In fact in his opinion, "breath of his lips" is to be rendered "at his command."[26] However, J. I. Packer takes a different view and cites Psalm 33:6 as evidence of the Spirit's activity of molding "*creation* into shape" and animating "created beings."[27] Yet for him, the verse is not evidence for the distinct personhood of the Spirit. He maintains that the distinct personhood of the Spirit was not part of the OT revelation. And so our verse is about God in action rather than the Third Person of the Trinity per se.[28] However, Boyd Hunt is more sanguine. Our verse is evidence of the Holy Spirit's work "in creation to create order and beauty."[29] Robert Gromacki is more cautious. Although he comes to the same conclusion as Hunt, he is sensitive to the issue of whether the text is "an anthropomorphism or a reference to the Holy Spirit."[30] For him it is "plausible to believe that the Holy Spirit actively energized the spoken decree of God in creation."[31] Suffice it to say at this stage that this verse raises the questions of metaphor, sense, and reference, as will some of the other biblical evidence that we shall consider in this discussion.

The book of Job contains three references germane to our interests. Two of them Abraham Kuyper took to be evidence of the Holy Spirit's work in creation (Job 26:13 and 33:4).[32] Job speaks in 26:13: "By his wind [*rûach*] the heavens were made fair; his hand pierced the fleeing serpent." Elihu adds in 33:4: "The Spirit [*rûach*] of God has made me, and the breath of the Almighty gives me life."[33] The third reference is Elihu once more saying, "If he [God] should set his heart to it and gather to himself his spirit [*rûach*] and his breath, all flesh would perish together, and man would return to the dust" (34:14–15). These ESV translations show the challenge of interpretation. In the first instance (26:13) God's creative wind is taken

25. Montague comments, "We note the association of word and spirit (breath) again. The verse reflects the theology of Genesis 1:1-3, where spirit and the word are both associated in the cosmifying of creation" (*Holy Spirit,* 70).

26. Moule, *Holy Spirit,* 18. He argues that it is not until the intertestamental period that *rûach* becomes "a mediating agent in creation," as in Judith 16:14.

27. J. I. Packer, *Keep in Step with the Spirit* (Leicester, England: Inter-Varsity, 1984), 57–58, emphasis original.

28. Ibid., 59.

29. Boyd Hunt, *Redeemed! Eschatological Redemption and the Kingdom of God* (Nashville: Broadman & Holman, 1993), 32.

30. Robert G. Gromacki, "The Holy Spirit: Who He Is, What He Does," in Charles R. Swindoll and Roy B. Zuck, eds., *Understanding Christian Theology* (Nashville: Thomas Nelson, 2003), 430.

31. Ibid.

32. Kuyper, *Work of the Holy Spirit,* 22 and 27. Gromacki is even more sanguine than Kuyper and contends that there are three verses which are "references to creation and to the Spirit of God": namely, Job 26:13; 27:3; and 33:4 ("Holy Spirit: Who He Is, What He Does," 430–431).

33. Strangely, Kuyper attributes the speech to Job, not Elihu (*Holy Spirit,* 33).

to be in view, although contextually it would seem to make more sense to translate *rûach* as "breath" (as in the NIV) to parallel the anthropomorphism of "hand" in the rest of the verse. In the second instance (33:4) the Holy Spirit appears to be in view, as evidenced by the capital "S". Since *rûach* belongs to the phrase "Spirit of God," there is a rationale for this rendering. In the final reference (34:14–15) *rûach* seems understood to be something like "vitality." In all three passages there are intracanonical resonances: in 26:13 and 33:4, with the creation narrative of Genesis 1; in the case of 33:4 and 34:14–15 there appear to be echoes of Genesis 2:7 also.

The Genesis resonances continue in Psalm 104. This great psalm blesses the Lord for his greatness as Creator and sustainer. The God who is both transcendent and immanent is in view. The creatures of the earth are contingent upon the will of the Lord. If he feeds them, they live (Ps. 104:27–28). But, "When you hide your face, they are dismayed; when you take away their breath [*rûach*], they die and return to the dust" (v. 29). However, "When you send forth your Spirit [*rûach*], they are created, and you renew the face of the ground [v. 30]." The Jewish Study Bible renders *rûach* as "breath" in both verses 29 and 30, while the NRSV has "breath" in verse 29 and "spirit" (lower case) in verse 30, with "breath" in the margin for verse 30. So again the question is whether in view is the Holy Spirit of God per se or God in action, more generally speaking, as breath. Be that as it may, as George T. Montague points out, there is a fascinating relationship in the text between God's face (*pānîm*) and his spirit (*rûach*) which is reinforced by the text's chiastic structure. The theological point that the text is making is that God is personally and actively at work in creation.[34]

A theologically maximizing approach to the verses we have considered would contend that in Genesis 1:2; Psalms 33:6; 104:29–30; Job 26:13; 33:4; and 34:14–15 there is evidence for the role of the Holy Spirit in creation or its shaping or its maintenance (Kuyper and Gromacki et al.). On the other hand, a minimizing approach would see these references as metaphor or anthropomorphisms of God in action as Creator and sustainer, but not of the Holy Spirit specifically (Packer, Ferguson, Green et al.). This latter view is not necessarily dismissive of the notion of God as Trinity and thus of the Holy Spirit as the Third Person of the Godhead. Rather the issue is one of responsible exegesis and not saying more than the OT text can bear.[35]

This diversity of scholarly opinion, which we shall simply continue to note for now so that its full weight might be felt, raises the crucial question of how such evidence is to be read as part of Christian Scripture canonically viewed, a subject to which we shall turn anon. But first some theological questions raised by our texts.

34. Montague, *Holy Spirit*, 71.
35. I chose Packer, Ferguson, and Green to illustrate this point as each is a committed Trinitarian.

Creatio ex Nihilo, Creatio Continuata, OR *Conservatio,* OR PERFECTING CAUSE?

Whether the material so far considered is about the Holy Spirit in particular, or more generally speaking, about God in action, there is an important
question to entertain: Do these verses speak of divine creation, or divine
shaping of creation, or divine maintenance of the created order, or divine
perfecting of creation? In classical theological categories, are they about
creatio ex nihilo (creation out of nothing), or *creatio continuata* (creation
continued), or *conservatio* (creation providentially preserved in being), or
a mix of these? Or is a fresh category needed? Let us review our texts with
these questions in mind.

In the Genesis 1:2 text the creation of the heavens and the earth are presupposed, as summed up in verse 1. And so the Spirit per se is not presented
as the agent of creation *ex nihilo*.[36] Kuyper sees the Spirit's work at this
stage as one of "ordering" by which "the formless took form, the hidden
life emerged, and things created were led to their destiny."[37] (In the text
the Spirit does appear to be opposed to the chaos that is "without form
and void.") He maintains that ". . . the material forces of the universe do
not proceed from the Holy Spirit [alone as a special work]. . . . His special
task begins only *after* the creation of matter with the germs of life in it."[38]
In terms of the classical categories, if Kuyper is right, the role of *rûach* in
Genesis 1:2 comports better with the idea of *continuata creatio* than with
either *creatio ex nihilo* or *conservatio*.[39] The Spirit is not presented as creating out of nothing, nor of simply maintaining the created order. Instead a
created platform is now in place for the unfolding of the days on which the
divine breath will carry the divine fiat into action, climaxing in the seventh
day of Sabbath rest (Gen. 1:3–2:3). Better than all three, in my view, is the
idea of the Spirit as perfecting cause leading creatures to their appointed
ends or destinies, as both Basil of Caesarea and Abraham Kuyper maintain.
We do see development in the Genesis story as it unfolds. According to
divine observation the creation moves from "good" (*tôb*) to "very good"
(*tôb mě'ôd*) over the course of the divine working week (cf. Gen. 1:4, 10,
12, 18, 21, 25 and then climactically, 31). God's good purposes are progres-
sively brought to completion.

However, the ideas of *creatio continuata* (or *continua*) on the one hand,
and *conservatio* on the other, are very relevant to the interpretation of

36. For a useful discussion of *creatio ex nihilo* see John Feinberg, *No One Like Him,*
352–357.

37. Kuyper, *Work of the Holy Spirit,* 30.

38. Ibid., 29, emphasis original.

39. For these scholastic terms and their import see Richard A. Muller, *Dictionary of Latin
and Greek Theological Terms: Drawn Principally from Protestant Scholastic Theology* (Grand
Rapids, Mich.: Baker, 1985), 81, 85, and 251–252, respectively.

Psalm 104:29–30. Without the breath of God, creatures cease to be. Here the Spirit's work is either that of continuing the creation in ever fresh ways, or, as a subset of divine providence, maintaining the created order in existence.[40] With relevance to our text, OT scholar Bernard W. Anderson comments, "Creation is not just an event that occurred in the beginning, at the foundation of the earth, but is God's continuing activity of sustaining creatures and holding everything in being."[41] Willem VanGemeren adds, "More usually this activity of God is referred to as Providence."[42] On the other hand, Bruce Milne sees our text as evidence for "continuing creation" and warns of the need to give it and others—he cites Job 9:8, 9; Isaiah 42:5; 44:24; and 45:18—their due weight in order to counteract any deistic tendencies on our part.[43] The thrust of the psalm is consistent with either view. Perhaps Karl Barth puts it best when in relation to our text he says of the OT testimony to the Holy Spirit, "But it describes Him (this is especially clear in Ps. 104:29f.) as the divine *conditio sine qua non* of the creation and the preservation of the creature."[44]

In general terms, C. F. D. Moule rightly contends that in the OT most commonly the Holy Spirit is ". . . not actually creative in the sense of making the substance of a thing but life-giving in the sense of animating it when made."[45] An exception in his opinion is Job 33:4: "But the fact remains that the only clear instance in the Old Testament itself of the spirit [note, lower case] as a creative force is in Job 33:4."[46] In this text Elihu states that, "The Spirit of God has made me, and the breath of the Almighty gives me life." Kuyper sees in this text evidence for the Spirit's "special work" in relation to the creation of the "human personality."[47] This special work, which results in the creation of humanity by the divine breath, is that which distinguishes us from animals. He links Job 33:4 and Genesis 2:7.[48] In the latter text, the divine breath makes Adam into "a living creature." Once again our text appears most amenable to the idea of the Spirit as the perfecting cause rather than to the ideas of creation *ex nihilo* or *continuata* or

---

40. Leslie C. Allen sees the divine work, described in this psalm, as one of sustenance. See his comments on Psalm 104:29–30 (*Psalms 100–150*, WBC).

41. Quoted in Willem VanGemeren, "Psalms," *EBC,* comment on Ps. 104:30.

42. Ibid.

43. Bruce Milne, *Know the Truth: A Handbook of Christian Belief* (London and Singapore: Inter-Varsity and S+U, 1983), 73. Appealing to the Genesius-Kautzsch *Hebrew Grammar,* Milne argues from the active Hebrew participles used in the texts he cites. The difficulty is that the argument also allows *conservatio* as well as perfecting cause, although it does effectively counter deism.

44. Barth, *CD,* III, 1, 57–59 quoted in McTavish and Wells, *Karl Barth,* 57.

45. Moule, *Holy Spirit,* 19. He specifically cites in evidence both Job 27:3 and Psalm 104:29 among other texts.

46. Ibid.

47. Kuyper, *Work of the Holy Spirit,* 33.

48. Ibid.

conservatio. Or to put it in Kuyper's quaint way, the Spirit leads creatures to their destinies.[49]

But again, are these texts about the Holy Spirit per se or about God the Spirit in action? This is the question that no longer can be postponed.

READING THE OT AS CHRISTIANS

As was said in the introduction, it is one thing to have a high view of biblical authority as God's Word written, albeit in inspired human words; it is quite another to know how to interpret those Scriptures aright. The challenge of interpretation becomes particularly acute when the question of how to read the OT responsibly as Christians comes to the fore. Our texts that deploy *rûach* (translated variously as "Spirit," "spirit," "wind," and "breath") provide a case in point, and we have already noted something of the challenge of translation, beginning with the second verse in the Bible.

Max Turner poses the problem succinctly. I quote *in extenso,* as his comments refer to all the texts considered thus far:

> Part of the problem was that the Hebrew word used—*rûach*—sometimes denotes a storm wind, sometimes 'breath', sometimes 'vitality' or 'life', and so it was not always easy to be sure whether or not a particular instance of *rûach* referred to God's Spirit. Anyone who has compared different English versions of Genesis 1:2 will have become acutely aware of the problem. . . . Similar ambiguities attach to other references usually quoted to support the view that the Spirit was involved in creation.[50]

To illustrate the last point he discusses in a footnote the following texts: Psalm 33:6; 104:30; and Genesis 2:7; then he cites Psalm 104:29; Job 27:3; 33:4; and 34:14–15 for further exploration.[51]

Significantly, all the OT texts that Turner finds problematical, Abraham Kuyper viewed as evidence of the work of the Third Person of the Trinity. So are the maximizers like Kuyper eisegeting (reading meaning into) the OT? Or are those who question the theological use of the texts unnecessarily reductionistic and therefore minimalist? Is there a way that the exegete, who wants to work with the natural sense and within the horizon of the original readership, the biblical theologian, who wants to work with the canon but using the canon's own categories, and the systematician, who wants the freedom to draw on the exegete, the biblical theologian, the canon, and the tradition, can all live in peace?

49. Ibid., 31.
50. Turner, *Holy Spirit and Spiritual Gifts,* 4.
51. Ibid., fn 2.

Evangelical systematic theologian J. I. Packer exemplifies such a way. He acknowledges that the exegesis of the OT texts regarding the Spirit shows *rûach* to mean "power in action" or "God at work."[52] He writes, ". . . the Spirit in the Old Testament is God active as *creator, controller, revealer, quickener,* and *enabler.*"[53] Furthermore, he maintains:

> You could truly say that references to God's *Spirit* signify God at work in resolute omnipotence, his *arm* and *zeal* acting together, but it would not be true to say that these references express any thought on the writer's part of a plurality of persons within the unity of the Godhead. The truth of the Trinity is a New Testament revelation.[54]

But having said the above, he goes on to argue that, "The right way for followers of Christ to read the Old Testament is in the light of all that was revealed in and through Christ and that now lies before us in the New Testament."[55] He contends that "Apostolic Christians" are to read their OT in the light of the NT's "revelation of the Spirit's distinct personhood." He sees a parallel with the Trinity and the OT. Christians are to view the OT insistence on the oneness of God with the Trinity in mind.[56]

Packer maintains that there is nothing arbitrary in his position and use of Scripture.[57] But this is the very issue that worries the exegete and the biblical theologian. His defense is to draw a distinction between "historical exegesis" and "Christian theological interpretation."[58] Historical exegesis stops once the method has uncovered the horizon of the original readership. Christian theological interpretation, on the other hand, recognizes that the Holy Spirit is the ultimate author of Scripture and was active in the OT as

52. Packer, *Keep in Step with the Spirit,* 57.
53. Ibid., 58, emphasis original.
54. Ibid., 59, emphasis original.
55. Ibid.
56. Ibid. Roman Catholic theologian Gerald O'Collins offers a slightly more modest proposal with regard to the Spirit and the OT: "The vivid personifications of Wisdom/Word/and Spirit, inasmuch as they were *both* identified with God and the divine activity *and* distinguished from God, opened up the way toward recognizing God to be tripersonal. The leap from mere personifications to distinct persons is already, to be sure, a giant one. Nevertheless, without these OT personifications . . . the acknowledgment of the Trinity would not have been so well and providentially prepared—by foreshadowings and by an already existing terminology" (*The Tripersonal God: Understanding and Interpreting the Trinity* [New York/Mahwah, N.J.: Paulist, 1999], 34).
57. Packer, *Keep in Step with the Spirit,* 60.
58. Ibid.

such.[59] He cites Mark 12:36 and Acts 1:16 and 4:25 as evidence.[60] He feels justified therefore in proceeding "on the basis that Old Testament references to the Spirit of God are in fact witnessing to the work of the personal Holy Spirit of the New Testament."[61]

The strength of Packer's argument lies in the high view of scriptural authority and inspiration (*theopneustos*) that it presupposes. Scripture is God's word in human words. There is a joint authorship. Scripture can be seen as the product over time of divine providence (government or *gubernatio*) and *concursus* (joint action, human and divine). Our Lord provides the key. He saw his Scripture as having more than one readership in view in the divine economy. His debate with the Sadducees makes this clear.[62] In Matthew 22 we find Jesus appealing to an OT text that originally was not addressed to the Sadducees but which Jesus saw as applicable to them as if they had been the first audience. The Sadducees had presented Jesus with a conundrum about the resurrection, which was a doctrine to which they did not subscribe. Theirs was an attempted *reductio ad absurdum* argument about a woman who had lost multiple husbands and, therefore, to whom would she be married in the life to come—if resurrection was real? Jesus countered by quoting from the Torah, which this sect of the Jews respected. He challenged them: "You are wrong, because you know neither the Scriptures nor the power of God" (Matt. 22:29). The Scripture he then quoted was Exodus 3:6 (see Matt. 22:32). In that text God emphatically is (*egō eimi*)—not was—the God of Abraham, Isaac, and Jacob. The implication is that these OT worthies still live in the presence of God. There really is a world and life to come. Of singular importance for our purpose, though, is how Jesus prefaced his quotation: ". . . have you not read what was said to you (*humin*)." The divine word has more than one readership in view. This word spoken so long ago was also addressed to the Sadducees centuries later. Paul and the book of Hebrews show a similar perspective (cf. Rom. 15:4; 1 Cor. 10:6, 11; and Heb. 3:7; 4:7).[63]

59. See also John Goldingay, "Was the Holy Spirit Active in Old Testament Times? What Was New about the Christian Experience of God?" *Ex Auditu* 12 (1996), who argues in a fascinating way that the Holy Spirit was at work in unnamed ways in the OT (16–19). See also Graeme Goldsworthy, *Preaching the Whole Bible as Christian Scripture* (Grand Rapids, Mich., and Cambridge: Eerdmans, 2000), 240, who is convinced by Goldingay's argument.

60. Packer, *Keep in Step with the Spirit*, 60.

61. Ibid., 61.

62. We return to this debate in our later chapter on the Spirit and knowing God, when we consider the role of the Spirit in enabling a text from the past to be God's word to the present.

63. The use of Psalm 110 in Hebrews 3–4 as "the Word of God is living and active" is highly instructive. It is the Holy Spirit's word in Hebrews 3:7 (*legei*, present aspect), God speaking in 4:3 (*eirēken*, perfect aspect), and God speaking through David in 4:7 (*legōn*, present aspect; and *proeirētai*, perfect aspect). The aspects show that for the writer, although the psalm was written long ago, it is a contemporary word from God. Hebrews 3–4 also shows the *concursus* at work in the inspiration of Scripture.

Paul Blackham insists on reading the OT as Christian Scripture even more strongly than Packer does. To a certain degree he endorses the argument of Margaret Bowker that, "The Trinitarian faith of the Church had grown from the older Hebrew belief in a pluriform deity."[64] The Hebrews did not worship "some divine monad in isolation." Blackham maintains that,

> When we adopt the theological convictions of exegetes such as Justin [Martyr], Irenaeus, Luther, Owen, Edwards, and moderns like Colin Gunton, we are able to follow the careful detail of the Hebrew text in its delineation of the identity and roles of the divine Persons. When we start with the truth that the God of Israel is a unity of God Most High, his Son, and his Spirit, then, we are free to give full exegetical weight to the distinctions between the three Persons made in the text, through its careful descriptions of divine titles and roles. God Most High sends his Angel with his Spirit to accomplish his work of creation, revelation, judgement and redemption.[65]

Indeed, he goes so far as to contend,

> The great Trinitarian theologians of the past were exegetes of these Scriptures [the Hebrew Scriptures], and it is as we sit and learn from *that most brilliant and careful Trinitarian theologian, Moses,* that we can go further and deeper into the God of Israel who is the Most High, the appearing Lord [Jesus], and the Spirit.[66]

Blackham has a point. Pre-critical exegesis may be full of genuine insight.[67] The God of OT presentation is no simple monad—although to describe Moses as "that most brilliant and careful Trinitarian theologian" is anachronistic in the extreme.

A further point needs to be made. Christians read Scripture this side of canon closure. This reality is laden with theological significance. As Stephen G. Dempster suggests, "Whatever may be said about the mystery of canonization, it is indisputable that the fact of canonization creates a new literary context for all the individual texts involved, and this fact makes one text out of many."[68] If canonization is taken seriously, then both the

64. Margaret Bowker, *The Great High Priest* (Edinburgh: T. & T. Clark, 2003), xi, quoted in Paul Blackham, "The Trinity in the Hebrew Scriptures," in Paul Louis Metzger, ed., *Trinitarian Soundings in Systematic Theology* (London: T. & T. Clark, 2005), 37.

65. Blackham, "Trinity in the Hebrew Scriptures," 45–46.

66. Ibid., 46, emphasis mine.

67. As David C. Steinmetz famously argued in "The Superiority of the Pre-Critical Exegesis," *Theology Today* 37 no. 1 (1980): 27–38. "Pre-critical exegesis" refers to the exegetical practices of the church prior to the Enlightenment of the eighteenth century.

68. Stephen G. Dempster, "Geography and Genealogy, Dominion and Dynasty: A Theology of the Hebrew Bible," in Scott J. Hafemann, ed., *Biblical Theology: Retrospect and Prospect* (Downers Grove, Ill.: InterVarsity Press, 2002), 67–68.

OT and the NT cease to be merely ancient writings but become instead Holy Scripture for the church. Harry Gamble maintains,

> In the nature of the case, canonization entails a recontextualization of the documents incorporated into the canon. They are abstracted from both their generative and traditional settings and redeployed as parts of a new literary whole; henceforth they are read in terms of this collection. In this way their historically secondary context becomes their hermeneutically primary context.[69]

Thus a reference to *rûach* in the OT such as in Genesis 1:2 is to be read as Christian Scripture in the context of the entire canon as its "hermeneutically primary context." Moreover, this way of reading Scripture appreciates that the Scripture has a dual authorship: God and the human authors (cf. 2 Tim. 3:16 and 2 Pet. 1:21). The human author's intention, therefore, does not necessarily exhaust the scope of intended meaning. Thus, according to this view, Genesis 1:2 when originally written may not have been a reference to the Third Person of the Godhead in the human author's mind—how could it have been?—yet such a meaning was in the mind of God.[70]

If there is merit in the above, and I believe there is, then those who have *ex hypothesi* a robust doctrine of biblical inspiration and of canonical integrity and a confidence in a providential deity will not be surprised at Packer's (and Blackham's) willingness to work with both historical exegesis and Christian theological interpretation.[71] Put another way, as Brevard S. Childs suggests, there is a "necessity of a multi-level reading of Scripture."[72] Integral to that approach should be the recognition that we read the OT in particular as Christians, if indeed that is our life stance. As Willem VanGemeren suggests, ". . . Christian students of the Old Testament *must pass*

69. Harry Gamble, *The New Testament Canon: Its Making and Meaning* (Philadelphia: Fortress, 1985), 75, quoted in Dempster, "Geography and Genealogy," 68, fn 8.

70. Caiaphas in the NT provides an example of someone who intended one meaning by his words while God intended another (John 11:49–53).

71. Colin Gunton makes a similar point. With regard to references to *rûach* in the OT, such as Ezekiel 37, he maintains, "This is not to claim there is to be found in the Old Testament a distinct *hypostasis*, alongside Father and Son, but that it is justifiable to interpret the language in the light of later understanding, just as it is right to interpret instances of divine immanence as anticipations of the incarnation" ("The Spirit in the Trinity," in Alasdair I. C. Heron, ed., *The Forgotten Trinity 3: A Selection of Papers Presented to the BCC Study Commission on Trinitarian Doctrine Today* (London: BCC/CCBI, 1991), 126.

72. For Childs's own approach to a responsible theological exegesis of Scripture, whether the Old or New Testaments or both are in view, see Brevard S. Childs, "Toward Recovering Theological Exegesis," *Pro Ecclesia* 6 no. 1 (Winter 1997): 16–26, esp. 22–25. He writes, ". . . a multi-level reading is required even to begin to grapple with the full range of Scripture's role as the intentional medium of continuing revelation" (24). Childs's Barthian debts don't undermine the value of his general point.

by the cross of Jesus Christ on their return to the Old Testament, and as such they can never lose their identity as a Christian."[73]

I would add that we must travel past Pentecost too on our return to the OT. Put another way, if Jesus could find himself spoken of in the OT testimony (Luke 24:44–47) and the NT writers could find Christ in the OT (e.g., Paul in 1 Cor. 10:1–4), why cannot the Christian reader find God the Holy Spirit there too?[74] All this raises huge hermeneutical questions that take us well beyond our brief. Suffice it to say that the academy is not the only setting for the study of Scripture. Scripture *qua* Scripture—as opposed to merely being the literature of ancient Israel together with some early Christian writings—finds its most appropriate home in the church as the people of God gather around the Word of God in the context of the worship of God. There is a way of studying Scripture that is an expression of that worship and yet is not hopelessly naïve.

The Creation, Its Preservation, and Common Grace: A Calvinian Note

B. B. Warfield, the great Princeton theologian, says of Calvin that, "The doctrine of the work of the Holy spirit [*sic*] is a gift from John Calvin to the Church of Christ."[75] In Warfield's view of the Reformation, ". . . Luther rose to proclaim justification by faith, and Calvin to set forth with his marvelous balance the whole doctrine of the work of the Spirit in applying salvation to the soul."[76] Be that as it may, what Warfield neglected to say was how Calvin extended our understanding of the Holy Spirit's work as the agent of the triune Godhead and as the one who is the key to the human pursuit of the true, the good, and the beautiful (the transcendental, as philosophers say). To this seminal contribution we now turn our attention.

Calvin in his *Institutes of the Christian Religion* draws a distinction between fallen humanity's grasp of earthly or inferior things and humanity's lack of grasp of heavenly or superior things.[77] Outside of Eden, human reason is still competent to varying degrees, as evidenced by the mechanical arts, manual arts, liberal arts, medical art, mathematical science, rhetoric,

---

73. Willem VanGemeren, *The Progress of Redemption: The Story of Salvation from Creation to the New Jerusalem* (Grand Rapids, Mich.: Baker, 2000), 21, emphasis original.

74. On rightly reading the OT in the light of NT readings of it see Peter Enns, *Inspiration and Incarnation: Evangelicals and the Problem of the Old Testament* (Grand Rapids, Mich.: Baker, 2005), 116: "The hermeneutical attitude they [the NT writers] embodied should be embraced and followed by the church today." In my view, Enns makes the concept of incarnation do too much theological work. Appeal to Calvin's idea of accommodation (*accommodatio*) would have served his purpose better.

75. B. B. Warfield, "Introductory Note," in Kuyper, *Work of the Holy Spirit*, xxxiii.

76. Ibid., xxxvii.

77. John Calvin, "Institutes of the Christian Religion," *CJCC*, II.2.13.

and so forth. These arts and sciences are the products of our natural endowments, which are the gift of God.[78] They also show "some remains of the divine image."[79] However, with regard to the knowledge of God and salvation, even the philosophers "are blinder than moles."[80]

The history of theological discussion has generated a technical term, "common grace," to sum up Calvin's theology of this general kindness of God toward his fallen image.[81] Special grace or saving grace, on the other hand—in Reformed thought at any rate—is God's unmerited kindness toward his elect in reconciling them to himself. With regard to common grace, Calvin traces whatever art, science, or skill fallen humanity shows to the work of the Holy Spirit. In fact, he asserts that in despising such gifts, we "dishonor the Spirit."[82] And further, he maintains, "if the Lord has willed that we be helped in physics, dialectic, mathematics, and the like disciplines, by the work and ministry of the ungodly, let us use this assistance. For if we neglect God's gift freely offered in these arts, we ought to suffer just punishment for our sloths."[83]

But how does Calvin justify this doctrine of common grace? As would be expected with Calvin, he turns to the Scriptures, but his evidence is surprising. He discusses the tabernacle of the wilderness period, and the skill and knowledge of Bezalel and Oholiab used in its construction (Ex. 31:2; 35:30). Their knowledge and skill came from the Spirit. The argument is cryptic: if their excellence comes from the Spirit, then so too does the highest excellence in human life.[84] There is a difference between the godly and the ungodly, though. The Spirit is said to indwell believers, making them holy temples by his presence. The ungodly are not so. Yet the Spirit has not left them bereft: "Nonetheless he fills, moves and quickens all things by the power of the same Spirit, and does so according to the character he bestowed on each kind by the law of creation."[85] For this latter proposition Calvin supplies no biblical evidence. But it appears to be his summary of the Holy Spirit's ongoing role in creation.

Calvin's biblical warrant for his idea of common grace is unconvincing. The tabernacle is part of Israel's history, as we shall see in the next chapter. God wants to be worshiped in his way and on his terms, not ours. The aesthetics of the tabernacle are important for understanding the God who is characterized by the beauty of holiness and who is the creator

78. Ibid., 14–16.
79. Ibid., 17.
80. Ibid., 18.
81. For a recent discussion of common grace see Earl D. Radmacher, "What Is Common Grace?" in Swindoll and Zuck, eds., *Christian Theology*, 846–853. See also Kuyper, *Work of the Holy Spirit*, who describes it as "ordinary or general grace" (634–635).
82. Calvin, "Institutes," *CJCC*, II.2.15.
83. Ibid., 16.
84. Ibid.
85. Ibid.

of color, shape, and imagination. Yet to generalize from the tabernacle's construction about human artistry per se is quite a logical leap. Calvin's point, however right, needs better biblical foundations than the ones he supplies.

IMPLICATIONS FOR BELIEF AND PRACTICE

The OT witness to the Spirit should lead to an appreciation of the Spirit's role in creation and a modesty about our claims concerning how much has actually been revealed concerning that role.

Appreciation of the Spirit's Role in Creation

The testimony to the Spirit's role in creation is scanty in the OT. As Gerald F. Hawthorne comments, ". . . this is a feature of the Spirit's activity that is easily overemphasized, as thoughtful scholars have pointed out."[86] Even so the Spirit's role in creation needs our appreciation. In Psalm 104 the fitting response to the goodness of God the Creator and sustainer of the created order is to bless and praise him (Ps. 104:1, 35, note the *inclusio*). But what does it mean to bless (*b-r-k*) and what does it mean to praise (*h-l-l*) him? For a start it does not mean to parrot empty words. Rather we speak out of a value judgment concerning the actions of God. His kingly actions show his greatness, majesty, and splendor (v. 1). They also demonstrate the divine wisdom (v. 24). Part of our appreciation lies in recognizing that without the Spirit we return to the dust (vv. 29–30). Reflection on the Spirit's role should form part of our meditation on God our Creator (v. 34) and find expression in our songs (v. 33) and be a source of our joy (v. 34). In this instance, biblical meditation is where we turn what we learn of the work of the Spirit into prayer and praise to God.[87]

Appreciating the Holy Spirit's work in creation should also keep us from confining his work to historic Israel and the church[88]—although,

86. Gerald F. Hawthorne, *The Presence and the Power: The Significance of the Spirit in the Life and Ministry of Jesus* (Dallas, London, Vancouver, and Melbourne: Word, 1991), 20. Hawthorne has in mind scholars such as A. B. Davidson, T. Rees, and W. D. Davies (ibid., 50, endnote 21).

87. See J. I. Packer, *Knowing God* (London, Sydney, Auckland, and Toronto: Hodder & Stoughton, 1973), 18, for a concise description of the practice of biblical meditation.

88. Clark Pinnock rightly chides the older work of W. H. Griffith-Thomas, *The Holy Spirit of God* (Grand Rapids, Mich.: Eerdmans, 1964) for this mistake (*Flame of Love: A Theology of the Holy Spirit* [Downers Grove, Ill.: InterVarsity Press, 1996], 54). Confining the Holy Spirit's role to the sphere of the saints is not a recent idea. See Origen, *De Principiis,* I.iii.5, in Henry Bettenson, ed. and trans., *The Early Christian Fathers* (Oxford: Oxford University Press, 1978), 238–239. Origen was not always consistent. In *De Principiis* he also suggested that when Genesis 1:2 is understood spiritually, it was the Holy Spirit who "moved over the water" in this creation text (ibid., 229).

as we shall see as our study proceeds, the people of God is where the revealed center of gravity is for the Spirit's ministry. We are not gnostics, who despise the material realm and wish to flee it. We believe in a Creator and not just a Redeemer. There are both an order of creation and an order of redemption. Ontologically speaking, we are creatures before we are Christians. Evangelical Christianity has not always appreciated these dual accents.

Modesty about Our Claims

When it comes to making claims about the Spirit's role in creation and its maintenance, there are two kinds of maximizers. One sort renders *rûach* as "Spirit" in key places rather than as "spirit" or "breath" or "wind" or "vitality" (e.g., Gen. 1:2; Ps. 33:6; 104:30; Job 27:3; 33:4; and 34:14–15). The other kind of maximizer then builds the maximum amount of theological superstructure on the references. Abraham Kuyper is in the latter group, as is Clark Pinnock.[89]

When I face the door to my apartment I cannot see the hinges that enable the door to work. But prior experience tells me that they are there. I have passed through that door before and have actually seen the two large hinges. Revelation tells me of the Spirit's role in creation and its preservation or continuance. But I can't see the Spirit's workings. I can't pass through that door and, looking back, see the hinges of divine connection. Consequently there is a certain epistemic modesty that should attend our speculations about the causal joint between the Spirit's workings and nature's own. Michael Green expresses that modesty well:

> The Old Testament *may* give these few hints of a Creator Spirit, and certainly this thought is found in the intertestamental period—where parallelism between Wisdom, Word and Spirit is important—but the paucity of instances that can be adduced, and the plausibility of taking them in another sense, does make one very cautious of building up a great doctrine of co-operating with the Holy Spirit in his on-going work of creation.[90]

89. For example, Kuyper, *Work of the Holy Spirit,* second chapter, 22–42; and Pinnock, *Flame of Love,* chapter 2, 48–77. Kuyper's sections include: "V. The Principle of Life in the Creature," "VI. The Host of Heaven and of Earth," "VII. The Creaturely Man," and "VIII. Gifts and Talents." In his discussion of the Spirit and creation, Pinnock surprisingly makes the Spirit the mediator between the Father and the Son in the Godhead, and the mediator between God and creatures (60). How this squares with Jesus Christ as the only mediator between God and humanity (1 Tim. 2:5) is never explained. Pinnock's theologizing is colorful and fertilely suggestive, although he does acknowledge the "relative scarcity" of biblical texts he is working with. Consequently, the chapter lacks a convincing biblical anchorage.

90. Michael Green, *I Believe in the Holy Spirit* (London, Sydney, and Auckland: Hodder & Stoughton, 1992), 32, emphasis original. I am more sanguine than Green in regard to how many OT references about creation are ones about the Holy Spirit, as my discussion shows. Green

Green offers this caution: "We would be wise not to build too high a build-ing on such a flimsy foundation."[91] The theologian may responsibly build a doctrine of the Holy Spirit's ongoing role in creation and its sustenance, but with the appropriate epistemic humility.

---

is right about the intertestamental developments. See Turner, *Holy Spirit and Spiritual Gifts*, chapter 1; and see also the discussion in Montague of Wisdom 7:22–8:1 (*Holy Spirit*, 106–110). Montague describes this book as ". . . the summit at which the Old Testament theologies of wisdom and of the spirit meet and are identified" (ibid., 106). As a Roman Catholic, of course, for him this apocryphal work is part of the canon of Scripture.

91. Michael Green, *I Believe in the Holy Spirit*, 32.

THE SPIRIT AND ISRAEL

The Spirit was and is active in creation and its maintenance. The last chapter made that clear. But the created order and ourselves as part of it are troubled. In fact according to Paul the creation itself experiences futility and vanity and longs for its own redemption, and that redemption is tied to the future of the children of God (Rom. 8:18–25). We live this side of what Augustine termed the fall (*lapsus*) or what Jacques Ellul brilliantly summed up as "the Rupture" (*"La Rupture"*).[1] Ruptures now exist between God and humanity, humans and humans, humans and the environment.[2] In fact, in the light of increasing human corruption God declares, "My Spirit [*rûachi,* or should it be translated, "my spirit"] shall not abide in man forever, for he is flesh" (Gen. 6:3).[3] The flood judgment soon follows. But the triune God will reclaim his creation.

1. See Augustine, *De Civitate Dei,* 12.8, in Henry Bettenson, ed. and trans., *The Later Christian Fathers* (Oxford: Oxford University Press, 1977), 195; and Jacques Ellul, *The Humiliation of the Word* (Grand Rapids, Mich.: Eerdmans, 1985), chapter 7.

2. There is no exegetical support for Jonathan Edwards's intriguing idea that Adam was indwelt by the Spirit before the fall and that the Spirit was withdrawn as a judgment. Salvation according to this view includes the restoration of the Spirit's indwelling presence to the elect. See the discussion in John H. Gerstner, *The Rational Theology of Jonathan Edwards in Three Volumes* (Powhatan, Va., and Orlando: Berea/Ligonier, 1992), 2:316–319. This idea was anticipated in Tatian in the second century; see his *Address to the Greeks,* chapter 15, http://www.newadvent.org/fathers/0202.htm.

3. Gordon Wenham points out that every word in this statement is controversial (*Genesis 1–15,* WBC, comment on Gen. 6:3). Is the Holy Spirit in view, or is the text speaking of "the life-giving power of God," as Wenham argues? Interestingly George Montague suggests that in this text is the first biblical contrast between "the spirit" and "the flesh," with the latter understood as opposed to life and the former as the promoter of life (*The Holy Spirit: Growth of a Biblical Tradition: A Commentary on the Principal Texts of the Old and New Testaments* [New York and Toronto: Paulist, 1976], 10).

Scripture tells the story of the divine project of reclamation. William J. Dumbrell expresses the divine goal of the project in this insightful way: "In very broad terms the biblical sweep is from creation to new creation by way of redemption, which is, in effect, the renewing of creation."[4] Or as I like to put it, the grand project is realized when God's people are in God's place under God's rule, living God's way in God's holy and loving presence as family.[5] The Spirit's work as perfecting cause who leads creatures to their divinely appointed ends must be seen against the backdrop of the Rupture and with the grand project in mind. Given the fall, the story is not one of a movement from perfection to even greater perfection (with perfection understood, not in the static categories of Platonic philosophy, but in dynamic ones). Rather it is the story of a movement from imperfection to perfection, with perfection understood as the complete realization of the divine purpose. The divine project will be actualized.

Integral to the recovery of creation, canonically understood, is the creation of a people—as the new Adam—to be the vehicle for the achievement of the divine purpose outside of Eden. Israel is that people, and as we shall see in this chapter the Spirit of God plays a vital role in the story. The centerpiece of that story lies beyond the scope of this part of our study but will loom large later on. Ultimately, Jesus will stand before us in the pages of Scripture as the definitive bearer of the divine purpose, the last Adam, the true Israel, the one who has the Spirit of God without measure. He is the linchpin of the divine project. But first we attend to Israel per se.

Pneumatology from Behind

Let me draw a parallel between how Christology can be done and pneumatology. The study of the person and work of Christ has been tackled largely along two main lines of inquiry. There are those who start where the Gospel of John starts: namely, with eternity and the Word who was with God, and who subsequently becomes flesh (John 1:1–2, 14). This is Christology from above. Using spatial metaphors, the movement is from above to below. The other approach starts where the Gospel of Mark does: that is to say, with the humanity of Jesus in full view (Mark 1:1, 9). Here the movement is from below to above, if there is to be any movement at all. This is Christology from below. A balanced Christology embraces both

4. William J. Dumbrell, *The Search for Order: Biblical Eschatology in Focus* (Eugene, Ore.: Wipf & Stock, 2001), 9.

5. My formulation betrays its debts to Graeme Goldsworthy, *Gospel and Kingdom* (Exeter, England: Paternoster, 1981), 47, who introduced me to biblical theology as a discipline when he taught me in theological college. See also Gordon J. Thomas, "A Holy God among a Holy People in a Holy Place: The Enduring Eschatological Hope," in K. E. Brower and M. W. Elliot, eds., *"The Reader Must Understand": Eschatology in Bible and Theology* (Leicester, England: Apollos, 1997), 53–69.

approaches. But Hendrikus Berkhof has helpfully suggested a third one: Christology from behind.[6] With reference to Jesus this means, ". . . we see him in the line of redemptive history, how he arises out of the Old Testament problematic, and gives and is the answer to it."[7] Again, this third approach ought not to be seen as displacing the others but as complementary to them. A pneumatology from above would begin with the evidences furnished by special revelation for the doctrine of God as the essential Trinity and then move to the orders of creation and redemption. A pneumatology from below would work from revelation concerning the orders of creation and redemption before drawing conclusions about the divine Holy Spirit. A pneumatology from behind focuses on the evidences for the Holy Spirit's person and work as unfolded in the OT presentation and especially in God's dealings with Israel.[8] On analysis, pneumatology from behind may legitimately be considered a subset of pneumatology from below in that it works with the record of God's words and deeds in history.

Pneumatology when done from behind exhibits two accents as far as our present chapter is concerned: the Spirit and the leadership of Israel, on the one hand; and the Spirit and the divine presence among God's people, on the other. (In the next chapter we will take up a third accent, which is that of the Spirit and the hope of Israel.) The first accent especially concerns the shaping of the divine project to reclaim creation. The second has to do with the divine goal of God at home with his people in his place, living under his rule, living his way, and in his holy and loving presence.

THE HOLY SPIRIT AND THE DIVINE PROJECT

After the great rupture of Genesis 3, the triune God is on a mission (*missio Dei*) to reclaim his creation in general and his image-bearer in particular. The *protoevangelium* of Genesis 3:15 signals as much. The Noahic covenant (Gen. 8:20–9:17) provides a promised stable platform for human existence, and soon—in the flow of the narrative—God calls Abraham to be the agent from whom he will create a nation and through whom ultimately that nation

6. The great strength of Berkhof's systematic theology is that it makes Israel a theological theme (Hendrikus Berkhof, *Christian Faith: An Introduction to the Study of Faith* [Grand Rapids, Mich.: Eerdmans, 1979], chapters 28–30). He also provides an excellent thumbnail sketch of how theologians past and present have dealt theologically with the phenomenon of Israel (ibid., 222–225).

7. Ibid., 267. He suggests a fourth approach, "Christology from before," which studies the impact of Jesus on human lives since the NT (ibid.). This "history of impact" approach is much less convincing than the other three, if it is meant to lead to some kind of normative Christology.

8. It might be argued that Berkhof's Christology from behind also dissolves into Christology from below. However, Christology from below, as he understands it, is particularly focused on the so-called historical Jesus as recovered by some historical-critical method.

will bless the world (12:1–3).[9] Indeed, Abraham stands in stark contrast to the pretensions of the Babel builders. They wanted to make a name for themselves (11:4). But God promises to make a name for Abraham (12:2). After the very few references to the Spirit in Genesis, the Spirit of God next comes into view in the Pentateuch in God's care for Israel, his governance of Israel, and his communication and presence with his people.[10]

Divine Care

God's care for his OT people—as Charles H. H. Scobie points out—is seen in his "deliverance and guidance" of them.[11] History provides the vehicle for care. Interestingly the account of Israel in the Torah does not show the Spirit at work in this way, but the later prophets do, as does the book of Nehemiah. Isaiah provides an example. Through a series of rhetorical questions, Isaiah speaks of the Spirit and the exodus deliverance: "Where is he who brought them [Israel] up out of the sea with the shepherds of his flock? Where is he who put in the midst of them his Holy Spirit?" (Isa. 63:11).[12] He also declares of the subsequent period in Israel's history that, "Like livestock that go down into the valley, the Spirit of the LORD gave them rest. So you led your people, to make for yourself a glorious name" (v. 14). In the book of Nehemiah, the Levites bless God for (and in so doing

9. Is the Noahic covenant to be understood as a reaffirmation of an assumed primal creation covenant as Dumbrell argues, or as "emergency orders" (*Notordnungen*) to preserve a stable cosmic context in a fallen world for the Redeemer who was to come, as Helmut Thielicke maintains? For Dumbrell, see his *Search for Order*, 30–32; for Thielicke, see his *Theological Ethics: Foundations, Volume 1* (Grand Rapids, Mich.: Eerdmans, 1966), 439–440. For a critique of the Dumbrell thesis see P. R. Williams, "Covenant," *NDBT*, 420–421.

10. Was Pharaoh speaking better than he knew—like Caiaphas speaking of Jesus' death in the NT (John 11:49–52)—when he declared of Joseph's wisdom, "Can we find a man like this, in whom is the Spirit of God?" (Gen. 41:38)? If so, then the Spirit—albeit recognized by the nations represented by Egypt, rather than by God's people—was using Joseph's helpfulness to Pharaoh to keep the Abrahamic promise alive in view of the famine to come. Interestingly, this is only the second reference to the expression "the Spirit of God" to be found in Genesis. The other is, of course, in Genesis 1:2.

11. Charles H. H. Scobie, *The Ways of Our God: An Approach to Biblical Theology* (Grand Rapids, Mich., and Cambridge: Eerdmans, 2003), 272.

12. This is one of only three references in the OT that use the expression "the Holy Spirit" (*qōdesh rûach*). The others are in Isaiah 63:10 and Psalm 51:11. In the intertestamental period the expression becomes more ubiquitous, as Gerald F. Hawthorne points out: ". . .the expression, 'the Holy Spirit,' occurs more frequently now (4 Ezr. 14:22; Asc. Is. 5:14; cf. Sir. 48:12; Pss. Sol. 17:37; Wis. 9:17; 1 QH 7:6, 7; 14:12b; 17:26; CD 2:11-13)" (*The Presence and the Power: The Significance of the Spirit in the Life and Ministry of Jesus* [Dallas, London, Vancouver, and Melbourne: Word, 1991], 22). As we shall see when we eventually consider the NT testimony, the expression will come into sharp relief by its frequency. In fact in the NIV, for example, 90 of the 93 times the translation has "Holy Spirit" are in the NT. Furthermore, according to Montague, *Holy Spirit*, 113, "The expression 'holy spirit,' which we occasionally encountered in the Old Testament, becomes a commonplace among the rabbis to express the divine revelation which is found in the words of the Torah or on the lips of the prophets."

remind Israel) of his care of his people during the wilderness episode: "You gave your good Spirit to instruct them and did not withhold your manna from their mouth and gave them water for their thirst" (Neh. 9:20).

Divine Governance

With respect to the divine governance of Israel, the Spirit first explicitly comes into prominence subsequent to the exodus. In the wilderness, Moses is worn out with the complaints of the people so the Lord instructs him to appoint seventy elders to "bear the burden of the people" with him (Num. 11:17). Divine enablement is needed and so God takes "some of the Spirit" that is on Moses and puts it on the elders.[13] As soon as he does so the elders prophesy, albeit temporarily (v. 25). Even the two elders who had remained in the camp prophesy (v. 26). What exactly the prophesying consisted of is not adumbrated. But the prophesying appears to have provided divine endorsement of the elders. Thus the people would know that Yahweh was behind their new role of helping Moses by bearing "the burden of the people" (v. 17). In other words, they were not arrogating power for themselves at their own instigation. Rather, these roles are by God's appointment.

The Spirit's connection with the leadership of Israel becomes far more prominent in Judges. These liberators of Israel are enabled by the Spirit: Othniel (Judg. 3:10), Gideon (Judg. 6:34), Jephthah (11:29), and supremely Samson (14:6, 19; 15:14–15). Of Samson, Max Turner writes: "Indeed, even at-first-sight bizarre eruptions of the Spirit of power through Samson . . . appear to have been understood as the divine protection of this champion of Israel, and for the routing of her enemies."[14] In this period the Spirit seems more like a "mysterious and quasi-physical power that broke in and took possession of a person, though only for a short time."[15] The raising up of various judges shows God's provision of charismatic leaders—in the sociological sense of charismatic—for his people when in "collective crisis," albeit of their own making.[16] It was a period of great disorder from the time of Othniel to the anointing of Saul as Israel's king.[17] The cycle of

---

13. As Max Turner comments, "Working at a more personal level (rather than as naked power), the Spirit of the Lord was perceived as an endowment on Moses (Num. 11:17, 29) through which he liberated and led Israel at God's direction. Joshua was understood to have had a similar endowment (Num. 27:18 and elsewhere)" (*The Holy Spirit and Spiritual Gifts: Then and Now*, rev. ed. [Carlisle, England: Paternoster, 1999], 5–6. In Numbers 11:16–30 we see some of that leadership of Israel devolved upon the seventy elders.

14. Ibid., 5.

15. Scobie, *Ways of Our God*, 272.

16. See Michael Welker, *God the Spirit*, trans. John F. Hoffmeyer (Minneapolis: Fortress, 1994), 52.

17. Brevard S. Childs, *Biblical Theology of the Old and New Testaments: Theological Reflection on the Christian Bible* (Minneapolis: Fortress, 1993), 149.

Israel's existence was a most unhappy one: lapse into sin, a cry to the Lord, provision of a deliverer, deliverance, order, and then relapse, as Judges 2:11–23 reveals. Dumbrell argues that, ". . . the judges continued the kind of Mosaic leadership to which Israel had become accustomed from Sinai days onward."[18] The Spirit's work was integral to that provision in the case of various judges: Othniel (Judg. 3:10); Gideon (6:34); Jephthah (11:29); and Samson (13:25; 14:6, 19; 15:14–15).

But Israel was not content with God's kingship and sought to be like the nations around her even though the Torah warned of such kings and their aggrandizing ways (cf. Deut. 17:14–17 and 1 Sam. 8:1–9). Israel got her king, Saul (1 Samuel 9). Once more the leadership of God's people, this time human kingship, and the Spirit come into high relief. As with the judges of long before, the Spirit came upon Saul, enabling him to lead and deliver Israel (1 Sam. 10:6–7; 11:1–11, esp. v. 6). Reminiscent of the experience of the elders in Numbers we see in 1 Samuel a link between leadership and prophecy as the Spirit gives Saul utterance on occasion (1 Sam. 10:9–13; 19:23–24).[19] There is a nexus between kingship and prophecy. (More anon.) But Saul—a king after the people's own heart—fails (13:8–15; 15). His disobedience costs him in the end his throne, his life, and his son Jonathan (1 Samuel 31). The Spirit's departure from Saul to David begins the sorry saga of the decline of the house of Saul (16:13–14).

Thus the Spirit also comes upon David—a man after God's own heart (as anticipated in 1 Sam. 13:14). He leads and delivers Israel from her enemies. The famous story of the battle between David and the Philistine giant, Goliath, in 1 Samuel 17 is a spectacular example. The pattern of messianic leadership is clear: the divine choice of the leader (1 Sam. 16:12), anointing (v. 13), endowment with the Spirit (v. 13), subsequent acts of delivering God's people (1 Samuel 17), and God's people eventually at rest from their enemies (2 Sam. 7:1). Brevard S. Childs says of David, "It is difficult to overestimate the importance for the biblical tradition of David who rivals Moses in significance for the entire canon."[20] In one of the psalms that is linked to David by superscription, we find the psalmist praying that the

---

18. Dumbrell, *Search for Order,* 59. Dumbrell argues that the editorial comment of Judges 21:25 that there was no king in the land in those days and everyone did as he wanted is not a plea for kingship as the remedy. Instead, the lesson to be drawn is that through Spirit-directed charismatic leadership Israel is preserved despite itself (ibid.). C. E. Armerding acknowledges that, "It is often claimed that Judges clearly rejects kingship, presumably in favor of the non-hereditary, charismatic model of leadership exemplified by the judges" ("Judges," *NDBT,* 175). However, he is persuaded that, ". . . it is difficult not to see in these statements [e.g., Judg. 21:25 inter alia] a longing for what was to come" (ibid.). The scholarly debate continues.

19. Scobie sees many examples of prophetic ecstasy in the OT. Saul's experience is but one of them (Scobie, *Ways of Our God,* 272–273). Wayne Grudem, however, argues that Saul's experience, narrated in 1 Samuel 19, was "unique" and the generalization from that one incident to the idea of an ecstatic band of prophets is unsupported ("Prophecy," *NDBT,* 703).

20. Childs, *Biblical Theology,* 133–134.

THE SPIRIT AND ISRAEL □ 121

Spirit be not removed from him (Ps. 51:11). If this psalm's *sitz im leben* ("situation in life") is David's sin with Bathsheba then what is at issue is not so much personal salvation as the possible loss of the kingship.[21] The specter of the Spirit's departure from King Saul and the subsequent declension of the house of Saul may be in mind. Once again, if this is the case, the Spirit is integral to the leadership of God's people. David does not want kingship without the Spirit.

Significantly, no other kings paraded before us in the OT Scriptures are said to be Spirit-enabled to lead and deliver God's people. Not even a reforming king like Josiah is an exception. William Dyrness suggests, "In the period of the monarchy the institutional aspects begin to predominate over the charismatic, and dependence upon the Spirit becomes less visible."[22] In Saul's early days, and then in David's reign par excellence, an ideal of kingship is presented that is not emulated by following kings, not even Solomon, although arguably in Solomon's reign the monarchy reached its *apogée* (1 Kings 4, esp. v. 25; and 1 Kings 10). The pattern of royal activity, in Saul then David, of election by God, anointing by the prophet ("messiahed," one might say, from the Hebrew *māšîah,* "to anoint"), gift of the Spirit, and public demonstrations of deliverance is theologically freighted. The rule of God is no longer direct as at Sinai; rather, a designated (anointed) agent will be the vehicle for the divine rule over his people, and ultimately the nations and the cosmos.[23] As Dumbrell contends, "These two monarchs are used to depict an ideal kingship—one impossible to duplicate in the experience of later northern and southern kings."[24] God will need to provide such a leader at a future date, as we shall see in the next chapter. Ultimately the NT will reveal the One in whom this ideal truly walks the earth.

Divine Communication

The Nicene Creed (A.D. 381, more accurately the Niceno-Constantinopolitan Creed) succinctly sums up the Spirit's role in the communi-

---

21. Not all are convinced that the superscription throws light on the genesis of this psalm. John Goldingay maintains, "If we leave the heading on one side for a moment . . . it makes good sense to see this psalm as a communal one, spoken by the community after the fall of Jerusalem" ("Was the Holy Spirit Active in Old Testament Times? What Was New about the Christian Experience of God?" *Ex Auditu* 12 [1996]: 21). In his view, the psalm would then be applicable to the Bathsheba incident as well as to many others that ordinary Israelites might experience. This suggestion is plausible but not compelling.

22. William Dyrness, *Themes in Old Testament Theology* (Carlisle, England: Paternoster, 1998), 173.

23. Dumbrell, *Search for Order,* 65. Hawthorne goes beyond the biblical evidence when he asserts, "The Old Testament kings were messiahs in that they were the anointed of the Lord (cf. 1 Sam. 24:6, passim), and as such they were bearers of the Spirit" (*Presence and the Power,* 18–19). He is right about the anointing, but with regard to historical Israel only Saul and David are described as bearers of the Spirit.

24. Ibid., 64.

cation of the divine will in these terms: "He has spoken through the prophets." The OT certainly provides evidence for such a view. As we have already seen, when some of the Spirit on Moses is placed on the elders of Israel they prophesy (Num. 11:24–25). Joshua takes exception to this. He wants them stopped (v. 28). He appears to be afraid that Moses' stature would somehow be lessened if others have the ability to prophesy. Moses responds by declaring, "Are you jealous for my sake? Would that all the LORD's people were prophets, that the LORD would put his Spirit on them!" (v. 29). The nexus between prophecy and the Spirit is clear. Later, Moses predicts that the Lord will raise up a prophet just like him (Deut. 18:15), a prophet to be listened to. The Spirit is not mentioned. But since this prophet to come is to be like Moses then the Spirit's activity as a prerequisite in that figure's prophetic ministry is a fair assumption.[25] As it was with Moses so it will be with this eschatological figure. Likewise when the Spirit comes upon Saul, Israel's first king, there is prophesying (1 Sam. 10:9–13). Again, David provided an oracle (*nĕʾum*) by the Spirit (2 Sam. 23:1).[26] But most probably the Creed has in mind the great prophets of Israel. Those covenant watchdogs had a basic message: "recalling Israel to her covenant faith."[27] For although kings like Saul and David may prophesy, as P. E. Satterthwaite suggests, "The consistent view of *Samuel* is that the king must be subject to the prophetic word."[28] Over and over again in the narratives and prophecies of the OT we see the prophets speaking God's truth to power. Samuel spoke the truth of judgment to Saul (1 Sam. 15:24–26), Nathan spoke the truth of sin and the abuse of power to David (2 Sam. 12:1–15), Elijah spoke the truth of God's displeasure and judgment to Ahab and Jezebel (1 Kings 21:17–24).

The prophetic word was not only directed to leadership. Wayne Grudem helpfully sums up the ministry of the OT prophets in the following terms:

25. I owe this observation to my student Sam Chan. But whether Chan is right to see the prophecy fulfilled in Jesus, the apostles, and the church is another question.

26. David is described in 2 Samuel 23:1 as "the sweet psalmist of Israel," or more probably, "the favorite of the songs of Israel" (ESV margin), and as "the man who was raised on high," and as "anointed of the God of Jacob." The oracle is about kingship, right rule, and the defeat of enemies (2 Sam. 23:3–7). Significantly the oracle is described as "the last words of David" (2 Sam. 23:1). Does this imply the last words as an oracle, suggesting that there were previous ones? Prophetic oracle, the Spirit, and kingship are thus linked. This is the only place in the OT that David is placed among the prophets. (It is worth noting in passing that the NT also links David to prophecy in Acts 2:30 in relation to Psalm 16.) Interestingly, the opening of 1 Samuel 23:1 is practically the same as that for Balaam's oracles (cf. Num. 24:3, 15). See A. A. Anderson, *2 Samuel*, WBC, comment on 1 Sam. 23:1.

27. Dyrness, *Themes in Old Testament Theology*, 183.

28. P. E. Satterthwaite, "Samuel," *NDBT*, 180, emphasis original. See also Dumbrell, *Search for Order*, 66; and Turner, who describes the Spirit as "the unseen sceptre" of God's rule (*Holy Spirit and Spiritual Gifts*, 6).

> Speaking through the prophets, God guided kings *and people* by tell-
> ing them how to act in specific situations, warned people when they
> disobeyed him, predicted events that he would bring about, interpreted
> events when they came about, and demonstrated that he was both
> ruler of history and a God who relates personally to people.[29]

All of God's people needed to heed the prophetic word, especially when
covenant faithfulness was at stake, and the Spirit of God was pivotally
involved with the prophets in making the divine will known.[30]

The Spirit impels the Word (*dābār*) of the Lord that is addressed to his
people. Micah, the eighth-century prophet, is an example. Micah begins
as so many of the writing prophets do: "The word of the LORD came to
. . ." (Mic. 1:1). Micah goes on to contrast his ministry with that of other
prophets who were leading the people astray: "But as for me, I am filled
with power, with the Spirit of the LORD, and with justice and might, to
declare to Jacob his transgression and to Israel his sin" (3:8). Word (*dābār*)
and Spirit (*rûach*) work together to enable the divine communication. The
exilic prophet Ezekiel provides another case in point of Word and Spirit
in symbiosis. The Spirit lifts him up and brings him to the east gate of
the temple (Ezek. 11:1). The glory of God is soon to depart because of
the southern kingdom's sin (11:22–25). Ezekiel as "son of man," is to
prophesy against the leaders of Judah (11:4). We read, "And the Spirit of
the LORD fell upon me, and he said to me, 'Say, Thus says the LORD . . .'"
(v. 5); and "Therefore thus says the Lord GOD" (v. 7). He goes on to say,
"And the word of the LORD came to me: . . ." (v. 14). These are standard
ways of prefacing the prophetic word. What is significant about Ezekiel at
this point is the thematization of the Spirit's direct role in the articulation
of that word.

Now it is true that mostly we read in the prophets, "Thus says the LORD"
or "The word of the LORD came" without there being any reference in the
text to the Spirit (e.g., Jer. 1:4; Hos. 1:1; Joel 1:1; Amos 1:3, 6, 9, 11, 13 inter
alia). But in the light of Micah 3:8, it is wrong for Moltmann to suggest that
in the preexilic prophets—Amos, Hosea, Micah, Isaiah, and Jeremiah—the
earlier ecstasy has given way to a formulaic "Thus says the LORD" that now
replaces the enthusiastic "in-spiration through God's Spirit."[31] This "inspiration," he argues, returns with exilic prophets like Ezekiel.[32] Postexilic
prophet Zechariah contributes a summarizing description of what brought

---

29. Wayne Grudem, "Prophecy," *NDBT*, 701, emphasis mine.

30. Turner argues that, "God's Spirit was typically related to God's *covenantal* activities *in
and on behalf of Israel* . . ." (*Holy Spirit and Spiritual Gifts*, 5, emphasis original).

31. Contra Jürgen Moltmann, *The Spirit of Life: A Universal Affirmation*, trans. Margaret
Kohl (Minneapolis: Fortress, 1994), 44. Hawthorne points out that in Hosea 9:7 (LXX) the
prophet is described as the man who bears the Spirit (*ho anthrōpos ho pneumatophoros*) (*Presence and the Power*, 19).

32. Ibid., 45.

about the exile: "They [Judah] made their hearts diamond-hard lest they should hear the law [*tōrāh,* meaning probably "instruction" or "teaching"] and the words [*dābār,* lit. "word," sing.] that the LORD of hosts had sent by his Spirit through the former ["earlier"] prophets" (Zech. 7:12).[33] So we find a preexilic prophet, Micah, an exilic prophet, Ezekiel, and a postexilic prophet, Zechariah, all connecting the Word and Spirit in God's communication with his people—albeit in judgment.[34]

Divine Presence

God's great goal in canonical perspective is to dwell among his people (Revelation 21–22). Even in the primal setting of the garden there are intimations of this as God walks in Eden seeking fellowship with Adam in the Edenic sanctuary (Gen. 3:8–9).[35] The divine desire to dwell with his people after the exodus deliverance is expressed in the narrative of the tabernacle. Willem VanGemeren maintains that, "The tabernacle, as the central symbol of God's presence, of his revelation, communion, and holiness, witnesses to something of much greater significance. Yahweh, the great King, has established *his kingdom on earth.*"[36] The blueprint for the tabernacle is a heavenly one (Ex. 25:9). This earthly sanctuary thus is to be a copy of the heavenly one. Israel indeed is to be a kingdom of priests (Ex. 15:17; 19:6). Yahweh is to dwell in the midst of the people, and when the tabernacle is completed, the glory (*kābōd*) of God takes up residence (Ex. 40:34). As Dumbrell explains, "Indeed, the erection of the tabernacle in chapters 35–40 [of Exodus] is the flourish with which the book concludes."[37]

The Spirit of God plays a key role in the establishment of the tabernacle in the midst of Israel's camp. It is the Spirit of God who enables Bezalel ". . . to devise artistic designs, to work in gold, silver, and bronze, in cutting stones for setting, and in carving wood, to work in every craft" (Ex. 31:4–5; 35:30–33). The Spirit is the source of Bezalel's genius: his skill ("wisdom," *hokmah*), his intelligence, his knowledge, and his craftsmanship

33. See Ralph L. Smith, *Micah—Malachi,* WBC.
34. The intertestamental period saw the efflorescence of literature connecting the Spirit and prophecy. So much so that as John Woodhouse points out, "'The Spirit of prophecy' was the favourite rabbinic expression for the Holy Spirit" ("The Spirit of Prophecy," in B. G. Webb, ed., *Spirit of the Living God: Part Two: Explorations* 6 [Homebush West, N.S.W., Australia: Lancer, 1992], 105). For a solid examination of the connection between Spirit and prophecy in intertestamental Judaism see Turner, *Holy Spirit and Spiritual Gifts,* chapter 1.
35. See Gordon J. Wenham, "Sanctuary Symbolism in the Garden of Eden Story," *Proceedings of the World Congress of Jewish Studies* 9 (1986): 19–25.
36. Willem VanGemeren, *The Progress of Redemption: The Story of Salvation from Creation to the New Jerusalem* (Grand Rapids, Mich.: Baker, 2000), 156–157, emphasis original.
37. Dumbrell, *Search for Order,* 48. Dumbrell's whole discussion of the tabernacle and its theological significance is first-rate.

(Ex. 31:3).[38] Both Calvin and Kuyper see in the Spirit's role a paradigm of his role as the source of human talent in general, whether that of a skilled laborer or of a military genius.[39] However, this supposition—though arguable on other grounds perhaps—is hardly to be established on the basis of the story of the erection of the tabernacle, which was peculiar to Israel's history and so clearly an element in redemptive history rather than in the order of creation, which is where Kuyper places it.

The Chronicler of Israel adds to the picture. In 1 Chronicles 28, David charges Solomon with the temple project. Solomon is to follow instructions that are even more detailed than the ones given to Moses.[40] David gives his son ". . . the plans of all that the Spirit [*rûach*] had put in his mind for the courts of the temple of the LORD and all the surrounding rooms, for the treasures of the temple of God and for the treasures for the dedicated things"(1 Chron. 28:12, NIV).[41] Like the tabernacle, the temple was a thing of beauty.

In the light of the glories of Solomon's temple one can understand the shock of the returnees after the exile.[42] The temple was in ruins (Hag. 1:9). Indeed the glory had departed (Ezekiel 10). The returnees began to rebuild but soon gave up and attended to their own comforts (Hag. 1:3–6). In that context the prophetic rebuke was heard once more. Haggai called for repentance and a return of the people to the Sinai covenant. He called upon the leadership to be strong: Zerubbabel, the governor; and Joshua, the high priest (2:4). He also called upon the people to be strong (2:4b). The point is clear: "Be strong and get back to work on the temple!" But what was the incentive to be so and to do so? The prophetic answer is pneumatological: "My Spirit [*rûchî*] remains in your midst" (2:5).[43] Zechariah adds to this postexilic picture.[44] The prophet encourages Zerubbabel not to lose heart over the temple rebuilding despite the recalcitrance of the people and external opposition (Zech. 4:6–10).[45] But on what grounds was the governor not to lose heart? The prophetic answer is that God is working: "Not by

38. See John I. Durham, *Exodus*, WBC, comment on Ex. 31:3.

39. For Calvin, see *Institutes of the Christian Religion*, II.2.16; and for Kuyper, see *The Work of the Holy Spirit*, trans. Henri De Vries (Grand Rapids, Mich.: Eerdmans, 1975), 38.

40. J. Barton Payne, "1 Chronicles," *EBC*, comment on 1 Chron. 28:12.

41. On analogy with the erection of the tabernacle and the role of the Spirit, I prefer to follow the NIV at this point. The ESV and NRSV omit any reference to *rûach*. The JSB does have "spirit," but all in lower case.

42. See Robert L. Alden's discussion of the occasion and purpose of Haggai ("Haggai," *EBC*).

43. Ralph L. Smith points out the parallelism between Haggai 2:4, "I am with you," and 2:5, "My Spirit is standing in your midst" (*Micah—Malachi*, WBC, comment on Hag. 2:5).

44. See Kenneth L. Barker's discussion of the occasion and purpose of Zechariah (*Zechariah*, WBC).

45. The external opposition was probably that of the regional administrator of Samaria and Tatenai (Montague, *Holy Spirit*, 79). Paul Hanson suggests that two groups among the returnees were struggling for control of "the restoration cult" (cited in Ralph L. Smith, *Micah—Malachi*,

power, nor by might, but by my Spirit [*rûchî*]" (4:6b). The promise of the divine presence is to be the key to fostering the morale needed for rebuilding the temple. According to George T. Montague, Zechariah's message to Zerubbabel is that, ". . . the work of rebuilding the temple is the work of God's spirit which nothing in the long run can resist."[46] God clearly had not abandoned his people nor his desire to dwell in their midst.

What may safely be surmised from the Spirit's role in turning the heavenly blueprints of first the tabernacle and then the temple into earthly realities is the Spirit's activity as the source of wisdom, implementer of the divine will, the perfecter of God's purposes (in this instance providing a place to dwell with his people), and the Spirit's willingness to enable human agents to carry out the divine intention.[47] The aesthetics of the tabernacle and temple also show that the Spirit of God is no Manichean. The Spirit is at home with matter, color, texture, and form. The Spirit is integral to preparing for the coming of God to dwell with his people, which reached its first great stage when the Word took flesh and dwelt (lit. *eskēnōsen* "tabernacled") among us, as we shall see (cf. Luke 1:35 and John 1:14), and which will find its ultimate expression in nothing less than a new heaven and new earth (Revelation 21–22).

IRENAEUS: A SEMINAL CONTRIBUTION

Irenaeus (130–200) has been described as "the first biblical theologian."[48] There is merit in the title. Irenaeus sought to work with the whole sweep of revelation, Old and New. Hendrikus Berkhof describes Irenaeus as one of the very few to show a systematic interest in the way of Israel before the Reformers.[49] The threat of gnosticism in its myriad forms sent Irenaeus back to the OT to affirm that the God of the older revelation and the Father of the Lord Jesus were the same God (contra Marcion inter alios). In fact it was Irenaeus who first described the Scriptures as consisting of Old and New Testaments.[50] Brevard Childs maintains that, ". . . [Irenaeus] established, once and for all, the centrality of the concept of the Christian Bible."[51] Moreover, he had a sense of redemptive history. God has a plan

---

WBC, comment on Zech. 4:7). If so, then there was not merely internal apathy to deal with but internal opposition.

46. Ibid.

47. With regard to the Spirit and wisdom, the intertestamental literature shows the connection between the two far more closely drawn than in the OT. See for example *The Wisdom of Solomon* 1:7; 7:21ff.; 12:1; and the discussion in Moltmann, *Spirit of Life*, 46–47.

48. Scobie, *Ways of Our God*, 10.

49. Berkhof, *Christian Faith*, 224.

50. See Phyllis A. Bird, "The Authority of the Bible," *New Interpreter's Dictionary of the Bible*, vol. 1 (Nashville: Abingdon, 1994), 33–64, http://www.prophetess.lstc.edu/~rkkin/Document/bird.htmhttp://www.Http://www, accessed February 23, 2005.

51. Childs, *Biblical Theology*, 32.

and Christ is its centerpiece. Jesus recapitulates in his own person (*in seipso recapitulavit*) all that Adam should have been and failed to be.[52] At every stage of life Jesus was the obedient one as opposed to Adam's primal and catastrophic disobedience. Jesus lived out a truly faithful human life from cradle to the grave.[53]

The OT, for Irenaeus, was an expression of the divine pedagogy.[54] God, like a great educator, was preparing the way with Israel for the coming of the Son. Irenaeus was thus an early pioneer of a typological approach to the OT. As he wrote in his classic work *Against Heresies,*

> Thus it was, too, that God formed man at the first, because of His munificence; but chose the patriarchs for the sake of their salvation, and prepared a people beforehand, teaching [the divine pedagogy] the headstrong to follow God; and raised up prophets upon earth, accustoming man to bear His Spirit [within him], and to hold communion with God: He Himself, indeed, having need of nothing, but granting communion with Himself to those who stood in need of it, and *sketching out, like an architect, the plan of salvation* to those that pleased Him. And He did Himself furnish guidance to those who beheld Him not in Egypt, while to those who became unruly in the desert He promulgated a law very suitable [to their condition]. Then, on the people who entered into the good land He bestowed a noble inheritance; and He killed the fatted calf for those converted to the Father, and presented them with the finest robe. *Thus in a variety of ways, He adjusted the human race to an agreement with salvation.*[55]

Irenaeus saw a unity in Scripture where Marcion had seen only a conflict. His seminal contribution in terms of our study of the Holy Spirit lies in his holistic approach to reading Scripture, which takes seriously the flow of redemptive history with its various covenants.

At times, though, Irenaeus's reading of the OT was fanciful. Is Mary really the counterpart to Eve?[56] Were the three spies whom Rahab received into her home really signifying the Father, Son, and Holy Spirit?[57] Again, when various OT figures experience wood in some way, ranging from Moses' use of a rod to Elisha's use of a stick, were they really pointing to Christ's reign

52. Irenaeus, *Adversus Haereses* III.xviii.1, quoted in Alister McGrath, ed., *The Christian Theology Reader,* 3rd ed. (Oxford, and Cambridge, Mass.: Blackwell, 2007), 344–345.

53. Irenaeus, *Adversus Haereses* III., xviii. 6–7, quoted in Henry Bettenson, ed. and trans., *The Early Christian Fathers* (Oxford: Oxford University Press, 1978).

54. Bird, "Authority," 33–64.

55. Irenaeus, *Adversus Haereses,* quoted in Gusto L. González, *Christian Thought Revisited: Three Types of Theology* (Nashville: Abingdon, 1989), 71–72. The italics are González's. But the words in square brackets are mine.

56. Irenaeus, *Adversus Haereses* III.xxi.10, cited in Bettenson, ed. and trans., *Early Christian Fathers,* 83.

57. Ibid., IV.xx.12, 88.

from the wood of the Cross?[58] I think not. However, such an approach to Scripture recognizes that revelation is progressive. Not everything is revealed at once. There is a plot line. As we are seeing, this is especially relevant to the study of the Holy Spirit's person and work. We will have to wait until we consider the ministry of the Spirit in NT perspective before the picture becomes more than a sketch. Or to change the metaphor, we will need to see "Act II" of the biblical *theodramatik,* as Hans Urs von Balthasar might say, before the full performance of the Holy Spirit can be examined.[59]

A more recent theologian who appreciated the divine pedagogy was Abraham Kuyper. He writes, ". . . the Holy Spirit performed a special work for the saints of God by giving them a temporary service of types and shadows."[60] For Kuyper those "types and shadows" included aspects of Israel's "ceremonies in the sanctuary," as well as "political, social and domestic life."[61] He contends that without this preparatory work of the Spirit in the history of the Old Covenant, Christ's coming would not have been understood. Israel "offered the Christ a place for the sole of His foot and a *base of operations.*"[62] Neither Athens, Rome, China, or India could have supplied such a base.[63] However, with Israel God had providentially seen to it. All this has a very Irenaean feel to it.

At this point in the discussion, though, a caveat may be in order. Christianity is no gnosticism. The divine intent cannot simply be reduced to instruction, as Irenaeus so clearly and rightly recognized. The great human need is for redemption and not only for enlightenment. As Richard B. Gaffin Jr. correctly maintains, "Revelation is not so much divinely given *gnosis* to provide us with knowledge concerning the nature of God, man and the world as it is divinely inspired interpretation of God's activity of redeeming men so that they might worship and serve him in the world."[64] He quotes with approval Geerhardus Vos, the Reformed pioneer of biblical theology: "The circle of revelation is not a school, but a covenant."[65]

One of the lasting legacies of Irenaeus is the challenge to the systematic theologian not to proof-text but to appeal to biblical texts in the light of the flow of redemptive history: texts in their contexts in their literary units

---

58. See Irenaeus, *Against Heresies,* in Philip Schaff, ed., *Apostolic Fathers with Justin Martyr and Irenaeus,* http://www.ccel.org/ccel/schaff/anf01.viii.iv.lxxxvi.html, accessed February 23, 2005.

59. For a splendid introduction to von Balthasar's theology see Edward T. Oakes, *Pattern of Redemption: The Theology of Hans Urs von Balthasar* (New York and London: Continuum, 1994), esp. part 3.

60. Kuyper, *Work of the Holy Spirit,* 53.

61. Ibid., 54.

62. Ibid., emphasis original.

63. Ibid.

64. Richard B. Gaffin Jr., ed., *The Shorter Writings of Geerhardus Vos: Redemptive History and Biblical Interpretation* (Phillipsburg, N.J.: Presbyterian & Reformed, 2001), xvii.

65. Geerhardus Vos, quoted in ibid.

in their books in the canon and with regard to the flow of redemptive history (*Heilsgeschichte*). Of course, there will always be a place for the proof text as evidence. There is not always the luxury of time that allows for the showing of the theologian's complete workings on every occasion. But if the systematician is challenged about whether the use of this text or that is a responsible one, then he or she needs to be able to bring such workings into view.

IMPLICATIONS FOR BELIEF AND PRACTICE

The story of the Spirit and Israel may seem like an archaeological dig to some. We live this side of the coming of Christ, and therefore, one might ask, what can be gained, practically speaking, by the examination of the Spirit's role as presented in the OT witness? Does not the NT provide a clearer window into the divine purpose and the Spirit's realization of it? In one sense, of course. Sinclair Ferguson suggests that B. B. Warfield's argument concerning the Trinity, in which he compares the OT to a dimly lit room, might *mutatis mutandis* apply to the Holy Spirit. Warfield had argued, ". . . the introduction of light [from the NT] brings into it nothing which was not in it before; but it brings into clearer view much of what is in it but was only dimly or not at all perceived before."[66] Again, Warfield: "Thus the Old Testament revelation of God is not corrected by the fuller revelation which follows it, but is only perfected, extended and enlarged."[67] Point taken. Even so, at another level reviewing the Spirit's role in implementing the divine project in its OT phase has the following practical merits.

For a start we can realize that as God's people we stand in a great stream of God's redemptive activity. Some evangelicals can give the impression that between St. Paul's conversion and their own—let alone anything prior to St. Paul's—very little has happened of a redemptive nature. But God has been at work reclaiming his creation. His covenants, his judges, his kings, his prophets, and his presence are part of the warp and woof of that story. The Spirit, as we have seen, has been integral to that story as well. We have great cause for thankfulness.

History is not ". . . a tale/Told by an idiot,/Full of sound and fury,/Signifying nothing."[68] History has been and remains the arena of the Spirit, the implementer and perfecter of the triune God's purposes. It has been said, "Without individuals nothing happens and without institutions nothing is preserved." The Spirit was at work in key individuals in OT times, whether a towering leader like Moses or an artist like Bezalel or a judge like

---

66. B. B. Warfield, *Biblical Doctrines*, quoted in Sinclair Ferguson, *The Holy Spirit* (Leicester, England: Inter-Varsity, 1996), 29.

67. Ibid.

68. William Shakespeare, *Macbeth*, Act 5, Scene 5, Macbeth speaking.

Samson or a king like David or a prophet like Micah. The Spirit was also at work in key covenant institutions such as prophecy and kingship. Thus were generated those paradigmatic figures (like a Moses) and events (like the exodus) and institutions (like the tabernacle for the divine presence) and Scripture (the OT) that were to be fundamental for understanding the coming and cross of the Christ.

The great American philosopher Josiah Royce (1855–1916) maintained that a people may be constituted by a shared memory.[69] He wrote of communities of memory. Evangelicals especially, because of an accent on the personal, individual, and immediate, may neglect to our hurt the memory of what the Spirit has accomplished in OT times. As the ancient Christian hymn known as the *Te Deum* ("To you, God") puts it, in our praise we join not only with "angels" and "Cherubim and Seraphim" but also with the "glorious company of apostles," "the noble army of martyrs," and "the goodly fellowship of prophets."[70]

Another practical aspect of the present discussion is to be reminded afresh that the Spirit is not antithetical to the aesthetic. The tabernacle—with its color, form, textures, and materials—is testimony to this. The language of Spirit may suggest in popular parlance the ethereal, the ascetic, and the unearthly. (The King James Version, which so often refers to the Holy Spirit as the "Holy *Ghost*," reinforces the ethereal impression.) But the biblical testimony to the Holy Spirit of God is otherwise. Christians are not Manichean. We do not posit two gods at war: one good and one evil. We do not believe that the material order and historical order have been abandoned by the Creator. Francis Schaeffer was right to chide fellow evangelicals for their neglect of the arts as though God were interested in only part of human existence—the so-called spiritual part. He wrote: "Evangelicals have been legitimately criticized for often being so tremendously interested in seeing souls saved and go to heaven that they have not cared much about the whole man."[71] Schaeffer saw in the tabernacle, and then Solomon's temple, a beauty wrought by God's Spirit through human agency that was to be celebrated but never to be worshiped per se.

69. Josiah Royce, "The Community and the Time Process," in John K. Roth, ed., *The Philosophy of Josiah Royce* (New York: Thomas Y. Cromwell, 1971), 366.

70. *An Australian Prayer Book: For Use Together with the Book of Common Prayer (1662)* (Sydney: AIO Press, 1978), 24. The hymn is attributed to Nicetas, Bishop of Remesiana (d. 414). It has been described as "the most famous hymn in the Western Church" (Robert C. Broderick, ed., *The Catholic Encyclopedia*, rev. and updated ed. [Nashville, Camden, and New York: Thomas Nelson, 1978], 572).

71. Francis Schaeffer, *Art and the Bible: Two Essays* (Downers Grove, Ill.: InterVarsity Press, 1973), 7. Happily there have been changes in the evangelical attitude since Schaeffer wrote, as can be seen in journals such as *Books and Culture* and *Christianity and Literature*. However, the attitude that he criticized can still be found in North America in print, on Christian radio and television, and in sermons.

SIX

THE SPIRIT AND THE HOPE OF ISRAEL

Josiah Royce, mentioned briefly in the previous chapter, maintained that a people may be constituted not only by a shared memory but also by a shared hope.[1] He wrote, therefore, not only of communities of memory but also of communities of hope. Israel was both a community of memory and a community of hope. Israel's memory centered on the exodus event and by means of it God's redemption of his people from Egyptian servitude. Israel expressed this memory in song (Psalm 106) and in prophecy (Jer. 2:4–9), and its Ten Commandments were prefaced with it (Ex. 20:1–2). Jürgen Moltmann rightly appreciates the interplay of memory and hope in the life of Israel. He writes,

> Through historical remembrance, the God of the Exodus, the covenant and the promised land become present to such a degree that as the Creator of the world and the Lord of human liberty he determines the present. The historical experience of God is always tensed between the remembrance and the expectation which frame that experience.[2]

As for Israel's expectations, by the end of the OT they were highly variegated, as we shall shortly see. But hope there was. God had made Israel his covenant people.

So often in OT Scripture, a divinely established covenant is the formalization and solemnization of a relationship founded on promise in the framework of sacrifice and oath expressed in a rite (Gen. 8:20–9:17; Genesis 15;

---

1. Josiah Royce, "The Community and the Time Process," in John K. Roth, ed., *The Philosophy of Josiah Royce* (New York: Thomas Y. Cromwell, 1971), 366–367.
2. Jürgen Moltmann, *The Spirit of Life: A Universal Affirmation*, trans. Margaret Kohl (Minneapolis: Fortress, 1994), 39.

Exodus 24).[3] Expectation or hope is intrinsic to covenant promise. Jürgen Moltmann goes so far as to say, "Israel's religion was from the outset a religion based on *the expectation of God.*"[4]

By the close of the OT canon, the hope of Israel is indeed multiplex and includes: a renewed Israel (Ezek. 37:1–14), a unified people of God (vv. 15–28), a new David (37:24–25), a new temple (Ezekiel 40–48), a new covenant (Jer. 31:31–34), Zion exalted (Isa. 2:2–4), the nations acknowledging Yahweh (Zech. 14:16–19), and even a new heavens and a new earth (Isaiah 65–66).[5] This list is not exhaustive. Thus Israel's experience on the historical plane of God's faithfulness in keeping his promises generated the incidents (e.g., the exodus) and symbols (e.g., the temple) which the prophets drew upon to articulate the hope of a people when the kingdom was split and both North and South declined.

But a wide-ranging discussion of the hope of Israel is beyond our brief, with its focus on pneumatology. Consequently we shall concentrate our attention on the work of the Holy Spirit in bringing about God's future for his people. In other words, eschatology broadly understood will be our focus, rather than the traditional but more narrow understanding that eschatology deals with the four last things of death, judgment, heaven, and hell.[6] In particular our attention will be on Israel's hope for a special agent of God, for a new beginning for God's people, and for a great outpouring of God's Spirit on all flesh. As Charles H. H. Scobie suggests, "The Spirit of God plays an important role in the promises of the dawning of a new order."[7]

The Spirit and the Agent of Israel's Future

In Israel's past God raised up various agents to achieve his purposes: e.g., Moses, judges, prophets, and kings. Likewise for Israel's future, the Lord would raise up agents of his purpose.[8] He will honor his covenants and keep

3. On various kinds of covenant, including divinely established ones, see Charles H. H. Scobie, *The Ways of Our God: An Approach to Biblical Theology* (Grand Rapids, Mich., and Cambridge: Eerdmans, 2003), 473–479.

4. Moltmann, *Spirit of Life*, 53, emphasis original.

5. Whether the OT canon in view is that of the Hebrew Bible which ends with 2 Chronicles 36 or the Protestant one which ends with Malachi 4, in both cases the canon closes on the note of expectation.

6. William J. Dumbrell, *The Search for Order: Biblical Eschatology in Focus* (Eugene, Ore.: Wipf & Stock, 2001), 9, describes the broad sense of eschatology in the following way: ". . . the broad sense of the goal of history toward which the Bible moves and of the biblical factors and events bearing on that goal."

7. Scobie, *Ways of Our God*, 274.

8. The focus in this chapter is on the Spirit and Israel's hope, rather than on a wide-ranging discussion of the nature of the kingdom and Israel's place in it. For a wider discussion of eschatology (especially corporate), see the forthcoming volume on eschatology in this series.

his promises, whether made to Abraham or to Moses or to David. Two of the promised agents to come are linked to the Spirit: the Branch of Jesse and the Servant of the Lord. These figures come before us in three important messianic texts found in Isaiah (Isa. 11:1–9; 42:1–9; and 61:1–11).[9] Let us consider each passage in turn.

The Branch of Jesse

On any reckoning the book of Isaiah is a high point of the OT. In the early chapters of the book a dismal picture of Israel's unbelieving leadership (Ahaz) and the house of David is presented (e.g., Isa. 7:2, 13). But God will raise up an agent of his purpose from the house of David: "a shoot [*chōter,* suggestive of a fresh start] from the stump [*nētser*] of Jesse" and "a branch from his roots" (Isa. 11:1). Upon this personage the Spirit of the Lord will rest (v. 2).[10] That Spirit is further characterized in terms of "wisdom," "understanding," "counsel," "might," "knowledge," and "fear of the LORD" (v. 2). This messianic figure is a person of integrity and an agent of divine justice (vv. 3–5). The outcome of this king's reign (vv. 6–10) will be nothing less than "universal peace and the restoration of Eden-like relationships in the animal kingdom."[11] In Israel's future then will emerge this idealized ruler of God's providing who will be Spirit-empowered.[12] As J. N. Oswalt comments, "Chapter 11 [of Isaiah] says that the coming King will rule not by the trappings of power, but in the power of righteousness."[13]

Significantly with this figure, his character and competencies are tied to his Spirit-endowment. For the text, having described his origins in the house of David (Isa. 11:1), then presents the Spirit as resting on him (v. 2), before outlining the branch's character, competencies, mission, and effectiveness (vv. 3–10). This king does not rule by his own wits and strengths alone. He has none of the fallibility of either Ahaz (Isaiah 7) or Ahaz's son Hezekiah (Isaiah 38–39).

9. Michael Welker observes that the earlier figures of judges delivered Israel from *"external danger"* by the Spirit, whereas each of the figures in the Isaianic texts to be considered "overcomes a situation of *internal danger* for Israel" by the Spirit ("The Holy Spirit," *Theology Today* 46 no. 1 [April 1989]: 10, emphasis original).

10. Max Turner suggests that when the Hebrew can be translated "Spirit of God/the LORD" or "my/his Spirit," then, "More usually, divine Spirit is denoted" ("Holy Spirit," *NDBT,* 551). In his view, a phrase such as "Spirit of the Lord" is "a synecdoche for God *himself* in action" (ibid., 558, emphasis original). Dumbrell, *Search for Order,* 91, argues that the reference to "rest" suggests that this agent of the Lord will "permanently possess the Spirit."

11. Dumbrell, *Search for Order,* 92.

12. Scobie, *Ways of Our God,* 316. The whole discussion in Scobie of messianic figures is highly instructive (see ibid., chapter 6).

13. J. N. Oswalt, "Isaiah," *NDBT,* 222.

The Servant of the Lord

The book of Isaiah presents the figure not only of the ideal Davidic king to come but also of a mysterious Servant of the Lord. However, the precise relationship between the two eschatological agents is nowhere spelled out in the prophecy. Let's look at the detail. In the first Servant Song, the Servant is introduced by the Lord in a mix of royal and prophetic categories (Isa. 42:1).[14] For example, William J. Dumbrell points out the "striking parallels between the appointment of the Servant and the royal messiah."[15] The parallels include similar designations used of the Servant and David in texts like 1 Samuel 16:1–13 and Psalm 89:3 (e.g., "servant" and "chosen one"). Importantly for our purposes, the Servant is presented as a Spirit-endowed agent of God's purpose (Isa. 42:1). God is the speaker and declares, "I have put my Spirit [*rûchî*] upon him" (v. 1b).[16] The mission of the Servant is to "bring forth justice [*mishpāt*] to the nations" (v. 1). This accent appears three times (vv. 1–4). But this mission will be carried out in such a way that "a bruised reed [battered Israel in exile] he will not break, and a faintly burning wick he will not quench" (v. 3). The mission of the Servant is summed up in verse 6: the Lord—identified as the Creator in the previous verse—will give the Servant "as a covenant for the people [Israel], a light for the nations." The blind will have their eyes opened and the prisoners will be set free (v. 7). The mission exhibits both prophetic and royal motifs. Geoffrey W. Grogan suggests, "Freeing captives suggests the conquest of the captors and so kingship . . . while the opening of blind eyes and the enlightenment of the Gentiles introduces a prophetic feature into the work of this Spirit-anointed Servant of God."[17] And so, the brief of the Servant extends well beyond Israel and her borders. Indeed, the Servant is part of the "new things" that God is about to do for his glory (vv. 8–9). The mission of the Servant of the Lord is predicated upon Spirit (*rûach*) endowment.

If Isaiah 61 is included among the Servant Songs of Isaiah—a controversial notion—then once again we see a linkage between the Servant, the Spirit's empowerment, and the future of Israel.[18] Even if this text is not about the

---

14. The identity of the servant figure is hotly debated in scholarship. Scobie helpfully discusses the four options: an individual, a collective, an ideal, or messianic (*Ways of Our God*, 407–409). He argues that these notions are not mutually exclusive and sees that ". . . there is clearly a progression from a collective toward a more individual understanding of the servant, especially in Song IV [Is. 52:13-53:12]" (ibid., 409).

15. Dumbrell, *Search for Order*, 115.

16. Again as previously noted, Turner suggests that "my Spirit" usually denotes the "divine Spirit" ("Holy Spirit," *NDBT*, 551). Of course, in places "my spirit" is that of the human agent who speaks, as in Isaiah 26:9. Context is critical.

17. Geoffrey W. Grogan, "Isaiah," *EBC*, comment on Isa. 42:7.

18. The four Servant Songs that are generally agreed on by scholars are: 1) Isaiah 42:1–7 or to v. 9 or to v. 12; 2) 49:1–6 or to v. 7 or to v. 13; 3) 50:4–9 or to v. 11; and 4) 52:13–53:12; see Charles H. H. Scobie, *Ways of Our God*, 406. Scobie himself thinks that the speaker of Isaiah 61:1–3 ought "probably also to be identified with the Servant" (ibid., 277). Dumbrell

Servant per se, what can be seen yet again is that there is a nexus presented between the mission of a future messianic agent of the divine purpose and Spirit-empowerment.[19] The opening speaker in our passage is anointed by the Lord and Spirit-endowed (Isa. 61:1).[20] As Grogan suggests, "His anointing with the Spirit of God provides a link with both the kingly and the servant prophecies of this book (11:1; 42:1)."[21] What is extraordinary about the speaker is that he knows that he is Spirit-endowed.[22] The figure in the passage is a preacher whose message is one of hope for the poor. These poor appear to be those Jews in Palestine awaiting the fulfillment of God's promises (Isa. 61:1).[23] Their poverty seems a mix of the physical ("poor") and spiritual ("brokenhearted"). The proclamation is that God's Jubilee year has come, and with it, freedom (v. 2)[24]—freedom for "the poor," "the brokenhearted," "the captives," and "those who are bound" (v. 1). The obverse side of such a liberation is judgment on others who remain unspecified (v. 2). Zion will be comforted and restored (vv. 2b–4). The nations will serve the restored people of God, who are now able to be the priestly kingdom envisaged at Sinai (cf. vv. 5–6 and Ex. 19:6). Once more the vision goes well beyond the borders of Israel. J. N. Oswalt sees in this passage links between the future Davidic king presented in Isaiah 11 and this proclaimer of Isaiah 61. He contends, ". . . the messianic figures in the two parts of the book are not contradictory, but complementary."[25]

Israel has a future because God will provide a ruler, a servant, and a preacher who will be instrumental in securing that hope. Each of the Isai-

---

describes the speaker in Isaiah 61 as Servant-like (*Search for Order*, 124); and Moltmann likewise (*Spirit of Life*, 53).

19. "Messiah" (*māshîach*) means anointed, and in the OT, prophets were anointed on occasion (e.g., 1 Kings 19:16, Elijah anoints Elisha), kings were anointed (e.g., 1 Kings 19:16, Elijah anoints Jehu), and priests were anointed (e.g., Ex. 28:41, Moses anoints Aaron and his sons). The anointed king is of particular interest for our purposes, especially the hope for a new David. Of the Davidic king in particular, Dumbrell maintains, "The Davidic king operates as Yahweh's vice-regent, who bears Yahweh's rule over the nations of the world. The Davidic covenant goes back to the divine intention not merely for Israel through Sinai but for humanity through Abraham, and thus to the manner in which the debacle of Genesis 3–11 is to be reversed and Eden to be restored" (*Search for Order*, 72–73).

20. John D. W. Watts identifies three speakers in the chapter: a preacher and healer in vv. 1–3; an administrator in vv. 4–7 and vv. 10–11; and Yahweh in v. 8a (*Isaiah 34–66*, WBC). His analysis seems over-elaborate at points.

21. Grogan, "Isaiah," *EBC*, comment on Isa. 61:1–3.

22. As does Jesus when he deliberately applied this passage to himself in the synagogue in Nazareth in Luke 4:16–30: "He unrolled the scroll and found [*heuren*, aorist aspect] the place where it is written" (Luke 4:17).

23. Watts describes them as "the dispirited Jewish community around the ruins of Jerusalem before Ezra returned" (*Isaiah 34–66*, WBC, comment on Isa. 61:1).

24. Ibid. Grogan comments, "Moreover the Hebrew word translated 'freedom' in v. 1 is *deror*, a technical term for the Jubilee release in the OT (cf. Lev. 25:10, 13; 27:24; Jer. 34:8–10; Ezek. 46:17)."

25. Oswalt, "Isaiah," *NDBT*, 222.

anic texts considered above describes the Spirit as remaining and resting on the figure concerned. There are similarities in their structure and subject matter. All three, as Michael Welker correctly points out, show that, "The power and authority of the person who bears God's Spirit lie in the fact that this person establishes *justice, mercy, and the knowledge of God and gives them a universal extension.*"[26] Ultimately only one figure in the future will instantiate the combination of these ideals: Jesus, ruler, servant, and proclaimer.

The Spirit and the Re-creation of God's People

By the prophet Ezekiel's day it was clear that Israel was dead. The kingdom had been divided (922 b.c.), the North fell to the Assyrians (722/721 b.c.), and later the South fell to the Babylonians (587/586 b.c.). The temple in Jerusalem was in ruins. The cream of the population of the South was in exile. The people of God had been judged for their sins. The psalmist could only lament, "By the waters of Babylon, there we sat down and wept, when we remembered Zion" (Ps. 137:1). And again, "How shall we sing the Lord's song in a foreign land?" (v. 4). Israelites in exile said, "our hope is lost" (Ezek. 37:11). The exile was a catastrophe.

But God! The people in exile may have lost hope, but the God of the people had not abandoned them, wayward though they had been. Ezekiel tells the reader that for the sake of his holy name the Lord would act (Ezek. 36:22).[27] God will regather his people as in a second exodus (v. 24). And with the regathering will come outward cleansing ("I will sprinkle clean water on you," v. 25) and inner transformation ("a new heart, and a new spirit I will put within you," 36:26a; see also 11:19–20). "The heart of stone" will be replaced by "a heart of flesh" (36:26b). The heart (*lēb*) to the Israelites, of course, represents the center of a person's cognition, volition, and affections. Moreover, the great covenant promise going all the way back to Sinai, "you shall be my people, and I will be your God," shall come to fruition (cf. Ex. 6:7 and Ezek. 36:28).[28] Israel will return to the Promised Land, and the land itself will flourish like Eden of old (36:35). The nations that observe all this shall know that this is the Lord's doing and that it has been done for his own name's

26. See Michael Welker, *God the Spirit*, trans. John F. Hoffmeyer (Minneapolis: Fortress, 1994), 109, emphasis original. He writes, "It is characteristic of the righteousness of God contained in the *messianic* promises that the creation of justice, mercy, and the knowledge of God spreads to the nations, that the nations are given a part in Israel's experience of righteousness and in Israel's knowledge of God" (ibid., 118, emphasis original).

27. L. John McGregor, "Ezekiel," *NBC*, describes this part of Ezekiel (Ezek. 36:16–38) as ". . . the core of the book. . . . Its message is a summary of the book" (740).

28. Ralph H. Alexander, "Ezekiel," *EBC*, comment on Ezek. 36:24–32.

sake as the holy God (vv. 23, 36). The people of God, in effect, are to be born again.

What then has the Spirit of God to do with this restoration of Israel's identity and fortunes? In Israel's past, the Spirit had come upon various individuals vital to her interests: judges, kings, and prophets, as we saw in the previous chapter. But in the future, the Spirit ("my Spirit," *rûchî*) will indwell all God's people, and his presence will be the cause of their new obedience (Ezek. 36:27). Dumbrell comments,

> What Ezekiel foresees—the occupancy of the land and obedience to the Torah—is in continuity with the Sinai covenant. By the action of renewal, the Promised land will become like the garden in Eden, where all Israel will exercise Adam's role and will become kings and priests (cf. Exod 19:6).[29]

God's creation purpose will stay on track.

The story of Israel's restoration is told another way in Ezekiel 37:1–14. The imagery is dramatic. The prophet finds himself placed by the Lord in the middle of a valley of dry bones (Ezek. 37:1). He is commanded to prophesy to the bones, which he does (v. 4). The Spirit as "breath" is in fact directly addressed by the prophet: "Thus says the Lord GOD: Come from the four winds, O breath [*rûach*], and breathe on these slain that they may live" (v. 9).[30] The scene then begins to echo the primordial one of Adam's creation (Gen. 2:7). The Lord puts breath into the bones, and they live (Ezek. 37:7–10). Further there is the promise which parallels that in the previous chapter: "And I will put my Spirit [*rûchî*] within you, and you shall live" (v. 14).[31] In the previous chapter the indwelling leads to obedience, and in this chapter it leads to new life. Alexander comments, "The vision clearly demonstrated the restoration to life of a people who had been dead for some time. It was in two stages: first physical (or national) restoration and then spiritual renewal."[32] This incredible transformation then is the product of the prophetic word and the Spirit. Israel is to be raised from the dead and spiritually renewed. Moltmann comments, "So in this way the people itself, in its historical and everyday life, is to become the 'temple' of God's

29. Dumbrell, *Search for Order*, 104.

30. This is yet another passage (Ezek. 37:1–14) where *rûach* allows a variety of translation possibilities: "breath," "wind," "spirit," and "Spirit." Interestingly, Leslie C. Allen allows only three of the aforementioned possibilities in his note on Ezekiel 37:5, which covers the entire section. He omits "Spirit" (*Ezekiel 20–48*, WBC).

31. Allen describes Ezekiel 37:14 in the following way: "The editorial rounding off of the unit wants also to tie it to the preceding piece . . . 36:27" (ibid.). As in Isaiah, "my s/Spirit" may in context be referring to the divine Spirit or the human spirit, depending upon the speaker. For example, Ezekiel 3:14 has a reference to the human speaker as well as to the divine Spirit.

32. Alexander, "Ezekiel," *EBC*, comment on Ezek. 37:11–14.

Spirit, and the Shekinah of the most high."[33] Again, the whole of a people is in view and not just individuals here and there within it.

THE SPIRIT AND THE GREAT OUTPOURING ON GOD'S PEOPLE

Part of Israel's hope was that at some future date in God's good keeping the Spirit would be poured out upon the people. Isaiah, Ezekiel, and Joel (most famously of all) speak of this day.[34]

In the second section of Isaiah, after a dire promise of judgment upon Israel—upon both the princes of the sanctuary and the people—Jacob (Israel) is addressed by the Lord: "But now hear, O Jacob my servant, Israel whom I have chosen" (Isa. 43:28–44:1). God will pour out his Spirit (*rûchî*, "my Spirit") upon the offspring of Jacob (44:3b). They will flourish like willows among the grass (v. 4). Above all they will know who they are: "I am the LORD's" (v. 5). As John D. W. Watts suggests, "The result will be a new enthusiasm among Israelites in Babylon and elsewhere to *belong to Yahweh* and to use the name *Jacob.*"[35] Or is verse 5 about the Gentiles, as some argue? If so, as Grogan contends,

> Isaiah is almost Pauline at this point, for the Gentile converts of v. 5 seem like an (adopted?) extension of the children of Israel to whom v. 4 refers. The statement, I will pour out my Spirit (v. 3) reminds us of Joel 2:29, with its fulfillment at Pentecost and the Gentile evangelization that followed it.[36]

Thus a link is established between vibrant life and knowing oneself as belonging to God, and the pouring out of the Spirit. After judgment, grace has come.

---

33. Moltmann, *Spirit of Life,* 55–56. In my opinion, Moltmann overdoes the Shekinah motif, retrojecting later rabbinic ideas (see ibid., 47–51).

34. It is worth noting that, generally speaking, dispensationalist theologians either see the texts we shall consider partially fulfilled in the church age and to be fully realized in the millennial kingdom, or to be fulfilled in the millennial kingdom. Generally speaking, non-dispensational theologians see these texts fulfilled in the church. For an excellent coverage of the issues see John S. Feinberg, ed., *Continuity and Discontinuity: Perspective on the Relationship Between the Old and New Testaments: Essays in Honor of S. Lewis Johnson, Jr.* (Westchester, Ill.: Crossway, 1988). Although I write from a non-dispensational perspective, a major strength of dispensationalism is that it takes the people of Israel seriously in the economy of God. Non-dispensationalist theologian Gabriel Fackre notes, "In systematics, the locus on Israel is regularly missing, demonstrating the effects of anti-semitism and anti-Judaism on theology, as well as the ahistorical temptations which regularly plague us" ("Bible, Community, and Spirit," *Horizons in Biblical Theology* 21 [1999]: 71). The volume on eschatology in this series will explore these matters. For this volume to do so is beyond its brief.

35. Watts, *Isaiah 34–66,* WBC, comment on Isa. 44:5, emphasis original.

36. Grogan, "Isaiah," *EBC,* comment on Isa. 44:1–5. Claus Westermann argues similarly that v. 5 is about the addition of "proselytes" to Israel's number (*Isaiah 40–66: A Commentary,* trans. D. M. G. Stalker [Philadelphia: Westminster, 1969], 136).

Ezekiel follows up his dramatic presentation of the battle between the mysterious Gog of Magog and the Lord with the divine promise that the fortunes of Jacob will be restored (Ezekiel 38–39, esp. 39:25).[37] Again, God is motivated by his holy name and its vindication (39:25 and 27). Israel will be brought back to the land. Their shame and treachery will be in the past tense (vv. 26–27). These events have epistemic consequences. Thus they will know that God is truly "the LORD their God" (v. 28). No longer will God's face be hidden from his people in judgment.[38] Instead his Spirit (*rûchî*, "my Spirit") will be poured out upon the house of Israel (v. 29).[39] The Spirit's donation is integral to God's becoming intimate with his people again. Significantly the last great section in Ezekiel follows, with the vision of the new temple (Ezekiel 40–48). God will be at home with Israel once more: "And the name of the city from that time on shall be, 'The LORD Is There'" (Ezek. 48:35b). As in Isaiah, after judgment has come grace.

The Joel prophecy concerning the outpouring of the Spirit is the most famous of them all (Joel 2:28–32), for this is the text that Peter appeals to on that first Christian day of Pentecost (Acts 2:17–21). Once more the promise of the Spirit is predicated upon a preceding judgment. The awesome day of the Lord is symbolized by an unprecedented plague of devastating locusts (Joel 1:2–2:11). God's people are invited to return to their gracious and merciful God (2:12–13). The Lord will have pity upon his disobedient people (v. 18). He will restore their fortunes: "the years that the swarming locust has eaten" (v. 25a). Again, these events have epistemic outcomes for Israel. They will know that the Lord alone is God and is their God (v. 27). Against that background stands the promise of the outpouring of God's Spirit (*rûchî*, "my Spirit"). What is added to the picture of the outpouring, which we saw delineated in Isaiah and Ezekiel, is the idea that this outpouring will be "on all flesh": that is to say, on that which is "frail, finite, and perishable" (v. 28).[40] No one appears to be exempt: sons and daughters, old men and young men, male and female servants (vv. 28–29).[41] What

---

37. Alexander, "Ezekiel," ibid., comments, "Ezekiel prophesied against Gog of the land of Magog, the chief prince of Meshech and Tubal (v. 2). The exact identity of each proper name has occupied many expositors and spawned many and varied interpretations of this text" (comment on Ezek. 38:1–3). Dumbrell is on safe ground to suggest that Gog is "the embodiment of Israel's foes" (*Search for Order*, 105).

38. God's face (*pānîm*) turned toward his people means blessing (Num. 6:22–26), but his face turned away is judgment (Isa. 59:1–2).

39. Over and over again in Ezekiel to this point, reference has been made to God pouring out his wrath, which makes the change to the Spirit in Ezekiel 39:29 all the more striking (cf. Ezek. 7:8; 14:19; 20:8, 13, 21; 21:31; 22:31; 30:15 with 39:29).

40. Welker, *God the Spirit*, 150.

41. Jürgen Moltmann goes well beyond the evidence to suggest that Joel envisages that the outpouring of the Spirit ". . . leads to the rebirth of all life, and to the rebirth too of the community of all living on earth" (*Spirit of Life*, 57). He is on much firmer ground when he argues that, "In the final presence of God's Spirit, the whole people will become *a prophetic people*" (ibid., emphasis original). Leslie C. Allen is more convincing than Moltmann with regard to the

previously had been the activities and experiences of a few in Israel now are "democratized": prophesying, dreams, and visions.[42] As for the "wonders in the heavens and on the earth" that accompany this outpouring, as delineated in verses 30–31, Richard D. Patterson comments, "Accompanying the outpouring of the Holy Spirit in those days and as visible signs of his supernatural and overseeing intervention in the history of mankind, God will cause extraordinary phenomena to be seen in nature. Thus the totality of man's experience will be affected."[43]

In sum, if God is going to live with his people, then they will need new life, intimacy with him restored, and what was the privilege of only some in Israel needs to be extended to all. The Spirit's outpouring is a necessary condition for any of this to take place.

THE SPIRIT AND A NEW CREATION

Thus far we have considered the relationship of the Spirit/Spirit of God/Spirit of the Lord/my Spirit to the provision of a Messiah/Servant/Proclaimer to achieve God's future for Israel and the world (e.g., Isaiah 11, 42, and 61), the rebirth of God's people (e.g., Ezekiel 36–37), and the making of Israel into a prophetic people (e.g., Joel 2). But God has a future for creation per se too. The earth itself will benefit from the eschatological largesse of her Creator. Once more Isaiah is the key.

Against the backdrop of a devastated Israel in Isaiah 32:9–14, God will bring renewal. The forsaken palace, the deserted city, the playground of wild donkeys and flocks will be transformed (Isa. 32:14–15). And the Spirit is the instrument of this renewal, "poured upon us [Israel] from on high" (v. 15a).[44] The Spirit brings "justice" and "righteousness" (v. 16). The effects of such justice and righteousness will be "peace," "quietness," and "trust forever" (v. 17). The wilderness will become "a home, giving protection and security."[45] The Lord declares, "My people will abide in a peaceful habitation, in secure dwellings, and in quiet resting places" (v. 18).

interpretation of "all flesh" when he maintains that, "'all flesh', here means 'everyone in Israel'" and that the promise of Joel 2:28–32 "takes up Moses' wish in Nu 11:29" ("Joel," *NBCRev,* comment on Joel 2:28–29).

42. Douglas Stuart, *Hosea–Jonah,* WBC, in his introduction to Joel uses "The Democratization of the Spirit" as a heading. See also Dumbrell, *Search for Order,* 109; and Scobie, *Ways of Our God,* 276: ". . . the emphasis is on the future reception of the Spirit by *all* God's people (v. 32a), without distinction of sex (sons/daughters, male/female slaves), age (old men/young men), or social status (male/female slaves, i.e., in addition to free persons)" (emphasis original).

43. Richard D. Patterson, "Joel," *EBC,* comment on Joel 2:30–31.

44. As Willem VanGemeren states, "Isaiah spoke of the work of renewal or restoration of the world as that of the Spirit (Isa. 32:15-20)" (*The Progress of Redemption: The Story of Salvation from Creation to the New Jerusalem* [Grand Rapids, Mich.: Baker, 2000], 409.

45. Welker, *God the Spirit,* 143, argues that the whole world is this home, but this is quite an extrapolation from the text itself.

Indeed, with regard to the ensuing economic prosperity, Grogan comments on v. 20, "The amount of produce given by the soil will be so great that the farmer can actually allow his working animals to browse in the fields, rather than feeding them with prepared foodstuff in their stalls."[46]

The other important passage is Isaiah 44:1–5. Once again the image is that of the poured out Spirit, and the Hebrew parallelism is striking: "For I [the Lord] will pour water on the thirsty land, and streams on the dry ground; I will pour out my Spirit [*rûchî*] upon your offspring, and my blessings on your descendants" (Isa. 44:3). The symbol used here of the Spirit is that of life-giving water that refreshes the parched earth. (The Spirit likened to flowing water is a symbol that will figure strongly in John's Gospel, as we shall see in a later discussion.) Michael Welker suggests that Isaiah 32:15–18 and 44:1–5, when viewed together, show how the heavenly connects with the earthly. In the former text the earth is renewed, and in the latter, the people of God, and through them the wider world.[47] God's concerns are not limited to the human domain. Nothing less than the wider creation provides his palette. And the poured out Spirit is the brush that returns the color to the canvas.

IMPLICATIONS FOR BELIEF AND PRACTICE

There are two practical implications that we shall draw from systematic reflection upon the hope of Israel in its OT unveiling.

Hoping in God

Lesslie Newbigin argues that there is a great divide in world religions. On one side there are religions that typically unify human experience using the image of the wheel (e.g., Hinduism).[48] On the other side are those religions that typically unify human experience using the image of the road (e.g., Christianity). In the former case, what is highlighted is a "cycle of birth, growth, decay and death," which endlessly recurs.[49] Plants, animals, humans, and even institutions are caught up in the cycle. History is "meaningless movement."[50] In the latter, the "perfect goal is not timeless reality hidden now behind the multiplicity and change we experience; it is

---

46. Grogan, "Isaiah," *EBC*, comment on Isa. 32:20. George Montague describes this text (Isa. 32:15–20) as "the high point in Isaiah's theology of the spirit" (*The Holy Spirit: Growth of a Biblical Tradition: A Commentary on the Principal Texts of the Old and New Testaments* [New York and Toronto: Paulist, 1976], 40).

47. Michael Welker, *God the Spirit*, 142–144.

48. Lesslie Newbigin, *The Finality of Christ* (Richmond, Va.: John Knox, 1969), 65. Newbigin develops the analysis of Nicol MacNichol.

49. Ibid., 66.

50. Ibid.

yet to be achieved; it lies at the end of the road."[51] Christians are roadies not wheelies. God has a project and he will achieve it, and history is the arena for that achievement. The OT reveals part of the road, some of the journey, and some of what is ahead. The best is yet to be, and so there is hope. Likewise there is no room in subsequent Christianity for a docetic pneumatology that removes the work of the Spirit—past, present, and future—from the realm of history.[52] The OT witness won't allow it, neither will the New as we shall see. So biblical hope is not escapist.

Living in Between

At first sight the differences between Abraham's life before God and our own in the twenty-first century seem so enormous as to make any identification with "father Abraham" highly questionable. Likewise with ancient Israel, King David seems a remote figure to us at a number of levels. In the United States, for example, there are presidents not kings. But at another level the modern Christian can identify with both an Abraham and a David, that is to say, with both wandering Abraham and settled-in-the-land David. For like Abraham and like David we live in between the divine promise and its ultimate fulfillment. The basis of salvation is the same whether in view is Abraham, David, or the contemporary Christian: the cross of Christ. The requirement is the same: faith. The object is the same: God clothed in his promises. But the content differs as the eschatological horizon, in the light of which the believer lives, becomes richer and more accented in content.[53] Because like Abraham and David we live within a promise-and-fulfillment theological framework, the great heroes of the past become our own, as Hebrews 11 makes plain. Indeed Abraham becomes, in NT terms, the paradigmatic believer (see Romans 4; Hebrews 11; James 2). With specific regard to the Holy Spirit, Israel lived between promise and fulfillment (Isaiah 11; 32; 42; 44; Ezekiel 36–37; 39; Joel 2). As we shall see in the next part of this study, so too does the NT believer, who has the down payment of the Spirit and the firstfruits of the Spirit. Yet there is so much more to come. "The best is yet to be," as the poet Robert Browning suggested. It is an interesting question, though, whether Abraham, or David for that matter, were not only believers—that they clearly were—but were

51. Ibid.

52. I owe the idea of docetic pneumatology to Welker, *God the Spirit*, 179, fn 87. The idea is a suggestive one. Just as in Christology, docetic ideas—from *dokein*, "to seem"—remove Christ from real flesh and turn him into some ethereal spirit merely appearing in the flesh. So too any doctrine of the Spirit that removes the Spirit from real action in time and space with flesh-and-blood humanity is to be rejected in the light of the biblical testimony.

53. See Charles Ryrie, *Dispensationalism* (Chicago: Moody, 1995), 115. One does not need to subscribe to dispensationalist theology to appreciate the theological wisdom of Ryrie on this point.

also regenerated by the Spirit. That question we now turn to and explore by way of an excursus.

EXCURSUS: WERE OT BELIEVERS REGENERATE?

OT believers were saved, as far as the NT writers are concerned. Paul tells us that Abraham was justified by faith (Rom. 4:1–12). Hebrews can appeal to a parade of OT figures starting with Abel and accenting supremely Abraham to illustrate the life of faith (Hebrews 11). Christian readers—probably ethnically Jewish—were to draw instruction from such exemplars (Heb. 12:1–2). Patently, then, there are continuities between Old and New Testament revelations. But were such OT believers regenerated by the Holy Spirit? On this question theologians disagree.[54]

Some maintain that saving belief is always a product of the Holy Spirit's regenerative work. Reformed theologian John Murray states, ". . . what is patent in the New is latent in the Old. The need is one, the covenant of grace and the way of salvation is one, the faith that saves is one."[55] According to this view the OT metaphor for new birth is the circumcision of the heart. The *locus classicus* of this view is the book of Deuteronomy (Deut. 10:16 and 30:6).[56] As in other places in the OT—for example, the Prophets—this book of the Torah knows that obedience is not a matter of mere outward conformity to the commandments of God. A profound inner transforming work is required. The Spirit, unmentioned but assumed, is the agent of this work. John Goldingay goes so far as to argue,

> . . . that the relationship between OT believers and God was essentially like that of NT believers rather than essentially unlike it. The argument of passages such as Romans 4 or Hebrews 11 depends on that assumption. It is, of course, the one which underlies much of the use of OT characters in Christian preaching.[57]

54. I am very much indebted to the excellent overview article by James M. Hamilton, Jr., "Old Covenant Believers and the Indwelling Spirit: A Survey of the Spectrum of Opinion," *TrinJ* 24NS (2003): 37–54. However, I have reduced the number of options in his taxonomy.

55. John Murray, "Regeneration," in *Collected Writings of John Murray: Volume Two, Select Lectures in Systematic Theology* (Edinburgh: Banner of Truth, 1977), 173. John Calvin, the fountainhead of the Reformed tradition, understood regeneration much more broadly than most Reformed theologians would today. For him regeneration was not simply the initial impartation of new life but the whole process of restoration of the believer to the righteousness of God from which the race fell in Adam ("Institutes of the Christian Religion," *CJCC*, III.3.9).

56. Ibid. See also VanGemeren, *Progress of Redemption*, 167. In his index, the reference to "Regeneration" directs the reader, "*See also* Circumcision of the heart" (ibid., 543, emphasis original).

57. John Goldingay, "Was the Holy Spirit Active in Old Testament Times? What Was New about the Christian Experience of God?" *Ex Auditu* 12 (1996): 19. See also Arthur H. Lewis, "The New Birth under the Old Covenant" (*The Evangelical Quarterly* 56 no. 1 [January 1984]:

Some in this tradition go as far as maintaining that OT saints were not only regenerated by the Spirit, they were also indwelt by the Spirit (e.g., Thomas Goodwin, John Owen, B. B. Warfield, and Sinclair Ferguson).[58]

Other theologians suggest that the Spirit was certainly the key to Abraham's faith but that it is going beyond the evidence to say that he was regenerated by the Spirit. Regeneration according to this view is an NT phenomenon (e.g., Lewis Sperry Chafer, D. A. Carson, and Michael Green).[59] René Pache even more strongly maintains that there was no regenerative work of the Spirit in the lives of believers prior to Pentecost.[60] To read it back into the OT is to ignore the flow of redemptive history, so the argument runs. What is clear is that NT believers are indwelt permanently by the Spirit. However, there is no evidence that OT believers were similarly indwelt by the Spirit in any permanent way. This is a new covenant blessing that Jesus promised his disciples in his Upper Room Discourse as found in the Fourth Gospel.

The diversity of opinion among scholars with a common high view of biblical authority suggests that there is a certain level of underdetermination of theory as far as the biblical evidence is concerned.[61] That raises the question of the dogmatic rank of the primary question about the regeneration of the OT believers.

My own view is that OT believers were regenerated by the Spirit, even though, as Graeme Goldsworthy points out, ". . . there is no word for regeneration in the OT."[62] Jesus expected Nicodemus as a teacher of Israel to understand the teaching about the new birth and the Spirit's role in it (John 3:10). His OT should have been sufficient. True, the exact expression "born again" (e.g., 1 Pet. 1:3, 23, *anagennaō*), "born from above" (e.g., John 3:3, 7, *anōthen*), or "regeneration" (e.g., Titus 3:5; Matt. 19:28, *palingenesia*) may not have appeared in the Hebrew Scriptures or the Septuagint. But, as Gottlob Frege has taught us, word and concept need to be distinguished.[63]

35–44). Lewis offers five arguments for continuity between Old and New Testament saints with regard to the experience of regeneration.

58. Hamilton, "Old Covenant Believers," 39 and 54.

59. Ibid., 49–50 and 54. Charismatic theologian J. Rodman Williams also appears to subscribe to this view: "Thus, through the Holy Spirit there is spiritual rebirth. The Old Testament looked forward to this" (*Renewal Theology: Systematic Theology from a Charismatic Perspective: Three Volumes in One* [Grand Rapids, Mich.: Zondervan, 1996], 2:35). According to Lewis, dispensational theologians are particularly attracted to this view ("New Birth under the Old Covenant," 36).

60. René Pache, *The Person and Work of the Holy Spirit* (Chicago: Moody, 1954), 29ff.

61. In philosophy a theory is "underdetermined" if the evidence is compatible (logically consistent) not only with it but also with at least one other theory. See "Underdetermination (of theory)," in Simon Blackburn, *Oxford Dictionary of Philosophy* (Oxford and New York: Oxford University Press, 1996), 385.

62. Graeme Goldsworthy, "Regeneration," *NDBT,* 721. See also J. Guhrt, "Birth, παλιγγενεσία," in *NIDNTT.*

63. As Gottlob Frege (1848–1925) has taught us, "sense" and "referent" must be distinguished. "Evening Star" and "Morning Star" have the same referent (Venus) but different meanings (the star that appears in the evening and the star that appears in the morning, respec-

With the OT language of "circumcised hearts," "hearts of flesh" replacing "hearts of stone," and "a new spirit," we are moving in the same conceptual field as the NT ideas of regeneration and new birth.[64] However, our Lord does make it plain that the indwelling of the Spirit was contingent upon his own return to the Father (John 16:7).[65] This is a permanent blessing for all God's new covenant people, not a temporary filling or a temporary coming of the Spirit upon a few as in the case of OT believers. According to this view, OT saints were regenerated but not indwelt by the Spirit.[66] So there are elements of continuity between the Testaments (regeneration) and elements of discontinuity (indwelling). Others who hold this position include Millard Erickson, Willem VanGemeren, and J. I. Packer.[67] This is a theological opinion (*theologoumenon*) that, I believe, is consistent with the scriptural testimony although not demanded by it. The debate continues.

---

tively). See Thomas Ricketts, "Frege," in Robert Audi, gen. ed., *The Cambridge Dictionary of Philosophy,* 2nd ed. (Cambridge: Cambridge University Press, 1999), 330.

64. Guhrt comments that these OT expressions give "rise to the suggestion that the NT idea of rebirth or regeneration has its roots in the OT prophecy of restoration and renewal in the messianic age" (Guhrt, ibid.).

65. Richard B. Gaffin Jr. takes a different view. He maintains that OT believers like David were both regenerated by and indwelt by the Holy Spirit. Indeed he argues that it is "wrong" to think otherwise. However, his own argument is somewhat forced, and the text he cites (Ps. 51:11) does not even mention the notion of indwelling and is compatible both with the idea of David being indwelt by the Spirit and as someone upon whom the Spirit has come (*Perspectives on Pentecost: New Testament Teaching on the Gifts of the Holy Spirit* [Phillipsburg, N.J.: Presbyterian & Reformed, 1980], 36–37). The reference to the Spirit of Christ (*pneuma christou*) at work in the OT prophets in 1 Peter 1:11 (*en autois*) does not settle the question of an OT indwelling of the Spirit since such internal work of the Spirit may have been temporary rather than a permanent gift.

66. As John Stott points out, "We sing the Psalms in Christian worship because we recognize in them the language of the regenerate" (*Baptism and Fulness: The Work of the Holy Spirit Today,* 2nd ed. [London: Inter-Varsity, 1975], 27, fn 5).

67. Hamilton, "Old Covenant Believers," 46. Abraham Kuyper also holds this view (*The Work of the Holy Spirit,* trans. Henri De Vries [Grand Rapids, Mich.: Eerdmans, 1975], 121). A. M Stibbs can be added to this list. See A. M. Stibbs and J. I. Packer, *The Spirit within You: The Church's Neglected Possession* (London: Hodder & Stoughton, 1967), 27.

III

THE MINISTRY OF THE SPIRIT—
NEW TESTAMENT PERSPECTIVES

CHAPTER

SEVEN

THE SPIRIT AND THE MESSIAH:
BEARER OF THE SPIRIT

A classic way of articulating the life and ministry of Christ is in terms of the so-called Christological mysteries.[1] According to this approach the key events in Jesus' life and work constitute the framework for understanding his person and work: the conception, the baptism, the temptations, the transfiguration, the passion, the resurrection, and the ascension. (We shall also include the mighty works of Jesus in the list, as the corollary of his messianic commission at the baptism by John and his surmounting of temptation as the true Israel of God and last Adam.) The great strength of this approach is that it preserves the narrative thrust of the scriptural presentation, although I prefer to describe these events as the key Christological moments as far as the presentation in the canonical Gospels is concerned.[2] The person of Jesus is no mere set of ideas. His work is no mere idealization of some religious notions.[3] Importantly—and for reasons we

---

1. As does, for example, John Macquarrie, *Principles of Theology,* 2nd ed. (London: SCM, 1977), 279–280.

2. Macquarrie describes these Christological events "as critical moments in the revelation given in Christ" (ibid., 280). His own discussion is somewhat vitiated by his distinction between "the historical Jesus" and "the Christ of faith," and by his belief that there are legendary and mythic elements in some of the biblical stories (ibid., 273–290). For example he says that, "The *ascension* is a purely mythical event and reflects a cosmology that has long since been abandoned" (ibid., 290, emphasis original).

3. It is interesting to read the account of Paul Williams's recent coming to Christian faith. This prominent British scholar of Buddhism, and former Buddhist, maintains that some Christian theologians are embarrassed by the miraculous in the NT accounts of Jesus (John Macquarrie might serve as an example) in a way that a number of Christian philosophers are not. In his view the kinds of stories we shall be considering in the pneumatological moments are not to be reduced to mere allegories. Instead we are dealing with fact (*The Unexpected Way: On Converting from Buddhism to Catholicism* [Edinburgh and New York: T. & T. Clark, 2002],

shall suggest—in all but two of these nodal points in the life and ministry of Christ, the Spirit comes into view as a key player in the story. So there seems to be a Spirit parallel to the Christological moments, namely, the pneumatological ones, which we shall soon explore—albeit as a heuristic strategy, to see what may be discovered. In so doing we shall also be taking up one of the strands in the hope of Israel: the expectation of the servant, king, and proclaimer of OT promise. It is important to note from the outset that nowhere in the OT is there a character like Jesus in whose life and work the Spirit is so prominent.

So very often these days the Spirit is subordinated to Jesus in our thinking. But pre-Pentecost the incarnate Son is very much under the empowerment of the Spirit, as we shall see. This fact has not often been noted by theologians, as Clark H. Pinnock correctly points out.[4] Some have noted it, however. For example, that empowerment is well described by J. Rodman Williams: "The ministry of Jesus in word and deed was carried forward in the power of the Holy Spirit. In everything He did, Jesus knew in Himself a mighty force working that was beyond Himself. . . . Jesus lived and moved in the presence and power of the Holy Spirit."[5] Abraham Kuyper makes the point even more strongly with regard to Jesus' consecration to the office of mediator:

> This ought to be carefully noticed, especially since the Church has never sufficiently confessed the influence of the Holy Spirit exerted on the work of Christ. The general impression is that the work of the Holy Spirit begins when the work of the mediator on earth is finished, as tho [sic] until that time the Holy Spirit celebrated His divine day of rest. Yet the Scripture teaches us again and again that Christ performed His mediatorial work controlled and impelled by the Holy Spirit.[6]

Finely said.

In this chapter we shall examine the "pneumatological moments," then draw out some important implications that may be summed up in the question, Is the Spirit-directed humanity of Christ the paradigm for us all?

114–117). Williams is Professor of Indian and Tibetan Philosophy, and Head of the Department of Theology and Religious Studies at the University of Bristol in England.

4. Clark H. Pinnock, "The Role of the Spirit in Redemption," *AsTJ* 52 no. 1 (Spring 1997): 55.

5. J. Rodman Williams, *Renewal Theology: Systematic Theology from a Charismatic Perspective: Three Volumes in One* (Grand Rapids, Mich.: Zondervan, 1996), 2:173. One does not have to subscribe to his charismatic theology to appreciate his fine point. See also his "Theological Comment" (ibid., 206–207).

6. Abraham Kuyper, *The Work of the Holy Spirit*, trans. Henri De Vries (Grand Rapids, Mich.: Eerdmans, 1975), 97.

THE SPIRIT AND THE INCARNATION

The Spirit is vitally involved in the Word becoming flesh in two ways. First, the Spirit prepares the way prophetically as the voice of prophecy is heard from the lips of Zechariah, Elizabeth, and Simeon explicitly, and implicitly from Mary and Anna. Second, the conception of the Messiah is Spirit-crafted, with possible echoes of the primordial creation narrative and probable ones of the glory that descended on the tabernacle. We shall examine each aspect in turn.

Luke provides the key references to the Spirit-inspired, prophetic preparation for the coming of the Messiah. To that end the Spirit of prophecy is restored to Israel.[7] An angel informs Zechariah that his wife, Elizabeth, will bear a child named John (Luke 1:13). This son will be Elijah-like in spirit and indeed will be filled (*plēsthēsetai,* future passive) with the Holy Spirit from his birth (vv. 14–17). The ministry of this son is to be that of a prophetic forerunner who prepares the way by making a people ready for the Messiah's coming (v. 17). Likewise Elizabeth, "filled with the Holy Spirit" (*eplēsthē,* aorist passive), greets the expectant Mary with these powerful identifying words: "And why is this granted to me that the mother of my Lord should come to me?" (vv. 41, 43). Following the birth and naming of John the Baptist, his father, Zechariah, filled (*eplēsthē,* aorist passive) with the Holy Spirit, prophesied (*eprophēteusen,* aorist) that this child ". . . will go before the Lord to prepare his ways" (vv. 67, 76). After Jesus' birth, he was presented to the Lord in the temple as the Law required. Simeon, a Jerusalemite, was present. He is described as "righteous and devout, waiting for the consolation of Israel" (Luke 2:25). Significantly, we are informed that "the Holy Spirit was upon him" (2:25), and furthermore that the Holy Spirit had revealed to him that he would not die before seeing the Lord's Christ (v. 26).[8] Moreover he comes into the temple "in the Spirit" (v. 27). He then speaks of the child as "a light for revelation to the Gentiles, and for the glory . . . [of] Israel" (v. 32). In addition he tells Mary that within Israel, the child will be opposed, though not universally (v. 34).

Clearly in the Lukan presentation what is unfolding is preparation for a key event in salvation-history. Thus by the end of the Lukan infancy narratives a theological framework has been established for understanding Jesus' messiahship. This child will prove to be the fulfillment of the promises to Abraham, a Davidic Savior, the restorer of Israel "to her covenantal vocation," and a personage whose ministry will impact the world beyond

---

7. See Max Turner, "Holy Spirit," *DJG,* 2.1.1. Turner defines "the Spirit of prophecy" as "the Spirit acting as the organ of communication between God and a person" (ibid., 1.1).

8. There are six references to the phrase "Holy Spirit" in the infancy narratives of Luke 1–2, whereas there are only three such phrases in the entire OT (cf. Ps. 51:11; Isa. 63:10, 11; and Luke 1:15, 35, 41, 67; 2:25, 26).

Israel.[9] But none of this will happen without conflict. And the nexus between Word and Spirit is also very much on display. What is happening on the plane of history has not been left uninterpreted.

There is a common view that with the cluster of prophetic activity surrounding the coming of Jesus—as outlined above—long generations of Spirit silence had been broken. Michael Green typifies this view when he contends, ". . . the age-long silence is ended. The heavens are no longer brazen and unyielding. The rabbis believed that when the Holy Spirit was withdrawn from Israel at the end of the prophetic era, God left them with a substitute, the *bath qol,* which means literally 'daughter of the voice' or 'echo.'"[10] In similar fashion, William J. Dumbrell states in relation to the Lukan infancy narratives, "The activity of the Spirit (1:41, 67; 2:25–27), the awakening of prophecy, which according to *tradition* had ceased at the close of the OT period until its revival in the messianic age, and the outbursts of joy combine to give the narratives an eschatological flavor."[11] The key question to ask is, Whose tradition exactly?

More recently, Max Turner has offered a much more nuanced and different view:

> It is often held that Judaism believed in the complete withdrawal of the Spirit following the last canonical prophets (cf. *Tosefta Soṭah* 13.3-4), a cessation that would last until the eschaton. This almost certainly rests on misunderstanding. . . . It would be nearer the truth to say that many Jews thought that experience of the Spirit of prophecy was relatively rare in their own day (except, perhaps, in the sense of pious wisdom), and comparatively lacking in quality and power.[12]

The problem is that first-century Judaism was such a variegated phenomenon. Rabbinic Judaism, which Green refers to, was only one of the kinds of Judaism present at the time.[13]

With regard to the Spirit and the incarnation per se, Sinclair Ferguson suggests, "Thus, as the inaugurator of the new humanity, the 'second man'

9. William J. Dumbrell, *The Search for Order: Biblical Eschatology in Focus* (Eugene, Ore.: Wipf & Stock, 2001), 208–210. On the restoration of Israel as the grand theme of Jesus' mission see James M. Scott, "Jesus' Vision for the Restoration of Israel as the Basis of a Biblical Theology of the New Testament," in Scott Hafemann, ed., *Biblical Theology: Retrospect and Prospect* (Downers Grove, Ill.: InterVarsity Press, 2002), 129–143.

10. Michael Green, *I Believe in the Holy Spirit* (London, Sydney, and Auckland: Hodder & Stoughton, 1992), 36.

11. Dumbrell, *Search for Order,* 210, emphasis mine.

12. Max Turner, *The Holy Spirit and Spiritual Gifts: Then and Now,* rev. ed. (Carlisle, England: Paternoster, 1999), 14. See also D. A. Carson, *Showing the Spirit: A Theological Exposition of 1 Corinthians 12–14* (Grand Rapids, Mich.: Baker, 2003), 154, fn 27.

13. As per Hebrew scholar Samuel Sandmel's happy term, we need to reckon with the "Judaisms" of the first century; see the reference to Sandmel's widely quoted term (to give only one example) in Bruce Chilton's review of Michael J. Gorman's book on Paul in *Catholic Biblical Quarterly* 66 no. 3 (July 2004): 474.

is brought into the world by the Spirit's agency. His virgin conception is therefore *essential* to our salvation and was, fittingly, brought to pass by the Spirit who is the executive of that salvation."[14] That the Spirit of God plays a crucial role in the coming into the world of the Messiah is beyond doubt, insofar as the Matthean and Lukan narratives are concerned.[15] But the question of the essential need for a virginal conception will raise some important theological questions, which we will consider shortly.

Both Matthew and Luke place the virginal conception of Jesus within an eschatological, promise-fulfillment framework.[16] As Welker suggests, "Just as every human being is born not as a merely biologically definable entity, but as the embodiment of a history and of a sphere of expectations, so this child too, is born as the embodiment of the messianic history and the messianic sphere of hopes and expectations."[17] The opening of Matthew's Gospel sets the scene: "The book of the genealogy of Jesus Christ, son of David, the son of Abraham" (Matt. 1:1). The climax of the carefully structured genealogy, which follows, leads "to the Christ" (v. 17). Next, the reader learns that this Christ of promise is to be born of Mary (*ex hēs*, out of whom) in a way that fulfills the ancient Isaianic promise of a deliverer child to be born to a virgin as a sign of the rescue of God's people (cf. Isa. 7:14 and Matt. 1:16, 23).[18] The child will be called "Immanuel," meaning

14. Sinclair Ferguson, *The Holy Spirit* (Leicester, England: Inter-Varsity, 1996), 42, emphasis mine.

15. A work of this kind is not the place to discuss, except in passing, critical questions that have been raised concerning the miraculous in Scripture. This is neither a work of Old or New Testament commentary and theology nor of Christian apology. The infancy narratives of Matthew and Luke provide particularly fertile fields for scholarly debate. For example, Raymond E. Brown accepts the fact of the virginity of Mary and the incarnation, but Wolfhart Pannenberg sees the story of the "virgin birth" as "legend" (cf. Raymond E. Brown, *The Birth of the Messiah: A Commentary on the Infancy Narratives in the Gospels of Matthew and Luke* [Garden City, N.J.: Doubleday, 1993], 697–712; and Wolfhart Pannenberg, *Jesus—God and Man,* trans. Lewis L. Wilkins and Duane A. Priebe [London: SCM, 1976], 141–15). But as a systematic theologian my task is to address, in the main, the content of the final form of the biblical text as the churches' canon. See also Frans Josef van Beeck, "Born of the Virgin Mary: Toward a *Sprachregelung* on a Delicate Point of Doctrine," *Pacifica* 14 (June 2001): 121–143; and James P. Sweeney, "Modern and Ancient Controversies over the Virgin Birth of Jesus," *Bibliotheca Sacra* 160 (April–June 2003): 142–158.

16. The traditional expression "virgin birth" is a theological misnomer. The miracle lies in the supernatural conception of Jesus, not in some physiological miracle that left Mary's virginity intact (*virgo intacta*). For example, one early church idea was that Mary's hymen was never ruptured and so consequently she remains the perpetual virgin. See the discussion of this idea and others in J. N. D. Kelly, *Early Christian Doctrines,* 5th rev. ed. (London: Adam & Charles Black, 1977), 490–499.

17. Michael Welker, *God the Spirit,* trans. John F. Hoffmeyer (Minneapolis: Fortress, 1994), 188.

18. D. A. Carson, having noted that the literature on the subject is "legion," comments on the difficult question of Matthew's use of the OT, in particular Isaiah 7:14 in Matthew 1:23: "In short [having canvassed various interpretations] there is a presumption in favor of rendering *almah* by 'young virgin' or the like in Isa. 7:14. Nevertheless other evidence must be given

"God with us" (Matt. 1:23). The Holy Spirit is said to have the causal role in the conception of this child: ". . . she was found to be with child from [*ek* has causal force here] the Holy Spirit" (v. 18), and the conception itself is "from [again, *ek* has causal force here] the Holy Spirit" (v. 20).[19]

In the Luke account, Mary is informed by the angel Gabriel that: "The Holy Spirit will come upon you, and the power of the Most High will overshadow you; therefore the child to be born will be called holy—the Son of God" (Luke 1:35).[20] The angel's address points both to the consequences of the Holy Spirit's role in the conception of Jesus (his holiness) and to his title, "Son of God." "Holy" accents the fact that this child is to be set apart for God's purpose. The presentation of Jesus to the Lord in the temple in the very next chapter reinforces this interpretation: "Every male who first opens the womb shall be called holy to the Lord" (Luke 2:23). "Son of God" has most probably, at the very least, Davidic king overtones (cf. 2 Sam. 7:11–19; Ps. 2:7; Ps. 89:26–29; 4QFlor 1.11) and possibly divine ones, given that he is also the "Son of the Most High" (Luke 1:32).[21] Some have suggested that the language of the angel's address alludes to the creation story with its description of the hovering of the Spirit over the waters (Gen. 1:2) and/or to the glory that filled the ancient tabernacle, which indicated the presence of God (Ex. 40:35, LXX).[22] The former suggestion is attractively possible, but the latter is probable given the vocabulary in the

---

a hearing. The LXX renders the word by *parthenos* which almost always means 'virgin.' Yet even with this word there are exceptions . . ." ("Matthew," *EBC*, comment on Matt. 1:23). Ben Witherington III argues that the term *almah* probably implies virginity ("Birth of Jesus," *DJG*). In short, Matthew's rendering of Isaiah 7:14 is defensible.

19. Gerald F. Hawthorne, *The Presence and the Power: The Significance of the Spirit in the Life and Ministry of Jesus* (Dallas, London, Vancouver, and Melbourne: Word, 1991), 70. Hawthorne also points out that in both the Matthean and Lukan infancy narratives the translation of the anarthrous *pneumatos hagiou* as "the Holy Spirit" is entirely warranted in context (ibid., 66).

20. Mary's response is highly instructive: "Behold, I am the servant of the Lord; let it be to me according to your word" (Luke 1:38). In Luke she is the archetypal believer who is receptive to the word of the Lord. However, she is hardly "the model charismatic" that Thomas Smail maintains (*The Giving Gift: The Holy Spirit in Person* [reprint of 2nd ed., Eugene, Ore.: Wipf & Stock, 2004], 22–29). To argue that Mary is a charismatic is anachronistic in the extreme.

21. Hawthorne, *Presence and the Power*, 74–75. Hawthorne allows both. He also speculates, although he acknowledges that the text is silent, that another consequence of the Spirit's involvement is that Jesus was filled with the Spirit from the womb on analogy with the Baptist, and that Jesus thus represents the new humanity (ibid., 89).

22. With regard to Genesis, Hawthorne, in his discussion of Luke 1:35, contends, "Just as the Spirit of God in the very beginning hovered over the primal waters and brought order out of chaos, cosmos out of waste and desolation (Gen. 1:2; Ps. 33:6), so the Holy Spirit in the fulness of time (Gal. 4:4) overshadowed the virgin Mary and brought forth a fresh order of humanity in the person of Jesus" (*Presence and the Power*, 86). The Lukan genealogy, which goes all the way back to Adam, strengthens Hawthorne's contention (Luke 3:23–38, esp. v. 38). As for the tabernacle, Walter L. Liefeld comments on Luke 1:35, "The word for 'overshadow' (*episkiazo*) carries the sense of the holy, powerful presence of God, as in the description of the cloud that 'covered' (Heb. *sakan*; NIV, 'settled upon') the tabernacle when the tent was filled

text. Mary is also informed on the occasion that her relative, Elizabeth, though barren, has conceived too (Luke 1:36). Elizabeth stands therefore in a long line of women who in the good purposes of God fall pregnant, although barren at the time or beyond childbearing age (for example, Sarah in Gen. 17:15–17; 21:1–7; the wife of Manoah in Judg. 13:3; and Hannah in 1 Sam. 1:6, 17, 19–20). The juxtaposition of the two conception stories shows—given the highlighted role of the Holy Spirit—that in Mary's case something very special indeed and qualitatively different was taking place, as the account is *sui generis* in the pages of Scripture.[23] Even so, there is no metaphysical speculation in evidence. This child is to be given "the throne of David" (Luke 1:32–33).

The frameworks of the Matthean and Lukan presentations are salvation-historical rather than speculatively metaphysical, as we have noted above. In Jesus' supernatural coming into the world, God is providing a fresh start for Israel in particular and humanity in general. The Holy Spirit is instrumental in the fashioning of the Messiah's humanity, as is Mary.[24] As Gerald F. Hawthorne notes, "He is Adam's Son and God's."[25] Importantly, there is no dissonance between the Matthean and the Lukan accounts on the one hand, and, on the other, the one-person-in-two-natures (fully divine and fully human, respectively) Christology which was to triumph much later at Chalcedon in A.D. 451. It took time and intense debate in the early church period, though, for the implications of revelation to be faithfully articulated.

As we saw, Sinclair Ferguson regards the virginal conception of Jesus as "essential to our salvation." The theological argument for this view usually appeals to the problem of the transmission of sin through the passing on of a corrupt Adamic nature through normal human intercourse and subsequent conception. Since Jesus did not have a human father, nor was he conceived through human sexual congress, then, so the argument runs, he escaped the corruption of original sin. John Murray exemplifies this view when he argues that the Holy Spirit effects a "supernatural preservation" of the sinless humanity of Christ in the incarnation, since "natural generation

---

with the glory of God (Exod 40:35; cf. Ps. 91:4)" ("Luke," *EBC*, comment on Luke 1:35). See also John Nolland, *Luke 1–9:20*, WBC, comment on Luke 1:35.

23. In the Lukan account Mary is virginal, as Luke 1:34 makes plain. But unlike the Matthean account, there is no clear reference to the Isaianic material, although Walter L. Liefeld comments on Luke 1:31 and Gabriel's address, "The wording here is virtually identical to the 'virgin' passage in Isaiah 7:14 (LXX) and to the assurance the angel of the Lord gave the fugitive Hagar (Gen. 16:11 LXX). The word 'virgin' is not, however, mentioned in the allusion to Isaiah, though Mary's question (v. 34) shows she was a virgin, a fact Luke has mentioned in v. 27" (Liefeld, ibid.).

24. Hawthorne, *Presence and the Power*, 95, endnote 89: "One should not overlook the fact that it is said of Jesus not only that he was formed *in* (*en*) Mary (Luke 1:31) as though she was merely a channel through which he came into this world, but that he was formed *from* (*ek*) her as well (Matt. 1:16)" (emphasis original).

25. Ibid., 79.

would have entailed depravity."[26] Thus he can be called "holy" (Luke 1:35). However, the Matthean and Lukan presentations move in a different orbit. The hope of Israel and hope for the Gentiles are being realized through the agency of the Spirit in the conception of Jesus. The accent is eschatological, not metaphysical. J. I. Packer displays an admirable restraint in theologizing about the virginal conception. He argues that the supernatural arriving into the world of Jesus "was entirely fitting."[27] However, he contends, ". . . we cannot affirm that a divine person could not have entered the world any other way than by virgin birth," and, ". . . we cannot affirm that God could not have produced sinless humanity apart from virgin birth."[28] Systematizing Scripture and drawing inferences can so easily lead well beyond the force of the biblical evidence.[29] Packer does not fall into that trap.

The Spirit and the Baptism

The next Christological moment, which is also a pneumatological one, is the baptism of Jesus in the River Jordan at the hands of John the Baptist. All four Gospels have an account of this event. Such is its importance. Interestingly, by way of contrast, there is precious little in the canonical Gospels about the boyhood of Jesus.[30] Hawthorne attempts valiantly to make some pneumatological sense of the Lukan descriptions of Jesus' development in strength, wisdom, and stature, as well as the story of the boy Jesus in the temple (Luke 2:39–52).[31] However, there are no Holy Spirit references in the Lukan account of Jesus as a boy. Consequently, Hawthorne has to make do with theological inferences about the Spirit's role, which may well be true. But there is not the textual evidence for us to be confident that they are true.

The prophetic ministry of John the Baptist has been ably summed up by Dumbrell: "John's prophetic voice urges the nation to go back to the beginning of its journey, back to the crossing of the Jordan, and once again to set out into the Promised Land, but this time in a new national direction

---

26. John Murray, *Collected Writings of John Murray: Volume Two, Select Lectures in Systematic Theology* (Edinburgh: Banner of Truth, 1977), esp. 135.

27. J. I. Packer, *Concise Theology: A Guide to Historic Christian Beliefs* (Australia, Singapore, and England: Anzea, Campus Crusade Asia, and Inter-Varsity, 1993), 112.

28. Ibid.

29. See again Bernard Ramm, "Biblical Interpretation," in Bernard Ramm et al., *Hermeneutics* (Grand Rapids, Mich.: Baker, 1974), 28.

30. It is significant that the gnostics sought to make up for this restraint with their own accounts of the boy Jesus. "The Infancy Gospel of Thomas," written around A.D. 150, is a case in point. See Ron Cameron, ed., *The Other Gospels: Non-Canonical Gospel Texts* (Philadelphia: Westminster, 1982), 122–130. Jesus' penchant for killing irritating playmates is not that attractive.

31. Hawthorne, *Presence and the Power,* chapter 3. As does Kuyper, *Work of the Holy Spirit,* 93–96.

into a new eschatological age."[32] With regard to the new eschatological age, the Baptist had prophesied that there was someone coming who was greater than himself (Matt. 3:11; Mark 1:7; Luke 3:16; and John 1:30). John baptized with water, but this coming one would baptize with the Holy Spirit (Mark 1:8) and fire (Matt. 3:11 and Luke 3:16).[33] Jesus is revealed to be that one. According to Mark, as Jesus comes up out of the water at his baptism, the Spirit descends on him in the form of a dove (Mark 1:10). The divine voice from heaven announces, "You are my beloved Son; with you I am well pleased" (Mark 1:11).[34] The symbolism of the opening heavens and the descent of the Spirit strongly suggests a grand revelatory moment is taking place. Heaven is embracing earth. Someone of immense significance now stands before Israel. This is the Son of messianic promise. The voice conflates Psalm 2:7 with its kingly overtones and Isaiah 42:1 with its Servant of the Lord overtones. Matthew amplifies the picture. The Baptist predicts that the coming one would baptize not only with the Holy Spirit but also with the fire of judgment (Matt. 3:11–12).[35] Moreover, in the account of the baptism itself, John's reluctance to baptize Jesus is highlighted, thus underscoring the superiority of the Son over the Baptist (vv. 13–14). Even so, as Michael Welker points out, "He [Jesus] has himself baptized. In other words, he consciously enters into solidarity with sinful human beings in need of repentance, purification, and the pouring out of the Spirit."[36] Still further we read that the Spirit not only descends on Jesus but then rests on him (*erchomenon ep' auton,* Matt. 3:16). Luke duplicates much of the Markan and Matthean pictures. The fresh detail in Luke is a reference to the "bodily form" (*sōmatikō*) of the Spirit's dove-like descent (Luke 3:22). In the Synoptics, the revelation of the Spirit's descent and the divine voice could be taken as private to Jesus, especially in Matthew, where we find that "the heavens were opened to him [*auto*]" (Matt. 3:16). But in the

32. Dumbrell, *Search for Order,* 161. Dumbrell sees great significance in the geographic hub of the Baptist's ministry. The Jordan was the place where Israel had renewed the covenant with Yahweh before entry into the land of promise.

33. There is considerable debate as to how the expression "with the Holy Spirit and fire" is to be understood, which will be discussed in the next chapter.

34. David Coffey argues that in Mark, "the bestowal of the Spirit brings about the divine Sonship of Jesus. The bestowal of the Spirit enters into the very constitution of his Sonship" ("The Holy Spirit as the Mutual Love of the Father and the Son," *TS* 51 [1990], 203). Coffey sees Mark as revising "an earlier theology in which the action of the Spirit and the 'designation' of Sonship are situated at the resurrection (Rom. 1:4)" (ibid.). Coffey believes that there are "overtones of adoptionism" in both Mark and Romans (ibid.). This is a classic example of theory outrunning the evidence. The divine voice at the baptism identifies Jesus as the Son but there is no textual evidence that the declaration makes him the Son.

35. On "the fire of purification and judgment" in this Matthean context see George T. Montague, "Holy Spirit," in Bradford E. Hinze and D. Lyle Dabney, eds., *Advents of the Spirit: An Introduction to the Current Critical Study of Pneumatology* (Milwaukee: Marquette University Press, 2001), 48.

36. Welker, *God the Spirit,* 189.

Johannine account, John the Baptist provides testimony to his seeing the descent of the Spirit and the Spirit's subsequent remaining (*emeinen*) on Jesus (John 1:32). The Spirit's involvement, therefore, is not privy to Jesus only. Furthermore, the Baptist accents the revelatory nature of the event: "that he [Jesus] might be revealed ["manifested," *phanerōthē*) to Israel" (John 1:31). The ensuing witness of the Baptist is to the sonship of Jesus: "this is the Son of God" (v. 34). And if John 3:34 is the Baptist speaking—rather than the author by way of editorial comment—then he also bears witness that Jesus has "the Spirit without measure [*ou . . ek metrou*]."[37] In Johannine terms, this gifting is displayed in Jesus' superiority as the messenger of God (*ta rēmata tou theou lalei,* "speaks the words of God") over any who had gone before.[38] Clearly, the Spirit figures prominently in all four Gospel accounts of Jesus' experience at the Jordan.

Theologically considered, what emerges in the accounts is the commissioning of Jesus as the Messiah of old covenant expectation.[39] A turning point in redemptive history has been reached, and with it the climactic moment in the history of redemptive revelation. James D. G. Dunn sums it up well: "The experience of Jesus at the Jordan is far more than something merely personal—it is a unique moment in history: the beginning of a new epoch in salvation-history—the beginning . . . of the End-time, the messianic age, the new covenant."[40] The symbol of the dove and Jesus' emerging from the waters, soon to reenter the land, possibly conjure up the old stories of Noah's flood and Israel's exodus from Egypt and its eventual crossing over the Jordan into the Promised Land.[41] God is about to do something of extraordinary significance in salvation-history. From the Matthean and Johannine accounts especially it is clear that the Spirit's role at the baptism was not episodic. The Spirit remains. Peter captures this thrust in his address to Cornelius in Acts. Speaking of the baptism, he interprets the event as God's anointing "Jesus of Nazareth with the Holy Spirit and power" (Acts

37. Turner argues convincingly (pace Thüsing, Porsch, and NRSV) that the subject is God and not Jesus. Therefore in view is not Jesus' *giving* the Spirit without measure but Jesus' *being given* the Spirit without measure (*Holy Spirit and Spiritual Gifts,* 59).

38. See Hawthorne, *Presence and the Power,* 152–154; and Max Turner, ibid., 59.

39. Ferguson argues that, "The coming of the Spirit . . . is an anointing for the three-fold messianic office prefigured by prophets, priests and kings" (*Holy Spirit,* 45). That Jesus is prophet, priest, and king may be established by a wide induction of NT evidence, but to see the baptism in those terms suggests more the needs of Reformed theology than of exegesis per se, especially when it comes to Christ's priesthood.

40. James D. G. Dunn, *Baptism in the Spirit* (London: SCM, 1977), 24.

41. For a helpful discussion of the range of possible meanings and backgrounds that "dove" has in these accounts see Hawthorne, *Presence and the Power,* 125–126. Possibilities include: a symbol for love (Patristic); Genesis 1:2 and the "hovering" image as background; Noah's flood as background; and Israel as a dove as in Hosea 7:11. Hawthorne is right to urge caution where the text is silent.

10:38a).[42] He immediately follows this claim with a summary statement of Jesus' public ministry: "He went about doing good and healing all who were oppressed by the devil, for God was with him" (v. 38b). Ferguson goes so far as to maintain that Christ's public ministry as Israel's Messiah was under the lordship of the Spirit.[43] This suggestive idea we shall return to at a later stage in the present discussion.

THE SPIRIT AND THE TEMPTATIONS

Jesus' messianic commission does not go untested. His vocation is soon challenged by the Devil. Once more the Spirit is integral to the accounts. In Mark, the language is breathlessly forceful: "The Spirit immediately drove [better, "drives," *ekballei*] him out into the wilderness" (Mark 1:12). There Jesus is tempted by Satan. He was with the wild beasts and was ministered to by angels (v. 13). The reference to "the wild animals" is suggestive of a restored harmony between the new Adam and the animal kingdom, previously estranged because of the fall.[44] The Markan account is tantalizingly brief. But as we shall see in subsequent discussion, the story has important questions to raise about our Trinitarian theology. Matthew enlarges the story considerably. We learn of Jesus' hunger and the precise nature of the temptations. The Spirit is described as the one who led (*anēchthē*) Jesus into the fray. The Devil attempts to lure Jesus into pursuing a different will than that of the Father by providing for himself in the wilderness (Matt. 4:3), by putting God to the test by leaping from the temple top (vv. 5–7), and by worshiping none other than the tempter himself to gain the world with its kingdoms (vv. 8–9).[45] But Jesus stays fully aligned with the Father's will throughout the ordeal. And in this account the angels come at the end of the ordeal to minister to Jesus (cf. Matt. 4:1 and 11). Luke adds that Jesus entered the fray, not only led (*ēgeto*) by the Spirit but full (*plērēs*) of the Spirit (Luke 4:1). He subsequently leaves the scene of his triumph "in the power of the Spirit" (v. 14). Hawthorne rightly suggests, "Thus at the outset of his ministry Jesus is depicted as overcoming the evil one who stands in opposition to the work of the kingdom ([Luke] 11:19, 20)

42. In contrast the *Catechism of the Catholic Church* states, "The Son of God was consecrated as Christ (Messiah) by the anointing of the Holy Spirit *at his Incarnation* (cf. Ps. 2:7)" (CCC, part 1, section 2, chapter 3, article 8, V, 745 [196], emphasis mine). This theological claim is hard to square with Acts 10:38.

43. Ferguson, *Holy Spirit*, 46.

44. See George T. Montague, *The Holy Spirit: Growth of a Biblical Tradition: A Commentary on the Principal Texts of the Old and New Testaments* (New York and Toronto: Paulist, 1976), 243.

45. Dumbrell points out that the wilderness, temple, and mountain were all key sites in Israel's eschatological expectations (*Search for Order*, 163).

through the all-sufficient energizing power of the Spirit of God."[46] Each of the Synoptic accounts has the Spirit playing a key role. But it is Luke who especially amplifies the story with pneumatological depth.[47]

The Matthean and Lukan accounts are highly suggestive. Given the genealogy that opens Matthew with its Abrahamic starting point (Matt. 1:1–17) and given the Jewish thrust of this Gospel, it is not too fanciful to see in Jesus' triumph in the temptations the very reverse of Israel's experience. Israel, God's son (Ex. 4:22), was tested in the wilderness also but failed.[48] If only Israel had lived the theology of Deuteronomy, which Jesus so strategically quotes in his encounter with the Devil, it would presumably not have fallen. The Lukan presentation of the temptations is also preceded by a genealogy (Luke 3:23–38). This time the genealogy goes all the way back to Adam. It is not too fanciful to see here an allusion to Adam's test in the paradise of God and subsequent failure in contrast to the testing of this son of Adam, Jesus, who in a very different setting—not a garden but a wilderness—does not fail.[49] In the power of the Spirit, Jesus is all that Israel should have been as God's son and all that Adam should have been as God's son. In other words, Jesus is the true Israel and the true Adam.

Clearly the temptations are not only a Christological moment but also a pneumatological one.

THE SPIRIT AND THE MIGHTY WORKS

Luke is especially interested in the connection between the Spirit and Jesus, as can be seen in the way that this Gospel expands the reader's understanding of Jesus' mission and his own perception of it. As we saw above in Luke's narrative, Jesus returns from the temptations to Galilee in the power of the Spirit (Luke 4:14). At the synagogue in Nazareth he reads from the prophet Isaiah. The passage from Isaiah 61 presents the eschatological proclaimer who bears the Spirit, and who thereby is anointed by the Lord to preach to the poor, to proclaim liberty to the captives, the recovery of sight to the blind, and to liberate the oppressed (cf. Luke 4:18–19 and Isa. 61:1–2). The eschatological year of Jubilee has dawned. Significantly Jesus omits the reference in the Isaianic text to "the day of vengeance of our God" (cf. Luke

46. Hawthorne, *Presence and the Power,* 139.

47. As Turner shows (*Holy Spirit and Spiritual Gifts,* 31).

48. Dumbrell, *Search for Order,* 163, a fine account. See also Donald A. Hagner, *Matthew 1–13,* WBC, comment on Matt. 4:1–11.

49. The Adam-Christ contrast is well brought out by Dunn, *Baptism in the Spirit,* 31. See also Nolland, who maintains with some caution, "In the final analysis Jesus is tempted neither as second Adam, nor as true Israel, but as Son. There is a touch of Adamic typology and considerable exodus typology, but that is because the experiences of Adam and Israel are paradigmatic cases of the testing of God's Son. Jesus' temptations are not uniquely messianic, though it is clear that his sonship is of a uniquely exalted kind" (*Luke 1–9:20,* WBC, comment on Luke 4:1–13).

4:19 and Isa. 61:2b). What Jesus says next (Luke 4:21) is startling: "Today this Scripture has been fulfilled in your hearing." This so-called Nazareth Manifesto—as though Jesus were launching a "political campaign"—is programmatic for his subsequent ministry in Luke's presentation. According to Turner, the account bristles with "both Christological" and "soteriological significance."[50] The Christological significance includes both messianic and prophetic accents.[51] Soon there is conflict, opposition, and expulsion from the town. A prophet is indeed without honor in the hometown (Luke 4:24). The narrative then unfolds with the story of an exorcism (vv. 31–37), the healing of Simon's mother-in-law (vv. 38–39), and multiple healings and exorcisms (vv. 40–41). But not only is messianic action in view, so too is his preaching. He is the proclaimer of the good news of the kingdom. Moreover, in terms of his mission the preaching has the priority. Preaching is a necessity (*euangelisasthai me dei*, v. 43). But clearly there is no either/or in Jesus' mind. Word and works belong together, but their relationship is asymmetrical in importance.

Matthew employs a different passage from Isaiah—compared to the Lukan account above—in connecting Jesus' mighty works to the Spirit. Jesus withdraws from confrontation with the Pharisees, who were intent on killing him because Jesus had healed a man on the Sabbath (Matt. 12:9–14). But many followed him, and he healed them all. The editorial comment establishes a nexus between the healings and the Servant of the Lord figure prophesied in Isaiah 42 by way of a lengthy quotation prefaced by, "This was to fulfill what was spoken by the prophet Isaiah" (Matt. 12:17). The quotation (Isa. 42:1–4) includes the pregnant phrase, "I will put my Spirit upon him."[52] D. A. Carson rightly observes that this accent on the Spirit—together with the reference to the Gentiles—becomes programmatic for the Gospel.[53] The very next incident related in Matthew's account further underscores the role of the Spirit in Jesus' public mighty works (Matt. 12:22–32). Jesus has cast out a demon. But some Pharisees who saw it put the event down to Beelzebul, the prince of demons. Jesus employs a *reductio ad absurdum*

50. Turner draws attention to the understanding of Isaiah 61:1–2 in contemporary Judaism, which saw in the passage an encapsulation of "New Exodus hopes" (11QMelch; 4Q521) (*Holy Spirit and Spiritual Gifts,* 34). In 4Q521 miracles cluster around the appearance of the Messiah (ibid., 33).

51. See Nolland, *Luke 1–9:20,* WBC, comment on Luke 4:18ff. Nolland contends initially that Luke is sending "confusing signals" in this passage, before he concedes that Luke may have both messianic and prophetic ideas in mind in his "promiscuous" use of Christological titles, although the prophetic predominates in this instance. I fail to see why having more than one accent is so confusing.

52. Welker also sees in the quotation a debt to Isaiah 11:10 (*God the Spirit,* 192). On the complex nature of the quotation's relation to the Masoretic Text and LXX, see the long and helpful endnote in Hawthorne, *Presence and the Power,* 173, endnote 1.

53. Carson, "Matthew," *EBC,* comment on Matt. 12:15–21. See also the discussion in Donald A. Hagner, *Matthew 1–13,* WBC, comment on Matt. 12:18ff.

argument to demolish their contention.[54] If Satan is at war with Satan, then what future for his kingdom? Then significantly he adds, "But if it is by the Spirit of God [*en pneumati theou*] that I [emphatic, *egō*] cast out demons, then the kingdom of God has come upon you" (Matt. 12:28; cf. Luke 11:20 and the reference to the finger of God). He warns them about blaspheming against the Holy Spirit. Blasphemy against the Son of Man is forgivable, but not blasphemy against the Holy Spirit (Matt. 12:31–32). We shall return to the questions that this passage raises about blaspheming against the Holy Spirit when we examine some implications for belief and practice later in this chapter. Suffice it to say that, as in Luke, Matthew presents Jesus' mighty works as Spirit-empowered.[55]

What is evident is that Jesus' public ministry, whether as preacher, healer, or exorcist, is not to be understood without reference to the Spirit of God. The classic creeds of Christendom exhibit an important lacuna at this point. All the great creeds of the early church period—Apostles', Nicene, and Athanasian—relate that Jesus was born of the virgin Mary and then jump to his suffering at the hands of Pilate. If one relied on these creeds alone for one's Christology then Jesus appeared to have marked time between his birth and passion. It is as though the life and mighty works of the Messiah have no part in the story of salvation. Of course, the creeds have specific historical contexts and burdens. But they are integral to the worshiping life of millions of Christians. Unless the fuller picture of Jesus' achievement in his "doing good and healing all oppressed by the devil" and his active obedience in fulfilling the will of God are thematized in the churches, then so much of the biblical testimony has been drained of its color and significance.

The mighty works of Jesus, the Messiah, do not constitute one of the traditional Christological moments. How can they, since they encompass years of activity? Consequently neither do they constitute a pneumatological moment per se. However, they do give content to that Christological and pneumatological moment where Jesus is commissioned for his public role in Israel and for the world at his baptism by John.

---

54. See Dallas Willard, "Jesus the Logician," *CSR* 28 no. 4 (1999): cf. 606 and 608–609, in relation to Luke 20:28–33. Willard's argument could have as easily been made from Matthew 12:22–32. However, describing Jesus as a logician is quite a stretch, as Richard Riesen points out in "Jesus the Logician: A (Very) Modest Proposal," *CSR* 34 no. 3 (2005): 341–351.

55. The miraculous element in these accounts of Jesus' public works is inescapable. How one deals with such accounts is very much dependent upon the worldview brought to the text. If one sees nature as a closed system, then other explanations have to be sought: legend, myth, exaggeration, or misunderstanding. Thus, an a priori is operative that sets limits to what constitutes a rationally acceptable reality. However, if one's universe is open and not closed, then one's estimate of Jesus, whether high or low, is the critical factor.

THE SPIRIT AND THE TRANSFIGURATION

The next Christological moment is the transfiguration. Each of the Synoptic Gospels has an account. In the Markan story, Jesus has just been acknowledged to be the Christ by Peter—albeit with limited understanding. Jesus defines his messiahship in terms of suffering before glory. He also informs the apostolic band that some of them would not taste death before experiencing the kingdom of God with power. Then follows the transfiguration. Only some are there: Peter, James, and John. Jesus is transformed before them on the mountain: ". . . he was transfigured before them, and his clothes became radiant, intensely white, as no one on earth could bleach them" (Mark 9:2–3). Elijah and Moses—representing, presumably, the Prophets and the Law—appear, talking with Jesus. A cloud overshadows the disciples, and a voice is heard: "This is my beloved Son; listen to him" (v. 7). Then only Jesus can be seen. Matthew adds that Jesus' face shone like the sun (Matt. 17:2). Luke informs the reader that the topic of conversation between Jesus and Moses and Elijah was the exodus (Gk. *exodus*) that Jesus was to accomplish at Jerusalem (Luke 9:30–31). Moreover, Luke relates that Moses and Elijah appeared in glory with Jesus (cf. 2 Pet. 1:17).

The theological import of these dramatic accounts is, in the first instance, Christological and soteriological. Jesus stands on another level to a Moses and Elijah. He is the Son. With regard to Christology, Jesus is revealed to be superior to both the Law and the Prophets in redemptive history. As for soteriology, an exodus is to be accomplished in Jerusalem, and Jesus is the linchpin to the project. But there are no references to the Holy Spirit in any of the accounts. To suggest a reason for this absence of reference requires some speculation and should be treated as such. If the point of the story is Jesus' preincarnate glory with the Father (see John 17:5), then there is no need for the Spirit to be thematized. The story is about the Father and the Son, as the voice appears to indicate. If the point is an anticipatory transformation of Jesus in the light of the glory to come in his resurrection, then again there is little need to accent the Spirit in the account.[56] With either explanation or a combined one, here is a Christological moment that breaks step with the pneumatological ones.[57]

56. Packer sees in these accounts both reference to Jesus' intrinsic glory as the divine Son and "a taste of things to come" (*Concise Theology*, 217).

57. An alternative reading is to regard the transfiguration as in some way an analogue—albeit superior—to the experience of Moses on the mountain. See the discussion by C. A. Evans, "Mark," *NDBT*, 269–270, where he suggests nine points of comparison (e.g., the shining face cf. Ex. 34:29–30 and Matt. 17:2; Luke 9:29).

The Orthodox tradition, however, sees the stories of the transfiguration as rich in pneumatological, indeed, Trinitarian content.[58] Kallistos Ware argues that the transfiguration ". . . is a Trinitarian happening."[59] He sees an analogy between the triadic structure of the baptism of Jesus and the transfiguration of Jesus. He contends, ". . . while as before [at the baptism] the Spirit descends upon the Son, this time [at the transfiguration, the Spirit descends] in the form of a cloud of light (Luke 9:34)." The cloud becomes a symbol of the Holy Spirit. Likewise the Orthodox Study Bible maintains, ". . . the Spirit is present in the form of the dazzling light surrounding Christ's Person, overshadowing the whole mountain."[60] One can appreciate the desire to read the biblical narrative in a Trinitarian fashion. But theology needs to be disciplined by the biblical evidence, and speculation needs to be called by its name, lest the speculation take on a theological life of its own. Responsible exegesis does not provide a platform for Ware's claims.[61]

The Spirit and the Cross

The atoning death of Jesus is central to all the Gospels, hence the merit in Martin Kähler's famous remark that the Gospels are passion narratives with extended introductions. Paul described the story of the death (and resurrection) of Jesus as of first importance (*en prōtois,* 1 Cor. 15:3). The practices of baptism and the Lord's Supper likewise accent the death of Jesus. The center of gravity in the gospel is not the incarnation or the Christmas story but the cross or the Good Friday story with the concomitant resurrection or Easter Sunday story. So the question needs to be asked as to what part the Holy Spirit plays in the story of Jesus' sacrifice for the sins of the world. Or as Moltmann puts it, "Can we discover any indication in the New Testament for a *pneumatologia crucis?*"[62] Is this traditional Christological moment also a pneumatological one? At first glance the

58. As does the Roman Catholic tradition. The official *Catechism of the Catholic Church* maintains, "On the mountain of Transfiguration, the Spirit in the 'cloud came and overshadowed' Jesus" (*CCC,* part 1, section 2, chapter 3, article 8, II, 554 [184]).

59. Kallistos Ware, *The Orthodox Way* (London and Oxford: Mowbray, 1981), 45–46. Orthodox hymnody also celebrates the role of the Spirit in the transfiguration, as can be seen in a hymn addressed to God on the feast of the transfiguration (August 6) (ibid.): *Lex orandi lex credendi* (Lat., "the law of praying is the law of believing").

60. *The Orthodox Study Bible: New Testament and Psalms* (Nashville: Thomas Nelson, 1993), 48.

61. With regard to reading Scripture responsibly, in our own case the use of devices like Christological moments—or pneumatological ones, for that matter—must remain heuristic rather than algorithmic, and thus entertained only insofar as they help to illuminate the biblical witness.

62. Jürgen Moltmann, *The Spirit of Life: A Universal Affirmation,* trans. Margaret Kohl (Minneapolis: Fortress, 1994), 62, emphasis original.

biblical evidence is meager, to say the least. To the evidence such as it is we now turn our attention.

The Synoptic Gospels have references to the human spirit in their passion narratives. For example, in Matthew's account of Jesus' praying in the garden, Jesus says of the sleepy disciples, "The spirit [*pneuma*] is indeed willing, but the flesh [*sarx*] is weak" (Matt. 26:41; see also Mark 14:38). Later in that same Gospel, Jesus in dying "yielded up his spirit" (Matt. 27:50; see also Luke 23:46). In John, Jesus' last words from the cross are, "It is finished" (John 19:30). The text then comments, ". . . and he bowed his head and gave up his spirit" (v. 30). Some have suggested that the *pneuma* Jesus gives up is the Holy Spirit, who had been the source of his mighty deeds. The argument is that "gave up" (*paredōken*) may be translated "handed over." Moreover there is no reference to "his" in the text. For example, in the ESV the translator has supplied the personal pronoun. The text literally states that "he handed over (or gave up) the *pneuma.*"[63] According to this view the Spirit had been with Jesus to the point of actual death. The loss of the Spirit thus underlines the horror of Christ's sin-bearing, just as the symbolism of the darkness surrounding the cross also suggests that creation is being undone and chaos is returning (Genesis reversed). By another interpretation, Jesus hands over the Holy Spirit to those disciples still with him at the end.[64] All this is very difficult to prove. There simply is not the evidence, and thus it must remain theological speculation.

We are on firmer ground when we turn from the silence of the four Gospels to the letter to the Hebrews.[65] The writer draws a contrast between the efficacy of the blood of calves, bulls, and goats under the old dispensation and the efficacy of the blood of Christ (Heb. 9:11–14). The argument is an a fortiori one. If the old system of sacrifice had some efficacy, how much more then the perfect sacrifice of Christ. The text runs, ". . . how much more will the blood of Christ, who through the eternal Spirit [*hos dia pneumatos aiōniou*, lit. "who through eternal S/spirit"] offered himself without blemish to God, purify our conscience from dead works to serve the living God" (v. 14). The argument is intriguing, and the language about

63. Matthew similarly presents Jesus as "letting go (*aphēken*, aorist) the *pneuma*" (Matt. 27:50, author's translation).

64. George T. Montague, "Holy Spirit," in Hinze and Dabney, eds., *Advents of the Spirit,* 50, adopts a variant of this line of interpretation. But this interpretation is problematic given the subsequent scene in the upper room where the risen Christ breathes the Holy Spirit upon the disciples in an act proleptic of Pentecost (John 20:22). See the discussion in George R. Beasley-Murray, *John,* WBC, 2nd ed., comment on John 19:30. We shall return to the discussion of John 19:30 in the next chapter.

65. On this silence see Hawthorne, *Presence and the Power,* 180; and as for Hebrews, Moltmann writes that the Epistle to the Hebrews "*stresses* the operation of the Spirit in Jesus' passion and death" (*Spirit of Life,* 62, emphasis mine). As we shall see, "stresses" is a little too strong.

pneuma rather odd. Some maintain that the *pneuma* in view is that of Christ's own spirit or "the spiritual aspect of Christ's sacrifice," or simply that the sacrifice is offered eternally "in the realm of spirit."[66] Leon Morris acknowledges the oddness of the language but contends, "While Christ's own spirit is involved in his sacrifice, the divine Spirit is involved, too. It seems that the writer has chosen this unusual way of referring to the Holy Spirit to bring out the truth that there is an eternal aspect to Christ's saving work."[67] Certainly, more often than not the writer to the Hebrews seems to prefer to refer to the Spirit as "the Holy Spirit" (Heb. 2:4; 3:7; 6:4; 9:8; and 10:15). He also does refer to the human spirit in apparent contrast to the human soul (4:12). And there is arguably one reference to the Holy Spirit as "the Spirit of grace" (10:29). So once more we face the question that has occurred more than once already in this project: Are we dealing with small "s" spirit or capital "S" Spirit? My own view is that the qualifier "eternal"—together with the context with its arguably Isaianic Servant of the Lord timbre—makes a reference to the Holy Spirit more probable than not.[68] If so, then in Hebrews we have the only biblical reference to the Holy Spirit's role in the atonement.

With only the Hebrews reference—albeit a controversial one—as a possible base, is the systematician condemned to virtual silence at this point on the question of the Spirit and the Cross? Not at all! There is only one biblical account of the Tower of Babel (Genesis 11) and of Pentecost (Acts 2). Frequency of a word or reference or allusion isn't necessarily determinative of theological importance. Otherwise "and" would be the most important word in Mark's Gospel. And as the *Westminster Confession* suggests, there are both Scripture and "good and necessary consequence" that "may be deduced from Scripture."[69] There is enough evidence to suggest as a theological opinion (technically, a *theologoumenon*) that the cross—as Moltmann has so forcefully argued—is indeed a Trinitarian event.[70] The Father gave up the Son (Rom. 8:32), the Son gave himself up (John 10:17–18), and

66. See Harold W. Attridge in his comment on Hebrews 9:14, in Wayne A. Meeks, gen. ed., *The HarperCollins Study Bible* (New York: HarperCollins, 1993), 2261. Attridge takes issue with the NRSV translation, which he is commenting on, because it uses a capital "S" for *pneuma*. See also Montague, *Holy Spirit,* 317. Montague dismisses any idea that this text involves a reference to the self or the Holy Spirit. For him it is "the realm of the spirit" that is in view.

67. Leon Morris, "Hebrews," *EBC,* comment on Heb. 9:14.

68. See also Moltmann, *Spirit of Life,* 62–63; Thomas Smail, *Reflected Glory: The Spirit in Christ and Christians* (London, Sydney, Auckland, and Toronto: Hodder & Stoughton, 1975), 114–115; and the extensive discussion in Hawthorne, *Presence and the Power,* esp. 179–184, for the Isaianic element. Coffey argues persuasively that the Holy Spirit is in view in Hebrews 9:14 ("Holy Spirit as the Mutual Love of the Father and the Son," 209–210).

69. *The Westminster Confession,* chapter 1, paragraph 6, quoted in Wayne Grudem, *Systematic Theology: An Introduction to Biblical Doctrine* (Leicester, England, and Grand Rapids, Mich.: Inter-Varsity and Zondervan, 1994), 1180.

70. Jürgen Moltmann, *The Crucified God,* trans. R. A. Wilson and John Bowden (London: SCM, 1982), 241. Moltmann quotes from B. Steffan's *Das Dogma vom Kreuz. Beitrag zu einer*

the Spirit kept the triune Godhead from imploding—as it were—when the barrier of sin went up between the Father and the Son, or when in Pauline terms the Son became sin for us (2 Cor. 5:21).

THE SPIRIT AND THE RESURRECTION

All four Gospels have resurrection stories. Without the resurrection the life of Jesus ends in sheer tragedy. For if he did not rise, then the truly good person is "mocked" by a universe indifferent to good and evil. Evil triumphs, injustice has the last say. The truly good person has no future. Moreover, Jesus prophesied that he would rise. If he did not, then he lived under delusion. The hope of Israel is extinguished. And as Paul argued at the personal level, if there was no resurrection, then there was no hope for Paul or the Corinthians (1 Cor. 15:19). They remained in their sins (v. 17). And as for Paul, if there was no resurrection of Jesus, then he had misrepresented God by claiming that an act of God had occurred which in fact had not occurred (1 Cor. 15:15). Intriguingly, however, there are no references in any of the Gospel accounts of the risen Christ that delineate the role the Holy Spirit played in Jesus' triumph over death.

The NT epistles, however, provide some clues. Romans is an important witness. From the start of the epistle Jesus is the one "declared to be the Son of God in power according to the Spirit of holiness by his resurrection from the dead" (Rom. 1:4). If this text is a reference to the Holy Spirit—with "the Spirit of holiness" as a Semitic equivalent—then we are dealing with a reference to the Spirit's role in Jesus' resurrection. Both the ESV translation quoted above and the NIV translation take this line, although the NIV has "spirit" as a footnoted alternative. However, here is yet another place where we may be dealing with small "s" spirit. The NRSV takes this approach, although it has a footnote with "Spirit" as an alternative reading. If so, the reference is to Jesus' own holiness of spirit. There is no reference then to the Holy Spirit.[71] There are three other Holy Spirit references before we come to the monumental eighth chapter, in which Paul refers to the Spirit twenty-one times (ESV). In one of these references an analogy appears to be drawn between the Spirit giving life to our mortal bodies and the Spirit having given resurrection life to Jesus' own body: "If the Spirit of him who raised Jesus from the dead dwells in you, he who raised Christ Jesus from the dead will also give life to your mortal bodies through his Spirit who dwells

---

staurozentrischen Theologie, who writes of the cross as "the shortest expression of the Trinity . . . in which the Father allows the Son to sacrifice himself through the Spirit" (ibid.).

71. Interestingly Leander E. Keck, in his comment on the NRSV text of Romans 1:4, takes issue with the translation on this point: "*Spirit of holiness* (a phrase found only here in the NT) probably refers to the Holy Spirit" ("Romans," in Meeks, gen. ed., *HarperCollins Study Bible,* 2116, emphasis original).

in you" (Rom. 8:11). However, it could be argued that the expression "the Spirit of him who raised Jesus from the dead" is simply a way of identifying the Spirit as the Spirit of God. According to this view it is God the Father who raised Jesus from the dead and not the Spirit in particular.[72] Even if this is granted, the text does maintain that God gives life to mortal bodies through the Spirit. And since Paul elsewhere argues that Christ's resurrection is the beginnings (*aparchē*, "firstfruits") of this eschatological harvest, then it is hard to resist the conclusion that the Spirit was integrally involved in the first in the series. One of the Pastoral Epistles adds to the picture: "He [Jesus] was manifested in the flesh, vindicated [*edikaiōthē*, "justified"] by the Spirit . . ." (1 Tim. 3:16).[73] Jesus' vindication was his resurrection.[74] The world's verdict about him was proved wrong. He was no blasphemer, no fraudulent claimant to royal dignity. One further reference needs our consideration. In 1 Peter 3:18 we learn, "He [Jesus] was put to death in the body but made alive by the Spirit" (NIV). It seems in this text that the Holy Spirit raised Jesus from the dead. However other translations carry a different suggestion. For example, the ESV has ". . . being put to death in the flesh but made alive in the spirit."[75] The NRSV takes a similar tack. Here the contrast is between flesh and spirit. There is no reference to the Holy Spirit at all.[76]

We may conclude that there is some, but not much, exegetical evidence in the Epistles to support the view that the Spirit was indeed involved in a special way in the raising of Jesus. Of course, a robust Trinitarianism would see the resurrection in triadic terms as the story of Father, Son, and Spirit. The meager nature of the evidence has not stopped some theologians, however, in attempting to claim that the Spirit "performed a peculiar work in the resurrection."[77] Abraham Kuyper, for example, writes in such

72. So Everett Harrison argues: "In v. 11 the Spirit is given yet another title: 'the Spirit of him who raised Jesus from the dead.' The reference is, of course, to God (cf. 4:24). Paul is not asserting, as some claim, that the Spirit raised Jesus from the dead. The title is simply a specialized variation of the Spirit of God" ("Romans," *EBC*, comment on Rom. 8:11).

73. The NIV also has "was vindicated by the Spirit," whereas the NRSV reads, "manifested in the flesh, vindicated in spirit," with the footnoted alternative "by the Spirit." The crucial questions are whether there is a flesh/spirit contrast in the text and whether *en* is to be rendered "in" or "by." Strangely, the NIV also translates *sarx* as "body" in 1 Timothy 3:16, although there is a footnoted alternative "in the flesh."

74. N. T. Wright describes this phrase as "likely . . . an oblique way of referring to the resurrection" (*The Resurrection of the Son of God* [Minneapolis: Fortress, 2003], 270).

75. Why the NIV translates *sarx* as "body" rather than "flesh" is strange.

76. Edwin A. Blum comments on the NIV translation in the following terms: "Behind the NIV translation stand a number of problems. The antithesis is between 'flesh' and 'spirit.' 'Flesh' and 'spirit' do not refer to two 'parts' of Christ, i.e., his body and his soul; nor does the 'spirit' refer to the Holy Spirit or Christ's human spirit. Rather, 'flesh' refers to Christ in his human sphere of life and 'spirit' refers to Christ in his resurrected sphere of life (cf. Dalton, 124–34; *TDNT*, 6:417, 447; 7:143). (For similar 'two sphere thinking,' cf. Rom. 1:3–4; 1 Tim. 3:16.) If this view is adopted, the exegesis makes good sense" ("1 Peter," *EBC*, comment on 1 Pet. 3:18).

77. Kuyper, *Work of the Holy Spirit*, 109.

terms and contends that the Spirit's role in raising Jesus from the dead was "similar" to his role in primordial creation.[78] Moltmann too maintains that the Spirit played a key role in Jesus' resurrection: "Where his own person is concerned, the Spirit of God is not only the one who leads Jesus to self-surrender to death on the cross. He is *very much* the one who brings Jesus up out of death."[79] But how does Moltmann know this? He appeals to texts which we have examined, such as Romans 1:4; 1 Timothy 3:16; and 1 Peter 3:18.[80] He sees behind the reference to Jesus' being raised "through the glory of the Father" a reference to the Holy Spirit under the symbol of glory (*doxa*). Likewise he regards another Pauline reference which asserts that Jesus was "crucified in (the) weakness (of God) but lives in the power of God (II Cor. 13:4)" as a reference to the Holy Spirit under the "image" of power (*dynamis*).[81] But there is no discussion of the ambiguities.

What theological proposals may be safely erected on this scanty exegetical foundation? The Spirit was indeed at work in the resurrection of Jesus. Our Trinitarian theology would teach us that. However, trying to detail a "special work of the Holy Spirit" soon outruns the evidence.[82] Hawthorne correctly observes that, "One might wish for an explicit statement such as, 'God raised Jesus from the dead by the Holy Spirit,' but it does not exist in the New Testament."[83] But then he goes on to conclude, "The Holy Spirit, then, was the divine agent by which God the Father raised Jesus from the dead."[84] Ryrie is rightly more cautious when he notes the lack of clarity in the biblical evidence as far as ". . . the Spirit's direct working in the death or resurrection of our Lord" is concerned.[85]

THE SPIRIT AND THE ASCENSION

The last of the traditional Christological moments is the ascension. Both in Luke and in Acts there is a brief description of Jesus' ascent to heaven. In Luke's account he is carried up into heaven in the very act of blessing the disciples (Luke 24:51). The book of Acts adds the detail of the cloud that took Jesus out of the disciples' sight and the angelic promise that Jesus

78. Ibid.

79. Moltmann, *Spirit of Life,* 65, emphasis mine.

80. Ibid., 66. Wright is also confident that in the Paulines "the resurrection [of Jesus] was accomplished by the Holy Spirit" (*Resurrection,* 245 and 256). He may well be right—I think that he is—but he does not sufficiently show that he is right.

81. Ibid., 66–67. He also sees the Spirit behind some of the references to light in the NT. Consequently he sees a pneumatological dimension to the transfiguration (ibid.).

82. The phrase is Kuyper's (*Work of the Holy Spirit,* 109).

83. Hawthorne, *Presence and the Power,* 194.

84. Ibid.

85. Charles C. Ryrie, *Basic Theology: A Popular Systematic Guide to Understanding Biblical Truth* (Paris, Ontario: ChariotVictor, 1997), 354. I would prefer to say "special working," rather than "direct working."

would return in the manner of his departure (Acts 1:9–11). The motion is upward, from earth to heaven. The physics need not detain us.[86] How else was Jesus to be seen as returning to heaven? If he were to simply vanish on earth before the disciples' eyes, then could he still be sought on the earth? There is a fittingness about the departure. Christ, the God-man, is not to be sought on earth. The doctrine of the ascension should teach us that Jesus is no longer accessible as one's best friend is accessible by sight, touch, and sound. Too many evangelicals speak, preach, and write as though relating to Jesus is just like relating to one's spouse. It is not. The rhetoric is fundamentally misleading and generates unrealizable expectations. There needs to be another way. As we shall see in the next chapter, the Spirit is integral to that other way. There are no references to the Holy Spirit in these accounts. As for the wider NT, some have seen in 1 Timothy 3:16 a suggestion of a link between the Spirit and the ascension. There we read that Jesus was "vindicated by the Spirit [*en pneumati*] . . . taken up [*anelēmphthē*] in glory."[87] Is the way the Spirit vindicated Christ that he took him up in glory?

Thomas Smail connects the Holy Spirit to the ascension by treating the resurrection, ascension, and Pentecost as one "complex event" in which "we see . . . the renewal of manhood in him [Jesus] by the Holy Spirit."[88] The ascension also signals both withdrawal of Jesus from the disciples and "the arrival of the Holy Spirit and of Christ's presence and power in him."[89] Smail is drawing out what he sees as a theological implication of the ascension. Yet just how these ideas are connected by way of implication remains puzzling because of the lack of elaboration. He also maintains that the ascension is part of the process of Jesus' return to the Father and a necessary condition for the subsequent outpouring of the Spirit from on high at Pentecost.[90] The attempt is valiant but as Abraham Kuyper rightly observes, "The work of the Holy Spirit in the exaltation of Christ is not so easily defined. Scripture never speaks of it in connection with His ascension, His sitting at the right hand of the Father, nor with the Lord's second

86. Philosophically speaking, stories like the ascension may be understood but not explained. We can see the *raison d'être* (i.e., suggest a final cause) but not explain (i.e., suggest an efficient cause which would satisfy a physicist). We are dealing with the mystery of the divine. See also the wise remarks on the ascension by Wright, *Resurrection*, 654–656. Wright points out some basic rules for reading ancient Jewish texts (ibid., 655). First-century readers were far more sophisticated than moderns and postmoderns often allow.

87. Ralph Earle points out with regard to 1 Timothy 3:16 that, "The last statement is that he 'was taken up in glory.' The same verb (*analambanō*) is used of Christ's ascension in Acts 1:2. This was the climax of his earthly ministry. Preaching Christ means preaching his life, death, resurrection, and ascension as the glorified Lord" ("1 Timothy," *EBC*, comment on 1 Tim. 3:16).

88. Smail, *Reflected Glory*, 119.

89. Ibid., 125.

90. Ibid., 126.

coming."[91] That the ascension is a Christological moment is undeniable. How it is also a pneumatological one is speculative at best.

IMPLICATIONS FOR BELIEF AND PRACTICE

There are two implications of our study which we shall now pursue: first, the "lordship" of the Spirit and the question it raises about order (*taxis*) within the triune Godhead; and second, whether Jesus' relationship to the Spirit during his earthly life and work is paradigmatic for our own.

The "Lordship" of the Spirit

Abraham Kuyper boldly contended that, ". . . the Church has never sufficiently confessed the influence of the Holy Spirit exerted on the work of Christ. . . . Yet the Scripture teaches us again and again that Christ performed his mediatorial work *controlled and impelled* by the Holy Spirit."[92] More recently, Sinclair Ferguson has used the provocative term "lordship" to sum up the relationship of the Spirit to Jesus prior to Jesus' glorification at the right hand of the Father.[93] Jesus lived under the authority of the Spirit. Our own study supports this contention. There is a subordination of the Son to the Spirit as the Son carries out his messianic vocation. The theological issue which this raises is whether such subordination was economic (a phase in the administration of the plan of salvation) or essential (intrinsic to the inner life of God as Trinity).[94]

The idea that the economic Trinity is a window into the inner life of the essential Trinity has become increasingly popular among theologians, both Protestant and Roman Catholic.[95] Hence some see in the Son's economic subordination to the Father in his messianic work a reflection of an eternal subordination within the triune Godhead. On the Protestant side, Karl Barth argues that, "In the condescension in which God gives himself to us in Jesus Christ, he exists and speaks and acts as the One he was from all eternity and will be to all eternity."[96] The obedience of the incarnate Son

91. Kuyper, *Work of the Holy Spirit*, 110.
92. Ibid., 97, emphasis mine.
93. Ferguson, *Holy Spirit*, 46. I understand what Ferguson is attempting to do but find the term "lordship" somewhat confusing when used in this way. Paul sees the lordship of Jesus as the *sine qua non* of the Spirit's work (1 Cor. 12:3), and "lordship" as a term, I believe, is best reserved for Christ.
94. For a careful discussion of various kinds of subordination that have been predicated of the Son in relation to the Father see Brian Edgar, *The Message of the Trinity* (Leicester, England: Inter-Varsity, 2004), 177–183.
95. Grudem, *Systematic Theology*, 248–257.
96. Quoted in Thomas A. Smail, *The Forgotten Father: Rediscovering the Heart of the Christian Gospel* (London, Sydney, Auckland, and Toronto: Hodder & Stoughton, 1987), 118–119.

is not "alien to God."[97] There is no God behind God. What is revealed in the economy of salvation is what pertains in eternity. On the Roman Catholic side, Karl Rahner's rule is, "The Trinity of the economy of salvation *is* the immanent Trinity."[98] For Rahner, Jesus' incarnate "submission to the Father's unfathomable will" is not to be explained simply by appeal to the hypostatic union.[99] Such submission is constitutive of Jesus' divine sonship. Fred Sanders explicates Rahner's Rule as follows:

> When we think about the Trinity itself, Rahner argued, we must begin with the trinitarian manifestations in the history of salvation, such as the incarnation of the Son and the sending of the Spirit. These events are to be taken with utmost and ultimate seriousness, because what takes place therein is nothing less than the appearance, in the history of the world, of one of the persons of the Trinity. *Such irruptions are trustworthy revelations of the eternal Trinity in itself.*[100]

Likewise, charismatic theologian Thomas Smail maintains, "If what Christ is on earth is what the Son is eternally with the Father, then we must see this functional subordination as being within the very nature of God's own life."[101] Reformed theologian Sinclair Ferguson says boldly, "It is axiomatic for the integrity of theology that God is as he reveals himself to be."[102] As we saw in the excursus on the Trinity in part 1, some draw important ethical implications from the idea. But if we too quickly move from the narrative of the economy to the inner life of the Trinity, what are we to make of the "lordship" of the Spirit over the Son prior to the glorification? What is the counterpart to this subordination in the eternal internal life of the Trinity? To pose the question is to see the problem. Moving from the economy to the essence is fraught with difficulty. Do we have to posit an eternal internal executive role to the Spirit within the essential Trinity? What then can be said?

The God who is essentially Trinity and who operates economically in a Trinitarian way is the same God (same referent). But the theological terms

97. Ibid., 119.

98. Karl Rahner, "Theological Investigations, Vol. 4," in Gerald A. McCool, ed., *A Rahner Reader* (London: Darton, Longman & Todd, 1975), 139, emphasis original. See also Karl Rahner, *The Trinity*, trans. Joseph Donceel (New York: Herder & Herder, 1970), 22. For a critique of Rahner's Rule see Randal Rauser, "Rahner's Rule: An Emperor without Clothes?" *International Journal of Systematic Theology* 7 no. 1 (January 2005): 81–94.

99. Quoted in Smail, *Forgotten Father,* 120. Smail's fine exposition of Rahner would have been strengthened by some reference to Rahner's Rule.

100. Fred Sanders, "Entangled in the Trinity: Economic and Immanent Trinity in Recent Theology," *Dialog: A Journal of Theology* 40 no. 3 (Fall 2001): 176, emphasis mine.

101. Smail, *Forgotten Father,* 120. I am indebted to Smail's excellent discussion of the question of the subordination of the Son, although I do not follow his conclusions.

102. Ferguson, *Holy Spirit,* 76. In his view, unless this principle is granted, "An agnosticism in relationship to God's actual being results" (ibid., 77). How his notion of the lordship of the Spirit over the Son squares with all this is not clear.

"economic Trinity" and "essential Trinity" have different meanings. For in the economy—the administration of the plan of salvation—the Second Person of the Trinity becomes the God-man. The essential Trinity now relates to himself—one struggles with language here—in a new way through the humanity of the incarnate Son. As Bruce Milne correctly maintains, "The biblical equation is . . . incarnation = God plus. In becoming incarnate the divine Word did not relinquish his deity; but added to it, if one may so speak, by taking a full human nature into hypostatic union with the Word."[103] The incarnation does make a difference. The subordination of the Son to the Spirit—during the state of humiliation, as classical theology might say—prior to the glorification is all of one piece with this. Jesus' human nature counts. The incarnation simply does not mean that the eternal subordination of the Son to the Father is now lived out in human flesh as though the incarnation does not really make any relational difference. After all, the NT tells us (pace Barth, Rahner, and Smail) that Jesus *"learned obedience [emathen . . . tēn hupakoēn]* through what he suffered" (Heb. 5:8). In other words there is an asymmetry between the inner workings of the Trinity (*ad intra*) and the external workings (*ad extra*) of the Trinity. The latter cannot simply be appealed to in order to illuminate the former. One of the theological values that emerges from the present discussion is to show the problem of facilely attempting to do so. Rahner's Rule that the economic Trinity is the immanent Trinity must be applied with care, lest referent and meaning be confused.

The Spirit and Jesus: How Prototypical?

Some theologians argue strongly that Christ comes before us in the Gospels as "the prototype" of all who are filled with the Spirit.[104] Hawthorne, for example, maintains that with regard to the Spirit, Jesus, and followers of Jesus, "Not only is Jesus their Savior because of who he was and because of his own complete obedience to the Father's will (cf. Heb. 10:5-7), but he is

103. Bruce Milne, *Know the Truth: A Handbook of Christian Belief* (London and Singapore: Inter-Varsity and S+U, 1983), 147. John 10:17 is an instance of the plus. Post-incarnation, there is now an additional reason (*dia touto*) for the Father's love for the Son: namely, the Son's sacrificial death on behalf of the flock.

104. So Smail, *Reflected Glory*, 71. The classic argument to this effect is found in Edward Irving of the nineteenth century. Smail is very much indebted to Irving's discussion and follows Irving's contention that in the incarnation Christ assumed a fallen human nature. That way Christ can indeed be prototypical, since we too have a fallen nature. Irving wrote, "Christ's flesh was as rebellious as ours, as fallen as ours" (in Gavin Carlyle, ed., *The Collected Writings of Edward Irving*, 5 vols. [London: Strahan, 1864], 5:138). Irving also used the term "prototype" (ibid., 5:133). For a fine exposition and critique of Irving's pneumatology see Narelle Jarrett, "The Spirit in the Teachings of Edward Irving," in B. G. Webb, ed., *Spirit of the Living God: Part Two*, Explorations 6 (Homebush West, N.S.W.: Lancer, 1992), 71–104. See also Donald MacLeod, "The Doctrine of the Incarnation in Scottish Theology: Edward Irving," *Scottish Bulletin of Evangelical Theology* 9 no. 1 (Spring 1991): 40–50.

the supreme example for them of what is possible in a human life because of his total dependence upon the Spirit of God."[105] James D. G. Dunn, in an early work, goes as far as contending that the baptism of Jesus at the Jordan was "a baptism in the Spirit" and that the NT *"imitatio Christi"* motif includes Jesus' Spirit experience at the river.[106] Indeed, the baptism of the Spirit at the Jordan represented Jesus' entry into the new covenant and eschatological sonship. So too for the disciples at Pentecost. More recently Pentecostal scholars Roger Stronstad and Robert P. Menzies see a paradigm for all believers in Jesus' empowerment by the Spirit for mission at his baptism.[107] Ferguson, writing from a strongly Reformed perspective, joins the chorus: ". . . so Jesus was baptized with the Spirit and lived under his lordship. So also do those who in turn receive Christ's baptism in order that they might be conformed to Christ."[108] Roman Catholic theologian George T. Montague takes a sacramental approach and sees in Jesus' baptism "a prototype for Christian baptism—where water, the Holy Spirit and divine sonship all play a part."[109] But long ago Abraham Kuyper highlighted the differences between Jesus' relation to the Spirit in his earthly life and ministry, and our own. Jesus is the Messiah. We are not. In fact the chapter in which Kuyper discusses these matters is entitled "Not Like unto Us."[110]

These differences of opinion raise acutely the question of the prototypical and paradigmatic nature of Jesus' Spirit experience. Was Jesus' experience of the Spirit at his baptism prototypical for entry into eschatological sonship (Dunn) or for Spirit fullness (Smail) or empowerment for service (Stronstad and Menzies) or for life under the lordship of the Spirit (Ferguson) or becoming a Christian (Montague) or none of these? Are these various suggestions category mistakes? Since the Jordan experience was programmatic

105. Hawthorne, *Presence and the Power,* 234, emphasis mine.

106. Dunn, *Baptism in the Spirit,* 24. Dunn actually uses the expression *imitatio Christi.* Dunn also equates Jesus' anointing with his baptism in the Spirit and argues that Paul draws a link between the two ideas and Christian conversion in 2 Corinthians 1:21: "The anointing of God which made Jesus the Christ is the same anointing which makes men Christians" (ibid., 133). I will dispute this view in the next chapter.

107. Roger Stronstad, *The Charismatic Theology of St. Luke* (Peabody, Mass.: Hendrickson, 1984); and *The Prophethood of All Believers: A Study in Luke's Charismatic Theology,* JPT Supplemental Series 16 (Sheffield, England: Sheffield Academic Press, 1999); and Robert P. Menzies, *Empowered for Witness: The Spirit in Luke–Acts,* JPT Supplemental Series 6 (Sheffield, England: Sheffield Academic Press, 1994).

108. Ferguson, *Holy Spirit,* 46. Irving also argued that Christ "received the baptism of the Holy Ghost" at the Jordan (Carlyle, ed., *Collected Writings of Edward Irving,* 5:524).

109. Montague, *Holy Spirit,* 242. Montague argues that, "Luke even more clearly [than Mark and Matthew] parallels the baptism of Jesus and Christian initiation by the manifestation of the Holy Spirit both at the Jordan and at Pentecost and in subsequent initiation scenes" ("Holy Spirit," in Hinze and Dabney, eds., *Advents of the Spirit,* 51). Dunn (*Baptism in the Spirit,* 23–37) offers an effective critique of this approach.

110. Kuyper, *Work of the Holy Spirit,* 97–101.

for Jesus' public life and ministry, we shall concentrate our discussion on this pivotal pneumatological moment and its lasting significance.

There is no suggestion anywhere in the NT that Jesus was baptized in the Spirit at the River Jordan.[111] Instead, the language of the Gospels about the Spirit, the baptism, and Jesus includes such expressions as "the Spirit of God . . . coming to rest on him" (Matt. 3:16), "the Spirit descending on him" (Mark 1:10), "the Holy Spirit descended on him" (Luke 3:22), and "the Spirit . . . remained on him" (John 1:32). Soon after the baptism and subsequent temptations, Jesus describes himself in the Isaianic categories of the Spirit "upon me" and the Spirit "anointed me" (*ep' eme* and *echrisen me,* respectively, Luke 4:18). The language of anointing (*echrisen*) is how Peter later describes Jesus' Spirit-impelled ministry (Acts 10:38). At the Jordan, Jesus was "Christed" and entered into his messianic labors. The Spirit was "upon him" (*ep' auton,* Matt. 12:18, again an Isaianic category). John's Gospel reinforces the picture of Jesus' uniqueness. Jesus alone had the Spirit without measure (cf. John 3:31–34).

The imitation of Christ is a *bona fide* NT theme. Jesus himself in John's account describes his washing of the disciples' feet as an example (*hupodeigma*) for them to follow (John 13:15). Moreover disciples are to love one another as he has loved them (John 13:34). Paul draws the Romans' attention to Jesus as someone who did not please himself (*ēresen*—the aorist appears to sum up Christ's lifestyle—Rom. 15:3). In Philippians, in a magnificent Christological hymn, Paul reminds his readers of the humility and other-person-centeredness of Christ (Phil. 2:5–11). Even the way Jesus conducted himself before Pilate at his trial becomes a model of making "a good confession" (1 Tim. 6:12–13). Outside the Paulines, 1 Peter argues that Christ's conduct in his sufferings is paradigmatic (*hupogrammon,* 1 Pet. 2:21–23). These examples don't exhaust the field but suffice to establish the point. However, there are no NT texts that draw the reader's attention to Jesus' experience of the Spirit as proto-typical or paradigmatic. Boyd Hunt is right to describe Jesus as "the unique . . . pneumatic"—there is only one Messiah—but where is the evidence for his claim that Jesus is the "exemplary pneumatic"?[112] Gordon Fee rightly

111. As R. W. Lyons rightly argues, "It should be noted that the coming of the Spirit upon Jesus is not the promised baptism in the Spirit, for Jesus is the One who shall baptize" ("Holy Spirit," *EDT,* 120). Moreover it would be difficult to argue that the language of "anointed," "the Spirit upon," "the Holy Spirit descending," "full of the Spirit," and "the Spirit coming to rest" are synonyms for "baptism in the Spirit." For example, Luke–Acts uses the language of filling of both Jesus and his disciples, but never baptism in or with or by the Spirit (cf. Luke 4:1 and Acts 7:55). This fact is easier to account for if Jesus was not baptized by or with or in the Spirit but the disciples were.

112. Boyd Hunt, *Redeemed! Eschatological Redemption and the Kingdom of God* (Nashville: Broadman & Holman, 1993), 34. Max Turner rightly points out that, ". . . there are clearly unique salvation-historical elements in Jesus' experience of the Spirit . . . and it is the church corporate rather than the individual, that is anointed to continue the task implied by Luke 4:18–21" ("Holy Spirit," *NDBT,* 555). I am not persuaded by Craig S. Keener's contrary

warns against facile arguments from "biblical analogies" that seek to draw parallels between the life of Christ and the Christian's own life.[113]

Jesus as the Messiah was anointed with the Spirit, and the Spirit remained on him. But in the Gospel accounts he not only bears the Spirit, it is also predicted that he would bestow the Spirit. A great reversal in roles is thus foreshadowed. Jesus is on a trajectory in the Gospels from the state of humiliation to the state of glory. And with the state of glory there will come the bestowal of the Spirit. To that foreshadowing, reversal, and bestowal we shall turn in the next chapter. But now we turn our attention to blaspheming the Spirit.

Blaspheming the Holy Spirit

Each of the Synoptic Gospels contains a reference to blaspheming (slandering) against the Spirit. Blasphemy against the Son of Man is forgivable, but not so with regard to the Spirit (cf. Matt. 12:31–32; Mark 3:28–29; and Luke 12:10). Blasphemy is slander directed against God. Because this sin finds no forgiveness, it has been described as the "unpardonable sin." In Matthew and Mark, the warning is addressed to outsiders (Pharisees and scribes). In Luke, however, Jesus warns disciples about it.

Historically the interpretation of these passages has fallen into two groups. Some argue that this sin was only possible while Jesus walked the earth.[114] However, if this interpretation is followed, it is difficult to see why the Synoptic Gospel writers, who wrote after the time of Christ's earthly life, included such stories in their accounts of Jesus. Others argue that this sin is still a real possibility. This view makes better sense of the inclusion of the warnings in the Gospels. What exactly then is this sin?

In my view, the sin is not simply opposing Jesus on a particular occasion. In Mark, Jesus warned the Pharisees that they were in danger of committing this sin. He did not declare that they had actually committed it (*enochos* may be translated "liable"). After all, he reasoned with them in an *ad hominem* way, pointing out the *reductio ad absurdum* nature of their accusation. If Satan is fighting against Satan then his kingdom is divided and doomed. This appeal to reason suggests that the Pharisees had not yet fallen into the abyss. As Packer argues, "Jesus saw that the Pharisees were getting close to committing this sin, and he spoke in hope of holding them

---

view (*Three Crucial Questions about the Holy Spirit* [Grand Rapids, Mich.: Baker, 1996], 29). In the next chapter I will argue that it is the anointed apostolic band that continues the task (cf. 2 Cor. 1:21).

113. Gordon D. Fee, *Gospel and Spirit: Issues in New Testament Hermeneutics* (Peabody, Mass.: Hendrickson, 1991), 108–109.

114. For example, Arnold G. Fructenbaum, "Israelology, Doctrine Of," in Mal Couch, ed., *Dictionary of Premillennial Theology: A Practical Guide to the People, Viewpoints, and History of Prophetic Studies* (Grand Rapids, Mich.: Kregel, 1996), 197–203.

back from fully lapsing into it."[115] Furthermore, speaking against Jesus on some occasion or at an earlier time in one's life is not to have committed this sin. Paul described himself as having been a blasphemer, but God made him his apostle to the Gentile world (cf. Acts 7:58–8:3 and 1 Tim. 1:12–17). Saul, the blasphemer, received mercy. Blaspheming the Spirit is the settled rejection of the Spirit's testimony to Jesus. Both the Pharisees and Saul of Tarsus were in danger of just that. Nor is blasphemy against the Spirit committed by the disciple who denies his or her Lord on occasion. Peter denied Christ three times yet he was restored to Christ's service (cf. John 18:15–27 and 21:15–19). Blaspheming the Spirit is not an episode but a way of life. Put another way, this is the sin of persistent impenitent unbelief. John Paul II was right to describe this sin as "the radical refusal to be converted."[116]

What then of those genuine Christians who worry that they have committed the sin against the Holy Spirit? As Packer points out, "Christians who fear that they have committed it [the unpardonable sin] show by that anxiety that they have not done so." [117]

115. Packer, *Concise Theology*, 217.

116. John Paul II, *The Holy Spirit in the Life of the Church and the World: Dominum et Vivificantem*, trans. Vatican (Boston: Pauline Books & Media, 1986), 79.

117. Packer, *Concise Theology*, 245. See also C. F. D. Moule, *The Holy Spirit* (London and Oxford: Mowbrays, 1978), 33.

EIGHT

THE MESSIAH AND THE SPIRIT:
BESTOWER OF THE SPIRIT

In the previous chapter we employed the idea of pneumatological moments as a heuristic device to see how it might illuminate the work of the Spirit in relation to Jesus, the Messiah of Israel. We looked at the traditional seven Christological moments, from the conception of Jesus to his ascension, and looked for their pneumatological analogues. As our focus changes to the risen Christ, Pentecost, and the rise of the Christian church, there is an eighth Christological moment—and its pneumatological counterpart—to consider.[1] That moment is Pentecost and the bestowal of the Spirit by the ascended and enthroned Christ. For at Pentecost we see the great reversal in the economy of salvation. The bearer of the Spirit becomes the bestower of the Spirit.[2] The state of Christological humiliation gives way to the state of Christological glory.[3] The bestowal of the Spirit at Pentecost is the dramatic sign of this.

1. These moments, including the eighth, are well articulated in *An Australian Prayer Book: For Use Together with the Book of Common Prayer (1662)* (Sydney: AIO Press, 1978). In part of the Litany there is a prayer entitled "Prayer Recalling Christ's Saving Work," which runs, "By the mystery of your holy incarnation; by your birth; by your circumcision and obedience to the law; by your baptism, fasting, and temptation. . . . By your agony and bitter grief; by your cross and passion; by your precious death and burial; by your glorious resurrection and ascension; *and by the coming of the Holy Spirit*, good Lord, deliver us . . ." (99, emphasis mine). The bestowal of the Spirit is seen as part of Christ's saving work.

2. See Miroslav Volf, "The Nature of the Church," *Evangelical Review of Theology* 26 no. 1 (2002): 9, for a concise statement of this reversal.

3. Hendrikus Berkhof goes too far in suggesting that, prior to the resurrection, "Jesus is the work of the Spirit," and after the resurrection, "the Spirit is the work of (the risen) Jesus" (*Christian Faith: An Introduction to the Study of Faith*, trans. G. F. Callenbach [Grand Rapids, Mich.: Eerdmans, 1979], 324). However he is right to see the great change in their respective roles in redemptive history after the resurrection (ibid.).

We begin by revisiting the prophecy of the Baptist concerning the One who will baptize with or in the Spirit. Next we explore Jesus' teaching concerning the coming Paraclete, his breathing the Spirit upon the disciples in the upper room, then the day of Pentecost itself and its theological importance. The dramatic bestowal of the Spirit raises large questions of the Spirit's relation to Christ. For example, is the Spirit simply Christ now accessible to his people in a new way? Spirit Christologies will need our critical attention. Our discussion then turns to the matter of Christ, the Spirit, and the mission of God (*missio Dei*). Christ sends the Spirit, but is this a purely economic affair that has no relevance to the eternal, internal life of God as Trinity? Or does the sending of the Spirit reflect the very order (*taxis*) within the Godhead? Does the mission of the Spirit *ad extra* isomorphically reflect the procession of the Spirit *ad intra*?[4] Thus we will need to consider *filioque* once more. This consideration is all the more urgent because some recent theologies suggest that if *filioque* is dropped, then a positive theology of Christianity and the other religions of the world becomes more feasible. According to this view the Father may be accessed by the Spirit without any necessary reference to the Son. A pneumatological understanding of how other religions may legitimately access God freed from Christological constraints makes a tolerant religious pluralism all the more possible. So the argument runs. But is it sound?

The Baptizer with the Spirit

In none of the Gospels does Jesus describe himself as the one who baptizes with the Spirit.[5] In the Synoptics it is John the Baptist who identifies Jesus as the baptizer, and in the Fourth Gospel it is God himself who does (cf. Matt. 3:11; Mark 1:8; Luke 3:16; and John 1:33). With regard to the Markan account, Robert A. Guelich suggests that, ". . . the Spirit would be the cleansing agent parallel to water-baptism."[6] With this view, it is as though John is claiming, "I work in your lives by word ("a voice") and

---

4. Daniel L. Migliore (*Faith Seeking Understanding: An Introduction to Christian Theology*, 2nd ed. [Grand Rapids, Mich., and Cambridge: Eerdmans, 2004]) usefully discusses this important distinction between mission and procession (231).

5. Intriguingly, when the risen Christ in Acts 1:5 refers to the baptism with the Spirit, he does not identify himself directly as the baptizer. Indeed one could be forgiven for thinking that the baptizer is the Father, whose gift of the Spirit is referred to by Christ in the previous verse. However the subsequent story of the day of Pentecost makes it plain that Jesus is the one who provides the promised Holy Spirit from the Father (Acts 2:33). It is worth noting that there is no suggestion in the scriptural testimony that the gift of the Spirit was purchased by Christ's death (contra Jonathan Edwards, "Misc. 1159," in *The "Miscellanies" 1153–1360*, ed. Douglas A. Sweeney, vol. 23 of The Works of Jonathan Edwards [New Haven, Conn.: Yale University Press, 2004], 72–74).

6. Robert A. Guelich, *Mark 1–8:20*, WBC, comment on Mark 1:8; and "Excursus: Baptism with the Spirit and/or Fire."

water (baptism), but he will work in your lives with Spirit (Spirit-baptism)." The forgiveness of sins is in view in both baptisms. With regard to the Matthean and Lukan accounts, we find in both an addition. As we saw in the previous chapter, Matthew's and Luke's accounts add "and fire." What did they mean by "fire"? Many—from Origen to Scobie—have seen in the expression "with the Holy Spirit and fire" a reference to two baptisms: one of blessing for some (Spirit) and one of judgment for others (fire).[7] Still others have seen only one baptism for blessing. The predicted fire finds its fulfillment in the tongues of flame at Pentecost (Chrysostom).[8] Others again, and more recently, have argued for one baptism that may be experienced either as blessing or as judgment (Beasley-Murray, Dunn). A variation on this later view is to regard the fire as a purging of God's people.[9] William J. Dumbrell, for example, maintains that the baptism with the Spirit signifies two coordinated effects: namely, "(1) Israel's cleansing and purification and (2) removal of the nation's dross."[10] Max Turner contends that "Spirit and fire" is a hendiadys for a single baptism, which "will cleanse/restore Israel in the fiery power of the Spirit."[11] D. A. Carson suggests with reference to the fire that, "There are good reasons, however, for taking 'fire' as a purifying agent along with the Holy Spirit. . . . Fire often has a purifying, not destructive, connotation in the OT (e.g., Isa. 1:25; Zech. 13:9; Mal. 3:2-3)."[12]

What is the systematician to do when the exegetes vary so much in opinion? Make a judgment call? The traditional view that both Matthew and Luke are referring to both blessing for some and judgment on others still has merit. In both contexts the Baptist's prophecy concerning the com-

---

7. Charles H. H. Scobie, *The Ways of Our God: An Approach to Biblical Theology* (Grand Rapids, Mich., and Cambridge: Eerdmans, 2003), 278. Likewise Robert G. Gromacki, "Holy Spirit: Who He Is, What He Does," in Charles R. Swindoll and Roy B. Zuck, eds., *Understanding Christian Theology* (Nashville: Thomas Nelson, 2003), 457–458. So also Craig S. Keener, *Three Crucial Questions about the Holy Spirit* (Grand Rapids, Mich.: Baker, 1996), 27. Some translations import a second "with" into the translation of Matthew 3:11 and Luke 3:16, which is unfortunate. In these instances the interpretative possibilities needed to have been left more open (as the NRSV does).

8. George T. Montague takes this approach—following Luke Timothy Johnson—in "The Fire," in Bradford E. Hinze and D. Lyle Dabney, eds., *Advents of the Spirit: An Introduction to the Current Critical Study of Pneumatology* (Milwaukee: Marquette University Press, 2001), 40 and 61–62, fn 8.

9. See the fine discussion in Donald A. Hagner, *Matthew 1–13*, WBC, comment on Matt. 3:11, which summarizes many of these views.

10. William J. Dumbrell, *The Search for Order: Biblical Eschatology in Focus* (Eugene, Ore.: Wipf & Stock, 2001), 162.

11. Max Turner, *The Holy Spirit and Spiritual Gifts: Then and Now,* rev. ed. (Carlisle, England: Paternoster, 1999), 28. Turner thinks that in Markan and Lukan thought, this purging of Israel began in Jesus' earthly ministry (ibid., 29). His evidence for this proposition is slight, especially in the light of Acts 1:4 and 11:16.

12. D. A. Carson, "Matthew," *EBC*, comment on Matt. 3:11. Calvin takes a similar view ("Harmony of the Gospels," *CJCC,* vol. 1, comment on Matt. 3:11): the fire is purificatory.

ing one is followed by the image of the sifting of wheat from chaff (Matt. 3:12 and Luke 3:17).[13] The winnowing fork is coming too. This is hardly accidental. Moreover the traditional view helps explain the Baptist's apparent *volte face* when he later inquires whether Jesus really is the Christ (Matt. 11:1–10). This makes sense if he expected the coming one both to bless with the Holy Spirit and judge with fire. Where's the judgment if John is in prison? Perhaps the answer to such a question lies in Luke. In the "Nazareth manifesto" Jesus quotes from Isaiah 61:1–2a but does not include the note of judgment (Luke 4:18–19). Likewise when the risen Christ (Acts 1:5) speaks of the Baptist and baptism with the Spirit, there is no reference to fire. Similarly when Peter recalls the day of Pentecost and the Baptist's words of prophecy, there is no reference to fire (Acts 11:16). In other words, first comes the opportunity for blessing but judgment is also coming. In fact the judge, Jesus, has been appointed, and yet there is forgiveness available now (e.g., Acts 10:42–43).[14] The eschatological rhythm has two major beats.

But what is meant by "baptize" in the expression "baptize . . . with the Holy Spirit"? The term has a range of possible meanings including, "to dip," "to bathe," or "to wash (by immersing)," or metaphorically, "to deluge with" or "to overwhelm."[15] Of these possibilities, Turner prefers "to wash (by immersing)."[16] However, the expression is metaphorical.[17] The Baptist sees some analogy between his rite and the work of the coming one. His medium is water but the coming one's medium will be the Holy Spirit. In my view, the way forward is to let the Acts account give the content. To that account we shall shortly turn.

The Quantum Leap

The progress of revelation takes a quantum leap as we turn from the Old Testament to the New. That leap is seen in the Gospels themselves. In particular, the name of the one God now needs to be understood as Father, Son, and Holy Spirit; the Father is revealed in relation to the Son and in

13. Matthew and Luke speak of "unquenchable [*asbestō*] fire" (Matt. 3:12 and Luke 3:17). Donald A. Hagner points out that in the Synoptics, the only other use of this Greek word for "unquenchable" is found in Mark 9:43 and refers to Gehenna, "the place of final punishment" (*Matthew 1–13*, WBC, comment on Matt. 3:12).

14. Sinclair Ferguson has an interesting, if not finally convincing, suggestion. The fire in the prophecy is the fire of judgment. But that fire was exhausted on the cross. Hence in Acts there is no reference to the predicted fire (*The Holy Spirit* [Leicester, England: Inter-Varsity, 1996], 59). But in Acts, the "fire" of judgment, for example, does fall on putative believers such as Ananias and Sapphira (Acts 5:1–11) and unbelievers such as Herod Agrippa (Acts 12:1, 20–23).

15. Turner, *Holy Spirit and Spiritual Gifts*, 28.

16. Ibid.

17. As Donald G. Bloesch correctly observes (*The Holy Spirit: Works and Gifts* [Downers Grove, Ill.: InterVarsity Press, 2000], 299).

relation to those who believe in him; the opposition of Satan to the kingdom comes to light and the Holy Spirit comes into high relief. The NT cannot be reduced to mere commentary on the OT.

The contrast between the former revelation and the new is so strong that there is a remarkable editorial statement in the Fourth Gospel to the effect that there was no Holy Spirit before the glorification of Jesus (John 7:39, NRSV). The scene is the last day of the Feast of Booths or Tabernacles (John 7:2). Jesus invites any of his hearers who are thirsty to come to him for drink through believing in him (vv. 37–38). Jesus refers to Scripture to explain the results of coming to him. Which particular Scripture is uncertain (possibly Isa. 44:2–3 and/or Zech. 14:8). The outcome will be rivers of living water flowing out of Jesus' belly (*koilias*, lit. "belly," John 7:38 as in the NRSV). Whether the rivers flow out of Jesus' belly or out of the believer's belly need not detain us at this point,[18] although most likely the reference is to Jesus as "the holy rock, the new temple from which rivers of living water will flow."[19] Then comes the striking editorial comment, in which the water is identified as the Spirit. But more than that. The NRSV renders the Greek well: "Now he said this about the Spirit, which believers in him were to receive; for as yet there was no Spirit [*oupō gar ēn pneuma*], because Jesus was not yet glorified" (John 7:39).[20] Glorification in John's Gospel appears to refer to a complex of events that includes Jesus' death, resurrection, and ascension. These events constitute Jesus' return to the Father.[21] Now the writer of John knows that the Spirit not only existed but was active already in the life and ministry of Jesus (John 1:32; 3:34). The statement then is an implied comparative. In comparison to what is coming concerning the Spirit's ministry, it is as though there is no Holy Spirit as yet.[22] As

18. The Greek is ambiguous. Ferguson points out that the Eastern view takes the believer as the source whereas the Western view takes Christ to be the source of the flowing water (*Holy Spirit,* 67). See also the discussion in George R. Beasley-Murray, *John,* WBC, comment on John 7:38. Beasley-Murray points out that *koilia* in the LXX can be a synonym for *kardia* ("heart"). See also Merrill C. Tenney, "John," *EBC,* comment on John 7:38.

19. As Dumbrell argues (*Search for Order,* 248). George T. Montague links John 7:37–39 with John 19:34 and argues that the latter text is the fulfillment of the prophecy of the earlier one. He maintains "there can be little doubt" about the nexus (*The Holy Spirit: Growth of a Biblical Tradition: A Commentary on the Principal Texts of the Old and New Testaments* [New York and Toronto: Paulist, 1976], 349). Where exegesis begins and imagination ends in this judgment is hard to determine.

20. Both the ESV and NIV take the easier course and add, following some of the early manuscripts, "for as yet the Spirit had not been given" and "up to that time the Spirit had not been given," respectively. But the correct textual critical procedure is to adopt the *lectio difficilior* (the more difficult reading) and also, as in this instance, the best manuscript support, as the NRSV does. Moreover, the NRSV gives the alternative in a marginal note. Neither the ESV nor the NIV offers an alternative. All this is to show that although we have some fine translations to work with, each has different strengths and weaknesses.

21. As Paul Barnett and Peter Jensen correctly observe (*The Quest for Power* [Sydney: Anzea, 1973], 21); and more recently, Max Turner, *Holy Spirit and Spiritual Gifts,* 76.

22. Ferguson, *Holy Spirit,* 68.

Sinclair Ferguson argues, "The statement must therefore carry economic, not ontological, significance."[23] Likewise James D. G. Dunn maintains, "The puzzling *oupō ēn pneuma* [my transliteration, Dunn has the Greek] is not to be interpreted ontologically but functionally."[24] In other words, John's Gospel is writing about the Spirit's work, not the Spirit's person. Jesus' extensive teaching on the coming of the Paraclete subsequent to his own return to the Father underscores the point that John 7:39 is making. To that teaching we now turn our attention.

The Promise of the Paraclete

The most sustained teaching on the person and work of the Holy Spirit to be found in the Gospels is from Jesus himself. The context is the Farewell Discourse in the second great part of the Fourth Gospel, in particular chapters 14–16.[25] Here we have the first mention of the Paraclete (*paraklētos*) who is coming (John 14:16). Translators are challenged to find the best way of rendering the term. Suggestions are manifold: "Helper," "Intercessor," "Comforter" (i.e., Strengthener, Lat. *con* "with" plus *fortis* "strength"), "Counselor," "Advocate," "Champion," "Advisor," to name a few suggestions that have been offered. Dumbrell helpfully suggests, "Though *paraklētos* has been translated in various ways (e.g., Counselor, Advocate, Helper), it is perhaps best to leave it untranslated and focus on the function of the one that will come."[26] My approach, following Dumbrell's, will be simply to retain the transliterated term "Paraclete" and to treat it as a logically proper name. With this approach the name is a tag for a cluster of

23. John Goldingay nuances the force of John 7:39 in a very stimulating article, "Was the Holy Spirit Active in Old Testament Times? What Was New about the Christian Experience of God?" *Ex Auditu* 12 (1996): 14–28.

24. James D. G. Dunn, *Baptism in the Spirit* (London: SCM, 1977), 180.

25. A weakness in Abraham Kuyper's magisterial work on the Holy Spirit lies in his lack of an extended, exegetically well-grounded discussion of the Spirit as Paraclete. His chapter entitled "Love and the Comforter" is a case in point (*The Work of the Holy Spirit,* trans. Henri De Vries [Grand Rapids, Mich.: Eerdmans, 1975], 532–537). A similar criticism may be directed at Gerald F. Hawthorne's otherwise excellent study of the significance of the Holy Spirit in the life and ministry of Jesus (*The Presence and the Power: The Significance of the Spirit in the Life and Ministry of Jesus* [Dallas, London, Vancouver, and Melbourne: Word, 1991]). If Hawthorne had included teaching as part of Jesus' ministry, then Jesus' teaching about the Paraclete would have figured prominently in his discussion. But as it is, Hawthorne did not.

26. Dumbrell, *Search for Order,* 255. See also J. I. Packer, *Keep in Step with the Spirit* (Leicester, England: Inter-Varsity, 1984), 61, for a wise comment on the difficulties of translation. Turner has a helpful discussion of the linguistic background and possibilities (*Holy Spirit and Spiritual Gifts,* 77–79). In contrast to Dumbrell, he argues for "Advocate" as the best translation of the verbal passive adjective (ibid., 79). However his subsequent discussion undermines his case. For example, he concludes in relation to John 16:8–11 that, *"It is thus as Teacher and Revealer, that the Spirit will also be 'Paraclete' or 'Advocate'"* (ibid., 87, emphasis original). "Advocate" simply does not adequately cover all the Johannine instances.

definite descriptions which apply to only one: namely, the one whom Jesus promised, who would be another of the same sort as he, and who would be characterized by a number of activities such as convicting the world of its sin.[27] Thus how the Fourth Gospel uses the term will give the content to the name, rather than exploring its possible etymology.[28]

In Jesus' first mention of the Paraclete, he informs the troubled disciples (John 14:1) that he will ask the Father on their behalf, and the Father will give another Paraclete (*allon paraklēton,* "another of the same sort of Paraclete as Jesus is") to be with them forever (v. 16).[29] This is none other than "the Spirit of truth." The world (*kosmos,* humanity in opposition to God) cannot receive (*labein*) the Spirit because it neither knows nor sees him (John 14:17). As Merrill C. Tenney colorfully puts it, "To use a modern metaphor, he would not operate on the world's wavelength."[30] Jesus is indeed returning to the Father but he will not leave them bereft. This Spirit already dwells with them but in the future shall indwell them (v. 17). In his next reference to the Paraclete, Jesus teaches the disciples that it will be the Paraclete, the Holy Spirit, who will bring to their remembrance all that he has said to them. This Paraclete will be sent by the Father in Jesus' name (v. 26). In his third mention of the Paraclete, Jesus is once more speaking of the world's opposition to himself and his disciples (15:18–25). However, Jesus will send the Paraclete, who proceeds from the Father (v. 26). The Paraclete will bear witness to Jesus, as will the disciples who have been with him from the beginning (vv. 26–27). The Spirit's focus will be Christocentric. J. I. Packer helpfully describes the Spirit's work as a "floodlight ministry," with Jesus as the one highlighted by the beam.[31] According to Jesus, the

27. In this approach I am indebted to the pioneering work of philosopher Bertrand Russell. However, the more recent approach of another philosopher, Saul Kripke, could also be applied and a causal link established between our current use of the term in the Christian community and Jesus' use of the term *paraklētos* in the upper room.

28. Charles H. H. Scobie wisely comments, "BT [biblical theology] is not concerned with possible origins of the term *paraklētos.* . . . but with its canonical usage" (*The Ways of Our God: An Approach to Biblical Theology* [Grand Rapids, Mich., and Cambridge: Eerdmans, 2003], 284, emphasis original).

29. In 1 John 2:1 Jesus is also described as a *paraklētos.* Beasley-Murray wisely comments on a key difference in roles: "That the Spirit-Paraclete is introduced [in John 14:16] as '*another* Paraclete' implies that Jesus himself is also a Paraclete. It has been common to interpret this in the light of 1 John 2:1, 'If anyone sins we have a Paraclete with the Father, Jesus Christ the Righteous One.' Here the ascended Lord is viewed as a Paraclete *in* the court of heaven, pleading the cause of his own; the Holy Spirit is then understood as the Paraclete *from* heaven, supporting and representing the disciples in the face of a hostile world" (*John,* WBC, comment on John 14:16). Of course, the Paraclete's role in John's Gospel is not reducible to a merely forensic interpretation but does include it, as I shall argue shortly. Stanley Grenz argues that the idea that "another" Paraclete "implies a similarity" between Jesus and the Holy Spirit is hardly strong enough to do justice to *allon* ("The Holy Spirit: Divine Love Guiding Us Home," *Ex Auditu* 12 [1996]: 5).

30. Tenney, "John," *EBC,* comment on John 14:16–17.

31. Packer, *Keep in Step with the Spirit,* 65–66.

disciples need to hear this teaching in order that (*hina*) they do not fall away (16:1). Moreover it is to the advantage of the disciples that Jesus is going away. The coming of "the Spirit of truth" is contingent upon Jesus' leaving them (v. 7). After his departure Jesus will send the Paraclete and "he will convict the world concerning sin and righteousness and judgment" (v. 8).[32] The sin is the sin of not believing in Jesus, the righteousness lies in Jesus' return to the Father, and the judgment is found in the judgment on the ruler of this world (v. 11). Jesus still has much to say to these disciples but they cannot bear it at that moment (v. 12). However, when "the Spirit of truth" comes he will "guide" (*hodēgēsei*) them into all the truth (v. 13). He will pass on to them what he hears. He won't speak "on his own authority" (ESV, lit. "from himself," *aph' heautou*). He will declare things to come. He will glorify Jesus by taking what is Jesus' and declaring it to the disciples (v. 14). Again, the Spirit's work is Christocentric.[33] Three times in our texts the Paraclete is "the Spirit of truth."[34] The truth, in this context, is the truth about Jesus, which is the burden of the Gospel. As Turner observes, "The Paraclete's task is not to bring *independent* revelation; first and foremost he explains and draws out the significance of the *historical* revelation."[35] So much for a brief overview, but what are the nuances?

Jesus' teaching about the Paraclete makes most sense when the Fourth Gospel is seen in terms of God's putting the world on trial. Jesus prosecutes the case in the first half of John especially (John 1–12). But with his return to the Father, it will be another like him—the Paraclete—who will continue the case (John 14–16). More than that, the Paraclete will continue the case through the disciples who had gathered in the upper room. Whoever embraces the divine verdict on Jesus—that he really is the Christ, the Son of God—has eternal life (John 20:31). Especially blessed are those who having never seen Jesus in the flesh yet believe in him. Jesus prayed for such (17:20) and pronounced a special blessing on them (20:29). Readers of John's Gospel are in this position. From one perspective the long discourse in the upper room is designed to underscore the truthfulness of this Gospel's witness. The reader is receiving the testimony of the signs of Jesus (20:30), the Paraclete (John 14–16), and a disciple who was an eyewitness (1:14; 19:35) and who

32. For a recent discussion of John 16:8–11 see John Alosi, "The Paraclete's Ministry of Conviction: Another Look at John 16:8-11," *JETS* 47 no. 1 (March 2004): 55–69.

33. Michael Welker observes with regard to the Paraclete, "In total selflessness the Paraclete represents Jesus, drawing attention to Jesus and to Jesus' words" (*God the Spirit*, trans. John F. Hoffmeyer [Minneapolis: Fortress, 1994], 222).

34. Before the NT, it appears that only the Qumran sectarians used the expression "the spirit of truth." In their literature it referred to an angelic being who helps the sons of light. See the helpful discussion in Montague, *Holy Spirit*, 351. Montague thinks that John definitely used motifs drawn from such angelology in his presentation of the Paraclete (ibid., 357). But since the Paraclete is another like Jesus, who is clearly not an angel according to John's account, this seems doubtful.

35. Turner, *Holy Spirit and Spiritual Gifts*, 83, emphasis original.

has the Spirit's promised enabling (chapters 14–16; 20:22–23). The Fourth Gospel itself is an extension of that truthful witness (20:30–31).

According to this view, much of the promise connected with the coming of the Paraclete has to do with those gathered in the upper room and is not as easily generalized. Thus there is a good case for seeing part of the fulfillment of the teaching about the Paraclete in the formation of the NT but not for some notion of a magisterium as found in the Roman Catholic Church, nor for wild claims to special Spirit-granted knowledge in the present based on an appeal to these texts in John.[36] This constraint on present-day application also applies *mutatis mutandis* to Jesus' teaching about extraordinary effectiveness in prayer (John 14:13–14; 15:7; 16:23–24) and the fruitfulness—in mission, rather than character—of abiding in him as a branch on a vine (15:1–11).[37] In the first instance, all this applies to those who were to be the spearhead of the *missio dei* ("mission of God") after Jesus' return to the Father and the sending of the Paraclete.[38] Here is yet another example of the need to place texts—in this case, Paraclete texts—in their contexts in their rhetorical units in their book in the canon in the light of the flow of redemptive history.

Of particular importance to our discussion is John 16:8–11. Our understanding of the passage here will affect our construal of the mission of the Spirit. Is the ministry of the Spirit to convict the world of sin, righteousness, and judgment (e.g., J. I. Packer), or is it to reveal to the disciples where the world had gone wrong with regard to Jesus (e.g., Raymond E. Brown), or a mix of the two (e.g., George T. Montague)?[39] If *elenchein* (cf. v. 8) is taken to mean either "to convict" or "to expose"—and it can be understood a number of ways depending on the context—and if the world is considered to be the object, then the Spirit is the great prosecutor who takes the world on—albeit through the disciples.[40] The core of the world's sin is unbelief in Jesus, and it needs to be convicted of Jesus' righteousness, despite the

---

36. See Ferguson, *Holy Spirit,* 70–71. With regard to the magisterium and the Spirit, see *CCC,* part 1, section 2, chapter 3, article 8, 688 (181).

37. Jesus is addressing those already made clean (cf. John 13:10, *ēdē,* and 15:3). The branch that is broken off and burned is Judas, by this line of interpretation (cf. John 15:6 and 17:12).

38. I say "in the first instance" because we must not preclude the idea that there are principles in the text that apply to God's dealing with any disciple (especially the vine and the branches, John 15:1–11). However, the details themselves in the text may be peculiar in their application to those in the upper room (e.g., John 15:27 clearly so).

39. See Packer, *Keep in Step with the Spirit,* 65; Raymond E. Brown as discussed in Turner, *Holy Spirit and Spiritual Gifts,* 86; and Montague, *Holy Spirit,* 354–355. Montague's view of the recipients of the Spirit's *elenchein* is not all that clear. On one page we read of the Spirit that "he prosecutes the world for its sin," and on the next, "The Paraclete makes this triumph obvious to the disciples" (ibid., cf. 354 and 355).

40. Earlier in the Gospel *elenchein* is best rendered "to expose," as in John 3:20, and "to convict," as in 8:46. Turner renders *elenchein* as "expose/convict" in his discussion of John 16:8–11 (*Holy Spirit and Spiritual Gifts,* 87). There is wisdom in this, given the usages in 3:20 and 8:46.

verdict of any earthly court and judgment. The ruler of this world does not have the final say with regard to Jesus. In fact, the ruler of this world stands condemned. But the world, we are told earlier in the Farewell Discourse, neither receives nor sees nor knows the Spirit (John 14:17). Thus Brown contends that the Spirit's role is to show the troubled and fearful disciples gathered in the upper room that the world has misread Jesus dramatically. Armed with that knowledge, then, the disciples can confront the world with their witness to the truth.[41] With this view, the reader of John's Gospel may be confident that the disciples got Jesus right and therefore likewise got right this Gospel account that he or she is reading. Montague believes that *elenchein* has at least two different meanings in the passage. With regard to sin the Spirit convicts, but with regard to righteousness and judgment the Spirit reveals.[42] In my view, the first option fits the context best. The world is on trial. The Holy Spirit will continue the prosecution begun by Jesus. The world won't receive, see, or know him, because he will prosecute the case through the disciples and not directly (John 14:17). The Paraclete's ministry is one of both convicting and exposing. The response of those cut to the heart on the day of Pentecost upon hearing the apostolic proclamation of the gospel is Exhibit A of this work (cf. 16:8–11 and Acts 2:36–39).[43] On that day the Holy Spirit did not confront the world in an unmediated way but through Peter.

"He Breathed on Them"

One of the most intriguing texts in John's account of the Spirit and the Messiah is John 20:19–22. It is the evening of the first day of the week. The risen Christ somehow comes to the disciples, who are behind locked doors out of fear of the Jewish authorities. This miracle is not explained. After a greeting of "Peace," Jesus displays his hands and side. They know it is Jesus and are glad. He announces, "As the Father has sent [*apestalken*, perfect] me, even so I [*kagō*, emphatic] am sending [*pempō*, present aspect] you" (v. 21). Next he breathes (*enephusēsen*, aorist) on them and declares, "Receive [*labete*, aorist] the Holy Spirit [lit. "Holy Spirit," no article]. If you forgive the sins of any, they are forgiven [*apheōntai*, perfect] them; if you withhold forgiveness from any, it is withheld [*kekratēntai*, perfect]" (vv. 22–23). What is going on here? Is this text presenting the story of the regeneration of these disciples as a new Adamic race or as a new Israel or as both? Or is this the commissioning of the church for mission? Or, as a variant of this, is this the revival of a remnant of Israel for prophetic ministry? Or is this John's version of Pentecost? Or is this an example of

---

41. Raymond E. Brown as discussed in Turner, *Holy Spirit and Spiritual Gifts,* 86.
42. Montague, *Holy Spirit,* 354–355.
43. A point well made by Ferguson, *Holy Spirit,* 69–70

enacted prophetic symbolism pointing to Pentecost which is to come? Or is this an act that is proleptic (anticipatory) of Pentecost—that is to say, a real taste of that which is to come?

Each of the above views of the theological import of the episode has its advocates. Some have seen in the passage the story of the regeneration of these disciples (J. Rodman Williams).[44] They are born again by the Spirit. Thus a new Adamic race is born.[45] Of those who hold this view, some maintain that Pentecost adds the promised baptism of the Spirit to give them power to witness to the risen Christ (J. Rodman Williams).[46] Another approach argues that Jesus fulfilled the promises of John 7:39 and 16:7 when he handed over the Spirit on the cross to those disciples still gathered there (19:30). The cross was the occasion of the sending of the Spirit. The incident related in John 20:21–23 is "the full revelation of what is simply presented as a fact in John 19:30" (David Coffey).[47] Others have seen in the story John's way of incorporating Pentecost into the presentation. The story then is theologically motivated as it adds a completeness to the Fourth Gospel's presentation of Jesus (Paul Barnett and Peter Jensen).[48] Still others maintain that the account is to be understood against the background of enacted prophetic symbolism (Merrill C. Tenney).[49] The breathing is such that it is observable. Like an Ezekiel, Jesus acts out what is to come (at Pentecost). Others again believe that the disciples received the Spirit on the occasion but did so in an act that was proleptic or anticipatory of the Pentecost to come.[50] The taste was real but the fuller experience of the Spirit was still to come (Calvin).[51] Yet another view sees the account as describing the appointment of the apostles to their apostolic office (Abra-

44. J. Rodman Williams, *Renewal Theology: Systematic Theology from a Charismatic Perspective: Three Volumes in One* (Grand Rapids, Mich.: Zondervan, 1996), 2:173, fn 61.

45. Turner appears to entertain a variant of this view. He contends that John 20:22 is "the climax in a *whole process* of life-giving experiences of the Spirit-and-word (through Jesus), extending from the disciples' earliest encounter with the one whose revelatory wisdom is Spirit and life (6:63)" (*Holy Spirit and Spiritual Gifts*, 97, emphasis original). This process is the means by which God brings into being a new humanity (ibid.).

46. Ibid., 174.

47. David Coffey, "The Holy Spirit as the Mutual Love of the Father and the Son," *TS* 51 (1990): 213–214. This is dubious given that the translation of *paredōken* that it assumes is so disputable.

48. Barnett and Jensen, *Quest for Power,* 24. They argue that, "John 20:19–23 is, in effect, Jesus' sign of Pentecost." However, this is a strange understanding of "sign," given John's use of *sēmeion* in the Gospel (e.g., John 2:23).

49. Tenney, "John," *EBC,* 1064.

50. Donald Guthrie, "John," *NBC,* 1064. Also Scobie, *Ways of Our God,* 286, who describes the "insufflation" as "a foreshadowing and anticipation of the Acts 2 giving of the Spirit."

51. John Calvin, "Commentary on John," *CJCC,* comment on John 20:22, where he says of the apostles that they were ". . . on this occasion only sprinkled by his grace but were not filled with full power; for, when the Spirit appeared on them in *tongues of fire,* they were entirely renewed" (emphasis original).

ham Kuyper).[52] Finally, some argue that the story is relating the revival of "remnant Israel" to its prophetic task (Dumbrell).[53]

In the light of the many competing interpretations adumbrated above, it is little wonder that Packer so aptly describes our passage as a "problem text."[54] My own view of this text synthesizes several of the aforementioned interpretations but excludes others of them. The thrust of Jesus' discourse is mission (John 20:21). He is sending the disciples in the same way that the Father sent him.[55] He was sent with the Spirit upon him (1:33). So too they will be sent with the Spirit upon them (20:22). The imperative, "Receive the Holy Spirit!" is to be understood as having future reference, which is not unusual in John.[56] The accent in Jesus' ministry fell on the forgiveness of sins.[57] This will be the accent in their ministry to come as well (v. 23). This is not so much John's version of Pentecost as John's version of the Great Commission. Indeed on the day of Pentecost the great benefits of the gospel held out to the hearers are the forgiveness of sins and the gift of the Spirit (Acts 2:37–38).[58]

What, then, happened to these disciples at Pentecost? To anticipate a discussion to come next, at Pentecost these disciples received the power to witness at a unique transitional moment in redemptive history.[59] In fact

52. Kuyper, *Work of the Holy Spirit*, 125.

53. Dumbrell, *Search for Order*, 256–257.

54. Packer, *Keep in Step with the Spirit*, 87.

55. I take *pempō* in this context to be present in aspect but future in force. This use of the present aspect is a feature of John (e.g., John 13:6, 27, 33; 14:3; 15:27; and 20:17). John 21 bears this out. There are no stories of mission to bring the Gospel to a close. Instead we find the disciples have returned to their former profession (John 21:1–3). Moreover, the re-commissioning of Peter has a future cast (John 21:15–19), as does the reference to Peter's fate and that of the beloved disciple (John 21:18–23).

56. Turner acknowledges this phenomenon but is not convinced that John 20:22 is an example (*Holy Spirit and Spiritual Gifts*, 90). Dumbrell contends that the imperative in John 20:22 "rules out any notion of a promise to be fulfilled later" (*Search for Order*, 257). I disagree. Strangely Hawthorne maintains that the idea of "receive" implies that whether the disciples receive the Spirit or not is a matter of their free choice (*Presence and the Power*, 236). This is hardly the point that the passage is making.

57. This is clearer in the Synoptics (e.g., Matt. 9:6; Mark 2:10; and Luke 24:47). Surprisingly, John 20:23 is the first explicit reference to forgiveness in John.

58. Like the Reformers of the sixteenth century, I understand John 20:23—a difficult text by any view—as referring to a declarative rather than a sacramental ministry (contra Rome). One looks in vain in the Acts narrative for any action resembling absolution by a priest. However, there are many examples of the forgiveness of sins held out as benefit in the declaration of the gospel (e.g., Acts 2:37–39; 3:19; 5:31; 10:43; 13:38; and 26:18). For a Reformation view, see John Calvin, "Commentary on John," *CJCC*, comment on John 20:23. For a clear presentation of the Roman Catholic view, see Pope John Paul II, *The Way to Christ: Spiritual Exercises,* trans. Leslie Wearne (New York: HarperSanFrancisco, 1984), 107–118. According to the Roman view, John 20:23 establishes priestly absolution, beginning with the apostles. But Thomas was not there on that occasion, and it is an open question as to whether only the apostles were in that room on that night and heard Christ's words (see John 20:24).

59. I agree with Dunn (*Baptism in the Spirit*, 178–181) and many others on this point.

placing this text in its redemptive-historical context makes attractive the view that in this commissioning Israel is being revived for the benefit of both the nation itself and those beyond it.[60] There are allusions to Genesis 2:7 and Ezekiel 37:9 in our passage which support this view.[61] The text is not about the individual regeneration of these disciples. Jesus had said that they were clean already (John 13:10; 15:3; 17:8). By this interpretation Jesus is not yet glorified, since in Johannine thought the glorification of Jesus appears to include the cross, the resurrection, and the ascension (7:37–39). This last event has yet to take place (20:17). Moreover Jesus had clearly taught that, ". . . if I do not go away [to the Father], the Helper [Paraclete] will not come to you. But if I go, I will send him to you" (16:7).[62] And so the absence of Jesus means the presence of the Spirit as another Paraclete like himself. But the presence of Jesus in that room with its locked doors means the absence of the Spirit as the Paraclete. Jesus' insufflation (observable breathing upon them) was "acted prophecy" of what the promise of the Father would make powerfully possible at Pentecost.[63] It was also, as Augustine argued, ". . . a demonstration, by a fitting symbol that the Holy Spirit proceeds not only from the Father but from the Son," or as I would prefer to say, "sent not only from the Father but from the Son" (15:26).[64]

PENTECOST AND BEYOND: THE BESTOWAL OF THE SPIRIT

If there is one event in the scriptural narrative that more than any other is associated with the Holy Spirit it is Pentecost, and the book of Acts is the key source for our knowledge of what happened on that first Pentecost

---

60. Dumbrell is persuasive here (*Search for Order*, 256–258). He sees in the Johannine text parallels with OT commissioning passages.

61. The verb for "breathed on" is a rare one in biblical literature but is found in Genesis 2:7 and Ezekiel 37:9. See the helpful discussion in Turner, *Holy Spirit and Spiritual Gifts*, 90.

62. For a contrary view, see D. Martyn Lloyd-Jones, who argues that John 20:22 is the constituting of the church by the bestowal of the Spirit rather than Acts 2, which is the more conventional idea. He maintains that whereas Jesus forbade Mary to touch him (John 20:17) but invited Thomas to do so (v. 27), Jesus, therefore, must have been glorified by then and able to bestow the Spirit in terms of John 7:39 (*Joy Unspeakable: The Baptism with the Holy Spirit* [Eastbourne, England: Kingsway, 1985], 262–263). However, the text does not say so. Moreover, if the story of John 20:22 is the founding of the church, it is an extraordinary lacuna on the part of Luke–Acts to omit it.

63. "Acted prophecy" is Packer's helpful expression. See Packer, *Keep in Step with the Spirit*, 88. The view I am espousing has not always been looked on kindly in Christian history. Theodore of Mopsuestia (c. 350–428) was condemned at the Council of Constantinople (Constantinople II) in A.D. 553 for the symbolic interpretation. See Ferguson, *Holy Spirit*, 261, endnote 6; and Turner, *Holy Spirit and Spiritual Gifts*, 88. But this condemnation may say more about the fate of Antiochian Christology over the previous hundred or so years than about the best exegesis of the text of John 20:22. Be that as it may, Turner effectively critiques Carson's revival of the Antiochian view (*Holy Spirit and Spiritual Gifts*, 89–91).

64. Augustine, *De Trinitate* 4.29, in Henry Bettenson, ed. and trans., *The Later Christian Fathers* (Oxford: Oxford University Press, 1977), 227.

after Christ's ascension. Often we are told that the Acts of the Apostles should really be named the Acts of the Holy Spirit.[65] There is some justification in this suggestion given its many references to the Spirit compared to the Gospels. However, the preface to the book is clear that it continues the story of what Jesus "began to do and teach" (Acts 1:1–3).[66] The book of Acts, if anything, is the Acts of the Risen Christ, to whom both the Spirit and the apostles bear witness (5:32). As for Pentecost, this festival of Israel, held some fifty days after the Passover, was associated with the giving of the Torah at Sinai and the wheat harvest (Ex. 23:16; 34:22; Num. 28:26; and Deut. 16:10).[67] According to the Acts account, Jerusalem was thronged with the devout from all over the known world (Acts 2:5). As for the disciples, they were awaiting the delivery of the promise of the Father. Christ himself had told them to wait (Luke 24:49; Acts 1:4, 8). Then it happened.

The story can be briefly rehearsed. The disciples were together in one place on that day when the Spirit came in a new way (Acts 2:1). The phenomena were extraordinary: the rushing wind, the tongues of fire, and then the proclamation (prophesying) of the mighty acts of God in diverse foreign languages (vv. 2–4).[68] The pilgrims heard about them, therefore, in their own tongues (v. 6). Babel is "reversed" for a moment (cf. Genesis 11 and Acts 2:1–13).[69] Peter proclaims that the ancient prophecy of Joel 2:28–32 has been fulfilled (Acts 2:16–21).[70] The Spirit has been poured out (Acts

65. For example, Brian Edgar, *The Message of the Trinity* (Leicester, England: Inter-Varsity, 2004), 213.

66. Richard N. Longenecker comments, "As such it [the use of *ērxato*] serves to stress Luke's intent to show in Acts what Jesus *continued* to do and to teach through his church, just as Luke had previously presented 'all that Jesus *began* to do and to teach' in his Gospel" ("The Acts of the Apostles," *EBC,* comment on Acts 1:1).

67. See Dumbrell, *Search for Order,* 223. The connection between Sinai and Pentecost is made in a number of intertestamental texts, such as Jubilees 1:1, 5; 6:1–21; 15:1–24 (ibid.). See also Montague, *Holy Spirit,* 275.

68. According to Dumbrell, ibid., the evidence that what was happening in that house was divinely effected is "revealed by language of wind and fire that was integral to Old Testament theophanies." Dumbrell gives no examples, but Ex. 19:16–19 and 1 Kings 19:9–18 provide cases in point. Longenecker suggests that the distribution of the fire so that each one present had a tongue of fire resting on him indicates that the Spirit is now for the individual believer and not just for a people per se ("The Acts of the Apostles," *EBC,* comment on Acts 2:3). As for their speaking in tongues, whether the glossolalia of the Paulines is likewise xenoglossia (uttering real foreign languages unknown to the speakers) is a question to which we shall return in a later chapter.

69. Montague maintains that Pentecost is "a reversal of the curse of Babel" (*Holy Spirit,* 282). Conrad Gempf argues that Babel is not so much "undone" by Pentecost as "redeemed" (*NBCRev,* comment on Acts 2:4–13). However, Dumbrell, *Search for Order,* 223, is not convinced that there is any Babel backdrop.

70. Strangely, J. I. Packer mistakenly attributes the speech to Paul (*Keep in Step with the Spirit,* 204).

2:33). The last days are here (v. 17). Like some of the bystanders on that day we too are asking, "What does this mean?"(v. 12).[71]

For a start, prophecies have come to pass. Jesus' own prophecy has been fulfilled (Luke 24:49; Acts 1:4–5, 8). The promise of the Father has been kept. The disciples are filled with the Spirit (2:4). The power from on high has been given. This is seen in the effective witness on that day. Three thousand believe Peter's proclamation, or perhaps it may be better to say his "prophesying"(v. 41).[72] Moreover, the prophecy of John the Baptist has come to pass (1:5). Jesus has been vindicated (2:36). Though put to death by humanity, Jesus was raised by the Father. The exalted Christ—now both Lord and Christ, and at the Father's right hand—has poured out the Spirit. The baptism with the Spirit was now a reality, not simply a promise. Lastly, the prophet Joel's vision for the future, that a prophetic community would arise, has been realized (Joel 2:28–32).[73] The Spirit of prophecy has indeed come.[74] Jesus is proved to be the bestower of the eschatological Spirit, promised for the end times.[75] Just as there had been with the Messiah's birth an outburst of prophesying by various people filled with the Spirit (e.g., Luke 1:41, Elizabeth; v. 67, Zechariah) or having the Spirit upon them (e.g., Luke 2:25–26, Simeon), so too at the birth of the Messiah's eschatological community (Acts 2:17–18). Clearly Pentecost represents a crucial event in the flow of redemptive history.

In three other key passages in Acts some of the phenomena of that first day reoccur. In Samaria too Christ is proclaimed (Acts 8:5). Miracles and signs happen at the hands of Philip (vv. 6–8). The Samaritans believe and are baptized, including one worker of magic named Simon (vv. 9–13). But the Spirit comes only after an apostolic delegation, consisting of Peter and John, travel down from Jerusalem (v. 14). With apostolic prayer and the laying

71. Some bystanders thought the disciples needed to be "breathalyzed" (Acts 2:13). But Peter soon pointed out that the "third hour of the day" was a little too early for that hypothesis to work (Acts 2:15). Providing naturalistic explanations for divine activity happened long before the Enlightenment.

72. Prophesying in this Acts 2 context is preaching the gospel. So whatever else prophesying in NT perspective may be, it can at least be this kind of communication. Indeed an element in NT prophesying appears to be the exposure of the moral state of the heart (cf. Luke 7:39; John 4:16–19; and 1 Cor. 14:24–25). In Acts 2:37, the hearers are "cut to the heart."

73. It is a moot point as to whether the Joel prophecy was fully or only partially fulfilled. Not all the phenomena promised in Joel 2:28–32 took place. The sun, for example, was not turned to darkness nor did the moon turn to blood. Of course, the language is apocalyptic and should not be over-pressed at the level of detail. See Kuyper, *Work of the Holy Spirit,* 129; and Paul D. Feinberg, "Hermeneutics of Discontinuity," John S. Feinberg, ed., *Continuity and Discontinuity: Perspective on the Relationship Between the Old and New Testaments: Essays in Honor of S. Lewis Johnson, Jr.* (Westchester, Ill.: Crossway, 1988), 126–127.

74. As Max Turner ably argues in numerous works, including "Holy Spirit," *NDBT,* 553–555.

75. As Peter's reworking of the Joel 2:28–32 text suggests, especially with the addition of "in the last days" (cf. Joel 2:28 and Acts 2:17). See Dumbrell, *Search for Order,* 224, for elaboration.

on of hands, the Spirit is received by the Samaritans (vv. 15–17).[76] There is power on display, and prophecy. Simon Magus is willing to pay for his share (vv. 18–19). What the manifested power is—Simon sees something—is not explained (v. 18). Probably the power is not tongues, since Simon sees rather than hears something. Simon soon learns that the Holy Spirit is not for sale (v. 20). Next at Caesarea, Peter, in response to a vision, is on an assignment directed by the Spirit (11:12). Soon he finds himself preaching the gospel not to Jews only but to a Gentile God-fearer and his household (10:34–43). Interestingly, there is no explicit reference to Cornelius's believing the proclamation about Christ. In fact the Spirit comes while Peter is preaching (v. 44)—a very different pattern of experience than that in Samaria. Tongues happen, and God is extolled (v. 46). Lastly at Ephesus, Paul finds some disciples of John the Baptist who had not caught up on the news of Jesus, Pentecost, and the Spirit (19:1–4). These disciples of John the Baptist soon join the new company of Christ's people, and they too experience the coming of the Spirit and speak in tongues (v. 6). What's more, they prophesy (v. 6). So in these various accounts we read of proclamation, tongues, and in some instances displays of power and what is described in the text as prophesying; but after Pentecost, there are no stories emanating from Samaria or Caesarea or Ephesus of the mighty rushing wind and the tongues of fire. What is going on?

Of these various places—Samaria, Caesarea, and Ephesus—it is Caesarea that is critical for understanding Pentecost. The reason is that Peter has to explain himself *post eventum* to the Jerusalem believers (Acts 11:1–2). There were critics (vv. 2–3). How come a Jew had eaten with a Gentile? So Peter tells the story from the beginning: the vision, his reluctance, the Spirit's directive to go, and how as he was speaking the Holy Spirit "fell on them" (vv. 4–17). His words are freighted with significance for our understanding Pentecost aright. Peter relates, "As I began to speak, the Holy Spirit fell on them just as on us at the beginning" (v. 15). Peter's memory was jogged: "And I remembered the word of the Lord, how he said, 'John baptized with water, but you will be baptized with the Holy Spirit'" (v. 16). He then draws this significant conclusion: "If then God gave the same gift to them, as he gave to us *when we believed in the Lord Jesus Christ,* who was I that I could stand in God's way?" (v. 17).[77] Jew and Gentile had

---

76. Thus there is a time lag between believing and Spirit-receiving, a matter to which we shall return when we consider some implications of the present study. For a contrary view, see A. M. Stibbs and J. I. Packer, who argue that the Samaritans were baptized with the Spirit upon believing and that the subsequent experience was a manifestation of a Pentecost-like phenomenon to show that the Samaritans too belonged to "the same covenant community" (*The Spirit Within You: The Church's Neglected Possession* [London: Hodder & Stoughton, 1967], 35). According to this view, Pentecost, Samaria, Cornelius, and Ephesus were one-step occasions as far as Spirit-reception is concerned.

77. The Greek is instructive: *hōs kai hēmin pisteusasin.* The particle *hōs* with the aorist participle *pisteusasin* is to be taken in a temporal sense. Max Zerwick and Mary Grosvenor suggest the

received the same baptism (with the Holy Spirit) and the same gift (of the Holy Spirit), and in both cases the same object of faith (the Lord Jesus) was crucial.[78] The baptism and the gift are predicated on the believing in the Lordship of Christ, which Peter dates in his case to Pentecost (v. 17).[79] To be sure, he was a disciple before that. The first volume, Luke, makes that clear. But now Christ is at the right hand of the Father, the place of preeminence (2:33). He is Lord and Christ (2:36). Now Jesus can be believed on as the risen, vindicated Lord. Pentecost was Peter's own baptism in the Spirit. In Pauline language, Peter was now a member of the body of Christ and indwelt by the Spirit of the risen Christ (1 Cor. 12:13).

A great epochal transition in salvation-history took place at Pentecost. J. I. Packer attempts to capture this transition in the following two statements: "Jesus' disciples [e.g., Peter] were evidently Spirit-born believers [regenerated] prior to Pentecost, so their Spirit-baptism, which brought power to their life and ministry (Acts 1:8), was not the start of their spiritual experience."[80] I agree at one level. Pentecost was not the start of the spiritual experience of these disciples who had been with Jesus in his earthly ministry. They were like OT saints in that respect. However, Packer seems to suggest the baptism in the Spirit was about power for service. I do not see the exegetical evidence for such a claim. The language of Acts 2:4 with regard to the disciples' effective proclamation of the mighty acts of God is that of the filling of the Spirit, which is also an idea found in the OT. Next Packer draws a contrast: "For all who have come to faith since that Pentecost

---

syntax should be seen as inceptive, i.e., "when we began to believe in the Lord Jesus Christ" (my translation) (*A Grammatical Analysis of the Greek New Testament,* vol. 1 [Rome: Biblical Institute Press, 1974], 387). See also Barnett and Jensen, *Quest for Power,* 23, 29–30; and Ferguson, *Holy Spirit,* 84 .The NIV has "who believed" but the ESV and NRSV are to be preferred here.

78. Thomas Smail argues that in the NT "baptism in the Spirit" is to be understood in two ways: initiation into Christ and an overwhelming of the Spirit (*Reflected Glory: The Spirit in Christ and Christians* [London, Sydney, Auckland, and Toronto: Hodder & Stoughton, 1975]). Initiation into Christ has good support, as our present discussion shows, but the idea of overwhelming is extremely dubious if made a defining characteristic of Spirit baptism. The apostles appear to have been overwhelmed in Acts 2—some onlookers thought that they were drunk—and Cornelius was arguably overwhelmed, but those who responded on the day of Pentecost to Peter's preaching do not appear to have been (cf. Acts 2:1–13; 10:44–45; 11:15–17; and 2:37–41). Spirit baptism, on my view, is always initiatory, but may be experientially overwhelming on occasion. See also G. R. Beasley-Murray, "Baptism, Wash," *NIDNTT,* 4. (d), who makes no mention of the idea of overwhelming although he does refer to the baptism in the Spirit. Those in Jerusalem who heard Peter's report, and with it the analogy he drew between his experience and that of Cornelius, were right to conclude that, "Then to the Gentiles also God has granted repentance that leads to life" (Acts 11:18). They judged the experience to be entry into the life of the age to come. In other words, initiatory.

79. See Bloesch, *Holy Spirit,* 288, who holds essentially the same view.

80. J. I. Packer, *Concise Theology: A Guide to Historic Christian Beliefs* (Australia, Singapore, and England: Anzea, Campus Crusade Asia, and Inter-Varsity, 1993), 145. Abraham Kuyper sees Acts 1:5 fulfilled in Acts 2:1ff. Pentecost is the apostles' baptism with the Spirit (*Work of the Holy Spirit,* 125). I agree with him here at one level (terminology) but our understanding of the baptism differs (meaning), as the next chapter will show.

morning, however, beginning with the Pentecost converts themselves, the receiving of the Spirit in full new-covenant blessing has been one aspect of their conversion and new birth (Acts 2:37; Rom. 8:9; 1 Cor. 12:13)."[81] In my view Packer is entirely and helpfully right on this point.

But how are we to understand the other phenomena such as the "mighty rushing wind" and "the tongues of fire"? In my judgment these phenomena are indicative that the Father's promise has been kept. The power to testify to the Lord Jesus Christ has come. The apostles were filled (*eplēsthēsan*, aorist) with the Spirit to this end (Acts 2:4). This fullness (empowerment) and the baptism with the Spirit (incorporation into Christ) should not be confused, although both happened to the apostles in the house where they were seated.[82] Prophetic Israel has been reborn. And that rebirth was to have an impact not just on Jerusalem and Judea but on Samaria and to the ends of the earth (Caesarea, Ephesus, and eventually Rome itself). That impact is not only on Jews but also on Samaritans and Gentiles, as well as on old-era disciples of the Baptist.[83] In other words, Samaria, Caesarea, and Ephesus demonstrate the inclusive nature of the gospel. They are Pentecost extended, not Pentecost as paradigm.[84]

So what is normative, if anything, of that day? If my argument holds, then the phenomena of that day and their reappearance to a limited degree later in the Acts narrative are not to be expected in our experience today. Where we stand in the flow of redemptive history is with the hearers of Peter's proclamation.[85] In the light of the kerygma (prophesying) about the risen Christ

81. Ibid.

82. In the OT, as we saw in an earlier chapter, God filled (empowered) with his Spirit selected members of his people for specific tasks. So too at Pentecost and elsewhere in Acts. Baptism with the Spirit, however, is a new covenant phenomenon. See Delbert R. Rose, "Distinguishing the Things That Differ," *Wesleyan Theological Journal* 9 (Spring 1974): 7. On this point I take a contrary position to that of Keener, *Three Crucial Questions*, 77, who understands the baptism of the Spirit as prophetic empowerment; and also to that of Bloesch who, exegetically speaking, stretches far too far the range of experiences covered by the expression (*Holy Spirit*, 299); and also to that of Smail, who tends to collapse together the baptism of the Spirit and the fullness of the Spirit (*Reflected Glory*, 138).

83. No one more than Jesus underscored both the importance of the Baptist as a prophet and yet that he belonged to a former age in God's redemptive dealings, which was passing away (Matt. 11:7–19).

84. This view is classically and often quaintly put by Kuyper, who carefully distinguishes between extraordinary outpourings of the Spirit as at Pentecost and ordinary outpourings of the Spirit as experienced in the church of his day. As for the relationship between the Jerusalem event and the one at Caesarea, he distinguishes between the "original outpouring" and a "supplementary" one, respectively. The Caesarean event is the Jerusalem one "in a weaker and modified form, but still extraordinary" (*Work of the Holy Spirit*, 125–127). For a contrary view, see Craig S. Keener, *Gift Giver: The Holy Spirit for Today* (Grand Rapids, Mich.: Baker, 2002), 95: "First, Luke presents the empowerment of the church at Pentecost as a normative experience for Christians."

85. Dunn is correct here: "If a norm is desired for the gift of the Spirit we have it not in John 20:22 or Acts 2:4, but in Acts 2:38" (*Baptism in the Spirit*, 182).

we too ought to say, "What shall we do?" (Acts 2:37). And like them we are to repent, be baptized, and receive the gift of the Spirit (vv. 38–39). Thus we too are baptized with the Spirit and become the Messiah's people. Needless to say, many will respectfully—and perhaps not so respectfully—disagree with these conclusions. Others will see in all of the Pentecost event, and the subsequent ones such as Samaria, Caesarea, and Ephesus, a normative pattern for today's church. But here our biblical theology method is crucial. Texts need to be placed in their contexts in their rhetorical settings in their books in the canon in the light of the flow of redemptive history. We shall explore this issue further under implications when we deal with the issue of subsequence. The term "subsequence" refers to the idea that the normative pattern of Spirit baptism or reception or release—the terminology differs from writer to writer—involves a chronological sequence of distinct steps in the Spirit's work, beginning with the new birth.

A host of questions remain concerning Acts 1–2. Do "the promise of the Father," "baptized with the Holy Spirit," "receive power," "filled with the Holy Spirit," and "receive the gift of the Holy Spirit" refer to the same experience, as some have thought?[86] I think not, and offer the following observations. On a positive note, "the promise of the Father" and "baptized with the Spirit" do appear to be referring to the same experience. The baptism with the Spirit has to do with the confession of Jesus as the Lord at the right hand of the Father. The baptism with the Spirit is about "conversion-initiation," as Dunn maintains.[87] However, being clothed with power from on high seems to have to do with the power to testify to the risen Christ, enabled by the filling with the Spirit. Pentecost, therefore, is a complex salvation-historical event. Let's explore that complexity a little further and attempt to be more precise.

In Acts 1 we learn that the Spirit is promised to disciples and that the Spirit will come upon disciples. Further, we find in Acts 2 that the Spirit fills those disciples and that the Spirit is poured out on those disciples. Peter is a case in point. There are other members of the cast of Acts 2, however. Those who respond to Peter's prophesying are not said to be baptized with the Spirit, or filled with the Spirit, or empowered by the Spirit, or to have the Spirit come upon them.[88] What they are told is that they are to repent, to be baptized, and to receive the gift of the Spirit. Distinctions appear to

86. For example, R. A. Torrey and D. L. Moody in Gromacki, "Holy Spirit," 494.

87. Dunn, *Baptism in the Spirit*, 102. See also Karl Barth, *CD*, IV, 4 (Fragment), 34. Charismatic theologian Smail takes a similar view (*Reflected Glory*, 141). Calvin has a very elastic understanding of the baptism with the Holy Spirit, ranging from a pre-Pentecost experience of the apostles, Pentecost itself, and a daily experience for all the elect ("Commentary on Acts," *CJCC*, comment on Acts 1:5).

88. In fact, the language about baptism with the Spirit appears only once more in Acts (Acts 11), and I have argued already that it has to do with entry into the salvation offered by the Lord Jesus Christ.

be needed to do justice to this complexity. There are lesser questions also of some interest: Where were the disciples seated? Was it the upper room or the temple or some other place?[89] The answer may depend on the answer to yet another question: Who received the clothing with power from on high at Pentecost? Was it the eleven or the 120? If the 120, then the upper room becomes problematic because of space limitations, one would think. This last question is worth pursuing a little further.

Many contend that 120 disciples were together on the day of Pentecost and the phenomena were experienced by them all (Acts 1:15 and 2:1). But there are good reasons for questioning this view. To begin with, our chapter divisions are artificial. The immediate antecedent of the "they" of Acts 2:1 is arguably the eleven apostles mentioned in 1:26. There is some textual evidence in support. Those who heard the tongues recognized the disciples as Galileans (cf. Acts 1:11; 2:7). It is reasonable to assume that the group of 120 was broader than just Galileans. Moreover when the thousands respond to Peter's message, they do not ask the 120, "What shall we do?" Instead, they ask "Peter and the rest of the apostles" (2:37).[90] In my view, the apostles were most likely those who were filled with the Spirit and prophesied on that day, perhaps as the nucleus of the prophetic community that would soon emerge.

To change the theological currency, in Johannine terms, the Paraclete had come to continue the prosecution of the world through them, just as Jesus had said (John 14–16). The vindication of Christ was proclaimed, and thousands were convicted of their sin and repented. Thus the promises of John 16:8–11 came to pass: sinners were convicted, Christ was vindicated, and the quotation in Acts 2:34–35 from Psalm 110:1 spoke of enemies being made a footstool.[91] Moreover the promise signaled by the insufflation narrated in John 20:21–23 had also come to pass. The forgiveness of sins was proclaimed in Christ's name (Acts 2:38).

IMPLICATIONS FOR BELIEF AND PRACTICE

A number of important implications of our present discussion need now to be teased out. These include: revisiting the *filioque* debate; the need for

89. In Stephen's speech in Acts 7:47, "house" refers to the temple in Jerusalem. Longenecker argues for the upper room, linking Acts 2:1 with Acts 1:12–26 ("The Acts of the Apostles," *EBC*, comment on Acts 2:1). But his argument is not decisive, especially if the "in those days" of Acts 1:15 indicates a separate occasion to Acts 1:12–14.

90. Gromacki, "Holy Spirit," 479–480. Gromacki succinctly adumbrates some five lines of argument for the apostles rather than the 120 as those described in Acts 2:1. Not all of his arguments are convincing. But enough are, in my opinion. Perhaps it is significant that in Acts 8, when the Samaritans come to faith and a delegation is sent down from Jerusalem to investigate, the delegation consists of apostles and not simply some of the 120. Further, it is only then that the Spirit comes. Pentecost extended.

91. Again, as Ferguson helpfully argues, *Holy Spirit*, 69.

a Trinitarian approach to Pentecost; and the issue of building doctrine on narrative, with the question of subsequence as a case in point.

The Spirit, Filioque, *and the World Religions*

At first glance this may seem an arcane issue to pursue in this context. As we saw in an earlier chapter, the question of the procession of the Spirit is one of long-standing debate. Does the Spirit eternally proceed from the Father and the Son, or does the Spirit eternally proceed from the Father only? How are Christology and pneumatology to be related in answering this question? My own position is more Eastern than Western. The Holy Spirit eternally proceeds from the Father through the Son.[92] In my view, this position preserves the nexus between Christology and pneumatology and does justice to the testimony of John 14–16. In his teaching on the Paraclete, Jesus made reference both to the Father sending the Spirit and to his sending the Spirit. What is of great importance is that whether one takes the Western approach or the Eastern one, in the economy of salvation pneumatology must not be divorced from Christology. The last chapter and the present one reinforce this point. As we saw in the last chapter, in the economy of salvation the Spirit directs the Son; and in this chapter the Son pours out the Spirit.

However, there are an increasing number of theologians who want to separate pneumatology from Christology. According to this view, if pneumatology is divorced from Christology then a new understanding of Christianity's relationship to the world religions might emerge. There can—so some argue—be access to God through the Spirit apart from the Son. As Thomas Smail observes of his own denomination (Anglican) and some of its theologians and bishops, "They do so [abandon *filioque*] be-cause it opens the door to an accepting attitude to other world religions, providing a basis for recognizing in them a valid spiritual relationship to God that bypasses Jesus."[93] Amos Yong observes "a growing agreement in the West regarding the dogmatic illegitimacy of the *Filioque*."[94] He further suggests that, "Rejection of the *Filioque* may free up some room for a development of a pneumatology of religions as a distinct or at least related stream in the history of salvation."[95] Indeed, Yong contends that,

92. As Gregory of Nyssa (d. ca. A.D. 395) argued in "On the Holy Spirit: Against the Fol-lowers of Macedonius," http://www.ccel.org/fathers2/NPNF2-05/Npnf2-05-26.htm#TopOfPage, accessed May 24, 2005.

93. Thomas Smail, *The Giving Gift: The Holy Spirit in Person* (reprint of 2nd ed., Eugene, Ore.: Wipf & Stock, 2004), 125–126.

94. Amos Yong, *Beyond the Impasse: Toward a Pneumatological Theology of Religions* (Grand Rapids, Mich.: Baker, 2003), 186, emphasis original.

95. Ibid., emphasis original. Yong is very much aware of the need for the development of some criteria of discernment with regard to this project, which he sees as still in its infancy (cf. 166 and 192). I find the project problematical.

"the religions of the world, like everything else that exists, are providentially sustained by the Spirit of God for divine purposes."[96] This is the very theological move that worried Karl Barth so much in a previous generation.[97] He had good grounds for his fears. Even so it must be emphasized again that the rejection of *filioque* does not necessarily lead to the embrace of religious pluralism.[98]

Chung Hyun Kyung's address at the World Council of Churches meeting in Canberra in 1991 serves as an important and noted example of the problem.[99] Chung began her provocative address by invoking the spirits of victims.[100] From the Bible she invoked the spirits of such figures as Hagar, Uriah, and many others. Next she invoked the spirits of figures from church and secular history such as the victims of the medieval crusades, Joan of Arc, the Jews of the Holocaust, and many others. Then followed the invocation of the spirits of creation such as the Amazonian rain forest, earth, fire, and others. Lastly she invoked the spirit of Christ ("the Spirit of the liberator"), whom she describes as: ". . . our brother Jesus, tortured and killed on the cross."[101] Her address combined her Asian and feminist concerns.[102] In particular she drew on her Korean heritage and spoke of the Han-ridden spirits. These are the spirits of the victims that injustice has made into wandering spirits. Their voices need to be heard. Indeed she argues, "Without hearing the cries of these spirits we cannot hear the voice of the Holy Spirit."[103] She said, "For us [Koreans] they [the spirits of the ancestors] are the icons of the Holy Spirit who became tangible and visible to us. Because of them we can feel, touch and taste the concrete

96. Quoted in Roger E. Olson, "A Wind That Swirls Everywhere," *Christianity Today*, March, 2006, 53–54. The subject of the article is Yong as a theologian. One wonders how the worship of Moloch with its child sacrifice, as described in the OT, fits into Yong's scheme (Lev. 18:21).

97. See the discussion of Barth's fears in George S. Hendry, *The Holy Spirit in Christian Theology* (Philadelphia: Westminster, 1956), 43–52.

98. The fact that some in rejecting *filioque* also embrace religious pluralism does not show that *filioque* is right. The validity of *filioque* needs to be decided on other grounds. For example, does careful exegesis reveal *filioque* to be a textless doctrine?

99. In 2002 Hyun Kyung dropped the name Chung (her father's name) for publication purposes because of its Korean patriarchal origins ("ZH Interviews [Chung] Hyun Kyung," http: www.zionsherald.org/Sept2003_interview.html, accessed May 20, 2005). Since I am referring to the 1991 address I will use her earlier name. Also note that Clark Pinnock, *Flame of Love: A Theology of the Holy Spirit* (Downers Grove, Ill.: InterVarsity Press, 1996), 208, wrongly places the conference in 1992.

100. Her address, "Come, Holy Spirit—Renew the Whole Creation," is found in Michael Kinnamon, ed., *Signs of the Spirit: Official Report of the Seventh Assembly* (Geneva: WCC, 1991), 37–47.

101. Ibid., 39.

102. Chung's feminist concerns may be seen in the way she consistently designates the Spirit in feminine terms. Her address concludes with, "Let us welcome her, letting ourselves go in her wild rhythm of life. Come Holy Spirit, Renew the Whole Creation. Amen!" (ibid., 46).

103. Ibid., 39.

bodily historical presence of the Holy Spirit in our midst."[104] Her address, according to one observer, was met with "passionate applause" by some and "passionate silence" by others.[105]

The Orthodox and evangelicals at the meeting were dismayed. The Orthodox argued in response that, "We must guard against a tendency *to substitute a 'private' spirit, the spirit of the world or other spirits for the Holy Spirit* who proceeds from the Father and rests in the Son."[106] Their next statement is even stronger: "Our tradition is rich in respect for local and national cultures, but we find it *impossible* to invoke the spirits of 'earth, air, water and sea creatures.'"[107] The evangelicals said, "We argued for a high Christology to serve as the only authentic Christian base for dialogue with persons of other living faiths."[108] There were good grounds for such responses. For example, there were relatively few references to Christ in the address and none to the Trinity.[109] Moreover it seemed so syncretistic.[110] Indeed Chung Hyun Kyung had said, "For me the image of the Holy Spirit comes from the image of *Kwan In*. She is venerated as the goddess of compassion and wisdom by East Asian women's popular religiosity."[111] The common complaint of both the Orthodox participants and the evangelical observers was that pneumatology had been severed from Christology.

In my view, Chung's address shows dramatically the problem if the nexus between Christ and the Holy Spirit is broken. But unlike Barth I am not convinced that *filioque* is needed to prevent the problem. He correctly maintained the *filioque* ties the Spirit irrevocably to Christ, since from all eternity the Spirit proceeds from the Father and the Son. However, as I suggested above, the Spirit eternally proceeds from the Father through the Son, but in time the Spirit is sent by both the Father and the Son, as Messiah, in the economy of salvation. Adhering to a Western understanding of *filioque* is not the only way to preserve the uniqueness and finality of

104. Ibid.

105. Reported in Molly T. Marshall, "Participating in the Life of God: A Trinitarian Pneumatology," *Perspectives in Religious Studies* 30 no. 2 (Summer 2003): 144.

106. See "Reflections of Orthodox Participants," in Kinnamon, ed., *Signs of the Spirit,* 281, emphasis original.

107. Ibid., emphasis mine.

108. See "Evangelical Perspectives from Canberra" (ibid., 282).

109. As Leonid Kishkovsky points out, "Ecumenical Journey: Authentic Dialogue," *Christianity and Crisis* 512 (1991), 228–229. Chung's references to Christ fell far below the high Christology of the NT. Her address stood in marked contrast with that of Parthenios, Orthodox Patriarch of Alexandria and All Africa, whose address "The Holy Spirit" was thoroughly Trinitarian (Kinnamon, ed., *Signs of the Spirit,* 28–37).

110. Hyun Kyung is happy to own the label of "syncretist." In her view, all Christians are syncretists and have been so from the beginning ("ZH Interviews [Chung] Hyun Kyung").

111. Chung Hyun Kyung, "Come, Holy Spirit," Kinnamon, ed., *Signs of the Spirit,* 36, emphasis original.

Christ as the Savior of the world.[112] Hence the strong Orthodox reaction to Chung's speech. And so even if *filioque* is understood only in economic terms, is not the Christocentric focus of the Spirit's ministry still preserved? But someone might object, "What of the Spirit's work in creation and the preservation of creation that was explored in part 2? Have you all too quickly forgotten that the Spirit is 'the Lord and giver of life,' as the ancient Nicene creed says?" Not at all! But Sinclair Ferguson so wisely observes, "Not all divine activity is saving activity."[113] Or put more sharply, not all Spirit activity is saving activity, just as not all grace is saving grace.

Pentecost: A Trinitarian Event

In Peter's explanatory address the Messiah pours out the Spirit, who is the gift from the Father (Acts 2:33). The event needs Father language, Son language, and Spirit language to do the occasion justice without confusing the Persons. A unitarian reading of Pentecost, whether of the Father or the Son or the Spirit, simply does not work. A Trinitarian reading does more justice to the evidence of the text.[114] Why is this important? It is important not only because yet again the description of divine activity falls into triadic form as it does so often at other points in the story of Christ (e.g., conception and baptism, to name just two). It is also important because Christology cannot be translated into pneumatology. There are Christologies that maintain that in his state of glory Jesus has become a Spirit and that the Holy Spirit language is another way of talking of Christ's presence with us now.[115] Given "the present revival of Spirit Christologies," let us explore this idea a little further.[116]

Those who argue for such a Spirit Christology center their attention on Paul's letters.[117] In places in Paul, "Spirit of God" and "Spirit of

112. Pinnock rejects *filioque* and argues that, by doing so, the Spirit's mission can be more broadly conceived, especially as far as the salvation of those who have not heard of Christ is concerned (*Flame of Love*, 196–197). None of this necessarily follows if it is the Father and the Son who send the Spirit in the economy of salvation, as I have argued.

113. Ferguson, *Holy Spirit*, 248.

114. As Edgar observes (*Message of the Trinity*, 225–226). A fine analysis. See also Max Turner's useful discussion, "'Trinitarian' Pneumatology in the New Testament?—Towards an Explanation of the Worship of Jesus," *AsTJ* 57/58 no. 2/1 (Fall 2002/Spring 2003): 177–180.

115. The most notable advocate of this position is Hendrikus Berkhof, *The Doctrine of the Holy Spirit* (Atlanta: John Knox, 1977), esp. chapter 1.

116. David Coffey, "Spirit Christology and the Trinity," in Hinze and Dabney, eds., *Advents of the Spirit*, 315.

117. There are three main kinds of Spirit Christology. The Hendrikus Berkhof kind offers a transformative model: Christ becomes Spirit. The Norman Hook kind presents Jesus as the quintessential, Spirit-possessed man ("A Spirit Christology," *Theology* 75 [1972]: 228). See also G. W. H. Lampe's still influential *God as Spirit* (Oxford: Clarendon, 1977), 117–119, 228, for a similar view. Lampe acknowledges that "Paul and John, however, and the other New Testament writers were unable" to settle for such a reduced Christology (119). The David Coffey

Christ"—so some argue—are interchangeable (Rom. 8:9–11). In his first Corinthian letter, Paul writes of the risen Christ in terms of "the last Adam [who] became life-giving spirit [*pneuma zōopoioun*]"(1 Cor. 15:45). Furthermore, in his second Corinthian letter, Paul identifies the Spirit with the Lord, asserting that, "Now the Lord is the Spirit, and where the Spirit of the Lord is, there is freedom" (2 Cor. 3:17). If this line of argument stands, then Acts and the Paulines are in great conflict. But the argument fails to convince. Recall our interpretative mantra of placing texts in their contexts in their rhetorical units in their books. The most compelling of the texts used to support the kind of Spirit Christology outlined above is the 2 Corinthians one. It is a difficult text on any reckoning.[118] However, considering 2 Corinthians as a whole, we find that the letter closes with one of the greatest Trinitarian texts. The benediction of 2 Corinthians 13:14 runs, "The grace of the Lord Jesus Christ and the love of God and the fellowship of the Holy Spirit be with you all." Consequently when exegeting 3:18 we need to assume that Paul wrote consistently. In other words, we need to adopt a hermeneutic of charity, which assumes that our neighbor knows what he or she is talking about—rather than a hermeneutic of suspicion. If we do, then it is clear that Paul does not confuse the Persons of the Son and the Spirit.

Narrative and Doctrine: The Subsequence Question

Subsequence is the term used by some for the idea that in Acts or Luke–Acts there is a normative pattern of Spirit baptism or reception or release which involves a chronological sequence of distinct steps in the Spirit's work, be-

---

kind argues for an approach that subsumes the Logos Christology of John 1:1–18 within a Spirit Christology ("Spirit Christology and the Trinity," in Hinze and Dabney, eds., *Advents of the Spirit,* 315–338). Another approach is that of Clark H. Pinnock, who advocates a Spirit Christology which is the recognition that Jesus was "a man filled with the Spirit" ("The Role of the Spirit in Redemption," *AsTJ* 52 no. 1 [Spring 1997]: 56). According to this view, such a Spirit Christology does not displace nor subsume a Logos Christology. The way forward is complementary or both/and. In my view, this last approach (Pinnock's) has some merit if understood within Chalcedon's "one person in two natures" framework.

    118. For example, the same evangelical dictionary can offer two incommensurate interpretations of the same passage in different articles. One scholar, R. B. Gaffin Jr., maintains that in the economy of salvation the Spirit is functionally the Lord to us. The identification is economic not ontological. The other scholar, T. Paige, contends that when Paul interprets Ex. 34:34 LXX he identifies Yahweh with the Holy Spirit, who is "the key to the knowledge of God" (see R. B. Gaffin Jr., "Glorification," 4:1, and T. Paige, "Holy Spirit," 5:3, respectively, *DPHL*). C. F. D. Moule offers yet another view, that the "Lord" in the text is "an allusion to the Lord Yahweh of Ex. 34, not to the Lord Jesus" ("The New Testament and the Doctrine of the Trinity: A Short Report on an Old Theme," *The Expository Times* 38 no. 1 [October 1976]: 18). Turner argues in a similar fashion to Moule. In his view, Paul is drawing an analogy between "the role" of Yahweh in Exodus 34 in old covenant times and the role of the Spirit in new covenant times (*Holy Spirit and Spiritual Gifts,* 115, fn 3).

ginning with regeneration.[119] Article 7 of the "Statement of Fundamental Truths" of the Constitution and By-Laws of the General Council of the Assemblies of God clearly exhibits the concept:

> All believers are entitled to and should ardently expect and earnestly seek the promise of the Father, the baptism in the Holy Ghost and fire, according to the command of our Lord Jesus Christ. This was the normal experience of all in the early Christian Church. With it comes the enduement of power for life and service, the bestowment of the gifts and their uses in the work of the ministry (Luke 24:49; Acts 1:4, 8; 1 Corinthians 12:1–3). *This experience is distinct from and subsequent to the experience of the new birth* (Acts 8:12-17; 10:44-46; 11:14-16; 15:7-9).[120]

The pattern of subsequence—so the argument generally runs—is to be found in the narrative of the Gospel of Luke and Acts. According to some, this pattern has two steps, as in the Assemblies of God quotation above, and for others, three steps.[121] The two-step pattern advocates argue that subsequent to regeneration comes the baptism of, with, or by the Spirit. According to this view regeneration is the first blessing and baptism of, with, or by the Spirit is the second blessing. This subsequent experience is

119. I first learned of the term from my old theological teachers, Barnett and Jensen, *Quest for Power*, 40. "Release," according to Packer, is the term more used in Britain by charismatic leaders—and by their German Protestant counterparts—than the one used in the United States. Those who use the term "subsequence" do so to preserve "the unity of salvation in Christ" (*Keep in Step with the Spirit*, 220). Smail illustrates his point. In his *Reflected Glory*, he uses it as a master metaphor covering "receiving," "being baptized with the Spirit," "being filled with the Spirit," and pouring out the Spirit (*Reflected Glory*, 138). Some recent Pentecostal scholars, however, prefer the term "separability" to that of "subsequence." For example, Douglas A. Oss maintains that although separable in theological thought, conversion and the baptism of the Spirit ideally occur together in NT faith ("A Pentecostal/Charismatic View," in Wayne A. Grudem, ed., *Are Miraculous Gifts for Today? Four Views* [Grand Rapids, Mich.: Zondervan, 1996], 255).

120. Quoted in Gordon D. Fee, *Gospel and Spirit: Issues in New Testament Hermeneutics* (Peabody, Mass.: Hendrickson, 1991), 105, emphasis mine. Fee, who is himself a Pentecostal NT scholar, argues that Pentecostalism speaks of a real biblical experience of the Spirit but with wrong biblical descriptors. Moreover he is not convinced that the subsequence argument is exegetically defensible (98, 104–119).

121. Gromacki provides a fair but critical account of the positions and their denominational advocates in "Holy Spirit," 494–496. Roman Catholicism has a two-step understanding of the Spirit's work. "Confirmation perfects Baptismal grace [which is given at an earlier date]" (CCC, part 2, section 2, chapter 1, article 2, V, paragraph 1316 [333]). The proof text for this pattern is found in the story of the Samaritans in Acts 8:14–17 (ibid., paragraph 1315, where the passage is quoted in full). In Orthodoxy the baptism of an infant is immediately followed by anointing with chrism (consecrated oil). This second act of initiation "corresponds to Confirmation in the Western tradition," according to Kallistos Ware (*The Orthodox Way* [London and Oxford: Mowbray, 1981], 133). This is the chrismation of the Holy Spirit or "The seal of the gift of the Holy Spirit" (ibid.). There is no solid exegetical foundation for either the Roman Catholic or the Orthodox positions.

either for sanctification or for power to serve or for both. The Wesleyan-Arminian tradition is an example of the last view. Charles W. Carter, for example, maintains that the disciples were converted before Pentecost, but at Pentecost were baptized with the Holy Spirit. This experience bestowed not only power but also purity.[122] The three-step proponents contend that subsequent to regeneration comes a distinctive experience of the Spirit for sanctification, and beyond that another distinctive Spirit experience for power to serve. For example, among Pentecostals, according to Robert Gromacki, about half, worldwide, advocate the three-step approach, while the Assemblies of God (as mentioned earlier) in 1914 rejected the three-step model and adopted a two-step pattern.[123]

However, others maintain that the narratives in Acts or Luke–Acts are not to be used to build doctrine (i.e., norms for belief and behavior). Put another way, it is methodologically flawed to build doctrine on narrative, unless, of course, the narrative has didactic elements embedded in it, as I shall argue shortly. I have already tipped my hand in this debate. The differences in the Acts accounts make our drawing a normative pattern from them too difficult. Just recall the Samaritans' experience, which appears to have involved two steps; and that of Cornelius, which appears to have been one step. Which one do we make a norm?[124] Furthermore, there is a good case for regarding the experience of the apostles as unique since they followed Jesus through the transition from the old to the new covenant. The contemporary Christian cannot do that. Still further, the dramatic accounts of Spirit-reception subsequent to Pentecost are arguably extensions of Pentecost rather than paradigms for today. As D. A. Carson observes, "The way Luke tells the story, Acts provides not a paradigm for individual Christian experience, but an account of the gospel's outward movement, geographically, racially, and above all theologically."[125]

---

122. Charles W. Carter, "Baptism with the Holy Spirit," in Richard S. Taylor, ed., *Beacon Dictionary of Theology* (Kansas City: Beacon Hill, 1983), 64–65. Interestingly John Wesley apparently never used the terms "baptism with or in or by the Spirit" with regard to sanctification. See Robert A. Mattke, "The Baptism of the Holy Spirit as Related to the Work of Entire Sanctification," *Wesleyan Theological Journal* 5 no. 1 (Spring 1970): 24–27.

123. Gromacki, "Holy Spirit," 495. It is curious that Veli-Matti Kärkkäinen lists some five theological motifs that characterize Pentecostalism but enduement with power for service is not one of them. Yet earlier on the same page he maintains that, "Empowerment through the Spirit for witnessing and service are emphasized." Of course, it is possible that he believes that such an enduement is analytically contained in his fifth motif, which is "the baptism of the Spirit evidenced by speaking in tongues." See his *An Introduction to Ecclesiology: Ecumenical, Historical, and Global Perspectives* (Downers Grove, Ill.: InterVarsity Press, 2002), 71.

124. The same problem attends any attempt to turn the Acts stories of the Spirit and water baptism into a normative pattern. The Samaritans were baptized well before receiving the Spirit (Acts 8), while Cornelius was baptized in or with water after receiving the Spirit (Acts 10). See Scobie, *Ways of Our God*, 283.

125. D. A. Carson, *Showing the Spirit: A Theological Exposition of 1 Corinthians 12–14* (Grand Rapids, Mich.: Baker, 2003), 150.

However, the controversy raises the important question of what to do with narrative, doctrinally speaking.[126] Do we ignore narrative when building doctrine? Do we use the Epistles to build doctrine and narrative for illustrative purposes? Bernard Ramm, for example, argues,

> To build a theology of the Holy Spirit primarily on the Book of Acts is contrary to the fundamental Protestant principle of interpretation: *Scripture interprets Scripture*. The great theology of the Holy Spirit is clearest in John's Gospel and Paul's letters. Here is where the great doctors of the church have built their doctrine of the Holy Spirit, and rightly so.[127]

Or again, Ferguson in his discussion of Acts maintains that, "We are to find doctrine that is already formulated elsewhere *illustrated* in the historical narratives."[128] Or is that approach unnecessarily restrictive, as both Grant Osborne and Craig S. Keener suggest?[129] Isn't it the genius of God to speak and act in history? Does not God have a story and does not his activity generate stories of his character, will, and ways? In other words, doctrine? If so, then does it not follow that all this is true for the Spirit? What is the way forward?

Scripture at times is merely descriptive. Jesus was crucified, but there is no norm to be drawn from the story for capital punishment and its methods. Scripture may be prescriptive. The love of God and neighbor are not optional. Scripture may be proscriptive. The worship of idols is never morally acceptable. Lastly, Scripture may be concessive, for example, Paul's careful discussion of singleness and marriage in the light of "the present distress" (1 Cor. 7:1–40, esp. v. 6 and v. 26). Narratives are descriptive but may also contain prescriptive or proscriptive or concessive elements. Moreover they may include didactic elements as actors in the narrative comment or command. When biblical narratives do so, they become significant for forming doctrine and not simply for illustrating doctrine formed from undeniably didactic portions of Scripture. As Paul Barnett and Peter Jensen rightly sug-

---

126. For a brief but useful presentation of the two main approaches to the Baptism with the Spirit question see Gregory A. Boyd and Paul R. Eddy, "Appendix," in *Across the Spectrum: Understanding Issues in Evangelical Theology* (Grand Rapids, Mich.: Baker, 2002), accessed at www.bakeracademic.com/acrossthespectrum, "Issue 7: The Debate over the Baptism in the Holy Spirit," 10–13. The website contains material not included in the book proper.

127. Bernard Ramm, *Rapping about the Spirit* (Waco, Tex.: Word, 1974), 113, emphasis original.

128. Ferguson, *Holy Spirit,* 84, emphasis original. For him, "This is a generally valuable principle" (ibid.). However, in his view: ". . . the structure and theological flow of Acts itself indicates that these events are not to be thought of as paradigmatic but, each in its own context, as *sui generis*" (ibid., emphasis original).

129. For spirited defenses of the appeal to narrative to establish doctrine see Grant Osborne, *The Hermeneutical Spiral: A Comprehensive Introduction to Biblical Interpretation* (Downers Grove, Ill.: InterVarsity Press, 1991), 172; and Keener, *Gift Giver,* 209–213.

gest, "We may indeed gather commands, promises, and doctrine from the words of an apostolic speech addressed to the public whether Christian or general."[130] Peter's interpretation in Acts 11 of the events of Pentecost and at Cornelius's house are an example of how narrative—in this instance, the story of his report to the Jerusalem leadership—may prove doctrinally instructive. From Peter's speech we learn that what happened to him at Pentecost was the promised baptism with the Spirit and that that too was Cornelius's experience. Apart from that comment there is no other text in Acts that explicitly and retrospectively links both the baptism with the Spirit and the events of Pentecost.[131]

This chapter and the last one explored the relationship between the Spirit and Christ. We have seen in them a story of successive subordinations. In the state of humiliation the Messiah is directed by the Spirit. In the state of glory, the vindicated Messiah directs the Spirit. But to what end? Answering that question is our next task.

---

130. Barnett and Jensen, *Quest for Power,* 15.

131. John Stott makes a wise general hermeneutical comment: "What I *am* saying is that what is descriptive is valuable only insofar as it is interpreted by what is didactic. Some of the biblical narratives which describe events are self-interpreting because they include an explanatory comment, whereas others cannot be interpreted in isolation but only by the light of doctrinal or ethical teaching which is given elsewhere" (*Baptism and Fulness: The Work of the Holy Spirit Today,* 2nd ed. [London: Inter-Varsity, 1975], 15, emphasis original). In Cornelius's case the narrative is in Acts 10 but the explanatory comment does not come until Acts 11.

NINE

THE SPIRIT, THE CHURCH, AND THE HOPE OF GLORY

God has a project. He won't let his fallen creation go. Jesus Christ is the linchpin of the divine plan. The primordial promise found in the *protoevangelium* has its fulfillment in him (Gen. 3:15). The promises to Abraham and their realization find their focus in him (cf. Gen. 12:1–3 and Gal. 3:16). The promise of Israel as the ideal servant of God is instantiated in him (cf. Isa. 53:4 and Matt. 8:17). The hope of Israel has indeed come, and he has now poured out his Spirit. And integral to that plan is the creation of a people who walk in the ways of God. The divine project involves nothing less than God's people living under God's rule, in God's way in God's place.[1] And God's place will be nothing less than a renewed heavens and earth, a restored creation.[2] The end point will be higher than the beginning one. Not so much paradise regained as Milton thought, rather paradise transfigured. The living God is on a mission.[3] The story of the church and the believers who make it up is generated by this mission. Pentecost is a crucial event in that story. The people of the Messiah have life in the Spirit. A new age has dawned but the best is yet to be. As Charles H. H. Scobie observes, "In keeping with the 'already–not yet' tension so characteristic of the NT, the presence of the Spirit not only is evidence that the new order has dawned, but also points forward to the final consummation of God's purposes."[4]

1. See Graeme Goldsworthy, *Gospel and Kingdom* (Exeter, England: Paternoster, 1981), 47. However, I have added "in God's way."
2. As Charles W. Carter argues, "The Holy Spirit in the History of Redemption," *Wesleyan Theological Journal* 5 no. 1 (Spring 1970): 35.
3. See Harry R. Boer, *Pentecost and Missions* (Grand Rapids, Mich.: Eerdmans, 1961).
4. Charles H. H. Scobie, *The Ways of Our God: An Approach to Biblical Theology* (Grand Rapids, Mich., and Cambridge: Eerdmans, 2003), 277.

In many works on pneumatology the approach is to devote a chapter to the Spirit and the individual, and another one to the Spirit and the church. However, in this chapter we will explore life in the Spirit as a corporate reality with individual implications. In other words the blessings for the individual will be discussed in the larger context of the blessings of the Spirit for the church.[5] As Richard B. Gaffin Jr. suggests,

> We must recognize that Scripture is just not interested in the question of individual religious experience in the way we are inclined to be preoccupied with it. What the New Testament does disclose of the individual repercussions of the Spirit's work largely results as it accents . . . broader Christological and ecclesiological concerns.[6]

In many ways evangelicalism is a printing press religion. So much of our practice would be very difficult without the invention of the printing press. Thanks to Gutenberg and Caxton we have our individual devotional time with a copy of the Scriptures open. We read books of spiritual worth in the privacy of our own home. This is a great boon in the providence of God. However, our first move in spiritual matters as a consequence may become so easily, "What's in it for *me?*" Likewise with regard to the Spirit. Our questions may revolve around me as an individual: "How can I be filled with the Spirit?" "What steps must I take to be filled with the Spirit?" And, sure enough, there will be a book on the subject. Again, this is not a complaint. But as we shall see, Paul's command to be filled with, or by, the Spirit is addressed in the first instance to the church, not the individual. Believers in earlier times understood this. As Mark Noll points out, "Up to the early 1700s, British Protestants preached on God's plan *for the church*. From the mid-1700s, however, evangelicals emphasized God's plans *for the individual*."[7] Sadly, a deep appreciation of ecclesiology has not usually been regarded as a modern evangelical strength.[8]

In this chapter we will begin with the *missio Dei* (mission of God) in the light of the exaltation of Christ. Pentecost will be revisited. Was it the

---

5. Interestingly, in Barth's Christology he discusses the work of Christ in the church in priority over that of Christ in the believer (*CD*, IV). I believe pneumatology needs a similar prioritizing. For those who want more on the individual and the Spirit, again, as I did in the introduction, I invite the reader to explore the excellent volume in this series by Bruce Demarest, *The Cross and Salvation: The Doctrine of Salvation* (Wheaton, Ill.: Crossway, 1997).

6. Richard B. Gaffin Jr., *Perspectives on Pentecost: New Testament Teaching on the Gifts of the Holy Spirit* (Phillipsburg, N.J.: Presbyterian & Reformed, 1980), 37.

7. Mark Noll, "Father of Modern Evangelicals?" *Christian History* 38 (vol. 12, no. 2, 1993): 44 (emphasis original).

8. Packer and Stibbs preserve the balance between the individual and the church. See A. M. Stibbs and J. I. Packer, *The Spirit within You: The Church's Neglected Possession* (London: Hodder & Stoughton, 1967).

birth of the church or simply another stage in the life of the people of God?[9] What place has Israel in the story? Next we will explore how God is making his children, and especially the Spirit's role. Then follows an examination of the idea of the body of Christ. Here the Pauline understanding of the baptism of the Spirit will figure prominently. So too will how the Spirit gifts the body for ministry and service. Next we will give thought to how ordinances (sacraments) of the Lord, that are features of the life of Christ's community, are related to the Spirit's work. But the body of Christ is not the only NT image of our corporate reality. We are corporately the temple of the Holy Spirit and individually temples of the same Spirit. The relationship of holiness and the Spirit will need our attention. Other important topics of interest to be considered are the role of the Spirit in reviving the church, in preserving the church in an unbelieving world, and in the worship of the church. Next we attend to the future as we examine the role of the Spirit and the hope of glory in its corporate, individual, and cosmic dimensions. Lastly we draw out some of the implications for life in the Spirit today.

PENTECOST REVISITED

In the previous chapter we considered Pentecost in relation to Christology. The ascended, enthroned Messiah is the bestower of the Spirit. Our focus now shifts to the relation between Christology, pneumatology, and ecclesiology. Was Pentecost the birth of the church as the new people of God in distinction to Israel? Or was Pentecost another stage in the unfolding history of the one people of God? Does Pentecost represent the restoration of Israel, albeit in remnant form? With any of these views Pentecost belongs to the *historia salutis* (salvation-history) and not the *ordo salutis* (order of salvation).[10] That is to say, Pentecost is to be understood as a salvation-history event and not simply an application of divine salvation that bears many repetitions.[11] As D. A. Carson finely says, "In short, Pentecost in Luke's perspective is *first of all* a climactic salvation-historical event."[12]

---

9. A. M. Stibbs speaks for many Protestants when he claims that, "The day of Pentecost has been rightly called the birthday of the Church" (*God's Church: A Study in the Biblical Doctrine of the People of God* (London: Inter-Varsity Fellowship, 1968), 44. The Roman Catholic Church takes a similar view: ". . . the Second Vatican Council speaks *of the Church's birth* on the day of Pentecost" (John Paul II, *The Holy Spirit in the Life of the Church and the World: Dominum et Vivificantem,* trans. Vatican [Boston: Pauline Books & Media, 1986], 38, emphasis original).

10. A point well made by Gaffin, *Perspectives on Pentecost,* 22.

11. Contra the Pentecostal view that, "This outpouring [Pentecost] is understood by Pentecostals to have been reenacted at Azusa Street in the early twentieth century, and continued all the way through to the present via the charismatic renewal, Third Wave, and Toronto Blessing movements" (Amos Yong, "The Marks of the Church: A Pentecostal Re-Reading," *Evangelical Review of Theology* 26 no. 1 (2002): 61.

12. D. A. Carson, *Showing the Spirit: A Theological Exposition of 1 Corinthians 12–14* (Grand Rapids, Mich.: Baker, 2003), 140, emphasis mine.

Recall that in a previous chapter I argued that apparent "repetitions" of Pentecost phenomena are extensions of the primordial event which show that the new community consists of all categories of humanity (Jews, Samaritans, Gentiles, and John the Baptist's disciples). In other words, I maintained that these events belong to the *historia salutis*. In my view, Pentecost is the birth of "the body of Christ," to use a Pauline descriptor, beginning with "the restored remnant of Israel" and extending thence to the world of the Gentiles in fulfillment of the ancient Abrahamic promises.[13] The community that emerges is new in that sense. The Spirit of the *risen* Christ now animates it.[14] This was not Abraham's experience under the old covenant but it is that of the believer post-Pentecost. As Packer and Stibbs argue,

> . . . the full activity of the Spirit under the New Covenant was one which in the nature of the case He could not begin till Jesus, having made atonement for our sins, was risen and ascended. For this new task was precisely to glorify before men's eyes the glorified Jesus of Nazareth—that is, to make them see the glory of His finished work of redemption, to make His presence with them, as the reigning Lord, a conscious reality, to unite them to Him in His risen life and make them understand what this union means, and to lead them into the wealth of the salvation which He won for them.[15]

Again, using a Pauline idea, as Acts unfolds we see the Gentiles grafted into the vine of believing Israel (Rom. 11:11–24). Put another way, the restoration of Israel has begun and Gentiles have a place at the table.[16] The God of the Bible is saving a people and not simply individuals here and there. Hence the importance of the Jerusalem Council of Acts 15.

13. See Donald Robinson, *Faith's Framework: The Structure of New Testament Theology* (Sutherland: Albatross, 1985), 97; and William J. Dumbrell, *The Search for Order: Biblical Eschatology in Focus* (Eugene, Ore.: Wipf & Stock, 2001), 225.

14. Raymond E. Brown points out that there are seventy references to *pneuma* in Acts, which is about one-fifth of NT instances (*The Churches the Apostles Left Behind* [New York: Paulist, 1984], 65). But surprisingly he misses somewhat the connection between Christology and pneumatology in Acts.

15. Stibbs and Packer, *Spirit within You*, 28–29. E. L. Mascall terms this union "adoptive union" and distinguishes it from two others: the essential union of Father, Son, and Holy Spirit in the triune Godhead, and the hypostatic union of Christ's divine and human natures in one Person (*Christ, the Christian, and the Church* [London: Longman, Green, 1963], 92). This analysis is helpful but his idea of baptismal regeneration as the means to establish the adoptive union is decidedly not.

16. The restoration theme is very ably argued by Dumbrell, *Search for Order*, 219–234; Luke Timothy Johnson, *The Writings of the New Testament: An Interpretation*, rev. ed. (Minneapolis: Fortress, 1999), 237–239; and Max Turner, *The Holy Spirit and Spiritual Gifts: Then and Now*, rev. ed. (Carlisle, England: Paternoster, 1999), 45–56. Others see Pentecost in terms of "empowerment for mission" (Menzies, Mainville, and Stronstad) or more generally the bestowal of "the charismatic empowerment of the church" (Mainville again, and Haya-Prat). See the discussion in Max Turner (ibid.).

The relationship between the Pauline communities and the Jerusalem church was a theological question and not merely a pragmatic one. Unity in fellowship although not uniformity in all practices is an Acts value, just as it is in the wider NT—a matter we will discuss at greater length at a later stage.

Importantly, the Spirit impels the Christian mission in Acts. With the Pentecostal outpouring comes boldness to proclaim the gospel in the face of hostility (Acts 4:23–31). The Spirit directs Philip to the Ethiopian eunuch and Peter to the house of Cornelius (8:29 and 10:19–20, respectively). It is the Spirit who commands the setting apart of Barnabas and Paul for outreach to the Gentiles (13:1–3). It not only seems good to the Jerusalem leadership that no hindrances be put in the way of the Pauline mission to the Gentiles. It is also good to the Holy Spirit (15:28). Again, the Spirit keeps Paul on track when he might have been deflected from the mission to Macedonia (16:6–10). Paul's mission plans are resolved in the Spirit (19:21–22). Raymond Brown concludes in his review of the Acts evidence, "Thus every essential step in this story of how witness was borne to Christ from Jerusalem to the ends of the earth is guided by the Spirit, whose presence becomes obvious at great moments where human agents would otherwise be hesitant or choose wrongly."[17]

THE SPIRIT AND THE MAKING AND SAVING OF GOD'S PEOPLE

The question now becomes, if Pentecost is the restoration of Israel in some sense to its prophetic role in mission to the entire world, how do individuals either Jew or Gentile join that people? Answering that question requires both a story of God's initiative and a story of our response. Put another way, how are individuals incorporated into the body of Jesus the Messiah? How does the triune God make a people for himself? Or again, to use what has been described as "probably the most general term in the Bible for the great gift which men receive by believing in Jesus Christ"[18]—how is salvation provided for the people of God? After all, it is the story of this salvation that Israel is to tell to the nations.

---

17. Brown, *Churches the Apostles Left Behind*, 68. I am much indebted to Brown for this paragraph. But I am also much surprised at his contention that a weakness in Acts is its triumphalism. The mission, he argues, shows constant numerical growth in its impact. But what if churches these days experience decline? However, Acts is more complex than he allows. There is great initial growth of believers among Jews, but the numbers of Gentiles converted never attain to the same numbers (cf. Acts 2:41, 47; 4:4; and 17:32–34). Israel was expecting a messianic age; the Gentile world was not. Church growth advocates in their appeal to numbers in Acts often miss this nuance too. Moreover, Acts ends with the great Apostle to the Gentiles in Rome under house arrest (28:16). This is a strange form of triumphalism.

18. I. H. Marshall, *Christian Beliefs: A Brief Introduction* (London: Inter-Varsity Fellowship, 1966), 58.

The Story of the Divine Initiative

The story of divine initiative accents the triune God's work in bringing individuals into his people and into his family.[19] Entry may be individual, but what is entered is corporate.[20] As argued in a previous chapter, Luke–Acts points to the baptism with or in the Spirit as the key concept for understanding this initiation-conversion. Baptism is an entry motif. Paul tells a similar story, in my view. The classical text is in 1 Corinthians 12:13, and it bears quotation in full: "For in [en] one Spirit we were all baptized into one body—Jews or Greeks, slaves or free—and all were made to drink of one Spirit." It is safe to surmise that Christ is the unnamed baptizer.[21] The Spirit is the element. Incorporation into the body of the risen Christ is the goal.[22] In Johannine terms, to become God's child requires nothing less than a new birth (or a birth "from above," gennēthē anōthen), as Nicodemus found out (John 3:3, 7). The Spirit is indeed the giver of life and new life, as the Nicene Creed affirms.[23] This too is a work of the Spirit, as Jesus argued with this teacher of Israel who should have known better (cf. John 1:11–12 and 3:5–8).[24] Barth writes, "Baptism with the Spirit is effective, causative, even creative action on man and in man . . . his [man's] being clothed upon with a new garment which is Jesus Christ Himself, his endowment with a new heart, controlled by Jesus Christ, his new generation and birth in brotherhood with Jesus Christ."[25] Barth thus synthesizes a number of biblical motifs, including not only baptism with the Spirit (Luke–Acts), and regeneration and birth (Johannine), but also being clothed with Christ (Pauline).

19. If this book were a general treatment of the doctrine of salvation, this objective story would start in eternity with the predestinating and elective purposes of the triune God. See Demarest, Cross and Salvation, chapter 3.

20. As Gordon Fee observes (God's Empowering Presence: The Holy Spirit in the Letters of Paul [Peabody, Mass.: Hendrickson, 2005], 846). The Pauline epistles are instructive here if one parallels Galatians 2:20, "the Son of God who loved [agapēsantos] me and gave [paradontos] himself on my behalf"(individual) and Ephesians 5:25, "the Christ loved [ēgapēsen] the church and gave [paredōken] himself on her behalf" (corporate) (my translation). Paul affirmed both the one and the many.

21. As John Stott forcefully argues (Baptism and Fulness: The Work of the Holy Spirit Today, 2nd ed. [London: Inter-Varsity, 1975], 38–43); Wayne Grudem, Systematic Theology: An Introduction to Biblical Doctrine (Leicester, England, and Grand Rapids, Mich.: Inter-Varsity and Zondervan, 1994), is excellent on this point also (766–773).

22. The verbs "were baptized" (ebaptisthēmen) and "were made to drink" (epotisthēmen) are aorist in aspect, suggesting some definitive event. Conversion is the best candidate, in context.

23. Daniel L. Migliore (Faith Seeking Understanding: An Introduction to Christian Theology, 2nd ed. [Grand Rapids, Mich., and Cambridge: Eerdmans, 2004], 228) is probably correct in suggesting that the Nicene Creed had both ideas in view.

24. See the helpful discussion in Dumbrell, Search for Order, 243–245, esp. the backdrop of Ezekiel 37.

25. Karl Barth, CD, IV, 4 (Fragment), 34, quoted in Thomas A. Smail, "The Doctrine of the Holy Spirit," in John Thompson, ed., Theology Beyond Christendom: Essays on the Centenary of the Birth of Karl Barth, May 10, 1886 (Allison Park, Pa.: Pickwick, 1986), 100–101.

In the Reformed tradition, theologians maintain that part of the objective work of salvation is the call of God in the gospel to the hearers to repent and believe. The call heard with the physical ears is termed the "external call," and with such a call there comes an effective, internal call by the Holy Spirit, who enables repentance and faith in the kerygma on the part of those who are elect. The famous *Westminster Confession of Faith* uses the language of effectual call by the Spirit. T. L. Wilkinson comments on chapter 10 of the *Confession,* which is entitled "Of Effectual Calling": "The CF describes this as effectual calling, because the word was accompanied by the inner working of the Holy Spirit in the hearts of the hearers, enabling them to repent and believe the Gospel."[26] However, there is no real exegetical evidence for this specialized role of the Spirit. There are NT references to God's call (e.g., Rom. 9:11) and to the Lord (presumably, the Lord Jesus) opening the heart, as in the case of Lydia, to pay attention to the apostolic word (e.g., Acts 16:14). Of course, one might appeal to the doctrine of appropriation and argue that it is fitting to describe this as the Spirit's work, rather than simply assume that it is.[27]

The Story of Our Response

This story concerns the human response to the gospel in repentance and faith. A long-standing debate in theology is whether regeneration (the impartation of new life) precedes repentance and faith, and indeed is the presupposition of the response (broadly speaking, the Reformed tradition) or whether regeneration is dependent upon repentance and faith (broadly speaking, the Arminian tradition).[28] With either view, the Spirit is usually regarded as intimately connected to human responsiveness to the gospel. Barth has an apposite comment:

> The change which God has made (in man) is in truth man's liberation.
> It comes upon him wholly from without, from God. The point is that

26. T. L. Wilkinson, *The Westminster Confession Now: An Exposition of a Reformation Document with a Message for Today, in Todays* [*sic*] *Language* (Australia: Wilkinson, 1992), 75. Many Reformed treatments of the objective work of the Spirit in salvation maintain that effectual calling is especially the work of the Spirit. For example see Louis Berkhof, *A Summary of Christian Doctrine* (London: Banner of Truth, 1968); 116 is typical: "The internal call is really the external call [through the preached or written gospel] made effective by the operation of the Holy Spirit." Likewise Demarest, *Cross and Salvation,* 221–227.

27. It is interesting to observe that when J. I. Packer treats the doctrine of effectual call he quotes the *Westminster Confession of Faith* and attributes the effectiveness of the call to the Holy Spirit. But not one of the Scripture references he cites refers explicitly to the Spirit. His discussion is typical (J. I. Packer, *Concise Theology: A Guide to Historic Christian Beliefs* [Australia, Singapore, and England: Anzea, Campus Crusade Asia, and Inter-Varsity, 1993], 152–153).

28. Demarest offers an interesting alternative. He contends that the effectual calling imparts to the sinner the ability to repent and believe, and regeneration follows (*Cross and Salvation,* 227).

here as everywhere, the omnicausality of God must not be construed as His sole causality. The divine change in whose accomplishment a man becomes a Christian is an event of true intercourse between God and man.[29]

The confession of Christ as Lord is a case in point. That confession is fundamental to Christian existence. As Paul argues in Romans, unless you believe God raised Jesus from the dead and confess him as Lord, then you are not saved (Rom. 10:9–10). Of course there is an intimate connection between the resurrection of Jesus and his Lordship. Hence the conjunction of these ideas is not surprising (Acts 2:32–36). But that is not the end of the story. Paul makes it clear to the Corinthians on a separate occasion that it is the Holy Spirit who enables the confession of Christ as Lord: "no one can say 'Jesus is Lord' except in [or "by"] the Holy Spirit" (1 Cor. 12:3).

To tell the story of the making of God's people requires two tracks: the divine one of what God has done for us in Christ and in us by the Spirit, as well as the human one of how the Spirit is intimately involved in facilitating our very human, but nonmeritorious, responses of repentance and faith. We are saved therefore by the merits of another, the Christ, as applied by His Spirit. These divine and human stories are well summed up by A. M. Stibbs: ". . . God makes us His people in Christ, by the Spirit, through faith."[30]

THE SPIRIT, CHRIST'S BENEFITS, AND GOD'S PEOPLE

A fresh question suggests itself: How are Christ's benefits accessed by both the church and the individual believer? The answer is pneumatological, as Calvin realized centuries ago. Calvin argued that as long as we are outside of Christ all his benefits are beyond us. But if the Spirit unites us to Christ then all is ours. He famously wrote,

> We must examine this question. How do we receive these benefits which the Father bestowed on his only-begotten Son—not for Christ's own private use but that he might enrich poor and needy men? First, we must understand that as long as Christ remains outside of us, and we are separated from him, all that he has suffered and done for the salvation of the human race remains useless and of no value for us. . . . all that he possesses is nothing to us until we grow into one body with him. . . . To sum up, the Holy Spirit is the bond by which Christ effectually unites us to himself.[31]

29. Barth, *CD*, IV, 4 (Fragment), 22–23, quoted in Smail, "Doctrine of the Holy Spirit," 101.
30. Stibbs, *God's Church*, 50.
31. John Calvin, "Institutes of the Christian Religion," *CJCC*, III.1.1. Calvin's heading for chapter 1 is, "The Things Spoken Concerning Christ Profit Us by the Secret Working of the

More recently, and in Calvin's wake, Robert Letham contends, "Union with Christ is, in fact, the foundation of all the blessings of salvation. Justification, sanctification, adoption and glorification are all received through our being united to Christ."[32]

Both Calvin and Letham have firm support in Paul. Paul, in particular, helps us understand the significance of union with Christ and the role of the Spirit in securing that union. First, in his discussion of the body of Christ, Paul writes, "For in one Spirit we were all baptized into one body—Jews or Greeks, slaves or free—and all were made to drink of one Spirit" (1 Cor. 12:13). It is unlikely that Paul is arguing that the Spirit is the baptizer, although some take this line. More likely this Pauline statement is all of a piece with those in the Gospels and Acts, that it is Christ who is the baptizer—as has been argued in previous chapters—and that the Spirit is the medium. Baptism with or in the Spirit is about entry into the new life and the new community of Christ's body. If so, Paul is arguing that the risen Christ unites members to himself through the agency of the Spirit. The intimacy of the union is underscored earlier in this same epistle when Paul writes to discourage immorality in the congregation. Members of Christ should never be made members of a prostitute (1 Cor. 6:15). Becoming one body with a prostitute is problematical in the extreme, given that "he who is joined to the Lord [Jesus] becomes one spirit with him" (vv. 16–18). An extraordinary claim! Sexual immorality, unlike other sins, is a sin against one's own body, and that body belongs to another, i.e., to God himself. Second, in Ephesians Paul makes it plain that believers have been blessed "in Christ with every spiritual blessing in the heavenly places" (Eph. 1:3). Paul locates the blessings of salvation such as redemption and the forgiveness of sins "in him [Christ]" (Eph. 1:7–10).

THE SPIRIT AND EMPOWERING GOD'S PEOPLE

God's empowerment of his people had a long history before the day of Pentecost described in Acts 2. We see such empowerment in leaders like Moses, in prophets like Elijah and Elisha, and in kings like David. We saw all this in an earlier part of this work. John the Baptist knew such empowerment and, supremely, so did Jesus. However, our present aim is to understand the nature of the Spirit's empowering work post-Pentecost.

Spirit," and that of the first section is, "The Holy Spirit as the Bond That Unites Us to Christ." Luther similarly saw unity with Christ as the key to obtaining the benefits of salvation. He drew an analogy between marriage and Christ and the believer. Becoming one flesh in marriage leads to a great exchange. The riches of the one become those of the other. See Martin Luther, "Freedom of the Christian Man," in John Dillenberger, ed., *Martin Luther: Selections from His Writings* (Garden City, N.Y.: Anchor, 1961).

32. Robert Letham, *The Work of Christ* (Leicester, England: Inter-Varsity, 1993), 80. He refers to Calvin's argument on the very next page.

Repeatedly in Luke–Acts we find references to those filled with the Spirit. Significantly, we find that this expression is often followed by the conjunction "and."[33] For example, right at the start of Luke we find that John the Baptist will be filled with the Spirit and will turn many to the Lord (Luke 1:15–16). Elizabeth was filled with the Holy Spirit and exclaimed a blessing upon Mary (vv. 41–42). Again, Zechariah was filled with the Holy Spirit and prophesied (v. 67). Similarly in Acts we read of those gathered together on the day of Pentecost that they were filled with the Spirit and spoke in other tongues (Acts 2:4). As the Acts narrative further unfolds, the believers face hostility. However, filled with the Holy Spirit, they continued to speak the word of God (the gospel) with boldness (*"parrēsia,"* Acts 4:31). At Paphos, Paul confronted Elymas the magician. We read that Paul was filled with the Holy Spirit and pronounced a rebuke (13:9–10). These examples show that the filling of the Holy Spirit and some kind of speech act are joined. This kind of fullness empowers the disciples.

The book of Acts contains another kind of conjunction, where the filling of the Spirit is conjoined to some aspect of character or personal life. In Acts 6 we read of the seven men of good repute who were sought to relieve the apostles from table duty. These men were to be full of the Spirit and wisdom (Acts 6:3). One of the seven gets special mention. Stephen is described as full of faith and the Holy Spirit (v. 5). Later in Acts, Barnabas is described in the same terms: full of the Holy Spirit and faith (11:24). In Acts 13 the disciples are presented as full of the Holy Spirit and joy (v. 52).[34]

The two kinds of fullness delineated above ("fullness and") need to be distinguished from the kind of fullness Paul writes about in Ephesians 5:18–21. Those verses are one long sentence in the Greek (correct in the ESV but broken up in the NIV):

> And do not get drunk with wine, for that is debauchery, but be filled [continuously, imperative, second person plural, present aspect] with the Spirit [lit., "in" or "by Spirit"], addressing [continuously, present participle] one another in psalms and hymns and spiritual songs, singing and making melody [continuously, both present participles] to the Lord with your heart, giving thanks [continuously, present participle] always and for everything to God the Father in the name

---

33. See D. Broughton Knox, in Tony Payne, ed., *D. Broughton Knox: Selected Works, Volume 1: The Doctrine of God* (Kingsford, N.S.W.: Matthias Media, 2000), 271–272. I am very much indebted to Knox for this paragraph.

34. Again, see ibid., 271–272. For another set of distinctions addressing the same textual phenomena see Delbert R. Rose, "Distinguishing the Things That Differ," *Wesleyan Theological Journal* 9 (Spring 1974): 3–12. His categories are "charismatic fullness" (e.g., Luke 1:67), "ecstatic fullness" (e.g., Acts 13:52), and "ethical fullness" (e.g., Acts 15:8–9). These are Rose's examples. I prefer my adaptation of Knox's descriptors. The use of "charismatic" to describe the experience of John the Baptist and Zechariah, for example, I find somewhat confusing in the light of 1 Corinthians 12–14.

of our Lord Jesus Christ, submitting [continuously, present participle] to one another out of reverence for Christ.[35]

In view, in this passage, is the congregation. In this congregational context, the fullness of the Spirit or by the Spirit shows itself in other-person-centered corporate activities as well as in relating to God. These are the sorts of activities that foster unity in the body of Christ.[36]

Among evangelicals the traditional understanding of Ephesians 5:18–21 is individualistic rather than congregational. Paul is drawing a contrast between being under the control of wine like the Gentiles and being under the control of the Spirit. In the congregation, being under the control of the Spirit (v. 18) shows in the behavior described in verses 19–21. Paul commands the individual reader to be continuously under the control of the Spirit—so the argument runs.

This common approach has been challenged by a newer view. According to this view, Paul is commanding the readers to let the Spirit fill the congregation with these other-person-centered practices. These practices constitute the filling rather than the Spirit's controlling presence per se.[37] Ephesians 5:18–21 is not about Christian sanctification or empowerment for service.[38] Put another way, Ephesians 5:18–21 is not about the indwelling of the Spirit in the individual and its consequences. The Pauline command to be filled with or by the Spirit is thus to be understood as an expression of Pauline ecclesiology, as Andreas J. Köstenberger argues.[39]

If the newer view is followed, then what of the Spirit's fullness and the individual? What can be said? These important questions we shall return to at a later stage in the discussion, when we consider the implications of our discussion for belief and behavior.

The Spirit and the Unity of Christ's Body

Unity in Christ or unity in the Spirit is an NT value that has not always been appreciated in the evangelical tradition.[40] But unity matters (John 17).

35. The NIV breaks up the Greek into four English sentences.

36. Note the phrase "with your heart" (*tē kardia humōn*), where "heart" is singular but the pronoun is plural (Eph. 5:19).

37. For a recent discussion of these two views see Timothy G. Gombis, "Being the Fullness of God in Christ by the Spirit: Ephesians 5:18 in Its Epistolary Setting," *Tyndale Bulletin* 53 no. 2 (2002), 259–271.

38. Grudem champions the common view. He argues that the passage is about the individual Christian and his or her increased sanctification and increased power for ministry (*Systematic Theology*, 781–784).

39. Andreas J. Köstenberger, "Filled with the Holy Spirit?" *JETS* 40 no. 2 (June 1997): 233–234.

40. Grudem's succinct but excellent treatment of this pneumatological theme (*Systematic Theology*, 645–647) is one exception.

The Pauline image of the church as a body underlines the point. Unity is essential to a body's healthy and harmonious working (1 Cor. 12:12–26). Unity, of course, does not mean homogeneity. A human body has a diversity of members. Members have different but complementary functions (Rom. 12:3–8; 1 Cor. 12:4–10). So too the body of Christ. Against the backdrop of congregational disunity and disorder, Paul's first epistle to the Corinthians shows that the Spirit is the key to the unity and integral to a harmonious diversity (cf. 1 Cor. 1–3 and 12–14). Likewise Ephesians makes it plain that the Spirit is "the architect of unity" in Christ.[41] Indeed it is through Christ but in or by the one Spirit (en heni pneumati) that both Jewish and Gentile believers have access to the Father (Eph. 2:18). Additionally, certain qualities of Christian character are requisite for unity: "all humility and gentleness, with patience, bearing one another in love" (4:2). Paul further instructs the Ephesian believers to "maintain the unity of the Spirit in the bond [syndesmos] of peace" (v. 3). A. Skevington Wood's comments on Ephesians 4:3–4 are apposite: "The 'one Spirit' (v. 4) is the agent of unity. What Paul envisages is not 'a vague spiritual identity, but rather a profound oneness made possible by God's Spirit.'"[42] But such oneness did not entail a bland uniformity in church life. Christianity in Jerusalem developed differently to Christianity in the Gentile world. Yet the right hand of fellowship between these communities was the great Pauline desideratum (Gal. 2:1–10). This is a subject we shall return to at a later stage, as it has practical implications for Christian fellowship today.

Swiss theologian Emil Brunner recognized that true Christian unity is found in the fellowship of the Spirit. He made a seminal theological distinction between the ekklēsia, which is the fellowship of believers in Christ, and the church as an organized social reality.[43] He wrote, ". . . the Ekklesia is never conceived of [in the NT] as an institution; but exclusively as a fellowship of persons, as a common life based in fellowship with Jesus Christ as a fellowship of the Spirit (koinōnia pneumatos) and a fellowship of Christ (koinōnia Christou)."[44] The church is to serve the ekklēsia or the fellowship of those who are bound together by the Spirit.[45] Sadly, the history of the church has not always shown such service. Brunner was on solid biblical

41. Michael Griffiths, Three Men Filled with the Spirit (London: Overseas Missionary Fellowship, 1970), 50.

42. A. Skevington Wood, "Ephesians," EBC, comment on Eph. 4:3–4.

43. Emil Brunner, The Christian Doctrine of the Church, Faith, and the Consummation, vol. 3 of Dogmatics, trans. David Cairns (Philadelphia: Westminster, 1962), section 1; and The Misunderstanding of the Church, trans. Harold Knight (London: Lutterworth, 1952). Veli-Matti Kärkkäinen describes Brunner as "the great ecclesiologist of the past generation" (An Introduction to Ecclesiology: Ecumenical, Historical, and Global Perspectives [Downers Grove, Ill.: InterVarsity Press, 2002], 231).

44. Brunner, Christian Doctrine of the Church, 21.

45. Ibid., 126–130. See also his Misunderstanding of the Church, 106; chapter 11 is titled "The Task before the Churches—To Serve the Growth of the 'Ecclesia'." One need not subscribe

ground for such a claim. In Paul's famous Trinitarian benediction at the conclusion of his second letter to the Corinthians, the great apostle writes of "the grace of the Lord Jesus Christ and the love of God and the fellowship [*koinōnia*] of the Holy Spirit" (2 Cor. 13:14). In this text *koinōnia* means either that the Corinthians share/participate in the Spirit or that they enjoy a fellowship created by the Spirit.[46] In Brunner's view the organized church is misunderstood if it is regarded as a substitute for this Spirit-inspired fellowship.[47] A. M. Stibbs makes a similar point about fellowship in the Spirit and the kind of unity it presupposes: "It is not dependent on, and does not interminably await, the organizational integration or harmonization of the institutional framework of man-made denominations."[48] Moreover the unity effected by the Spirit and which is expressed in Christian fellowship is one that encompasses both men and women and the generations. This fellowship does not split men from women nor the young from the old. The Spirit after all was poured out on all flesh on the day of Pentecost.[49]

THE SPIRIT AND GIFTING CHRIST'S BODY

The risen Christ provides for his body's health. Gifts are given to the church to that end. The Spirit is the great distributor of these gifts. The sovereignty of the Spirit in this task is accented in 1 Corinthians 12:11 ("as he wills," *kathōs bouletai*) and possibly in Hebrews 2:4 ("distributed according to his will," *kata tēn autou thelēsin*).[50] Importantly, according to the Pauline testimony, these gifts are not given for personal and individual aggrandizement. They are to be used to edify, that is to say, to build up the church (1 Cor. 14:12,

---

to Brunner's idea that the institutionalizing process of church as opposed to *ekklēsia* began with the Pastoral Epistles to appreciate the merit in his distinction between church and *ekklēsia*.

46. Scholarship divides over whether the genitive "of the Holy Spirit" is to be taken as objective or subjective or intentionally both (Murray J. Harris, "2 Corinthians," *EBC*, note on 2 Corinthians 13:13, favors "fellowship engendered by the Spirit." Colin Kruse, "2 Corinthians," *NBC*, in his comment on 2 Corinthians 13:14 argues for both ideas: "participation in the Holy Spirit through being his temple and participation in the fellowship of believers created by him" (1205). R. P. Martin suggests, "The last phrase ["fellowship of the Holy Spirit"] may mean either that fellowship which he promotes between believers (Eph. 4:3) or the Christian's fellowship with him as a Person (John 14:17). A third view is preferable, namely, that the Holy Spirit's work is to create a true 'fellowship of believers' to share in that work, which in turn is a sign of the new age (1:22; 5:5)" (*2 Corinthians*, WBC, comment on 2 Cor. 13:13).

47. Interestingly an accent on fellowship is seen by Kärkkäinen as the basic model of Pentecostalism (*Introduction to Ecclesiology*, 75).

48. Stibbs, *God's Church*, 46.

49. This point is well argued by Jürgen Moltmann, *The Source: The Holy Spirit and the Theology of Life*, trans. Margaret Kohl (Minneapolis: Fortress, 1997), 89–102.

50. In the Hebrews 2:4 text, is it God per se who distributes the gifts of the Holy Spirit or is it the Spirit? Leon Morris discusses the two possibilities but decides that God is in view as the distributor of the gifts, including the gift of the Spirit (see "Hebrews," *EBC*, comment on Heb. 2:4). William L. Lane takes a similar view (*Hebrews 1–8*, WBC, comment on Heb. 2:4).

pros tēn oikodomēn tēs ekklēsias). There is a diversity of gifts but a common goal. They are to be used for the common good (12:7, *sumpheron*). However, although all gifts matter, not all the gifts have the same value for edifying the church (12:22–23). But what exactly are these gifts? What is their nature? How many are there? And which of them are at the center, if any, and which are not? Moreover, there is great controversy today as to whether all the gifts delineated in the pages of the NT are still given by the risen Christ to today's churches. This controversy is important enough to be given a separate treatment by way of an excursus at the conclusion of the present discussion.

Although a fuller discussion of the gifts awaits our excursus, as I have just said, it is worth reminding ourselves, at this stage of the discussion, of the other-person-centeredness of the gifts of the Spirit. They are to serve the congregational good. The gifts are not given to promote personal psychic growth or for personal therapy's sake. Least of all are they given to foster Christian celebrity, as though the gifts were an unfailing index of the depth of Christian character. The Corinthians had all the gifts (1 Cor. 1:4–8, *charismati*), but where was their Christian character? Instead, there was a party spirit at Corinth (1:10–17; 3:1–23), a notorious instance of immorality (5:1–13), litigation by Christian against Christian (6:1–11), gluttonous abuse of the Lord's Supper (11:17–34), disorder in the conduct of worship (chapters 12–14), and some even had wrong doctrine concerning the resurrection (15:12). Yet it remained the church of God in that place (1:2), as the Reformers noted.[51]

THE SPIRIT AND THE CHRIST'S ORDINANCES

The most striking feature of the two dominical ordinances are their christocentric nature. They are not pneumacentric. Baptism as practiced in the earliest church period was in the name of either Jesus or the Trinity (cf. Acts 2:38 and Matt. 28:18–20, respectively). Paul views baptism in terms of dying with Christ to an old way of life (that of this age) and rising to a new life (that of the age to come) with Christ (Rom. 6:4). And the Lord's Supper is a proclamation of Christ's death until he comes again (1 Cor. 11:26). In these ordinances the gospel is preached to our senses. To use Kevin J. Vanhoozer's language, they are "theo-dramatic."[52] How Christ is present in these ordinances generates immense debate in the churches.[53]

---

51. See the discussion in Paul D. Avis, *The Church in the Theology of the Reformers* (Atlanta: John Knox, 1980).

52. See the discussion in Kevin J. Vanhoozer, *The Drama of Doctrine: A Canonical Linguistic Approach to Christian Theology* (Louisville: Westminster/John Knox, 2005), 410–413.

53. See my "Lord's Supper," in Kevin J. Vanhoozer, gen. ed., *Dictionary for Theological Interpretation of the Bible* (Grand Rapids, Mich., and London: Baker and SPCK, 2005), 464–465.

Our focus, however, is on the Spirit's role in them, and there is a surprising lack of biblical evidence to help us.

With regard to baptism, apart from clear references to baptism with or by the Spirit, as in the case of 1 Corinthians 12:13, and in Acts 2:38, there is little explicit linkage between water baptism and the Spirit in the Scriptures. The same is true of the Lord's Supper. Even so, the Orthodox, Roman Catholic, and increasingly the Anglican traditions make much of the notion of *epiclesis*.[54] God is formally called upon to send the Spirit to make the elements of bread and wine effectively the body and blood of Christ. For example, in the Liturgy of St. John Chrysostom we find the following prayer:

> Send down the Holy Spirit upon us and upon these gifts here set
>   forth:
> And make this bread the precious Body of thy Christ,
> And what is in this cup the precious Blood of the Christ,
> Transforming them by the Holy Spirit.[55]

Kallistos Ware sees in the Supper "the extension of Christ's incarnation" because of the Spirit's role.[56] Likewise the Roman Catholic Church has a robust doctrine of *epiclesis:* "The Holy Spirit makes present the mystery of Christ."[57] According to this tradition: ". . . in each celebration there is an outpouring of the Holy Spirit."[58] Again, "The *Epiclesis* ('invocation upon') is the intercession in which the priest begs the Father to send the Holy Spirit, the Sanctifier, so that the offerings may become the body and blood of Christ."[59] The Reformed tradition, following Calvin, also answers the question of the Lord's presence at the Supper in pneumatological terms:

> Even though it seems unbelievable that Christ's flesh, separated from
> us by such great distance, penetrates to us, so that it becomes our
> food, let us remember how far *the secret power of the Holy Spirit*
> towers above all our senses, and how foolish it is to measure his
> immeasurableness by our measure. What then, our mind does not

54. A Baptist evangelical who makes much of the notion of *epiclesis* is Clark Pinnock (*Flame of Love: A Theology of the Holy Spirit* [Downers Grove, Ill.: InterVarsity Press, 1996], 124–129). He believes that the idea applies both to water baptism and "the Eucharist" (his preferred term).

55. Quoted in Kallistos Ware, *The Orthodox Way* (London and Oxford: Mowbray, 1981), 46.

56. Ibid.

57. CCC, 287.

58. Ibid.

59. Ibid. Gerald O'Collins, *The Tripersonal God: Understanding and Interpreting the Trinity* (New York/Mahwah, N.J.: Paulist, 1999) points out that after Vatican II there are two *epicleses* in the Roman liturgy (3). In the first *epiclesis* the Spirit is invoked before the consecration of the elements in order "that gifts be changed," and in the second *epiclesis,* which occurs after the consecration, that the communicants be changed.

comprehend, let faith conceive: that the Spirit truly unites things separated in space.[60]

The Lord Jesus, who according to this view is at the right hand of the Father, is present by his Spirit. Therefore, in this tradition there is no thought that the Supper is an extension of the incarnation. But again there is little, if anything, in Scripture to give these very different claims solidity.

Given the paucity of biblical evidence with regard to the Holy Spirit's role in the ordinances, the question must be raised about their theological importance (dogmatic rank) in a study of pneumatology. Indeed this question is a subset of the more general one of their importance per se. The idea that the theological value of the ordinances of baptism and the Lord's Supper might be overestimated would be a scandalous thought in some Christian traditions. Indeed, for some Christian traditions, baptism is essential to begin a Christian life, and the Eucharist or Lord's Supper or Mass is central to the sustenance of the Christian life. If this were rightly so, then Paul's lapse of memory with regard to baptisms at Corinth and his insistence that Christ sent him not to baptize but to preach the gospel is baffling (1 Cor. 1:14–17). Furthermore when Paul does at a later stage discuss the Lord's Supper at Corinth, the great abuse lies in not "discerning the body" (11:29). The "body" arguably in context is the congregation, which Paul will go on to describe in the very next chapter as the body of Christ (12:12–13). The disorder at Corinth, when they gathered to eat and remember Christ's sacrifice, was a consequence of the disregard shown to other members of the body. This disregard, in my view, was how Christ's "body and blood" (his historic sacrifice) was despised at Corinth (cf. 11:22 and v. 27) .

In the light of the above there are good reasons for adopting a moderate skepticism toward overinflated claims concerning the specifics of the Holy Spirit's role in the administration of the dominical ordinances.[61]

The Spirit and the New Life of God's People

The Spirit brings new life to a person. This life is a liberated life, a foretaste of the freedom of the world to come. Moreover it is a fruitful life as the

60. Calvin, "Institutes of the Christian Religion," *CJCC*, IV.17.10, emphasis mine. For a contemporary Reformed defense of the Calvinian view see Sinclair Ferguson, *The Holy Spirit* (Leicester, England: Inter-Varsity, 1996), 202–205.

61. Contra Pinnock, *Flame of Love*, 124–129; and Donald G. Bloesch, *The Holy Spirit: Works and Gifts* (Downers Grove, Ill.: InterVarsity Press, 2000), 274–285. For a fine evangelical exposition of the doctrine of the Lord's Supper see A. M. Stibbs, *Sacrament, Sacrifice and Eucharist: The Meaning, Function, and Use of the Lord's Supper* (London: Tyndale Press, 1962). Stibbs preserves the right balance between Christology and pneumatology in his treatment.

Spirit reshapes moral character. Regeneration may not change our tempera-
ments but should lead to changes in character. The Spirit's mission is not to
make an extrovert of every Christian. Rather the fruit of the Spirit is about
Christlike character. Further the new life that the Spirit brings is a sanctified
life. God's people are to be holy. However, there is opposition to this new
life from within (the flesh) and from without (the world, persecution, and
the Devil). Let us explore each of these claims in turn.

The New Life, Which the Spirit Brings to God's People, Is a Liberated Life

One of the great Pauline insights into the Spirit's ministry is that the Spirit
brings freedom in Christ (2 Cor. 3:17). As Daniel L. Migliore suggests,
"the work of the Spirit is *liberative*."[62] Romans 8:2 strikes this freedom
note: "For the law of the Spirit of life has set you free [*ēleutherōsen*] in
Christ Jesus from the law of sin and death."[63] The believer lives a life that
fulfills the righteous requirements of the law by walking according to the
Spirit rather than the flesh (Rom. 8:4). Earlier in his letter Paul makes it
plain that, "we serve in the new way [*en kainotēti*, lit., "in newness"] of
the Spirit and not in the old way of the written code" (Rom. 7:6). This
freedom is the freedom of the children of God. J. I. Packer rightly argues
that although justification is "the *primary* and *fundamental* blessing of the
gospel . . . adoption . . . is *the highest privilege that the gospel offers*: higher
even than justification."[64] Paul is clear. The Spirit the believer received is
not "the spirit of slavery to fall back into fear" (Rom. 8:15a). For him the
contrary state to freedom is one of fear. Instead the Spirit that now indwells
the believer is "the Spirit of adoption [*pneuma huiothesias*] as sons" (Rom.
8:15b).[65] Like our Lord, we pray "Abba" when addressing the Father (cf.
Mark 14:36 and Rom. 8:15c). This exalted status and extraordinary freedom are such that the groaning creation itself longs to see "the revealing
of the sons of God." That revelation will signal creation's own liberation
from bondage to decay and futility, which is its present condition this side
of the fall (Rom. 8:18–25).

According to Stibbs and Packer, the freedom that the Spirit brings is both
external and internal.[66] The external freedom is a freedom in relation to

---

62. Migliore, *Faith Seeking Understanding*, 228, emphasis original.

63. Douglas Moo argues that "law" in this text means "power" ("Romans," *NBC*, 1139).
This exegetical suggestion makes good contextual sense.

64. J. I. Packer, *Knowing God* (London, Sydney, Auckland, and Toronto: Hodder & Stoughton, 1973), 186, emphasis original.

65. "Sonship" is an idea drawn from the Greco-Roman world where legally the adopted
child is given thereby "all the rights and privileges that would accrue to the natural child" (Moo,
"Romans," *NBC*, 1140).

66. Stibbs and Packer, *Spirit within You*, 46–47.

God's law. The believer does not obey God's moral demands to win salvation. Christ has secured the believer's salvation on the cross. This freedom from the law as an instrument of salvation provides no rationale for moral license, though. Whatever view one takes of the third use of the Law and the question of the continuity and discontinuity between the Testaments on the matter of the Mosaic law, for Paul every believer lives under "the commandments of God" (1 Cor. 7:19) and "under the law of Christ" (1 Cor. 9:21 and Gal. 6:2). The same imperative—for example, "Honor your father and mother!" a commandment which Paul repeats in Ephesians 6:2—which under the Mosaic law condemns us in Adam because of our failure to comply perfectly, becomes a commandment and a law in Christ that gives moral eyes to Christian obedience within a secured relationship with God. Internally, the Spirit changes "our nature and heart's attitude to God." The believer is freed from sin as his or her "ruling drive."[67] The expression "ruling drive" is important. Neither Stibbs nor Packer is advocating a sinless perfectionism in this life, as though the Spirit places the believer beyond the conflict between the flesh and the Spirit.[68] In the light of the liberty the Spirit brings, either licentious evangelicalism or legalistic evangelicalism would represent a sad falling away from the liberty that Christ's Spirit brings.[69]

The New Life, Which the Spirit Brings to God's People, Is a Fruitful Life

It is an old adage but true that God in the gospel meets us where we are but does not leave us where we are. The great apostolic desideratum is maturity in Christ (Col. 1:28). That maturity shows itself in many ways, but Christian character is a key index. The Galatian Christians needed to hear that. Contemporary evangelical Christianity needs to hear that. The evangelistic may all too easily be divorced from the ethical—a danger to which the apostle Paul never succumbed.[70] Moreover, concentration on gifts of the Spirit may lead to the neglect of the virtues that the Spirit fosters.

67. Ibid., 47.
68. "Sinless perfection" is not to be confused with the Wesleyan notion of "Christian perfection." Wesley maintained, "Sinless perfection I do not contend for seeing it is not scriptural" (quoted by Neil E. Hightower, "Sinless Perfection," in Richard S. Taylor, ed., *Beacon Dictionary of Theology* [Kansas City: Beacon Hill, 1983], 486). See also Robert W. Burtner and Robert E. Chiles, eds., *A Compend of Wesley's Theology* (New York and Nashville: Abingdon, 1954), 205–216. Whether Wesley's idea of Christian perfection (freedom from known sin) is scriptural is another question.
69. Stibbs and Packer, *Spirit within You*, esp. 48–50.
70. For Paul, the NT evangel brought with it an ethic that flowed out of a new relationship to Christ. The Thessalonians, for example, not only heard Paul's call to turn away from idols to serve the living and true God, and to wait for his Son from heaven whom God raised from the dead and who would deliver them from the wrath to come (1 Thess. 1:9–10). They also heard

Not so with Paul and the idea of the fruit of the Spirit, which is sadly much neglected in evangelical systematic accounts of the Holy Spirit. In his fifth chapter of the Galatian letter, Paul contrasts life in the old era and that in the new.[71] The old era is life according to the flesh (*kata sarka*). Flesh is that principle of opposition to the will and ways of God. The new era is life according to the Spirit (*kata pneuma*). Within the believer both are at work still (Gal. 5:17).[72] However, if the Spirit is followed then the law is fulfilled and the flesh is trumped (v. 18). The flesh is replete in vices, including "sexual immorality, impurity, sensuality, idolatry, sorcery, enmity, strife, jealousy, fits of anger, rivalries, dissensions, divisions, envy, drunkenness, orgies and things like these" (vv. 19–20). In contrast the fruit that should be evident in the new life of the Christian is an impressive list of personal moral qualities (e.g., love, patience, kindness, goodness, faithfulness, gentleness, and self-control) and experiential states (e.g., joy and peace). Importantly, as Gordon Fee observes, ". . . the decided major-ity of these items have to do not with the internal life of the individual believer, but with *the corporate life of the community*."[73] According to Fee's analysis, self-control would be an example of a fruit that has to do with the internal life of the believer, while love would involve others besides oneself. I would slightly modify Fee's analysis and rephrase it as follows: the decided majority of these items have to do not *solely* with the internal life of the individual believer but with the corporate life of the community. In my view it is hard to imagine how any one of the Pauline fruit does not have an internal aspect. For example, surely the genuine exercise of Christian love issues from the internal moral character of the believer even though it is directed beyond him or her. However, be that as it may, whatever fruit is in view, the said fruit is the Spirit's doing, un-

---

his call to sanctification: namely, to abstain from fornication (4:1–8). In Paul's short three weeks with them (Acts 17:1–9), he preached an evangel and taught an ethic. The ethic he describes as a lifestyle they learned from him. Its content was concerned with pleasing God. Its source was the Lord Jesus. The apostle, Silvanus, and Timothy provided the living conduit between Christ and his people by which the ethical instruction was conveyed.

71. Ferguson has a fine discussion of the contrast between the old era (flesh) and the new (Spirit) (*Holy Spirit*, 153–156).

72. Traditionally Romans 7:13–25 has been viewed as the classic location for this internal conflict. But much recent exegesis has argued that the "wretched man" of whom Paul writes is the man or woman under either the OT law or any moral law rather than the Christian one. For a discussion of the issues, see the appendix in J. I. Packer, *Keep in Step with the Spirit* (Leicester, England: Inter-Varsity, 1984), 263–270; and Ferguson, *Holy Spirit*, 156–162. Both argue for the traditional perspective. For contrary views, see Luke Timothy Johnson, *Writings of the New Testament*, 354–356; and Fee, *God's Empowering Presence*, 508–515. Interestingly Fee regards the absence of explicit reference to the Spirit in the passage as evidence that the Christian is not in view (ibid., 514). In my view, whatever the outcome of the exegetical debate with regard to Romans 7, Galatians 5 remains a testimony to a conflict that believers know all too well.

73. Gordon Fee, *God's Empowering Presence*, 445, emphasis original.

like indulging the flesh, which is a human work (*ta erga*).[74] Paul does not elaborate on the how of the Spirit's working.[75] However, he does describe the style of life he is envisaging in terms of living by the Spirit, walking by the Spirit, and being led by the Spirit (Gal. 5:18, 25).

The New Life, Which the Spirit Brings to God's People, Is a Sanctified Life

One of the common ways of referring to the Holy Spirit during the course of church history has been to describe him as the sanctifier. After all, Scripture presents the Spirit in so many places as the *Holy* Spirit. Indeed, fundamental to the biblical characterization of God is the idea that God is holy. Holy in two senses. The Creator is separate from creation (Isa. 40:25). He is transcendent. He stands apart from it. God stands in an asymmetrical relation to creatures. They depend upon him. He does not depend upon them. God minus creation = God. But creation minus God = 0. In philosophical terms the Creator is externally related to creatures, but creatures are internally related to him. The other sense is the more important one for our purposes. Holiness is also a moral quality. God is morally pure (Hab. 1:12–13). God's people are to image his character (Lev. 19:2). He is holy, and so should we be. The new life which the Holy Spirit brings to God's people is a holy life.[76]

With regard to the doctrine of sanctification, or Christian holiness, some careful distinctions need to be made. Positional or definitive sanctification refers to the gracious move of God to set a people and a person apart for himself.[77] The Corinthian Christians for all their faults were still the saints (*hagiois*)—those who had been sanctified (*hēgiasmenois*, aorist participle)—in that place (1 Cor. 1:2). Indeed corporately and individually they were the temple of the Holy Spirit (3:16–17 and 6:19–20, respectively).[78] Yet they needed progressive sanctification, which refers to the process by which God works to make his children holy in character and

---

74. Ibid., 443–444.

75. In the next chapter I will offer a suggestion concerning the how.

76. Origen limited the Spirit's ministry to sanctifying God's people. However, this creative early church thinker is way off the mark given the Holy Spirit's work in creation, as we saw in an earlier chapter. For a discussion of Origen's restrictions on the ministry of each Person of the Trinity see J. N. D. Kelly, *Early Christian Doctrines* (San Francisco: Harper & Row, 1978).

77. See the fine discussion in John Murray, *Collected Writings of John Murray: Volume Two, Select Lectures in Systematic Theology* (Edinburgh, and Carlisle, Pa.: Banner of Truth, 1977), 277–293.

78. There are over a hundred NT descriptors of the new social reality that emerges after Pentecost. Three particularly important ones are that believers are children of the Father, the body of the Messiah, and the temple of the Holy Spirit. These three images are at the heart of a fully Trinitarian ecclesiology.

not just position.[79] This process is concursive, which is to say that more than one agent is involved. God is at work and so too is the believer, as Philippians 2:12–13 shows: "Therefore, my beloved, as you have always obeyed, so now . . . work out your salvation [note, not work *for* your salvation] with fear and trembling, for it is God who works in you, both to will and to work for his good pleasure." But that is not the end of the story of sanctification. As Wayne Grudem helpfully points out, there is "complete" sanctification, which refers to the final state of Christlikeness which is the divine desideratum for his wayward images who have been reclaimed.[80]

With regard to the Spirit, progressive sanctification—in contradistinction to positional and complete sanctification—is the arena where his work is particularly thematized in the scriptural testimony. Negatively, the deeds of the body need to be put to death. This mortification involves the Spirit's work, according to Paul. He presents this contrast in Romans: "For if you live according to the flesh [*sarx*] you will die, but if by the Spirit [*pneuma*] you put to death the deeds of the body, you will live" (Rom. 8:13).[81] Combatively, "the schemes of the devil" are to be opposed, which requires believers to be clothed in the armor of God (Eph. 6:10–20). That armor includes "the sword of the Spirit, which is the word [*rhēma*, spoken word in the context] of God, praying at all times in the Spirit" (vv. 17–18). The offensive weapon of the Christian is the gospel itself proclaimed in the face of unbelief. The praying which is in keeping with the mind of the Spirit (*en pneumati*) is probably illustrated when Paul calls upon the Ephesians to pray for him that, "words may be given me in opening my mouth boldly to proclaim the mystery of the gospel" (v. 19). Positively, progressive sanctification is an increasing transformation into the likeness of Christ. The key Pauline text, 2 Corinthians 3:18, is a difficult one, as we saw in an earlier chapter. But by any view, because of the Spirit's work, the believer is in process as he or she beholds or reflects the Lord's glory. How the Spirit effects these changes positively and negatively is not revealed. Mystery remains. Scripture is non-postulational. It does not offer theories concerning the nature of realities or processes. Instead it affirms that certain realities are so, and the believer by faith lives as if they are so, and in so doing finds that they indeed are so (*solvitur ambulando*, Lat., "It is solved by walking").

79. See Murray, *Writings 2*, 294–304.
80. Grudem, *Systematic Theology*, 749–750.
81. Fee takes the view that "flesh" in this context and in Galatians 5:16 does not refer to an indwelling sinful nature opposed to God but to the way of life of those outside of Christ (*God's Empowering Presence*, cf. 431, 556, and 822). For a contrary view that takes "flesh" as a reference to "man's innate tendency to selfishness and evil," see George T. Montague, *The Holy Spirit: Growth of a Biblical Tradition: A Commentary on the Principal Texts of the Old and New Testaments* (New York and Toronto: Paulist, 1976), 199, 206–208.

THE SPIRIT AND "DEIFICATION"?

The Orthodox tradition in its various forms (Greek, Russian, Antiochian, among others) understands the divine project in very bold terms. God is making little gods. The theological terms typically used to capture this idea are *"theosis,"* "deification," and "divinization." These terms are synonyms. This idea has had a long history in Christian thought. We find it in Irenaeus, in Athanasius, in the Cappadocians, Hilary of Poitiers, and Symeon the New Theologian, to name a few.[82] Irenaeus is the Patristic fountainhead of the idea: "If the Word is made man, it is that men might become gods."[83] The crucial biblical text is 2 Peter 1:3–4:

> His divine power has granted to us all things that pertain to life and godliness, through the knowledge of him who called us to his own glory and excellence, by which he has granted to us his precious and very great promises, so that through them you may become partakers of the divine nature [*genēsthe theias koinōnoi phuseōs*].

The Orthodox position must not be misunderstood, however. In Orthodoxy, as Kallistos Ware makes plain, *theosis* is not taken to mean that believers share the essence of God, but rather that believers share in the energies of God with which God relates to creatures.[84]

Recently, a number of evangelicals have been attracted to the Orthodox position. Clark H. Pinnock, for example, writes of *theosis* (a term he uses) in the following way: "This category invites us to think of the goal of salvation as participation in the divine nature, in a way that preserves distinctions proper to Creator and creature without losing sight of their union."[85] He further argues that the "classic expression" of this idea is in 2 Peter 1:4.[86] The Spirit is vitally involved in enabling such a participation, according to Pinnock's view.[87] Charles Sherlock argues similarly: *"The Spirit makes me a participant, not a mere observer.* This third act [God's gift of the Spirit in the divine drama of salvation] not only shows us God's nature, it enables

---

82. See John Meyendorff, *Living Tradition: Orthodox Witness in the Contemporary World* (Crestwood, N.Y.: St. Vladimir's Seminary Press, 1978), esp. chapter 10. See also Daniel B. Clendenin, "Partakers of Divinity: The Orthodox Doctrine of Theosis," *JETS* 37 no. 3 (September 1994): 365–379; and Robert V. Rakestraw, "Becoming like God: An Evangelical Doctrine of Theosis," *JETS* 40 no. 2 (June 1997): 257–269.

83. Irenaeus, *Against Heresies* VI.i.1, quoted in Rakestraw, "Becoming like God," 259. See also Henry Bettenson, ed. and trans., *The Early Christian Fathers* (Oxford: Oxford University Press, 1978), 77, for a similar statement.

84. Ware, *Orthodox Way,* 28; and esp. 98.

85. Pinnock, *Flame of Love,* 150–151.

86. Ibid., 151.

87. Ibid., chapter 5, passim.

us to share it."[88] Again, he writes: ". . . we are called to be participants, not just spectators, *in God's being* and work."[89] It is a strange claim, that sounds as if Sherlock is arguing that the believer shares in God's essence in some way.

Some evangelical treatments of this idea do not appear to make the careful distinction between the essence or being of God and the divine energies which the Orthodox make to prevent any suggestion of our becoming idolatrous rivals to our Creator, even if only in our own minds. The Orthodox faith understands the term "essence" as referring to "the substance, nature and being of God," whereas in its view "energies" refers to "that which radiates from the hidden essence or nature of God."[90] Moses, so the argument runs, saw the energies of God on Mount Sinai but did not see God's hidden essence. God's grace is another example of such an energy, according to Orthodoxy.[91] What are we to make of such claims about deification?

In an evidence-based approach we must ask if 2 Peter 1:4 is able to bear the weight that the Orthodox and some evangelicals place on it. Barth certainly would not have thought so. He understood the text to be simply asserting the reality of "the practical fellowship of Christians with God and on this basis the conformity of their acts with the divine nature."[92] Who is right? Exegete and theologian Richard J. Bauckham's commentary on this fascinating text shows the way forward: ". . . it is not very likely that participation in God's own essence is intended. . . . To share in divine nature is to become immortal and incorruptible."[93] The Petrine argument accents the role of the knowledge of God made available through the divine power, which provides the believers the promises to be believed, which promises in turn transform believers through faith in them. This bedrock of faith (v. 5, *tē pistei humōn*) is to be built on by the addition of qualities which, if embodied in the believer, make the believer fruitful in the knowledge of Christ (e.g., "brotherly affection," *tēn philadelphian*). The keys to understanding the argument are the emphases on "knowledge," "promises," and "faith." Rakestraw persuasively concludes his discussion of *theosis*:

> To speak of divinization, deification, and human beings "becoming God" seems to violate the historic Christian understanding of the essential qualitative distinction between God and creation. "Becom-

---

88. Charles Sherlock, *God on the Inside: Trinitarian Spirituality* (Canberra: Acorn, 1991), 98 (italic text was bold in the original).

89. Ibid., 106, emphasis mine.

90. *The Orthodox Study Bible: New Testament and Psalms* (Nashville: Thomas Nelson, 1993), 797. Interestingly, this annotated Bible links the account of Moses on Sinai (Exod 33:18–23) with 2 Peter 1:4.

91. Ibid.

92. Quoted in Rakestraw, "Becoming like God," 258.

93. Richard J. Bauckham, *Jude, 2 Peter*, WBC, comment on 2 Pet. 1:4.

ing like God" appears to express more Biblically the concept of the Christian's union and communion with God in sanctification.[94]

What is striking to me about the 2 Peter 1:4 text is the absence of any reference to the Holy Spirit. This Petrine text simply cannot bear the pneumatological weight which Pinnock and Sherlock want it to carry.

THE SPIRIT AND THE REVIVAL OF GOD'S PEOPLE

Christians may easily romanticize the early church. If only we could return to the halcyon days of Acts, to the unity, to the miracles, to the joy. But even the NT tells a more complex story. Many of the Pauline letters were written because of troubles in the churches. At times wrong doctrine is the key issue (e.g., Galatians and Colossians). At other times, wrong doctrine and wrong living feature strongly (e.g., 1 Corinthians). Indeed in the famous seven letters to the churches found in the book of Revelation, five of the churches are problematical (Revelation 2–3). Only two receive unqualified endorsement from the risen Christ. The subsequent history of the churches tells a similar story. At times a reformation of doctrine is needed, at other times, a revival of spiritual life, and at times, both. From an evangelical perspective, the Reformation of the sixteenth century and the Evangelical Awakening of the eighteenth century are cases in point.

Some theologians see that first day of Pentecost after Jesus' resurrection as the "archetypal" biblical account of revival. D. Martyn Lloyd-Jones boldly maintains that, "Every revival is a repetition of Pentecost."[95] In his view, revival is to be understood as ". . . God pouring out his Spirit on an assembled church or company, or many churches or countries even, at a time. What he did at the beginning [Pentecost] he has done again."[96] According to Lloyd-Jones, subsequent examples of such repetitions include the Montanists of the second century, the Donatists of the third, the Reformation of the sixteenth, the New England awakening of the eighteenth, North America in the nineteenth, and Wales and Korea in the twentieth.[97] Packer likewise takes Pentecost as an example of revival, as can be seen in his proof texts drawn from Acts 2.[98] Revival is the divine revitalization of the church, the divine stirring of the hearts of God's people, and the display of divine sovereignty.[99] Packer distinguishes revival and renewal.

94. Rakestraw, "Becoming like God," 266.
95. D. Martyn Lloyd-Jones, *Joy Unspeakable: The Baptism with the Holy Spirit* (Eastbourne, England: Kingsway, 1985), 280.
96. Ibid., 275.
97. Ibid., 275–278. I have truncated his list.
98. Packer, *Keep in Step with the Spirit*, 256–257. For example, he cites Acts 2:17–21, 46–47; 4:32; and 8:8.
99. Ibid., 255–258.

A feature of revival is a deep sense of sin and consequent repentance. According to Packer, renewal does not exhibit this feature, even though it is characterized by genuine joy.[100] Sinclair Ferguson also regards Pentecost as the archetypal revival account. He describes the event as "the inaugural revival of the New Testament epoch."[101] He quotes Jonathan Edwards's description of revival with approval: "remarkable effusions [of the Holy Spirit] at special seasons of mercy."[102] He argues that Acts 3:19—he surely meant Acts 3:19–20—which speaks of "times of refreshing" from the Lord, is justification for expecting occasions of revival subsequent to Pentecost.[103] He does not elaborate. Presumably the plural "times" (*kairoi*) is for him the evidential basis for his point. Lloyd-Jones and Packer argue that the Holy Spirit's work in reviving God's people cannot be organized but may be prayed for and prepared for by deep repentance. A sense of the awesome holiness of God and revival are intimately connected.

My respect for the above-mentioned theologians is profound, and like them I believe that a sovereign God has revived and may indeed again revive his people. Like them I believe "revival" refers in the first instance to a corporate phenomenon. Moreover like them I believe God's people need constantly to be aware of the purity of a holy God and to wait upon his sovereign grace in revitalizing his church—and in waiting, they must indeed deeply repent and earnestly pray. However, describing Pentecost in "archetypal" terms as the paradigm case for revival—my language note, not theirs—runs the risk of missing the unique salvation-historical features of that event (features previously highlighted).[104] There may be family resemblances between Pentecost and, for example, the Welsh revival of 1904–1905, but not identity. We must be careful not to read the phenomenology of events in church history subsequent to the NT into the NT testimony itself.[105]

---

100. Ibid., 234. The charismatic movement he regards as a genuine renewal of the church but not a revival. In an earlier work he brings the ideas of revival and renewal together, when he argues that revival is ". . . a work of God by his Spirit through his Word bringing the spiritually dead to living faith in Christ and renewing the inner life of Christians who have grown slack or sleepy" (J. I. Packer, "Puritanism as a Movement of Revival," *Evangelical Quarterly* 52 no. 1 [January–March 1980]: 2).

101. Ferguson, *Holy Spirit,* 90.

102. Ibid., 91.

103. Ibid.

104. Ibid. Ferguson does not explain how his discussion of Pentecost as "epoch crossing, and consequently atypical and non-paradigmatic in nature" comports with his claim that Pentecost was "In some respects . . . the inaugural revival of the New Testament epoch" (cf. 80 and 90). The "some respects" needs teasing out. I have argued elsewhere that Packer faces the same question ("Renewal: Catholic, Charismatic, and Calvinist," *RTR* 44 [January–April 1985]: 8, fn 31).

105. Lloyd-Jones would dissent from this conclusion. But he would have been pleased to see a systematic theologian, at the very least, discussing revival. His policy was to check any new work on the Holy Spirit to see if revival even received mention (*Joy Unspeakable,* 269). He rarely found what he was looking for. Likewise William Porter laments the ignorance or rela-

The Spirit and the Worship by God's People

For many Christians, "worship" is about Sunday or those occasions when God's people gather to sing. So we speak of "worship services," "worship time," and "worship leaders." We learn from a dictionary that "worship" in English has behind it the idea of "worthship." Hence, it is argued, our worship has to do with recognition and expression of the worth of God. There is indeed a biblical case for such an understanding. In Revelation 4 and 5, those creatures who surround the throne of God and the Lamb express the worth of God. "You are worthy!" is the cry in heaven. And if our theology of church is that every local church is an actual assembly of God's people, which in some ways ought to mirror the heavenly one, then such a vertical notion of worship is totally in order.[106] However, this is only half of the NT story. Paul, for example, is free to use language associated with the OT tabernacle and temple worship or, as David Peterson helpfully expresses it, "engagement with God" in fresh ways.[107] To look no further than Romans, Paul uses such language of the whole of the Christian life lived in response to the gospel (Rom. 12:1–2) and even of his mission to the Gentiles. They become his priestly offering to God (15:15–16). Thus the NT presentation of engagement with God ties Sunday and every other day of the week together in the light of Revelation 4–5 and Romans 12 and 15.[108] But what of the Spirit? Does the Spirit play any particular role in both dimensions of this more biblically nuanced understanding of worship? This question we shall now explore in relation to the more traditional notion of worship, and we shall do so with the help of insights from a recent theologian. The question of the Spirit's general role in the life of the people of God as they live out the gospel, which is also worship broadly understood, I shall leave to a later stage of our discussion.

The recent theologian I have in mind is James B. Torrance.[109] In particular, Torrance sees in our union with Christ by the Spirit the key to understand-

---

tive disinterest in the subject across much of the British church ("Study Article: Revival—The Surprising Work of the Spirit?" *Epworth Review* 33 no. 3 [July 2003]: 30).

106. G. Delling, *Worship in the New Testament* (London: Darton, Longman, & Todd, 1962), 45.

107. David G. Peterson, *Engaging with God: A Biblical Theology of Worship* (Leicester, England, and Grand Rapids, Mich.: Apollos, 1992).

108. Ibid. This broader understanding of worship is excellently brought out by Peterson, who concludes his study in the following way: "Above all, we must come to grips with the New Testament perspective that acceptable worship is an engagement with God, through Jesus Christ, in the Holy Spirit—a Christ-centred, gospel-serving, life-orientation" (293).

109. Another theologian who has recently accented the theme of union with Christ by the Spirit is Clark H. Pinnock. However, his discussion takes strange turns at times. He seems to argue for creation itself as included in union with Christ, and not simply believers: "The aim [of God] is to integrate creation into the life of God which is the goal of creation" ("The Role of the Spirit in Redemption," *AsTJ* 52 no. 1 [Spring 1997]: 59). This appears confused at the very least.

ing the worshiping life of the believer in general and his or her prayer life in particular. Drawing upon the NT presentation of Christ as our great High Priest, and with debts to Nicene Trinitarianism and Patristic Christology, Torrance argues that the Holy Spirit enables the believer to participate by way of union in the worship and prayer life of God incarnate: "As Christ was anointed by the Spirit in our humanity to fulfill his ministry for us, so we are united by the same Spirit to share his ministry."[110] According to his view the God-man is the archetypal worshiper and prayer. With regard to worship he argues, ". . . that worship is the gift of participating in the incarnate Son's communion with the Father, and in so worshiping we worship and glorify the Father, the Son and the Holy Spirit."[111] In reference to prayer he maintains, "He [Jesus] pours out his Spirit on the Church at Pentecost to lift us up into that life of communion with the Father that we might participate in his glorified life, in his prayers, his intercessions, his mission to the world."[112]

There is strong NT evidence to back Torrance's approach. Christ is our great High Priest, who ever lives to intercede for us, and the leader of our worship, according to Hebrews (cf. Heb. 7:23–26 and 8:1–2, *leitourgos tōn hagiōn*).[113] The Spirit of the Son enables us to pray like the Son, as far as Paul is concerned in Romans and Galatians. Indeed the distinctive intimacy with which Jesus prayed to the Father, when he prays "Abba" Father, becomes our privilege because the same Spirit that animates his life of communion with the Father animates our own. Galatians is particularly instructive because of the syntactical parallelism between the sending of the Son and the Spirit of the Son (cf. Gal. 4:4 and 4:6–7). The Son is sent in order that (*hina,* purposive) we might have the status of sons (and daughters). The Spirit is sent so that (*ōste*) we might, as a consequence, have the experience of sonship (*tēn huiosthesian*). Indeed, elsewhere in his writings Paul describes the Holy Spirit as the Spirit of adoption (Rom. 8:15). But even though we may be the adopted sons and daughters of God, prayer does not always come easily. At times it is exceptionally hard to know what to pray, especially when we are spiritually winded, as it were, by the circumstances of life (e.g., an illness, a bereavement, a redundancy). However, the apostolic consolation is that Jesus intercedes [*entunchanei*] for us at the right hand of the Father and likewise the Spirit intercedes [*entunchanei*] within us (cf. Rom. 8:26–27 and 8:34).

110. James B. Torrance, "Christ in Our Place: The Joy of Worship," Gerrit Dawson and Jock Stein, eds., *A Passion for Christ: The Vision That Ignites Ministry* (Edinburgh: Handsel, 1999), 51.

111. Ibid., 42.

112. James B. Torrance, "Prayer and the Priesthood of Christ," ibid., 58.

113. James B. Torrance, *Worship, Community, and the Triune God of Grace* (Carlisle, England: Paternoster, 1996), 10. See also Robert Doyle, "The One True Worshipper," *The Briefing,* April 29, 1999, 7–9, who writes, "In the context of the epistle's [Hebrews's] argument, Jesus is the One True Worshipper, the leader of our worship, who has gone ahead to lead us in our prayers and intercessions."

Both Son and Spirit pray according to the Father's will. Their prayers will be heard, although the answers will presumably be according to our needs and not necessarily according to our wants.[114]

There is thus a Trinitarian shape to our prayer life. The Father is approached through the Son by the Spirit. In this way we worship the Father in spirit and in truth (John 4:24): in "spirit" because we need to approach God, who is spirit, in a way that is in keeping with his nature; and in "truth" because without the self-disclosure of God in Christ our prayers are blind. The worship of God in spirit and truth, according to Kevin J. Vanhoozer, keeps the worshiper from the twin dangers of hypocrisy, if without spirit, and idolatry, if without truth.[115] The true worshiper is fueled by the living water that Jesus gives, which in this Johannine context is most probably none other than the Holy Spirit.[116] The Spirit's ministry of uniting us to Christ is integral to the worship and prayer life of the people of God. In the bold language of Basil of Caesarea, "It is impossible to worship the Son except in the Holy Spirit; it is impossible to call upon the Father except in the Spirit of adoption."[117]

THE SPIRIT AND THE PERSECUTION AND PRESERVATION OF THE PEOPLE OF GOD

There is an intriguing—because so cryptic—apocalyptic passage in one of the earliest documents of the NT that many see as a veiled reference to a ministry of the Holy Spirit. Paul warns the Thessalonians in his second letter to them that the Day of the Lord will be preceded by rebellion or apostasy (*apostasia*).[118] The rebellion or apostasy will also be the revealing of the man of lawlessness, who is the "son of destruction" (2 Thess. 2:3–4). Paul reminds the Thessalonians that, while with them, he had alerted them about this coming person. He also reminds them that they know "what is restraining [*to katechon*, neuter] him" (v. 6). Indeed even at the time of his writing, the mystery of lawlessness is at work. Then Paul writes, "Only

114. For a useful discussion of the Spirit's intercessory ministry see Peter O'Brien, "Romans 8:26, 27: A Revolutionary Approach to Prayer," *RTR* 46 no. 3 (September–December 1987): 65–73. Given the force of O'Brien's argument, it is highly unlikely that the groanings of the Spirit is a reference to tongues.

115. Kevin J. Vanhoozer, "Worship at the Well: From Dogmatics to Doxology (and Back Again)," *TrinJ* 23 NS no. 1 (Spring 2002): 3–16.

116. Ibid., 7. David G. Peterson contends that, in the argument of John's Gospel, to worship God in spirit and truth involves both receiving the Holy Spirit and acknowledging the truth about Jesus ("Worship," *NDBT*, 860).

117. Basil of Caesarea, *On the Holy Spirit*, St. Vladimir's Seminary Press Translation (New York: St. Vladimir's Seminary Press, 1980), 48. See also Vanhoozer, "Worship at the Well," 15.

118. Dumbrell, *Search for Order*, argues for apostasy since *apostasia* as also found in Acts 21:21 is a religious term and not a political one (313).

he who now restrains [*ho katechōn,* masculine] it will do so until he is out of the way. And then the lawless one will be revealed . . ." (vv. 7–8). For our purposes, the intrigue surrounds identifying the one who restrains the mystery of lawlessness for a time.

Scholarly suggestions as to the identity of "he who now restrains" are multiple and include, "the preaching of the gospel (Calvin), the Jewish state, the binding of Satan, the church, Gentile world dominion, and human government."[119] A popular suggestion is that Paul has in mind the Roman empire itself (Chrysostom). A variant of this proposal is that the restraining force is "the principle of law and order" and that the restrainer is "Roman control."[120] An important suggestion and one with a long history in the church is that the restrainer is the Holy Spirit.[121] Identifying the restrainer requires a weighing of probabilities. Either the Roman Empire or the Holy Spirit appears to be the main contender, if one does not want simply to leave the question open, which is also an option. If the Spirit is in view then the Spirit has a secret role in the public sphere in restraining both ultimate wickedness and societal dissolution. This ministry of the Spirit would be yet another expression of that kind grace of God that has not left a rebellious creation to its own destructive devices but stays engaged with the created order and does so with the ultimate end in mind of creation regained.

Whoever the restrainer may be, what is clear from the pages of the NT is that in this life the people of God face hostility in the world and from the world. Jesus warned as much, as we shall shortly see, and certainly the fate of NT characters like Stephen in the book of Acts testifies to the truth of Jesus' warnings (Acts 7). However, God's people are not left abandoned *in extremis.* Jesus promised that the Spirit would give disciples the words needed when they were hauled before governors and kings for his sake. No forethought would be needed insofar as the right thing to say is concerned. This is the Spirit's task (Mark 13:9–13). Luke describes the Spirit's activity as teaching (*didaxei*) disciples what to say (Luke 12:11–12).[122] Matthew identifies the Spirit who is at work as "the Spirit of your Father [*to pneuma tou patros humōn*] speaking through you" (Matt. 10:20).[123] The illocutionary force of the utterance in each Synoptic context is to encourage disciples not to be anxious when such a circumstance of hostility

---

119. Robert L. Thomas, "2 Thessalonians," *EBC,* comment on 2 Thess. 2:7.

120. Dumbrell, *Search for Order,* 314.

121. Robert G. Gromacki, "The Holy Spirit: Who He Is, What He Does," in Charles R. Swindoll and Roy B. Zuck, eds., *Understanding Christian Theology* (Nashville: Thomas Nelson, 2003), argues that the Spirit is the restrainer and works restraint through the church (533).

122. Donald A. Hagner, *Matthew 1–13,* WBC, comments on Matthew 10:20 that this text is well illustrated by Acts 4:1–22 and Peter's speech to the rulers, elders, and people.

123. Ibid. Hagner comments on Matthew 10:20 that this text speaks with an intimacy that is unique in the NT.

arises (Matt. 10:19; Mark 13:11; and Luke 12:11). Stephen exhibited that courage and equanimity (Acts 7).

The Spirit and the Hope of Glory

In NT perspective, believers live in a particular space and time frame. We are located in the groaning creation which itself longs for redemption (Rom. 8:18–25) and in this present evil age (Gal. 1:4). The best is yet to be. The ultimate eschatological horizon is nothing less than a new heavens and a new earth (2 Peter 3). Thus, God's reclamation project does not leave creation behind. The future, therefore, is not some ethereal realm of swirling clouds and endless harp muzak. Rather, as Ferguson argues, ". . . the Spirit's task is to restore glory to a fallen creation."[124] Indeed something of God's future for believers, the church, and the creation may be experienced now. In the present age—even though it is passing away—the Spirit is the down payment, the firstfruits, and the seal of the glory to come. Significantly, it is both the bride (church) and Spirit who long for that future (Rev. 22:17). These ideas bear further examination.

The Pauline ideas are particularly important for our present discussion: the Spirit as down payment, as firstfruits, and the hope of glory.[125] Let us begin with the Spirit as down payment on the life of the world to come. According to Paul the Spirit is the *arrabōn*. This Greek word may be translated variously: "deposit" (NIV) or "first installment" (NRSV) or "guarantee" (ESV).[126] In commercial transactions in Paul's day the term described a sum of money paid in advance to validate a legal contract or secure an article of some kind. Unlike a pledge, this earnest money was not returnable. In 2 Corinthians 1:22 Paul asserts that God has given believers the Holy Spirit "in our hearts as a guarantee (*arrabōn*)." Later in this same epistle (2 Cor. 5:1–5) Paul deals with the Christian hope of the life to come, both its nature ("a heavenly dwelling") and certainty ("we know"). God has prepared believers for this future and "has given the Spirit as a guarantee" (v. 5, *arrabōna*). Furthermore, we find in Paul's discussion in Romans that it is through the Spirit that God will give our mortal bodies life (Rom. 8:11). Still further, for Paul it is the promised Spirit who is the *arrabōn* of our inheritance until such time as we take possession of it (Eph. 1:13–14). The Spirit brings something of the future that God has in store

---

124. Ferguson, *Holy Spirit*, 91.

125. Some may be surprised at this point that I have not included the Pauline idea of the Spirit as seal. However, I take it that this idea belongs more usefully in a discussion of assurance. Hence I shall examine it in the next chapter when dealing with the question of how we can be assured that we are God's children.

126. I prefer "guarantee" as the translation. The idea of a guarantee seems to be the key one, as the NIV paraphrase suggests: "put his Spirit in our hearts as a deposit, guaranteeing what is to come" (2 Cor. 1:22).

for his people into our lives in the here and now. Even so the best is yet to be for the people of God.[127] The idea of firstfruits (*aparchē*) is similar in this respect. The firstfruits represent the beginning of the harvest. There is so much more to come in the future. Romans 8:23 is the *locus classicus*. The creation itself longs for release and for freedom. Our own bodies share that groaning. Paul writes, "And not only creation, but we ourselves, who have the firstfruits [*tēn aparchēn*] of the Spirit, groan inwardly as we wait eagerly for adoption as sons, the redemption of our bodies." There may be a link between Paul's use of the idea of firstfruits, his appeal to the Spirit, and the day of Pentecost. The day of Pentecost was the occasion for the Jews to present their firstfruits. That of course was also the day on which the eschatological Spirit came in a dramatic fashion.[128]

If the gift of the Spirit is the down payment (*arrabōn*) of the future and its beginnings (*aparchē*), what is the content of our hope? After all, according to Paul, it is the Spirit whose power enables believers to abound in hope (Rom. 15:13). The answer in Pauline terms is glory, as Romans 8 shows. "The Spirit of life" will give us life (Rom. 8:1–13).[129] "The Spirit of adoption" will give us status (vv. 14–17). And the "Spirit of glory" will ultimately usher us into the final state of glorification. Then we shall be Spirit-shaped into the likeness of Christ. In the world to come our resurrection bodies will be Spirit-directed (*pneumatikon*, 1 Cor. 15:44). As Ferguson maintains, ". . . the task of the Spirit may be stated simply: to bring us to glory, to create glory within us, and to glorify us together with Christ."[130]

What is surprising about the biblical testimony is how little is said about precisely how the Spirit as "the perfecting cause"—to use Basil's language—will bring about the end and secure "the destiny of the universe to glorify God," as Abraham Kuyper argues.[131] What we do find is that as the canon closes, the bride of Christ and the Spirit issue a joint appeal: "'Come.' And let the one who hears say, 'Come'" (Rev. 22:17). This is an appeal to the risen Christ to return from heavenly glory in the light of his

127. For the substance of the paragraph I am indebted to Scobie, *Ways of Our God*, 293. Interestingly Ferguson is comfortable with the idea of *arrabōn* as "pledge" (*Holy Spirit*, 177). But I think that Scobie is to be preferred, given Genesis 38:20, 23.

128. Again I have followed Scobie's discussion (ibid., 294). For a classic discussion of the eschatological Spirit in Pauline thought see Geerhardus Vos, "The Eschatological Aspect of the Pauline Conception of the Spirit," in Richard B. Gaffin Jr., ed., *The Shorter Writings of Geerhardus Vos: Redemptive History and Biblical Interpretation* (Phillipsburg, N.J.: Presbyterian & Reformed, 2001), 91–125.

129. "Spirit of Life," "Spirit of Adoption," and "Spirit of Glory" are the headings that Moo adopts in his very fine discussion of Romans 8:1–30 ("Romans," *NBC*, 1139–1142).

130. Ferguson, *Holy Spirit*, 249.

131. Abraham Kuyper, *The Work of the Holy Spirit*, trans. Henri De Vries (Grand Rapids, Mich.: Eerdmans, 1975), 25. Contrast the restraint of the biblical testimony with the discussion of "The Ecology of the Creative Spirit" in Moltmann, *Source*, 111–124; and of the Spirit, the Rapture, the Tribulation, and the Millennium in Gromacki, "Holy Spirit," 532–535.

promise, "Behold, I am coming soon" (v. 12).[132] As in the case of the Old Testament, so too the New: the biblical testimony closes in longing. Thus God's people live in hope as we live in the tension of the now of firstfruits but the not yet of glorification (Rom. 8:18–30), and for those who suffer for their faith in Christ, their coming vindication (Rev. 6:9–10).

IMPLICATIONS FOR BELIEF AND PRACTICE

The risen Christ's gift of the Spirit is replete with implications for the people of God and their life in the world. In this section we will explore only some of them: appreciating our union with Christ; unity in the Spirit as an apostolic value; the Spirit as the primary agent in Christian mission; properly understanding the fullness of or by the Spirit; the importance of holiness of life; and the need to live in the light of God's ultimate eschatological goal for the church, of which the Spirit is the guarantee.

Appreciating Our Union with Christ by the Spirit

The Reformers Luther and Calvin regarded the doctrine of justification by faith alone (*sole fide*) through Christ alone (*solus Christus*) by grace alone (*sola gratia*) as at the heart of the Christian gospel. Luther wrote that justification is "the centerpiece of our teaching" and Calvin "the main hinge on which religion turns."[133] These metaphors (centerpiece and hinge) are eloquent of the dogmatic rank that these towering figures of the past gave to the doctrine. However, theologian J. I. Packer has argued persuasively that while the "fundamental" and "primary" blessing of the gospel is justification, the "highest" blessing is sonship.[134] By "justification" he means that Pauline doctrine that the believer's sins have been forgiven on account of Christ's finished work of atonement on the cross and that the believer is clothed in the righteousness of Christ. This righteousness is imputed to the believer, not imparted. "Sonship" refers to that Pauline doctrine that by the grace of God the believer is adopted into the family of God. Believers are the children of God. Packer contends, "Adoption is higher [than justification], because of the richer relationship with God that it involves."[135] These claims have firm biblical backing.[136] But arguably if justification is foundational and sonship is preeminent, then union with Christ by the Spirit, as discussed earlier, is the *central* blessing of the gospel since all the blessings of salvation are found in Christ. Union with Christ

132. Alan F. Johnson, "Revelation," *EBC*, comment on Rev. 22:17.
133. Quoted in Migliore, *Faith Seeking Understanding*, 236–237.
134. Packer, *Knowing God*, 186–187.
135. Ibid., 187.
136. See Demarest, *Cross and Salvation*, chapter 9.

by the Spirit relocates the believer from Adam to Christ. Significantly, our union with Christ by the Spirit not only brings us into relationship to God as Father but also to one another as Christ's body. As John Stott correctly argues, union with Christ is "indispensable to our Christian identity" and is "central to the New Testament gospel."[137] Without the Spirit there is no union with Christ.

Recognizing Unity as an Apostolic Value

I recently was in conversation with a new member of the church which I attend. He told me that his father was a pastor and had recently left the denomination in which he was pastor. He spoke of the bellicose ethos of his father's former tradition in terms of one that was willing to fight fellow Christians anywhere. Unity is a dominical value, as our Lord's prayer in the garden shows (John 17). And unity in the Spirit is an apostolic value, as both Paul's writings and his practice show. Recall that Paul instructs the Ephesian believers to "maintain the unity of the Spirit in the bond of peace" (Eph. 4:3). To live this way is to walk in a manner worthy of their calling to be Christians (Eph. 4:1). Paul practiced what he preached. His espoused theology and his operational theology were one. And so he entreats Euodia and Syntyche—both of whom were gospel workers with him—"to agree in the Lord" (Phil. 4:2–3). These women need to heed his earlier general admonition to the Philippians that if they have "any encouragement in Christ, any comfort from love, any participation in the Spirit (*ei tis koinōnia pneumatos*), any affection and sympathy," then the way to complete Paul's joy was to be unified in mind and in love (Phil. 2:1–2). Humility needs to replace rivalry and conceit (v. 3). To give a different Pauline example, what the Jerusalem church thought of the Gentile mission mattered to him. He rejoiced that "the right hand of fellowship" with its leadership had been extended to him (Gal. 2:1–10)—even though it is clear from the argument of his Galatians letter that, if he had thought that the Galatian leaders' approval would have risked the integrity of his message of grace, he would not have mentioned it (Gal. 1:6–10; 2:11–14).

However, the NT nowhere mandates that a dull uniformity of Ecclesiastical polity is to be pursued. There is every indication that the Pauline communities developed differently from that in Jerusalem. "The right hand of fellowship" does not mean organizational homogeneity, nor that one

137. John Stott, *Focus on Christ: An Enquiry into the Theology of Prepositions* (Glasgow: Collins, 1979), 54–58. For good or ill, the theology of prepositions has had a long history in Christian thought. See Basil of Caesarea, *On the Holy Spirit*, chapters 1–8, for a Patristic example. He laments the way the heretics (the Pneumatomachi, "fighters against the Spirit") appeal to prepositions in the biblical text to erect differences between God and the Spirit that don't exist in reality. I don't believe that Stott falls into the error of misusing prepositions of which Basil writes.

apostolic leader such as Peter rose above all others (contra the claims of the church of Rome). In fact even the Pauline communities themselves may have differed in organization. The first letter to Timothy, for example, speaks of elders and deacons (1 Tim. 3:1–13), but the letter to Titus refers only to elders (Titus 1:5–9). His Corinthian correspondence refers neither to elders nor to deacons. In contrast the Jerusalem church seems to have ultimately come under the presidency of James the brother of Jesus (Acts 15:1–21). Indeed there is some extrabiblical evidence that the leadership of that church may have been kept within Jesus' own family.[138]

The Spirit, Mission, and Persecution

Some years ago I was having dinner with two Christians from different continents when I found myself party to a startling conversation. One was from Pakistan, and he was a giant (around six foot eight and three hundred pounds). The other was from Nigeria, and he was tiny in comparison. Soon both were to graduate from the theological college in Australia where I was teaching at the time. They began to talk about their return home. The Pakistani Christian said that after a time he expected that he would be killed for doing evangelism in that setting. The Nigerian thought that he would only be beaten and his house would be burned down, and that more than once, for doing the same thing. I lived in another world to both of them. For such disciples, Jesus' promise of the Spirit's aid in defending one's faith and giving an account is not a matter of looking for the principle underlying the text (e.g., Mark 13:9–12) so that it might be applied to a very different cultural setting. For them such texts speak with literal forcefulness and are redolent with comfort. In an era in which estimates suggest that more believers die for confessing Christ than at any time in church history, we should remind ourselves that the Spirit will be with the faithful even *in extremis*.[139]

Just What Is Jesus Doing Now?

As a new Christian, I was puzzled by the evangelists whom I heard in those days. They rightly pointed me to the cross and the great act of redemption accomplished there. Sometimes they also spoke of the resurrection. But rarely did they go beyond those fundamental assertions and their implications. And so I found myself asking, "What is Jesus

138. J. Stevenson, ed., *A New Eusebius: Documents Illustrative of the History of the Church to A.D. 337* (London: S.P.C.K., 1970), 8–9. See also "Jerusalem," in F. L. Cross, ed., *The Oxford Dictionary of the Christian Church*, 2nd ed. (Oxford: Oxford University Press, 1978), 733.

139. See Charles Colson's forward to Nina Shea, *In the Lion's Den* (Nashville: Broadman, 1997), ix.

doing now?" Over the years, answers came. For example, I learned that the risen Christ is our great High Priest in heaven who intercedes for us, that he is our advocate at the right hand of the Father, that when the gospel is preached it is the risen Christ who is preaching through human agents, and that he is vitally involved in the life of the churches by his Spirit. Moreover, I learned that the mission of the risen Christ is prosecuted by the Spirit he has sent from the Father. We have not been abandoned to our own devices. We are not orphans. Instead we have been enlisted in the divine project to reclaim creation and, in particular, God's wayward images.

Understanding the Fullness of and by the Spirit: Ephesians 5:18–21

The only place in Scripture that commands that believers be filled with or by the Spirit is in Ephesians 5:18–21, as we have seen. Traditionally the command is interpreted as being about control. Who is to be in charge of the believer's life? Will it be the Spirit? Or will it be something other than the Spirit, such as wine in excess?[140] (In this and the next section, I will be proposing an alternative view.)[141] Significantly, no conditions are set out as to how to obey this command, nor are any steps to fullness mandated. Consequently the advice on how to obey varies. Robert G. Gromacki argues for three conditions based on other Pauline texts: "walk in the Spirit," "don't grieve the Spirit," and "don't quench the Spirit."[142] If we live that way we will be filled with the Spirit. A. W. Tozer argues for four conditions based on a variety of NT texts, including some that are Pauline: "present your vessel [body]," "you must ask," "you must be willingly obedient," and "you must have faith in God."[143] K. Neill Foster offers a more expansive list of conditions. His six conditions are: "be saved," "have a right motive," "have a deep desire to be filled," "be obedient," "put the flesh to death," and "believe God."[144] But the biblical fact is that no conditions and no steps are in the text, as Stanley Toussaint observed.[145] Likewise Boyd Hunt wisely comments,

140. For a brief but clear presentation of the traditional view, see the volume in this series by Demarest (*Cross and Salvation*), 424–428.

141. For a fuller presentation of the alternative view and critique of the traditional one, see my *Engaging with the Holy Spirit: Six Crucial Questions* (Nottingham, England: Inter-Varsity, 2007; and forthcoming, Wheaton, Ill.: Crossway, 2008).

142. Gromacki, "Holy Spirit," 503–504.

143. A. W. Tozer, *The Counselor: Straight Talk about the Holy Spirit from a Twentieth Century Prophet* (Camp Hill, Pa.: Christian Publications, 1993), 80–84.

144. K. Neill Foster, *Six Conditions for the Filling of the Holy Spirit* (Camp Hill, Pa.: Christian Publications, 1999), 3–13.

145. Stanley D. Toussaint, "The Filling of the Spirit," in John R. Masters and Wesley R. Willis, eds., *Basic Theology Applied* (Wheaton, Ill.: Victor, 1995), 213; cited in Gromacki, "Holy Spirit," 503.

> No set of pre-determined conditions to the Spirit-filled life, however arduous and demanding, guarantee the fulness of the Holy Spirit. Christianity, unlike Gnosticism, teaches no secrets for persons to master in order to lead infallibly to lives of unbroken, unclouded fellowship with God.[146]

An evidence-based approach to making theological assertions pays attention to such lacunae in the text. What then are we to make of this absence of conditions for Spirit-fullness in the Ephesians text?

In Ephesians, Paul writes about the corporate life of God's people as the church. In this great company both Jews and Gentiles have their place as the new temple of the holy God indwelt by the Spirit of God (Eph. 2:11–22). The unity established by Christ's death needs maintenance, though. Indeed the Ephesians ought to be "eager to maintain the unity of the Spirit in the bond of peace" (4:3). When they gather, they are not to behave as the Gentiles do (5:6–11). Christian meetings are not to be debauched as though all were drunk with wine and out of control (5:18).[147] In contrast, the Spirit is to fill them as God's temple with group practices that are other-person-centered. In relation to one another, they are to address one another in psalms, hymns, and spiritual songs and submit to one another out of reverence for Christ. In relation to the Lord Jesus himself, they are to sing and make melody in their collective heart to him. And as for the Father, they are to give thanks to him for everything. A congregation where such practices are found, motivated by other-person-centered regard—whether vertically in a Godward direction or horizontally in a fellow believer's direction—is a Spirit-filled reality, a true temple of God. Understood as above, Ephesians may provide better tests for evaluating a church's health than the acreage of the church's parking.

The Individual Believer and the Fullness of the Spirit

I can imagine someone who has read thus far becoming quite frustrated with the discussion about the fullness of the Spirit. Does the previous section suggest or imply that Ephesians has nothing to say about the individual believer outside the context of a congregational meeting? Not at all! A transition takes place between Ephesians 5:18–21 (the congregational meeting) and Paul's discussion of the various relationships to be found in the

---

146. Boyd Hunt, *Redeemed! Eschatological Redemption and the Kingdom of God* (Nashville: Broadman & Holman, 1993), 62. Hunt's foil is R. A. Torrey, who delineated seven steps to the baptism of the Spirit.

147. C. J. Rogers, Jr., "The Dionysian Background of Ephesians 5:18," *Bibliotheca Sacra* 136 (1979): 249–257, suggests the passage needs to be read against the backdrop of Dionysian reveling with its sexual and drunken debauchery. But it is hard to be this specific given the lack of detail in the text, as Gombis, "Being the Fullness of God," convincingly argues (264, fn 15).

Christian household in 5:22–6:9: husbands and wives (5:22–33), children and parents (6:1–4), and slaves and masters (6:5–9). This is Paul's version of the household code (see also Col. 3:18–4:1). In fact, the three sets of relationships just mentioned are discussed in Greek literature as early as Aristotle's *Politics* 1.3.[148] In the structure of Ephesians, Paul has clearly turned his attention away from the congregation per se from Ephesians 5:22 on (or from Eph. 5:21 on according to the NRSV, which heads that section "The Christian Household").

A second question comes to mind. If the only command to be filled by the Spirit in the NT is about congregational life, can nothing then be said about the individual believer and the fullness of the Spirit? After all, in the book of Acts it is quite clear that believers filled with or by the Spirit were empowered in the service of God or exhibited Christlike character. Stephen is an example of both (cf. Acts 6:5, 8, 10; 7:55). The Spirit's filling in Acts is the Spirit giving the believer what he or she needs for the next step of obedience to the divine will and service in God's kingdom.

The biblical answer to the question of how I as an individual may be filled with the Spirit is subtle. One of the stories in Acts provides the way forward, I believe. In Acts 4:23–31 we find Peter and John rejoining their friends after a brief stay in custody. They had been interrogated by the chief priests and elders about a healing incident in the temple and about their preaching Christ (Acts 4:1–22). In a unity of response to the apostles' report the disciples call upon the sovereign Lord in prayer to "look upon their threats and grant to your servants to continue to speak your word [the gospel] with all boldness" (v. 29). The Lord answered their prayer: "they were all filled with the Holy Spirit and continued to speak the word of God with boldness" (v. 31). Significantly these disciples did not pray that they might be filled with the Spirit in order to respond appropriately to the hostility they had encountered. Instead they prayed for the boldness they needed, and in so praying they were filled with the Spirit. When they made the object of their prayer the godly need in that hour (*parrēsia*, boldness), then the fullness came.[149] If I want to be filled with the fullness of the Spirit, then let me set my heart on doing the will of God and call upon him for the enablement to do so (e.g., to preach the gospel faithfully and effectively next Sunday). Unlike idols, the living God answers prayers (cf. Isa. 46:1–7 and Ps. 116:1).

---

148. See the very helpful discussion of the Christian household in comparison and contrast with non-Christian ones in James S. Jeffers, *The Greco-Roman World of the New Testament: Exploring the Background of Early Christianity* (Downers Grove, Ill.: InterVarsity Press, 1999), 80–88, esp. 86, which cites Aristotle's *Politics*.

149. I thank Dr. David G. Peterson, who is the Principal of Oak Hill College in London, for pointing out to me in private conversation this text and its implications.

Holiness of Character Matters

The holy God wants a holy people, who image his character. Believers rightly emphasize the love of God in a broken world. But the loving God of scriptural presentation is also the holy God who is of purer eyes than to behold iniquity. Christian character matters. And the Spirit's ministry is key to Christian character, as the Pauline idea of the fruit of the Spirit shows. Virtue ethics is about the character of the moral agent and has a solid biblical anchorage. Evangelicals have tended to focus on moral acts as to whether they are right or wrong according to moral rules. This deontological approach too has strong biblical support. The Ten Commandments provide a case in point. Moral outcomes also count, as the book of Proverbs makes clear. Good fruit is indicative of a good tree, according to Jesus himself. Consequentialism also has some biblical support. The holy God is interested in the moral agent, the moral action, and the moral aftermath.

However, when right and wrong are reduced simply to whether the moral law has been obeyed or the outcomes of an action are happy ones, while at the same time the question of Christian character is neglected, then something is radically amiss. Moral rule keeping without development of character may lead to censorious legalism, and an outcomes orientation alone may lead to the worst forms of religious trickery, where the end justifies the means. I recall hearing an evangelist appeal for a response. All heads were to bow in an attitude of prayer and those who wanted to respond were to raise their hands. I was at the back in the amphitheater and could see all. No hands were raised until the evangelist started to thank nonexistent people here and there for raising their nonexistent hands. Only then did real people raise their real hands. The Holy Spirit is the architect of Christian integrity. Evangelism divorced from ethics is Spiritless.

The Spirit May Be Grieved

We saw in earlier discussion on progressive sanctification that the Holy Spirit may be grieved (*lupeō*) by certain Christian behaviors such as slander (Eph. 4:30).[150] This is not a new idea in the biblical testimony. Psalm 78 rehearses the history of Israel's disobedience up until the rise of David. Speaking of the wilderness period, the psalmist says, "How often they rebelled against him in the wilderness and grieved him in the desert" (Ps. 78:40). Isaiah 63:10 is more precise: "But they [Israelites] rebelled and grieved his Holy Spirit." How are we to understand this language? Does the Holy Spirit really grieve?

---

150. Elsewhere in the Paulines *lupeō* is used straightforwardly of human sorrow (2 Cor. 2:2, 4; 1 Thess. 4:13).

The classical answer is that God cannot grieve. If God were to grieve then he would be less than perfect and therefore disqualified to be the deity. God is impassible. God is not subject to emotion or emotion-like states. He cannot suffer anything analogous to our experience of mental hurt or anguish. Therefore, the language of the psalm, the prophet, and the epistle must be understood as a way of speaking. The typical way to sum up such language is to call it anthropomorphic. God is spoken of in very human terms (anthropomorphism, i.e., *anthrōpos* "human," *morphē* "shape").[151]

Calvin's sermon on Ephesians 4:30 illustrates the traditional approach, when with his typical lucidity he writes,

> For we know that there are no passions in God. . . . God is unchangeable. Nevertheless, because we do not conceive that he is most high, and his majesty is so infinite that we cannot approach it, the apostle therefore uses a comparison, even for the sake of our ignorance. . . . The Scripture then does not mean to make God subject to any change, when it says that he is angry or is grieved, but it leads us to our own doings, in order that our voices should grieve us so much more, and that we should abhor them.[152]

Calvin understands the reference to the Spirit's grief as a convention of speech. Although the reference is apparently telling the reader something about God, in fact it is saying something about ourselves and how we ought to respond to our behavior that displeases God. "Grieving the Spirit" is accommodated speech. God graciously stoops down to our level in order to communicate.[153]

However this approach, although traditional, is fraught with difficulty. Why read only Scriptures that ostensibly speak of divine grief in this way? Why not read those that speak of divine love and wrath similarly? In my view the Pauline reference to grieving the Spirit is the Achilles' heel of any attempt to discount the idea that Scripture presents a God who knows suffering from the inside.[154]

151. I have argued elsewhere that there is merit in distinguishing between anthropomorphism (human shape) and anthropopathism (human emotion). Since God is Spirit (John 4:24) we recognize the figure of speech involved in Scripture referring to God's hand (i.e., strength, as in Isa. 59:1). It is an anthropomorphism. However, there is no obvious reason to think that the Spirit may not have human-like emotion. See my "The Living God: Anthropomorphic or Anthropopathic?" *RTR* 59 no. 1 (April 2000): 16–27.

152. Quoted in ibid., 19.

153. See the brilliant article on Calvin's *accommodatio* by F. L. Battles, "God Was Accommodating Himself to Human Capacity," *Interpretation* 31 (January 1977): 19–38.

154. Interestingly the ablest defender of the traditional doctrine of divine impassibility, Thomas Weinandy, acknowledges that God is grieved and angered by human sin. However, although God has emotional states, he does not change from one such state to another. He is not mutable (Thomas Weinandy, "Does God Suffer?" *First Things* 117 [November 2001]: 35–41). There is much to commend here. However, it is hard to see how Weinandy is able to

The Horizon of Life

Some years ago Ronald Conway wrote a book about Australia, my home-land, with the title, "The Land of the Long Weekend." His thesis was that the mind-set—or if put into theological categories, the eschatology—of most Australians goes no further than the next public holiday. (I suspect many Americans have the same attitude.) Christians may fall into the same mind-set and forget that we are to pray as our Lord has taught us to do, "Your kingdom come." We can become culturally captive on this point. In other words, we can lose our sense of the imminence of Christ's return for his people. In fact, we can fall into a complacency like that of those scoffers of which 2 Peter 3 speaks. The scoffers argued that "all things are continuing as they were from the beginning of creation" (2 Pet. 3:4). However, as we saw in an earlier section of this chapter, the eschatological Spirit is the firstfruits and guarantee of a future far beyond anything the next long weekend might offer. The best is yet to be, for believers and for the created order. Creation will be reclaimed and transfigured (cf. Rom. 8:18–25 and Revelation 21–22). The Spirit and the Bride are still saying, "Come!" In the meanwhile we live in between the promises of God and their ultimate fulfillment, as Hebrews 11 with its parade of the heroes of faith makes plain. In this we live in the same tension that believers have in every age, whether Abraham, David, Mary, or Paul. The tension is between the now and the not yet.

EXCURSUS: Are All the Gifts of the Spirit for Today?

One of the controversial questions facing churches today is whether all or only some of the gifts of the Spirit, adumbrated in the NT, are still the risen Christ's gift to the church. The tone of discussing such a question needs to be irenic. This is an intramural issue on which believing Christians differ. Dispute concerning the Spirit's person and work is not new, however. Nor is the heat. In the Patristic era, Basil of Caesarea wrote in the midst of debate over the deity of the Spirit,

> Those who judge the erring are merciless and bitter, while those judg-ing the upright are unfair and hostile. This evil is so firmly rooted in us that we have become more brutish than the beasts: At least they herd together with their own kindred, but we reserve our most savage warfare [which he compared earlier to a naval battle] for the members of our own household.[155]

argue consistently that God is "grieved" and yet does not "suffer," unless an unusual definition of both terms is assumed.

155. Basil of Caesarea, *On the Holy Spirit*, 117. For an example of an irenic approach see Wayne Grudem, ed., *Are Miraculous Gifts for Today? Four Views* (Grand Rapids, Mich.: Zondervan, 1996).

This writer has attempted throughout this work to avoid the very belligerency of which Basil complains. Our present task is no exception. Not all will agree with my conclusions, but all should recognize the in-house nature of the issue.

Let us begin with some basic questions.

What Is a Spiritual Gift?

Boyd Hunt offers a useful working definition: *"Spiritual gifts are God empowering His people through the Holy Spirit for kingdom life and service, enabling them in attitude and action to live and minister in a manner which glorifies Christ."*[156] Some gifts appear to be closely related to natural talents and/or Christian character (e.g., the gifts of helps and generosity, respectively). Others seem to be out of the ordinary (e.g., speaking in tongues, especially if understood to be ecstatic). Still others may involve a native ability to speak, together with the involvement of the supernatural (e.g., prophecy).[157] Some theologians write with confidence about the precise nature of each gift mentioned in the NT. Others are far more cautious.[158] The fact is that the NT writers do not define their terms, and why should they? They were writing in a pastoral mode to congregations, not to an academic audience as though they were writing for a peer-reviewed journal.

What Spiritual Gifts Are There?

There are three important NT passages that adumbrate spiritual gifts. The Romans list includes: prophecy, service, teaching, exhortation, generosity, leading, and acting mercifully (Rom. 12:6–8). This passage sources the diversity of these gifts in the grace of God, and their use is tied to faith. The Corinthians list is more extensive: the utterance of wisdom, the utterance of knowledge, faith, gifts of healing, working of miracles, prophecy, ability to distinguish between spirits, various kinds of tongues and the interpretation of tongues (1 Cor. 12:4–11).[159] The gifts are described as

156. Hunt, *Redeemed!* 48–49, emphasis original. Hunt offers his "working definition" in the light of Kenneth S. Hemphill's *Spiritual Gifts: Empowering the New Testament Church* (Nashville: Broadman, 1988). It is important to note, however, that, ". . . there is no precise Hebrew/Greek equivalent to the English phrase 'spiritual gift'" and that the term is used as "mainly a collective label [by] *interpreters* . . . to pigeonhole certain phenomena" (Max Turner, "Spiritual Gifts," *NDBT*, 789–790, emphasis original).

157. Turner carefully discusses the difficulty of working out the degree to which the gifts are "almost entirely the work of God's Spirit" as opposed to "natural abilities" at the Spirit's service ("Spiritual Gifts," *NDBT*, 790–791).

158. Hunt, *Redeemed!* 47.

159. Although *pneumatika* in 1 Corinthians 12:1 may be translated "spiritual gifts" as in the ESV, that is an interpretation. It could also mean "spiritual persons," as the ESV footnote correctly observes.

charismata in 1 Corinthians 12:4.[160] They are given Trinitarianly. Father, Son, and Spirit are involved in gifting the church, but the Spirit's sovereign role in their distribution is highlighted. They are given for the common good. Later in the same chapter, Paul adds to the list gifts of helping and administering (12:27–31). The Petrine list includes: speaking the oracles of God and serving (1 Pet. 4:10–11). These gifts are for serving others and have their source in the grace of God.

Some include Ephesians 4:11 in their accounts of spiritual gifts.[161] It is a nice question as to whether apostles, prophets, evangelists, and pastors-teachers are better discussed under the head of the foundation of the church (apostles and prophets) or offices of the church (evangelists and pastor-teachers) than under that of *charismata*. Attempting to answer that question, however, is beyond our present purpose.[162]

What is clear is that there is no reason for thinking that the lists of gifts in the various passages are meant to be exhaustive. As Peter O'Brien argues,

> The New Testament contains five such lists (Rom. 12:6-8; 1 Cor. 12:8-10, 28-30; Eph. 4:11-12; cf. 1 Pet. 4:10-11) which between them number more than twenty different gifts, some of which are not particularly spectacular (cf. Rom. 12:8). Each list diverges significantly from the others. None is complete, but each is selective and illustrative, with no effort to force the various gifts into a neat scheme. Even all five do not present a full catalogue of gifts.[163]

O'Brien's five lists include, of course, not just gifts of the Spirit but also those of the risen Christ (cf. 1 Cor. 12:8–10 and Eph. 4:11–12), and he separates 1 Corinthians 12 into two lists.

Two Controversial Gifts Then and Now: Prophecy and Tongues

Paul singles out prophecy and tongues-speaking for special consideration in his first letter to the Corinthians. Those who exercised these two gifts

---

160. Turner argues convincingly that the popular idea that etymologically *charismata* is derived from *charis*, meaning "grace," is mistaken ("Spiritual Gifts," *NDBT*, 792). Rather, it simply means "thing given" or "gift."

161. I part company with Hunt, *Redeemed!* 45 on this point. Interestingly charismatic theologian J. Rodman Williams recognizes the uniqueness of the original apostles and the "original" NT prophets in his own discussion of ministry (*Renewal Theology: Systematic Theology from a Charismatic Perspective: Three Volumes in One* [Grand Rapids, Mich.: Zondervan, 1996], chapter 5 of vol. 3 [164–174]). He discusses *charismata* in chapter 14 of vol. 2, following his treatment of gifts of the Spirit in the previous chapter. Thus he separates the two themes. See also Turner, "Spiritual Gifts," *NDBT*, 795, for a helpfully nuanced treatment.

162. See the brief discussion of offices and spiritual gifts in Carson, *Showing the Spirit*, 184–185.

163. Peter T. O'Brien, *The Letter to the Ephesians*, The Pillar New Testament Commentary (Grand Rapids, Mich.: Eerdmans, 1999), 298.

needed to hear that God was a God of order and not of strife, and that love for others should impel the exercise of such gifts. Defining what each of these gifts actually was is very difficult, and the suggestions are manifold. Let me put them in question form, starting with tongues-speaking. Are tongues ordinary languages but unknown to the speaker at the time of their exercise in the congregation? Or are tongues ecstatic speech with no known human counterparts? Or are tongues the language of angels (as 1 Cor. 13:1 might suggest)? These are just a few of the suggestions.[164] One thing is clear from the Greek of 1 Corinthians 12:30, and that is that Paul did not expect all to speak in tongues.[165] Of course he wished that the situation were otherwise: "Now I want you all to speak in tongues" (14:5). But he also wished that all the Corinthians were unmarried (7:7). An apostolic wish is not an apostolic command.[166] Those who insist that all Christians ought to be tongues-speakers or that tongues-speaking is initial evidence of salvation are exegetically adrift and, pastorally speaking, exceedingly unhelpful.[167]

As for NT prophecy, there are a number of suggestions, and again I will put them in question form. Was such prophecy revelatory and therefore on a par with the writing prophets of the OT era? Or was such prophecy a lesser form of Spirit-directed communication? Could prophecy have simply been the proclaimed gospel or have been inspired applications of the apostolic gospel, or even an apostolic letter embodying the gospel and its application?[168]

These are huge and controversial questions. On Monday to Wednesday my own view is that the tongues at Pentecost and those at Corinth differ. The former were unknown languages (xenoglossa) and the latter were ecstatic (glossolalia). For the rest of the week I feel the force of the argument that in both places tongues were the same (xenoglossa). But even this view

164. There is an excellent discussion of the possibilities in Carson, *Showing the Spirit*, 77–88. He argues that the tongues spoken at Pentecost and those spoken in Corinth were not essentially different. That is to say, they were real languages with cognitive content but serving different functions. For example, the tongues of Pentecost could be understood by bystanders. However, the tongues at Corinth needed interpretation and consisted of a special form of coded utterance, 83–86.

165. Paul uses *mē* in 1 Corinthians 12:30, which indicates that he expects a negative answer to his question. If he had used *ou* or *ouchi* then the reverse would apply.

166. A point well made by Paul Barnett and Peter Jensen, *The Quest for Power* (Sydney: Anzea, 1973), 84.

167. Craig S. Keener argues that "those who require tongues for salvation—are becoming an increasingly small minority" (*Gift Giver: The Holy Spirit for Today* [Grand Rapids, Mich.: Baker, 2002], 92–93).

168. As Barnett and Jensen imply (ibid., esp. 103–104). They argue with regard to OT prophecy that, "It is an inadequate reading of the Old Testament which separates prophecy from preaching or the exposition of Scripture" (ibid., 101). Their argument suggests that they see an analogy between Old and New Testament presentations of prophecy. Packer argues similarly (*Keep in Step with the Spirit*, 215). For a contrary view, see Michael Green, *I Believe in the Holy Spirit* (London, Sydney, and Auckland: Hodder & Stoughton, 1992), 211.

admits of subdivision. One might argue that in both places unknown but actual earthly languages were spoken, which to those who did not know them might sound like gibberish or slurred speech (hence the accusation of drunkenness at Pentecost). Or one might argue that in both places the tongues were ecstatic (hence the bystanders at Pentecost thought the speakers were drunk).

As for prophecy, whatever else it may have been as a form of communication, at Pentecost its content was forth-telling the mighty works of God in the gospel (Acts 2:11, *ta megaleia tou theou;* the ESV and NRSV are better than the NIV here, which has "wonders") and at Corinth prophetic activity could disclose the secrets of the heart (1 Cor. 14:25).[169] Interestingly, knowing or exposing the moral state of the human heart seemed to be a defining characteristic of a prophet, according to Luke 7:36–50 and John 4:1–38. In the former case, Simon the Pharisee thought to himself that if Jesus were a prophet, he would know the moral state of the woman showing him such deference (Luke 7:39). And in the latter case the woman of Samaria when confronted with Jesus' knowledge of her marital and extramarital history declared him to be a prophet (John 4:19). Peter's prophetic discourse on the day of Pentecost confronted the hearers with "this Jesus . . . you crucified and killed by the hands of lawless men" (Acts 2:23). The hearers "were cut [*katenugēsan*] to the heart" (v. 37). Paul instructed the Thessalonian believers not to despise prophecies and yet called for discernment on their part (1 Thess. 5:19–21). He instructed those at Corinth similarly (1 Cor. 14:29). In my view there is an argument, then, that even regular preaching might become prophetic when used of the Spirit to so expose the hearts of the hearers.[170]

The Gifts and Today

Are all the gifts of the Spirit, including prophecy and tongues, intended for the church today? There are two main views: cessationist and continuationist.[171] Both cessationists and continuationists are supernaturalists. Their

169. Like OT prophecy, NT prophecy exhibits both the forth-telling of God's word and foretelling the future (ibid., 101–102).

170. My view is consistent with that of Anthony C. Thiselton, *The First Epistle to the Corinthians*, New International Greek Testament Commentary (Grand Rapids, Mich.: Eerdmans, 2000), 1094; and indeed with Calvin's view (John Calvin, *The First Epistle of Paul to the Corinthians*, trans. John W. Fraser [Grand Rapids, Mich.: Eerdmans, 1960], 271). I owe these references to Dr. Sam Chan. Carson asks, "What preacher has not had the experience, after detailed preparation for public ministry, of being interrupted in the full flow of his delivery with a new thought, fresh and powerful, interrupting him and insinuating itself upon his mind, until he makes room for it and incorporates it into his message—only to find after the service that the insertion was the very bit that seemed to touch the most people, and meet their needs? Most charismatics would label the same experience a 'prophecy'" (*Showing the Spirit*, 168–169).

171. I draw the categories from Gregory A. Boyd and Paul R. Eddy, *Across the Spectrum: Understanding Issues in Evangelical Theology* (Grand Rapids, Mich.: Baker, 2002), 212.

differences lie in differing assessments of the importance for today of the gifts of the Holy Spirit. On the one hand, the cessationists—as the name for this position implies—argue that certain *charismata* belonged to the period of the open canon, and once the canon of Scripture was closed then they disappeared from the life of the church.[172] Therefore, not all the NT *charismata* are operative today. Richard Gaffin Jr. maintains, "The issue of cessation needs to be focused. I certainly do not hold that all the gifts of the Spirit have ceased or that the church is devoid of such gifts today. . . . Suffice it here to say that the question is not *whether* but *which* spiritual gifts continue today."[173] According to Gaffin, tongues is an example of a gift that has ceased. And so whatever tongues-speaking today might be, it is not the NT phenomenon.[174] On the other hand, the continuationists believe that all the charismata mentioned in the NT continue today—as the name for this position implies. But there is a subdivision of opinion among continuationists. The cautious argue that there is no convincing theological reason to think that the risen Christ may not still be gifting his church with the *charismata* but they are somewhat skeptical about many contemporary claims, especially Pentecostal, charismatic, and Third Wave, for their present existence and use.[175] They are also aware of the definitional difficulties and the problem of knowing that a claimed phenomenon of today (e.g., tongues-speaking) really is the same as the one referred to in the NT. This view has been described as the "open but cautious view."[176] The other kind of continuationist is enthusiastic about both the existence of the *charismata* and their contemporary use, even though mindful of many present-day abuses.[177]

Let's now examine more closely—albeit in broad strokes—the cases for cessation and for continuation.

The case for cessation rests on a number of considerations.[178] The biblical argument for cessation is based on texts such as Ephesians 2:18–22; Hebrews 2:2–4; and 1 Corinthians 13:8–13. Ephesians 2:18–22 speaks of "the household of God, built on the foundation of the apostles and

172. The ranks of cessationists include not only Gaffin, *Perspectives on Pentecost*; but also John F. MacArthur Jr., *Charismatic Chaos* (Grand Rapids, Mich.: Zondervan, 1992); and Daniel B. Wallace, "Who's Afraid of the Holy Spirit?" *Christianity Today,* September 12, 1994, 35–38.

173. Gaffin, in Grudem, ed., *Are Miraculous Gifts for Today?* 41, emphasis original.

174. For example, Gaffin, *Perspectives on Pentecost,* chapter 5.

175. For a brief description of the these three views see Grudem, "Preface," in *Are Miraculous Gifts for Today?* 11–12. See also the Glossary.

176. For example, Robert L. Saucy in Grudem, *Are Miraculous Gifts for Today?* 97–148.

177. For example, Douglas A. Oss, in ibid., 239–283, 313; and Keener, *Gift Giver,* esp. chapter 5.

178. For the purposes of our discussion I am going to follow the case for cessation set out in Boyd and Eddy, *Across the Spectrum,* 219–224. One lack in Boyd and Eddy's discussion is that *no* attention is given to the cessationist argument that the Pastoral Epistles "most prominently, address and make specific provision for our post apostolic situation" (see Richard Gaffin Jr., *Perspectives on Pentecost,* 113).

prophets, Christ Jesus himself being the cornerstone." A foundation is only built once, and the charismatic gifts were part of God's design for securing the foundation. In Hebrews 2:2–4, the writer "draws a parallel between the attestation of the revelation given in the Old Testament and the attestation of the revelation given in the early church."[179] God secures his revelation through the miraculous. Hebrews 2:3–4 states that the great salvation "declared at first by the Lord" and "by those who heard" was also witnessed to by God "by signs and wonders and various miracles and by gifts of the Holy Spirit." For example, Paul's ministry was characterized by the signs of an apostle, including "signs and wonders and mighty works" (2 Cor. 12:12). But is this revealing activity of God to continue from the apostolic age to our own era? No! Paul in 1 Corinthians 13:8–13 writes of the charismatic gifts such as prophecy and tongues ceasing "when the perfect comes" (1 Cor. 13:10). The Greek word (*teleion*), translated as "perfect" (e.g., ESV), could justifiably be translated as "complete" (NRSV). What is in view is not the return of Christ but the completion of God's special revelation in its canonical form.[180] The biblical argument is supported by an appeal to early church history. Early church history shows the decline of references to the miraculous and to the gifts of the Holy Spirit. Once the canon was complete, there was no need of them.

The case for continuation likewise rests on a number of considerations.[181] The biblical argument for continuation parades the various passages delineating the gifts of the Spirit, such as 1 Corinthians 12:8–10, 28–30; Romans 12:6–8; Ephesians 4:11; and 1 Peter 4:10–11, then raises the questions: Where is it stated that God did not intend for these gifts to continue throughout history? Isn't it arbitrary to suppose, for example, that the gift of teaching is still valid but the gift of tongues is not? Moreover, earlier in 1 Corinthians, Paul made it plain that he expected the gifts to operate until the return of Christ: ". . . you [Corinthians] are not lacking in any spiritual gift, as you wait for the revealing of our Lord Jesus Christ" (1 Cor. 1:7). On the continuationist view, the cessationist position is an unwarranted inference from a cluster of biblical texts that either point in a different direction (e.g., 1 Cor. 13:10 is about Christ's return, and not the canon) or are irrelevant to the debate once properly exegeted (Heb. 2:2–4). The continuationist case also finds support in such references to the gifts of the Spirit as are found in early church literature (e.g., Justin Martyr, Irenaeus,

179. Ibid., 220. The present paragraph summarizes the main thrust of Boyd and Eddy's argument (219–224).

180. Ibid., 221. Boyd and Eddy correctly point out that not all cessationists exegete 1 Corinthians 13:10 in this fashion. Gaffin is an example of a cessationist who does not (*Perspectives on Pentecost*, 109–112).

181. Again, I am summarizing the main thrust of Boyd and Eddy's most helpful setting out of the two sides of the debate (ibid., 214–219).

Tertullian, Origen).[182] These references show that the gifts did not die out after the apostolic era had passed.

Open but Discerning

In my view one's eschatology is crucial with regard to the question of the *charismata* and today. Something of the world to come has broken into the Christian's life (Heb. 6:5). But the best is yet to be, and that best lies beyond this "present evil age," to use Paul's idiom (Gal. 1:4). Those who hold such inaugurated eschatology as I do cannot foreclose on what a sovereign and gracious God might do to gift the church. Moreover, broadly speaking, in a very real sense all Christians are charismatics because every genuine Christian has been incorporated into the body of Christ and gifted in some way by the Spirit.[183] The cessationist arguments that canon closure is in view in 1 Corinthians 13:10 ("when the perfect comes") and that the Pastorals (1 Timothy, 2 Timothy, and Titus) show the eclipse of the *charismata* by the absence of reference to them do not persuade me. With regard to the former argument, the reference in 1 Corinthians 13:10 appears more likely to be a reference to the return of Christ, and additionally, 1 Corinthians 1:4–8 places the Corinthians and the exercise of their gifts in the framework of life between the cross and the second coming of Christ, and not that of the cross and canon closure.[184] Moreover, I find it hard to imagine that the charismatic gift of faith (*pistis en tō autō pneumati*, 1 Cor. 12:9) no longer remains among God's people. Since faith is a necessary condition for being a Christian, a special capacity for faith is in view (cf. Rom. 5:1 and Heb. 11:6). James 5:15 with its reference to the "prayer of faith" and healing the sick may be an example of how this charismatic gift of faith shows itself, as C. Samuel Storms suggests.[185] Interestingly, a cessationist such as Richard Gaffin Jr. believes that James 5:14–15 is still applicable to today's church.[186] Cessationists therefore aren't necessarily anti-supernaturalist or bound by Enlightenment presuppositions—contrary to some of

182. See the section entitled "Gifts of the Spirit" in David W. Bercot, ed., *A Dictionary of Early Christian Beliefs: A Reference Guide to More than 700 Topics Discussed by the Early Church Fathers* (Peabody, Mass.: Hendrickson, 2002), 298–304. Note, this work only deals with the Ante-Nicene Fathers. See also Chad Owen Brand's own contribution to the volume he edited, *Perspectives on Spirit Baptism: Five Views* (Nashville: Broadman & Holman, 2004), 1–14, for a discussion of the evidence provided by the early church period. Carson, *Showing the Spirit*, 165–169, is also very useful on the evidence of history.

183. A point well made by both Keener, *Gift Giver*, 93–94, as a continuationist; and Gaffin, *Perspectives on Pentecost*, 47–48, as a cessationist.

184. I note that in Gaffin's fine presentations of the cessationist case, at no point does he discuss 1 Corinthians 1:4–8 with regard to gifts and eschatology. See his *Perspectives on Pentecost* and his contribution to Grudem, ed., *Are Miraculous Gifts for Today?* This lacuna is a major weakness.

185. See C. Samuel Storms, "A Third Wave View," in ibid., 213–214.

186. For example, Richard Gaffin Jr., *Perspectives on Pentecost,* 114.

their critics.[187] With regard to the Pastoral Epistles, the absence of evidence is not necessarily the evidence of absence. Otherwise one could argue, for example, that James knew nothing of the Lord's Supper because he does not mention it in his brief letter. An argument based on the silences of the Pastoral Epistles is dubious.

With regard to those who are enthusiastic about *charismata* for today's church, some seem all too ready to define NT terms for gifts too precisely and identify present-day phenomena with NT realities too facilely. As John Owen "contends," according to Packer's putting words in Owen's mouth,

> Since one can never conclusively prove that any charismatic man- ifestation is identical with what is claimed as its New Testament counterpart, one can never in any particular case have more than a tentative and provisional opinion, open to constant reconsideration as time and life go on.[188]

There is then the need for discernment. Certainly Scripture gives every reason for thinking that false teaching and false prophecy will continue to plague the church (Matt. 24:24; 2 Pet. 2:1; and 1 John 4:1). And so Christian gullibility—a long-standing problem—must be avoided.[189]

Open but discerning is the way forward that I would advocate. This is one of the versions of continuationism. In practical terms, for me thus far that has meant adopting a position in the debate that is little different from cessationism. Experience has taught me to be discerning. Over the years I have heard "tongues" spoken on more than one occasion. I have seen the ecstasy on the faces of those who so spoke. I do not begrudge their ecstasy. I do not deny that God may have blessed them and others through their ut- terances. I have also heard the interpretations of some of them. In the main these interpretations have been pastiches of Scripture phrases expressed in a fervent praise mode. These interpretations have been unexceptional. I have also heard prophesyings in a congregational setting. I have no reason to doubt the sincerity of the "prophets," but the actual "prophecies" were vague and loosely based on Scripture passages which I recognized. But are these the tongues, interpretations of tongues, and prophesyings of which Paul wrote?

Pentecostal scholar Gordon Fee has his doubts too with regard to con- temporary tongues-speaking. He writes,

187. Gaffin, in Grudem, ed., *Are Miraculous Gifts for Today?* 25–26. For the critical view see Keener, *Gift Giver,* 89–91, esp. the reference to "Bible Deists" borrowed from Dallas Wil- lard with acknowledgment.

188. This is Packer's imaginative reconstruction of what Owen might have said if confronted with the claims of *charismata* operating today (J. I. Packer, *A Quest for Holiness: The Puritan Vision of the Christian Life* [Wheaton, Ill.: Crossway, 1990], 221).

189. Lucian on Peregrinus is a second-century instance (see Stevenson, ed., *New Eusebius,* 134–136).

The question as to whether the "speaking in tongues" in contemporary Pentecostal and charismatic communities is the same in kind as that in the Pauline churches is moot—and probably somewhat irrelevant. There is simply no way to know.[190]

He settles for the notion that contemporary speaking in tongues is "at the very least analogous" to that of the Pauline churches.[191] Because of the analogy, there is no need for the Pauline phenomenon and the contemporary one to be identical in order for the contemporary practice to be embraced by the churches—because, in his view, the analogy lies in both being the result of the supernatural activity of the Spirit, which simply begs the question. Is the analogy a real one? How does he know that contemporary tongues-speaking is the result of the Spirit's activity?

However, it may be objected, "Doesn't continuationism necessarily entail the idea that there are apostles today of the same sort as Peter and Paul were in New Testament times?" I think not. Paul makes it clear that those NT apostles were integral to the foundation of the church (Eph. 2:20). With regard to the apostles, D. A. Carson argues,

> As long as 'apostles' are understood to refer to a select group (the Twelve plus Paul) whose position or functions cannot be duplicated after their demise, there is a prima facie case for saying *at least one* of the *charismata* [the original quote has the Greek as well] passes away at the end of the first generation, a gift tightly tied to the locus of revelation that came with Jesus.[192]

In my view, this argument also applies *mutatis mutandis* to the prophets Paul refers to in Ephesians 2:20. If Wayne Grudem is correct, then Paul is writing of the apostles who were also prophets.[193] More likely though, these prophets were foundational NT ones.[194] Some of these may also have been apostles. For example, if the book of Revelation was written by the apostle John, as traditionally supposed, then there is indeed evidence that apostles also could function as prophets in a self-aware way (cf. Rev. 1:3–4 and 22:18–19).

Positively speaking, great expectations of God is a defining characteristic of the charismatic movement in mainline churches and of Pentecostal

190. Gordon D. Fee, *Listening to the Spirit in the Text* (Grand Rapids, Mich., Cambridge, and Vancouver: Eerdmans/Regent College Publishing, 2000), 115, fn 18.

191. Ibid.

192. Carson, *Showing the Spirit*, 88, emphasis original. Carson is well aware that the NT in places uses the term "apostle" in the broader sense of messenger (e.g., Epaphroditus, Phil. 2:25). Even so he cogently argues that there is no good reason to think that any present-day person is an apostle like the Twelve and Paul (ibid., 88–91).

193. Wayne Grudem, *The Gift of Prophecy in 1 Corinthians* (Washington, D.C.: University Press of America, 1982), 82–105. For criticisms of Grudem's view, see Carson, *Showing the Spirit*, 90, fn 49; and more generally of this view see Gaffin, *Perspectives on Pentecost*, 93–95.

194. Richard Gaffin Jr., *Perspectives on Pentecost*, 93–102.

and Third Wave churches.[195] In the light of this, the open but discerning position means a certain generosity toward those who are enthusiastic for Christ and who believe in a living God who acts in history today, but whose theological skill in articulating the nature of their experiences, ministries, and gifting may be lacking. For example, someone may speak of how the Holy Spirit has given them the gift of prophecy, whereas to my mind when I hear them speak, it seems more like an expression of Christian wisdom. Genuine gifts from God and experiences of the Lord may simply be misdescribed. It is all too easy to dismiss the experience rather than to explain the way of the Lord more accurately as Priscilla and Aquila did with Apollos (Acts 18:26).

195. See the insightful article by Chris Armstrong, "Embrace Your Inner Pentecostal," *Christianity Today*, September 2006, 88.

TEN

THE SPIRIT AND KNOWING GOD

A great challenge to any worldview is securing its epistemological basis. Why believe its claims? How can we have confidence in its truth? In the first instance Christianity is not commending a worldview but a relationship. It is a religion (a binding relationship). At the center of that relationship is the living God who is Father, Son, and Holy Spirit. But the relationship also comes with a worldview. By that I mean a set of answers to our most basic questions: What is real? What is ultimate? Where do we come from? What is the matter with humankind? What hope is there for us? Christianity claims a special revelation from God that informs its construal of reality and its answers to these fundamental questions. In other words, supernaturalism.[1] The relationship to God it claims is predicated on revealed truth.[2] As we shall see, the Holy Spirit plays the pivotal role in making God knowable and known. He is the searcher of the depths of God.

Classically, the theological sources for the knowledge of God have been construed as general or natural revelation (Ps. 19:1–6) and special reve-

---

1. I distinguish two kinds of worldview. An existential worldview answers the set of basic questions already listed. An encyclopedic worldview is a much grander project. It attempts a synoptic view of all things: art, craft, science, social sciences, humanities, popular culture, and so forth. God has this view. Our grand metaphysical schemes are attempts to reconstruct, as it were, the mind of God. For more on this distinction see my "Christianity as a Relational Religion," in Michael Schluter and John Ashcroft, eds., *Jubilee Manifesto: A Framework, Agenda, and Strategy for Christian Social Reform* (Leicester, England: Inter-Varsity, 2005), 37–49. For an important recent discussion of the concept of worldview see David K. Naugle, *Worldview: The History of a Concept* (Grand Rapids, Mich., and Cambridge: Eerdmans, 2002).

2. Once supernaturalism is allowed to slip, Christianity becomes yet another example of the human search for transcendence, rather than a response to the divine search for us. A theologian of the past who saw that supernaturalism—including a supernatural revelation—is at the heart of the Christian Faith was B. B. Warfield. See his chapter entitled "Christian Supernaturalism," in his *Biblical and Theological Studies* (Philadelphia: Presbyterian & Reformed, 1968), 1–21.

lation (vv. 7–11). The term "general" in the expression "general revelation" refers to its putative recipients: that is to say, all people everywhere and at any time. The synonym "natural revelation" includes "natural" to indicate the medium of revelation: that is to say, revelation through the natural order. Both of these concepts are to be distinguished from the concept of natural theology. Natural theology is a project of unaided human reason that attempts to establish what, if anything, may be successfully argued with regard to the existence and character of God or gods. The earliest philosophical example of this project known to me is found in book 10 of Plato's *Laws*.[3] An issue of frequent and long-standing debate is whether the Scriptures reflect this project or embody it in any way. Special revelation refers to what God has made known of his character, will, and ways to some people in particular—most notably, prophet and apostle—through specific words and interpreted deeds, which now finds its definitive crystallization in inspired Holy Scripture.

With regard to general revelation, there is simply too little scriptural evidence of the Spirit's role in leaving fallen humankind without excuse (Rom. 1:18–23). This has not stopped some from pursuing the question, a subject to which we shall return at a later stage. However when it comes to special revelation and the Holy Spirit, there is much biblical evidence to consider. To that evidence and its implications we now turn.

THE SEARCHER OF THE DEPTHS

There is a certain fittingness in the Spirit's playing the pivotal role in our knowing God. The classic text to explore here is Paul's discussion of the Spirit in 1 Corinthians 2:6–13. In his examination of the wisdom of God displayed in the gospel, Paul argues that it is the Spirit who makes that wisdom known. He draws an analogy between our self-knowledge and God's self-knowledge. "Like knows like" is the ancient epistemic principle of connaturality, and that principle is assumed by Paul.[4] The spirit (*pneuma*) in a man and a woman (Paul uses *anthrōpos*) knows the person from the inside in a way that the outsider does not. There is privileged access. Likewise with God and God's Spirit (*pneuma*), there is privileged access. However, that Spirit can make that knowledge available and has done so through the gospel. The depths (*ta bathē*) that Paul refers to appear to be the gospel as the wisdom (*sophia*) of God that the world does not recognize.[5] As B. B.

---

3. See the extract in D. Elton Trueblood, *Philosophy of Religion* (Grand Rapids, Mich.: Baker, 1985), 307–312.

4. See Gordon D. Fee, *God's Empowering Presence: The Holy Spirit in the Letters of Paul* (Peabody, Mass.: Hendrickson, 2005), 99.

5. Ibid., 100. See also Peter Jensen, *The Revelation of God* (Downers Grove, Ill.: InterVarsity Press, 2002), 251.

Warfield suggested long ago in reference to our passage, the Spirit "appears as the substrate of the Divine self-consciousness, the principle of God's knowledge of Himself."[6] Put another way, we might say that the Spirit is the epistemic bond in the triune Godhead, and not only the love bond as Augustine argued. If Christ is the redemptive mediator, then arguably the Spirit is the epistemic mediator.[7] Gordon Fee puts it well:

> In terms of his relationship to us, the Spirit is first of all the *revealer* (vv. 10-11), the one who, to use John's language, "takes the things of Christ and makes them known to us." He is therefore the *instructor* in the ways of God and Christ (vv. 2-13).[8]

There is no knowing God without the continual searcher (*erauvaō* is in the present aspect in the text) of the depths of God, namely the Spirit. Therefore it is no surprise to find the Spirit thematized in other places in Scripture when God's making himself known is in view. To a consideration of that revelatory word we next turn.

THE SPIRIT AND THE REVELATORY WORD

The God of revelation is no mime artist who simply acts to create and redeem but leaves his creatures to grope for the interpretation. God has made himself known in prophetic word, gospel word, and supremely the incarnate Word. The crystallization of such revelation is found in the scriptural word. And the Spirit is pivotally involved in each, as we shall see.

To start with, Scripture makes it plain that in OT times messianic prophecy came by the instrumentality of the Spirit. In 1 Peter 1:10–12 the foretelling mode of prophecy is in view. The prophets prophesied of the salvation that was to come at the instigation of "the Spirit of Christ in them" (1 Pet. 1:11). Indeed the Spirit predicted the two states of Christ: the state of humiliation ("the sufferings of Christ") and the state of glory ("the subsequent glories"). In prophesying such grace, the prophets were not serving themselves but Peter's readers (v. 12).

The same passage from 1 Peter is also important for understanding the Spirit's relationship to the gospel word as proclaimed by the apostles. The Spirit is pivotally involved in this proclaiming activity, since it is by the Spirit that the good news has been preached. The prophetic word is fulfilled "in the things that have now been announced to you [Peter's readers] through those who preached the good news to you by the Holy Spirit" (1 Pet. 1:12). Thus

6. B. B. Warfield, *Biblical Foundations* (London: The Tyndale Press, 1958), 110.

7. On the epistemic importance of the Spirit see Thomas F. Torrance, "The Epistemological Relevance of the Holy Spirit," in R. Schippers et al., eds., *Ex Auditu Verbi* (Kampen: J. H. Kok, 1965), 272–296.

8. Fee, *God's Empowering Presence*, 98, emphasis original.

the Spirit who spoke in OT prophesying also speaks in NT gospel proclamation.[9] Paul likewise gives the Spirit a prominent role in the proclamation of the gospel. In fact in the NT, "word," "word of God," and "word of the Lord" language applies most frequently to the oral communication of the gospel rather than to a written text (cf. 1 Cor. 15:2; 2 Cor. 2:17; and Acts 8:25). Paul's first letter to the Thessalonians is a case in point. In chapter 1 he rehearses what has happened to them when the gospel came—how they "turned to God from idols to serve the living and true God"; how they are "wait[ing] for his Son from heaven" (1 Thess. 1:9–10). It is this Son, who is now raised from the dead, who will deliver them "from the wrath to come" (v. 10). This gospel he describes in the next chapter as "the word of God," which they had received as such and not as "the word of men" (2:13).[10] Significantly, this word came not as mere word but with the Spirit (1:5). Word with Spirit had transformed the Thessalonians. As Fee finely says, "What is finally significant, of course, is that in both cases—his [Paul's] preaching and their [the Thessalonians'] conversion—the Spirit is the key."[11] Moreover, according to Paul this word was still actively at work within them as believers ("continually works," *energeitai,* present aspect, 2:13).

The definitive Word of God is the Son, who as the Logos became flesh and dwelt among us (John 1:1 and 1:14). He was able to sum up his entire ministry as that of definitively manifesting the name of the Father ("manifested," *ephanerōsa,* aorist aspect, 17:6) and passing the Father's words to them (John 17:8). Jesus as the one sent by God utters the words of God and can do so because the Spirit has been given to him "without measure" (3:34). Indeed Jesus' words are "spirit and life" predicated on "the Spirit who gives life" (6:63). The Son is the exegete of the invisible Father by the Spirit ("definitively made known," *exēgēsato,* aorist aspect, 1:18) and the Spirit as Paraclete is the exegete of the Son. It is the Spirit who "will teach you [apostles] all things and bring to your remembrance all that I have said to you" (14:26). He is the supreme witness to Christ, his glorifier and the declarer of what is his (16:13–17). He is "the Spirit of truth" (15:26 and 16:13).

The work of the Spirit is also integral to the production of the scriptural Word of God. Kevin J. Vanhoozer sums up the theological claim well:

> The Scriptures are the Spirit's work from first to last. The Spirit is involved in the very messy historical process of producing Scripture—prompting, appropriating, and coordinating human discourse to present God's Word—as well as in the process of bringing about

9. George T. Montague, *The Holy Spirit: Growth of a Biblical Tradition: A Commentary on the Principal Texts of the Old and New Testaments* (New York and Toronto: Paulist, 1976), 313, says, "The continuity of the New Testament with the Old is thus assured not only because the same God speaks in both but also because the same Spirit acts in both."

10. In 1 Thessalonians "word of God" (*logon theou,* 2:13) as the gospel is to be distinguished from an occasional "word from the Lord" on a particular subject (*en logō kuriou,* 4:15).

11. Fee, *God's Empowering Presence,* 45.

understanding of Scripture among present-day readers. The traditional names for these modes of participation are *inspiration* and *illumination*, respectively.[12]

There is strong biblical backing for such claims. For example, from 2 Peter 1:19–21 we learn that no prophecy of Scripture is a merely human product.[13] Men impelled by the Spirit spoke like a boat moved by the breeze.

As is so often the case with the scriptural testimony, we would love to know the psychology of this phenomenon. Were the prophets always conscious of the Spirit at work in them? What did it feel like? How did his work present itself to their consciousness? But Scripture is non-postulational. Theories aren't given us in Scripture as to the essences of things.[14] The fact is asserted, but no theory is offered to explain it. Nor is there any explanation of the precise relationship between the Spirit's agency and human agency in the inscripturation of God's word. This *concursus* is clearly claimed but never explained. Thus in Hebrews 3–4 we find that Psalm 95, which the writer is applying to the consciences of his readers, is what "the Holy Spirit says" (Heb. 3:7), and yet the psalm is also David's work (Heb. 4:7). Thus, through double agency, both human and divine, Scripture has been provided. (The doctrine of providence understood as God's provision through his wise *gubernatio* or government, utilizing *concursus* is the best theological framework for discussing Scripture.[15]) Scripture is indeed God-breathed (*theopneustos*, 2 Tim. 3:16) but there is a human story to it as well.

The Spirit and Receiving and Understanding the Revelatory Word

For the revelatory word to be effective it needs to be embraced. Not all who hear or read that word embrace it. This should not be surprising. In

12. Kevin J. Vanhoozer, *The Drama of Doctrine: A Canonical Linguistic Approach to Christian Theology* (Louisville: Westminster/John Knox, 2005), 226, emphasis original.

13. This Petrine text should not be used to suggest that all Scripture is prophecy or that the Spirit is limited to prophetic texts. That is not the logic of the text. In fact in the last chapter of 2 Peter we find that Paul's letters are described as Scripture—albeit hard to understand in places (2 Pet. 3:15–16). Moreover there is some evidence that prophecy in Judaism was a wide enough category to cover the range of OT genres. See Gordon D. Fee, *God's Empowering Presence*, 794. In his discussion of the reference to Scripture in 2 Timothy 3:16, Fee also refers to 2 Peter 2:21 (*sic*, surely a misprint). The theological concept of inspiration covers all scriptural genres.

14. To see the difference between postulational literature and non-postulational literature in the ancient world, compare Genesis 1 and Plato's *Timaeus*.

15. See Kevin J. Vanhoozer, *First Theology: God, Scripture, and Hermeneutics* (Downers Grove, Ill., and Leicester, England: InterVarsity Press and Apollos, 2002), 127–158, esp. 131: "[N]o doctrine of Scripture without a doctrine of providence." Strangely this chapter is headed with a quotation from 1 Thessalonians 2:13, as though Paul were speaking of Scripture as the word of God rather than the gospel. This jump can be made theologically in my view but does need to be explained rather than assumed.

the Lord's famous parable of the sower—or would it be better titled "the parable of hearing the word"?—four kinds of hearers are presented (Mark 4:1–20). Some show no interest (v. 15). Some show interest for a while, until hard times come (vv. 16–17). Still others welcome the word for a time but this world eventually snuffs out the interest (vv. 18–19). Finally and happily there are those who not only hear but embrace that word and prove fruitful (v. 20).

According to Paul, those who understand the gospel and receive its wisdom are those taught by the Spirit (1 Cor. 2:12–13). The tenor of Paul's argument suggests that the problem in receiving the word does not reside in the receptor's cognitive disability but in his or her affective disinclination. A transformation needs to take place at the deepest level, the heart. The heart (Heb. *lev*; Gk. *kardia*) in biblical terms is the core of the person where cognition (thinking), volition (willing), and affections (feeling) have their locus.[16] The affections are the keys. In contrast, the natural person does not welcome the things of the Spirit. "Welcome" (*dechetai*) indicates a positive reception like greeting a friend at the door and is used, or its cognates are used, consistently in the NT of the proper embrace of the word (cf. Mark 4:20; Acts 17:11; 1 Thess. 2:13).[17] The Thessalonian Christians are a case in point. The gospel that Paul preached to them came in both word and power (1 Thess. 1:4–5). The Spirit was much in evidence (v. 5). A new clustering of humanity had been preached into existence, which was characterized by the virtues of faith, love, and hope (v. 3). Paul's preaching was received as the word of God and not merely a human artifact (2:13). The Spirit had been at work.

Embracing the scriptural word of God is, by analogy, a similar story of the Spirit's work. There is a consistency in God's revelatory action. Both hands of God are involved—to use Irenaeus's famous phrase. He reveals by Word and Spirit, whether in gospel proclamation or Scripture. But the role of the Spirit ought not to be misunderstood. The Spirit does not infuse new brain power into an individual's life in regenerating him or her. In fact, unbelief can rehearse the propositional content of the gospel heard or the Scripture read. I have heard it done. But without the Spirit there is no affection for the message. There are no faith, hope, and love in response. The existential significance of the scriptural word is not seen, only its linguistic

16. Wilber T. Dayton, "Heart," in Richard S. Taylor, ed., *Beacon Dictionary of Theology* (Kansas City: Beacon Hill, 1983), 249.

17. On the idea of "welcome" see Millard J. Erickson, *Christian Theology*, unabridged, one-volume ed. (Grand Rapids, Mich.: Baker, 1993), 248. Erickson is to be commended for his lengthy discussion of illumination (247–259). Some systematic treatments are exceedingly brief. For examples see J. Rodman Williams, *Renewal Theology: Systematic Theology from a Charismatic Perspective: Three Volumes in One* (Grand Rapids, Mich.: Zondervan, 1996), 1:24–25; and Wayne Grudem, *Systematic Theology: An Introduction to Biblical Doctrine* (Leicester, England, and Grand Rapids, Mich.: Inter-Varsity and Zondervan, 1994), 644–645, 1041–1042.

meaning. However, how the Spirit does this work we are not told. There is mystery here. The Spirit eludes our epistemological nets.

The traditional way to describe the work of the Spirit in enabling understanding of the word is illumination.[18] The Spirit brings light. According to this view, the doctrine of illumination is concerned with understanding Scripture. Charles C. Ryrie captures this position well: "Specifically, the doctrine of illumination relates to that ministry of the Holy Spirit that helps the believer understand the truth of Scripture."[19] But the scriptural evidence for this doctrine of the Spirit's particular involvement in the process of understanding Scripture is slim.[20] Four texts are typically adduced for the doctrine: Psalm 119:18; 1 Corinthians 2:6–16; Ephesians 1:15–21; and 1 John 2:20.[21] These texts are then connected to the Spirit's teaching ministry as the promised Paraclete (John 14–16). However, in all these texts a nexus between the Scriptures and the Spirit is not directly in view. Instead it is the law and Yahweh in focus in the Psalms text (cf. Ps. 119:12 and 18) and in the NT texts it is the gospel that is the focus.[22] In 1 Corinthians 2:6–16 it is the gospel wisdom of God, in Ephesians 1:15–21 it is gospel hope, and in 1 John 2:20 it is gospel truth as opposed to the antichrist's lie. Moreover, John 14–16 is addressed to the disciples in the upper room who had been with Jesus from the beginning (John 15:27) and ought not to be applied too quickly to Christians in general.

Scripture does make it clear that the unregenerate person is blind to God's truth, dead to its claims, and has a darkened understanding due to a hardened heart (cf. 2 Cor. 4:3–4; Eph. 2:1–3; 4:18). But when the heart is opened to God's revelation, as in the case of Lydia, we find that it is the Lord's work (Acts 16:14), presumably the risen Christ. There is no specific reference to the Spirit. Further, when it comes to the gospel and human blindness, it is "God [the Creator], who said, 'Let light shine out of darkness,' [who] has shone in our hearts to give the light of the knowledge of the glory of God in the face of Jesus Christ" (2 Cor. 4:6). The move from gospel illumination to Scripture illumination by the Holy Spirit specifically

18. For a comprehensive discussion of the doctrine of illumination see Kevin D. Zuber, *What Is Illumination? A Study in Evangelical Theology Seeking a Biblically Grounded Definition of the Illuminating Work of the Holy Spirit* (doctoral dissertation, Trinity Evangelical Divinity School, 1996).

19. Charles C. Ryrie, "Illumination," *EDT*, 544–545.

20. For example, in Clark H. Pinnock's discussion of the doctrine of the Spirit and illumination there are frequent references to "Scripture" but no actual text of Scripture is cited in support (*Flame of Love: A Theology of the Holy Spirit* [Downers Grove, Ill.: InterVarsity Press, 1996], 227–231). I owe this observation to my student Tom Wiebe.

21. Edwin H. Palmer, *The Holy Spirit*, rev. ed. (Philadelphia: Presbyterian & Reformed, 1971), 53–61, provides a good example.

22. As the commentators make clear; see, with regard to 1 Corinthians 2:6–16, Fee, *God's Empowering Presence*, 100; Ephesians, Andrew T. Lincoln, *Ephesians*, WBC, comment on Eph. 1:18–19; and 1 John, Stephen S. Smalley, *1, 2, 3 John*, WBC, comment on 1 John 2:20.

must not be made too hastily. There is a theological case for such a move. The move could be argued for on the basis of an analogy between God's work in the proclaimed word and his work in the written word. That is to say, there is a consistency in God's ways of dealing with us. Thus, a more general epistemological principle may be assumed to be operative in a particular instance. In other words, if from examining other NT texts (e.g., 1 Cor. 2:6–16) we find that the Spirit is principally involved in our knowing God, then why not with regard to our knowing God through the Scripture? This argument could be reinforced by an appeal to the concept of appropriation. There is a certain fittingness in attributing revelatory work to the Spirit even where the text of Scripture is not explicit.[23]

"Understanding" is a problematic term in the doctrine of illumination. If "understanding" is defined as both the ability to recognize the linguistic meaning of the word and its existential value, then there is an argument. Such an argument may be based on 1 Corinthians 2:6–16 and the notion of transformed affections. As Walter C. Kaiser Jr. contends with reference to these verses, ". . . the Spirit's ministry is one of aiding the believer to apply, to see the value, worth, and significance of a text for his own person, situation, and times."[24] D. Broughton Knox maintains,

> An intellectual apprehension of what the scriptures are saying is not difficult [what about 2 Pet. 3:16, one may ask] and does not require an outside interpreter. However, the acceptance of the truth of what is being said, and apprehension of our own relationship to it, is another matter and comes about only when the Spirit of God writes his word on our heart, that is, touches the inmost point of our personality so that we align ourselves with what is being said. This in turns leads to a much deeper apprehension and understanding of what the Bible is about.[25]

However, if "understanding" is merely the ability to state the linguistic content of the word heard or read, then there is no real biblical support for the idea that there needs to be a special work of the Spirit to enable it. Jesus told Nicodemus he needed to be born again (John 3:7). But he also expected this teacher of Israel to have understood what he had been talking about (John 3:9–10).

23. See J. Theodore Mueller, "The Holy Spirit and the Scriptures," in Carl F. H. Henry, ed., *Revelation and the Bible: Contemporary Evangelical Thought* (London: The Tyndale Press, 1969), esp. 267–268. See also Millard J. Erickson and James L. Heflin, *Old Wine in New Wineskins: Doctrinal Preaching in a Changing World* (Grand Rapids, Mich.: Baker, 1997), part 2.

24. Walter C. Kaiser Jr., "A Neglected Text in Bibliology Discussions: 1 Corinthians 2:6-16," *WTJ* 43 no. 2 (Spring 1981): 301–319. Note how Kaiser applies the passage to a text, whereas Paul has the proclaimed gospel in mind.

25. D. Broughton Knox, in Kirsten Birkett, ed., *D. Broughton Knox: Selected Works, Volume 2: Church and Ministry* (Kingsford, N.S.W.: Matthias Media, 2003), 122.

The Spirit and the Contemporaneity of the Scriptural Word

The Enlightenment thinker Gotthold Lessing famously wrote of the "ugly ditch" of history. According to Bernard Ramm, to Lessing "events of the past were forever gone and could never be retrieved."[26] Ramm helpfully illustrates the implication of Lessing's idea.[27] In the eighteenth century, George Washington defeated the British. He is a hero to the American psyche to this day. He is revered. However, no contemporary American has a personal relationship to the General. Washington is dead. However, as Ramm, among others, has contended, when it comes to Christ, who is now at the Father's right hand, the theological key to bridging the gap between past and present, heaven and earth lies in pneumatology.

Ramm is on good biblical ground to see in the Holy Spirit the answer to connecting the past and the present. According to Jesus, Paul, and the writer to the Hebrews, Scripture is God's contemporary word and not merely his past word.[28] In his debate with the Sadducees about the resurrection, Jesus says to them, "[H]ave you not read what was said *to you* [Sadducees] by God" (Matt. 22:31). He then quotes from the Torah to make his point (cf. Matt. 22:32 and Ex. 3:6). Likewise Paul in dealing with the behavioral problems in the Corinthian congregation draws their attention to the example of the grumbling Israelites in the wilderness and argues, "Now these things happened to them as an example, but they were written down *for our instruction,* on whom the end of the ages has come" (1 Cor. 10:11). Clearly for both Jesus and Paul, in the providence of God, Scripture has more than the original one readership in view. Scripture is a contemporary word. In neither Jesus' words nor Paul's is there any reference to the Spirit. But in the letter to the Hebrews the work of the Spirit with regard to the contemporaneity of Scripture is explicit. In Hebrews 3–4 the writer applies Psalm 95 to the life context of his readers. He warns them of the dangers of unbelief and of not heeding the warning of God. For the writer, Psalm 95 is not simply what God said once in the past but is the Spirit's present word to the Hebrews. In Hebrews 3:7 we read, "Therefore, as the Holy Spirit says ["is saying," *legei,* present aspect] . . ." This accent on the present speaking of the Spirit through the past word is expanded in 4:7, where we find that it is through David that the Spirit is warning the readers: "[A]gain he appoints a certain day, 'Today,' saying [*legōn,* present participle] through David . . ." Subsequently, the writer describes Psalm 95 as the "living" word of God (*zōn . . . ho logos tou theou*), which is like a sword in its effectiveness. Psalm 95 is no dead letter. However, this is not some sort of ancient

26. Bernard Ramm, *Rapping about the Spirit* (Waco, Tex.: Word, 1974), 172.
27. Ibid.
28. It was my theology teacher, D. Broughton Knox, who first drew my attention to this phenomenon in the text.

anticipation of Barthianism, as though the word is only the word of God when it becomes so though the Spirit's use of it. There is no suggestion of such subjectivity in the Hebrews text. Rather we see that past Scripture is the vehicle for God's contemporary ministry to his people.

Thomas Smail has called the Holy Spirit "God in the present tense."[29] And it is God in the present tense who makes the past word of God the present word of God in the present tense. The work of the Spirit with regard to the past word of God, as seen in the testimony of Hebrews, and in Jesus' and Paul's recognition that past Scripture has more than one audience in mind, makes appeals to the need for a contemporary word of God dubious to say the least. God has not left his people bereft and in silence. The Spirit leaps Lessing's "ugly ditch."[30]

THE WITNESS OF THE SPIRIT

The expression "witness of the Spirit" covers two different but related ideas. The concept is found in Scripture in Paul's letter to the Romans, where assurance of our relationship to God appears to be in view; and historically, Calvin wrote of the internal testimony or witness of the Spirit in relation to our confidence that Scripture is indeed the word of God. Both are concerned with an epistemic claim, and in that lies their similarity. We shall examine both ideas.

The Witness of the Spirit and Assurance of Adoption

How confident we may be that we are in a saving relationship to God is a vital question and has been the subject of much controversy through the course of church history. Are believers eternally secure and able to know it, or may salvation be lost under certain conditions? These are huge questions that take us well beyond our present task.[31] But the role of the Spirit in assuring the believer of his or her present status as a child of God is within our task. And with regard to that role there are several key Pauline texts to consider (Rom. 8:12–17; 2 Cor. 1:21–22; Eph. 1:13–14; 4:30) because in them we find two important concepts to examine: the Spirit as a witness and as a seal.

The Spirit's ministry as witness is an important part of the story of Christian assurance. The subject of Christian assurance is much debated.

29. Thomas A. Smail, *The Forgotten Father: Rediscovering the Heart of the Christian Gospel* (London, Sydney, Auckland, and Toronto: Hodder & Stoughton, 1987), 14.

30. Ramm, *Rapping about the Spirit,* 172–173.

31. For a fine discussion of the issues see Bruce Demarest, *The Cross and Salvation: The Doctrine of Salvation* (Wheaton, Ill.: Crossway, 1997), chapter 11. See also D. A. Carson, "Reflections on Christian Assurance," *WTJ* 54 (1992): 1–29.

Are believers eternally secure as in the Calvinian tradition, or may they fall away as the Wesleyan tradition argues? That large debate, as just stated, is beyond our brief. However, we need to note in passing that the main part of the story of assurance, as John Calvin argued, lies in the finished work of Christ upon the cross. Furthermore, the subjective correlate to that objective work of the cross is our faith. Faith is a necessary condition for the experience of assurance. No faith, no assurance. The witness of the Spirit and exhibition of good works are secondary and corroborative. In fact, good works, or more to the point their absence, operate rather as a negative test of whether faith is real. For example, if someone claims to be God's child and lives a transparently ungodly life, then there are no grounds for confidence in the claim that this person is truly God's son or daughter.[32]

As for the witness of the Spirit, there is a magnificent passage in Romans in which Paul draws a contrast drawn between the way of the flesh, which leads to death, and the way of the Spirit, which is life-giving (Rom. 8:12–13). Indeed all who are led by the Spirit are God's sons (v. 14). By "led" Paul does not mean "guided" but a life under the Spirit's direction. Douglas Moo comments, "To be *led by the Spirit of God* (14) means not to be guided by the Spirit in decision-making, but to be under the dominating influence of the Spirit."[33] Believers have not received the spirit of slavery but the Spirit of adoption (*pneuma huiothesias,* v. 15). This exalted status is "the crowning blessing" of the gospel, as J. I. Packer argues, while justification is "the basic blessing."[34] This adoption not only brings status, it also brings a future.[35] As believers we are heirs with Christ, provided we are prepared to follow his path of suffering before glory (v. 17). But how can we be sure that we are adopted children of God? The Spirit is the answer. The Spirit jointly bears witness with our spirits (*summarturei,* "continually bears joint witness," present aspect) that we are the children of God (v. 16).[36] How do we know? Paul does not say how in so many words. Fee cautions, "Paul is almost certainly not speaking to some deep, interior witness that the Spirit makes within us."[37] Perhaps the clue lies in the prayer life of the

32. For this paragraph I am very much indebted to my colleague D. A. Carson's discussion of Calvin and 1 John in particular ("Johannine Perspectives on the Doctrine of Assurance," in R. J. Gibson, ed., *Explorations 10: Justification and Christian Assurance* [Adelaide, South Australia: Openbook, 1996], 59–97).

33. Douglas J. Moo, "Romans," *NBC,* 1140, emphasis original.

34. J. I. Packer, *Concise Theology: A Guide to Historic Christian Beliefs* (Australia, Singapore, and England: Anzea, Campus Crusade Asia, and Inter-Varsity, 1993), 167.

35. As Moo, "Romans," *NBC,* comment on Rom. 8:1, concerning sonship: "the legal institution whereby one could adopt a child and confer on that child all the rights and privileges that would accrue to a natural child."

36. The Greek in context is better rendered "continually bears witness *with*" rather than "continually bears witness *to*" (my emphases). For the argument see Sinclair Ferguson, *The Holy Spirit* (Leicester, England: Inter-Varsity, 1996), 184.

37. Fee, *God's Empowering Presence,* 569.

Christian who prays, "Abba, Father" (v. 15).[38] This is Jesus' own prayer language. The Aramaic has been transliterated into Greek; such was the importance of "abba" to these early Christians like Paul (cf. Mark 14:36 and Gal. 4:6). The very fact that the Christian can pray as a child of the Father rather than address God like a slave addressing a master is evidence of the Spirit's witness and adoption.

In the 2 Corinthians text and the two from Ephesians, Paul writes of the seal of the Spirit. The concept of the Spirit's sealing, based on these texts, has played an important role in the discussion of Christian assurance at least from Reformation times, if not before. The concept of the sealing of the Spirit has to do with God's authenticating believers as truly his. When the Ephesians believed the gospel they "were sealed [*esphragisthēte tō pneumati,* aorist aspect] with the promised Holy Spirit" (Eph. 1:13). The Spirit is also the guarantee of the inheritance that is coming (v. 14).[39] Later in this same epistle Paul exhorts the readers—probably hearers, as Scripture was presumably read aloud, whether by individuals privately or in a congregational setting—"not [to] grieve the Holy Spirit of God, by whom you were sealed [*esphragisthēte,* aorist aspect] for the day of redemption" (4:30). In both texts the reference to the sealing of the Spirit is set within an eschatological framework. The 2 Corinthians text also speaks of the Spirit as the guarantee of the coming inheritance, but it is not as clear that the sealing spoken of refers to the Spirit (*ho sphragisamenos,* "the one who sealed," aorist participle, 2 Cor. 1:22). However, given the analogical pressure of the Ephesians texts, it is hard to resist that conclusion.

What does the sealing of the Spirit have to do with knowing that we are God's children and therefore that we belong to him? According to D. Martyn Lloyd-Jones, everything. In his view the baptism with the Spirit, the witness of the Spirit, and the sealing of the Spirit are synonyms which refer to the gift of "the highest form of assurance of salvation."[40] From this experience comes the power for Christian service. And so this experience is not to be identified with either conversion or sanctification, he argues. In the Puritan tradition, which Lloyd-Jones knew so well, some important divines in earlier centuries indeed argued that believing and sealing refer to two different events separated in time. Sealing is subsequent to believing and may or may not be experienced by the believer. Richard Sibbes (1577–1635)

38. This is well brought out by Montague, *Holy Spirit,* 197, in relation to "abba" in Galatians 4:6–7: "The Christian 'knows' his sonship by the experience of Christian prayer."

39. In the Greco-Roman world, seals "denoted ownership and authenticity; this thereby guaranteed the protection of the owner," according to Fee, *God's Empowering Presence,* 292.

40. For example, "the sealing of the Spirit and the baptism with the Spirit are the same thing" (D. Martyn Lloyd-Jones, *Joy Unspeakable: The Baptism with the Holy Spirit* [Eastbourne, England: Kingsway, 1985], 156–157).

especially comes to mind.[41] However, Fee is on far more solid exegetical ground—in contradistinction to Lloyd-Jones—in arguing that the sealing, for example, refers to conversion.[42] Paul is stating a fact, not describing a conscious Christian experience. Our response to Paul's statement ought to be to believe it rather than to attempt to find it in experience.[43]

There is in moral philosophy a paradox known as the hedonistic paradox. If you seek pleasure, you won't get it. Pleasure is produced by seeking other than itself. Philosopher D. Elton Trueblood describes the hedonistic paradox well:

> This paradox, long acknowledged by philosophers, is the observation that the surest way to miss happiness is to seek it directly. When happiness comes to a person, it usually comes as a by-product rather than as something at which the individual directly and expressly aims.[44]

There is a similar paradox in the spiritual realm. In seeking the Father in prayer the assurance comes, the witness of the Spirit takes place. But to seek assurance of adoption per se may be to miss it.[45] Real assurance comes when the focus is elsewhere.

The Witness of the Spirit and the Scriptural Word

Calvin has been described as the theologian of the Holy Spirit.[46] His accent on the Spirit's work is nowhere stronger than in his treatment of the believer's confidence in the authority of Scripture as the authentic Word of God over against the claim of the Catholicism of his day that it is the church that provides that confidence.[47] His heading to chapter 7 of book 1 of his *Institutes* makes this clear: "Scripture Must Be Confirmed by the

41. See the brief discussion in Ferguson, *Holy Spirit*, 181–182; and the extensive collection of extracts from "English Divines" in J. C. Ryle, *Holiness* (Cambridge and London: James Clarke, 1956), 126–134. See also J. I. Packer, *A Quest for Godliness: The Puritan Vision of the Christian Life* (Wheaton, Ill.: Crossway, 1990), 179–189.

42. Fee, *God's Empowering Presence*, 670. Paul's consistent use of the aorist points strongly in this direction. The alternative view, popular in some circles, that the sealing refers to Christian water baptism (for example, Montague, *Holy Spirit*, 186), fails to convince because these Pauline texts are silent as to such a connection.

43. Ferguson suggests that the sealing of the Spirit, which he sees as "two aspects of one and the same initiation event," should register in consciousness in some way (*Holy Spirit*, 182). How so, he does not make at all clear.

44. D. Elton Trueblood, *General Philosophy* (Grand Rapids, Mich.: Baker, 1976), 271–272.

45. For a contrary view, see Lloyd-Jones, *Joy Unspeakable*, 162.

46. Peter Jensen, "The Spirit of Revelation," in B. G. Webb, ed., *Spirit of the Living God: Part Two* (Homebush West: Lancer, 1992), 9.

47. William J. Abraham argues strangely that the idea of the internal witness of the Spirit in the *Institutes* is Calvin's attempt to deal with "the problem of canonicity" when clearly Calvin in context is dealing with the problem of authority, contra Abraham's "The Epistemological

272 OF THE MINISTRY OF THE SPIRIT—NEW TESTAMENT PERSPECTIVES

Witness of the Spirit. Thus May Its Authority Be Established as Certain."[48] Here we find Calvin's seminal contribution to theological thought of the idea of the internal witness of the Spirit (*testimonium Spiritus sancti internum*).[49] This witness he judged to be stronger than reason. He argues, "we ought to seek our conviction in a higher place than human reasons, judgments, or conjectures, that is, in the secret testimony of the Spirit." Again, he contends,

> But I reply: the testimony of the Spirit is more excellent than all reason. For as God alone is a fit witness of himself in his Word, so also the Word will not find acceptance in men's hearts before it is sealed by the *inward testimony of the Spirit*. The same Spirit, therefore, who has spoken through the mouths of the prophets must penetrate into our hearts to *persuade* us that they faithfully proclaimed what had been divinely commanded.[50]

He develops the argument further:

> Let this point therefore stand: that those whom the Holy Spirit has inwardly taught truly rest upon Scripture, and *that Scripture indeed is self-authenticated;* hence, it is not right to subject it to proof and reasoning. And the certainty it deserves with us, it attains by the testimony of the Spirit. For even if it wins reverence for itself by its own majesty, it seriously affects us only when it is sealed upon our hearts through the Spirit. Therefore, *illumined by his power,* we believe neither by our own nor by anyone else's judgment that Scripture is from God; but above human judgment we affirm with utter certainty (just as if we were gazing upon the majesty of God himself) that it has flowed to us from the very mouth of God by the ministry of men.[51]

Here are familiar themes in Calvin: the witness of the Spirit, its inward nature, its secret character, the Spirit's illuminative work vis-à-vis Scripture, and the self-authenticating nature of Scripture.

The notion of a self-authenticating Scripture is puzzling given the tenor of Calvin's argument. If anything it is an argument for Word and Spirit, and for Spirit authentication of the Word. He leaves the impression that Scripture has a life of its own whereas his argument is that the Spirit with the Word is the key. Indeed, the Spirit is the great persuader that this Scripture is in fact

---

Significance of the Inner Witness of the Holy Spirit," *Faith and Philosophy* 7 no. 4 (October 1990): 443.

48. John Calvin, "Institutes of the Christian Religion," *CJCC*, I:7.

49. George S. Hendry maintains that Calvin's notion of the internal testimony of the Spirit is "one of the best known elements in the Reformed tradition," and even though the notion was not original to Calvin, his classic articulation of it has been of lasting influence (*The Holy Spirit in Christian Theology* [Philadelphia: Westminster, 1956], 72).

50. Calvin, "Institutes of the Christian Religion," *CJCC*, I:7:4, emphasis mine.

51. Ibid., emphasis mine.

the Word of God.[52] The objective Spirit working with the objective Word has a role in shaping the believer's subjectivity. The Spirit brings certitude.

Calvin finds the scriptural support for his proposals in Isaiah 59:21 and 2 Corinthians 1:22.[53] How he justifies his move from these texts to claims about Scripture per se is not clear. Writing in the Reformed tradition, R. C. Sproul correctly acknowledges that,

> The New Testament does not provide us with a thoroughgoing exposition of the "internal testimony" as such. This, at face value, could expose Calvin, Martin Luther, and a host of other theologians to the charge that the doctrine has been constructed on the basis of speculative philosophy or by a "system" of theology imposed on the Scriptures arbitrarily.[54]

Sproul's approach is to argue that the idea of the internal witness of the Spirit can be safely based on "allusions" to the Spirit's work in texts such as "2 Corinthians 4:3-6; 1 John 1:10; 2:14; 5:20; Colossians 2:2; 1 Thessalonians 1:5; Galatians 4:6; Romans 8:15-16; and others."[55] In his view, "a classic text for the *testimonium*" is 1 Corinthians 2:4–11.[56] But as we have argued previously, Paul is writing about the gospel, not Scripture. Interestingly, Calvin knew that.[57] Be that as it may, the historic importance of Calvin's formulation of the idea of the internal witness of the Spirit cannot be gainsaid. In my view, Calvin's doctrine of the internal testimony of the Spirit to Scripture's authority is consistent with Scripture. I am not convinced that it is demanded by Scripture, even though it is arguably a safe inference from Scripture.

DISCERNING THE SPIRIT

Discerning what is a genuine work of God's Spirit in today's world is a tricky matter.[58] Claims concerning the Spirit need sifting. This was also

52. On the Spirit as persuader, and with acknowledged indebtedness to Calvin, see the discussion in Bernard L. Ramm, *The God Who Makes a Difference: A Christian Appeal to Reason* (Waco, Tex.: Word, 1972), 38–44.

53. Calvin, "Institutes of the Christian Religion," *CJCC*, I.7.4.

54. R. C. Sproul, *Scripture Alone: The Evangelical Doctrine* (Phillipsburg, N.J.: Presbyterian & Reformed, 2005), 115.

55. Ibid.

56. Ibid., emphasis original.

57. For example, John Calvin, "1 Corinthians," *CCJC*, comment on 1 Corinthians 2:11: "*For what man knoweth?* Two different things he intends to teach here: *first*, that the doctrine of the Gospel cannot be understood otherwise than by the testimony of the Holy Spirit; and *secondly*, that those who have a testimony of this nature from the Holy Spirit, have an assurance as firm and solid, as if they felt with their hands what they believe, for the Spirit is a faithful and indubitable witness" (emphasis original).

58. For this section I am drawing upon my article, "Religious Experience and Discernment Today," *RTR* 56 no. 1 (January–April 1997): 10–12. See also the discussions in A. M. Stibbs

the case in NT times. Paul argued that prophecies need to be tested but in such a way as not to quench the Spirit (1 Thess. 5:19–21). John was aware that many spirits are at large in the world. But any that denies the incarnation is actually the antichrist at work (1 John 4:1–3). Gullibility is not a Christian virtue. Deception, either self-deception or devilish, is a real possibility.[59] So what criteria may be brought to bear on this question of discernment?

The first criterion is the scriptural test. Does that which is claimed have a *prima facie* analogy with some phenomenon found in the pages of Scripture? For example, a claim to have carried out an exorcism in the name of Jesus and by the Spirit of God has a real possibility of genuineness. Even so, discernment is still required (Matt. 7:21–23).[60] But such a claim is not to be dismissed a priori. Again a claim along the lines that someone came to a real Christian faith after becoming convinced of their sinfulness, and therefore their need of Christ, through reading a contemporary Christian book is consistent with what we know of the Spirit's work from our NT, even though C. S. Lewis' *Mere Christianity* isn't mentioned in Scripture.

A second criterion is Christological. Any claimed experience of the Spirit that detracts from the dignity of Christ as truly God and truly human and from the integrity of his saving work is not of the Spirit (1 John 4:1–3). We might ask of such a claim questions such as, What place has Christ (both his person and his work) in the alleged experience of the Spirit and in the rhetoric used to explain it? Does the experience preach Christ (as Luther might say)?[61] When Paul thought that the value of Christ's work was being undermined by the false teachers troubling the Galatians, he said, "let [them] be accursed" (Gal. 1:6–10). But when others preached the right gospel about Christ at Philippi—albeit for the wrong reasons (to make life in prison for him even harder)—he rejoiced (Phil. 1:15–18). Christology is at the heart of Paul's quality assurance. So also with us, especially if the Holy Spirit is invoked. After all, the Spirit is the Spirit of Jesus (v. 19). He has not come, as we have seen in previous chapters, to thematize himself but Christ (John 14–16). Christology is at the center, not pneumatology.

---

and J. I. Packer, *The Spirit within You: The Church's Neglected Possession* (London: Hodder & Stoughton, 1967), 21–25; Craig S. Keener, *Three Crucial Questions about the Holy Spirit* (Grand Rapids, Mich.: Baker, 1996), chapter 3; and A. W. Tozer, *How to Try the Spirits: Seven Ways to Discern the Source of Religious Experiences* (Camp Hill, Pa.: Christian Publications, 1997).

59. See the stimulating discussion of deception and lying spirits in Michael Welker, *God the Spirit*, trans. John F. Hoffmeyer (Minneapolis: Fortress, 1994), 84–98.

60. Clearly the mere parroting that "Jesus is Lord" is no necessary indication that the Spirit of God is at work (cf. 1 Cor. 12:1–3 and Matt. 7:21–23).

61. See Luther's "Preface to the Epistles of St. James and St. Jude," in John Dillenberger, ed., *Martin Luther: Selections from His Writings* (Garden City, N.Y.: Anchor, 1961), 36.

A great Christian leader of an earlier century, Bishop J. C. Ryle, suggested that the gospel may be spoiled in a number of ways.[62] We can spoil the gospel by substituting for Christ's saving work on the cross (for example, our good deeds, as Pelagius did). We can spoil Christ's work by adding to it (for example, faith plus circumcision, as in the Galatian error). We can also spoil the gospel by disproportion when secondary biblical accents become primary (for example, clerical clothing). This latter problem is particularly relevant to the present discussion. We can spoil the gospel when the NT sense of proportion is lost and pneumatology becomes our primary emphasis rather than Christology. The idea in some charismatic circles, for example, that "the major compass point for moving ahead in active ministry" is not "the cross" but "charisma" is extremely troubling.[63]

The last important test for our purpose is the moral one.[64] The NT presents not only an evangel but also an ethic. So when Paul preached to the Thessalonians and then moved on, he left behind the Word of God (the gospel, as in 1 Thess. 1:2–10 and 2:13) and instruction in how these new Christians were to live and please God (an ethic, as in 4:1–8). The gift of the Holy Spirit means a sanctified life (esp. vv. 7–8). Christians are expected to be "a community of character," as Stanley Hauerwas suggests. Indeed one of the problems with which John deals in his first letter concerns a schismatic community, which had set itself up over against that of John's readers (1 John 2:18–19). The schismatics were claiming to love God but in fact were exhibiting a hatred toward John's readers. How can disciples claim to love God whom they cannot see, when so evidently despising the brothers and sisters in Christ whom they could see (1 John 4:7–21)? John drew attention to the anomaly.

All sorts of claims are made these days about the Spirit's present activities. Some even claim that the Spirit has spoken to them or that a vital part of a Christian's devotional life is allowing the Spirit to speak in the quietness of one's room. There are books that discuss what the Spirit is saying to the churches and that encourage the reader to hear him.[65] After all, didn't

62. See his classic essay "Evangelical Religion," in J. C. Ryle, *Knots Untied* (London: Thynne, 1885), esp. 16–17. The examples are mine, though, not his.

63. See C. Peter Wagner, *Seven Principles I Learned after Seminary* (Ventura, Ca.: Regal, 2005), 19–20. How this squares with Paul's ministry to the Corinthians is not at all clear (1 Cor. 2:1–5).

64. This test is particularly important to Welker, *God the Spirit,* 85, who draws out its communal application.

65. For example, Henry Blackaby, *What the Spirit Is Saying to the Churches* (Sisters, Ore.: Multnomah, 2003). There is much that is edifying in this book. There is a healthy accent on searching the Scriptures. But readers are invited to, "Hear Him afresh" (53). However, what that would mean in practical terms is not made clear. Expectations are raised. Yet the reader is left with generalities. The same question may be asked of Keener, *Three Crucial Questions,* 151–153, where he writes of, "Hearing God's Voice: A Personal Account." However, his more recent *Gift Giver: The Holy Spirit for Today* (Grand Rapids, Mich.: Baker, 2002) is more restrained.

the Spirit speak to Philip and command him to go to the chariot of the Ethiopian eunuch (Acts 8:29), and didn't the Spirit tell those at Antioch to set Saul and Barnabas apart for ministry (13:2)? However, so little is described of what such speaking was like in those scriptural contexts that it is extremely hazardous to generalize from such incidents or from texts addressed to first-century churches.[66] I suspect that those who relate how the Spirit has spoken to them today are talking about certain strong impressions they have to do X or Y or to say X or Y, and that is the Spirit's speaking to them today. Sometimes the rhetoric evangelicals, charismatics, and pentecostals use to articulate Christian experience, whether of the Spirit or Christ, is fundamentally misleading because it is left unnuanced and unexplained.[67]

Implications for Belief and Practice

There are many implications for belief and practice that arise from the Spirit's role as the searcher of the depths. For our purposes we shall follow out just two: appreciating the Spirit's role in our knowing God, and our engagement with what the Spirit has made known of God.

Appreciating the Christian's Epistemological Base

To know the God of the Bible means to have relied upon God to have made himself known. The living God holds the initiative in revelation. Without special revelation from God we are able only to grope after him, as Paul makes plain in his speech to the pagan intelligentsia at the Areopagus (Acts 17:16–34). The Spirit plays a vital role in that revelation, its various forms of delivery, and its ultimate inscripturation. The Spirit also is crucial to our right reception of that revelation whether delivered in proclaimed gospel form or in the text of Scripture. To cut ourselves adrift from that special revelation is folly. Other authorities do operate in the Christian life. Tradition does shape us. We are legatees of a great history of God's dealings after the close of the canon. Towering figures from the Christian past, such as Athanasius, Augustine, Aquinas, and Calvin, may still teach us. We also rightly appeal to discursive reason. Argument is important to a rational Christian life. The contrast in Paul, for example, is not between faith and discursive reason,

66. A point well made by Jensen, "Spirit of Revelation," 16–17.
67. See my "Experiencing the Lord: Rhetoric and Reality," in Webb, ed., *Spirit of the Living God,* 49–70. In this piece I address the problem arising from rhetoric that suggests that speaking to God and God speaking to us is just like relating to one's best friend or spouse. Our spouse and friends are embodied, and we read their body language as well as hear their words. But God is unembodied except for the incarnate Christ, and he is at the right hand of the Father. The doctrine of the ascension matters as far as unrealistic expectations of personal dealings with God are concerned.

but between faith and sight (2 Cor. 5:7). Christian experience matters too. The wise person learns from the ups and downs of life but does so within a particular attitudinal framework so that it is godly wisdom, namely, the fear of the Lord (Prov. 1:7). However, all these norms are ruled by an even greater one. They are *norma normata* (ruled norms). Scripture trumps them all, as it is special revelation. It is the ruling norm (*norma normans*). The wise Christian recognizes the epistemologically privileged position of Spirit-provided and inspired special revelation.

Engaging Revelation

Engaging the revelation of God does call for an active response of our own. Meditating on that Word is part of the story. In the practice of "holy thought," as Packer expresses it, we turn what we learn about God from special revelation into prayer and praise to God.[68] This practice is the one advocated in the very first psalm, where the blessed person is the one who meditates (*hāgāh*) on the instruction of God day and night (Ps. 1:2). This kind of meditation is very different from the forms of meditation found in Eastern religions, which are so often journeys inward to the still point where there is nothingness or nothing but pure consciousness. In contrast, biblical meditation is a journey outward and upward. We are to lift up our eyes to the hills because our help comes from the Lord who made heaven and earth (Ps. 121:1–2). In the Reformation era, Luther put it so well when he argued that *lectio* (reading), *oratio* (praying), and *tentatio* (struggling in obedience) are integral to making a theologian. Packer agrees, and with Luther's dictum in mind he writes, "The way to benefit fully from the Spirit's ministry of illumination is by serious Bible study, serious prayer, and serious response in obedience to whatever truths one has been shown already."[69] But what ought we to pray as we engage revelation? The Litany, which is a part of the Anglican tradition, suggests that we pray that God deliver us "from hardness of heart, and contempt of your word and commandment."[70] We pray for right affections that appreciate the extraordinary kindness in God making himself known to us in Jesus Christ. Such a transformation of our affections is the Spirit's work (1 Cor. 2:13).

68. J. I. Packer, *Knowing God* (London, Sydney, Auckland, and Toronto: Hodder & Stoughton, 1973), 18–19.

69. Packer, *Concise Theology*, 155–156.

70. *An Australian Prayer Book: For Use Together with the Book of Common Prayer (1662)* (Sydney: AIO Press, 1978), 98.

THE MAGNIFICENCE OF DIVINE SELFLESSNESS

ELEVEN

The Magnificence of Divine Selflessness

We began this study with a number of methodological observations. Doing theology appeals to the normative Word of Revelation foundationally. But it does so with attentiveness to the Witness of Christian Thought down the ages. Doing theology also recognizes that the context of the task is the World of Human Predicament since we live outside of Eden in the midst of the groaning creation. Bringing these elements together is the Work of Wisdom, which is an activity of careful thought done within a particular attitudinal framework, which is the fear of the Lord. When this task is seen as an offering to God, then it is done in the Way of Worship.

In part 1 we explored the elusive nature of the Spirit and the Spirit's place in the triune Godhead. Dietrich Bonhoeffer argued that in Christology the "what" of Christ's achievement must be understood through the "Who" of his identity.[1] In other words, consideration of the Work of Christ needs to be predicated on an understanding of the person of Christ. Likewise in pneumatology, the "what" of the Spirit's work needs to be seen through the lens of the "who" of the Spirit. And so our first part examined the person of the Spirit. We began with the mystery. The Spirit is like the wind, in Jesus' symbolism of the Spirit. We distinguished mystery from a puzzle, a riddle, and a problem. The category of mystery preserves the "Godness" of God. We are to be neither evangelical rationalists who dissolve mystery through facile overanalysis nor evangelical mystics in the sense that we

---

1. Dietrich Bonhoeffer, "Positive Christology," in E. J. Tinsley, ed., *Dietrich Bonhoeffer* (London: Epworth Press, 1973), 56. Tinsley confuses *anhypostasia* and *enhypostasia*. He argues that *enhypostasia* is "[t]he idea that in the Incarnation Christ assumed human nature in general rather than the human nature of an individual" (56, fn 1). But *enhypostasia* is the idea that all that is true of the human person inheres in the divine person of the Son.

hardly do analysis at all, and use the category to foreclose prematurely on hard thinking.

The mystery of the Spirit needs to be seen in terms of the mystery of the triune God as revealed in Scripture. Consideration of the biblical presentation of the person and work of the Spirit—his descriptors and activities—showed that he is as much God as the Father is God and as the Son is God. Yet there is only one God. The Spirit cannot be reduced to a mere creature or to an impersonal influence. The nature of the Godhead is spirit. But, to use classic categories, to speak of the Holy Spirit as a person is to speak *personaliter* rather than *essentialiter*. Two important motifs emerged from this part of our study: the Spirit as bond (Augustine) and the Spirit as perfecting cause (Basil of Caesarea).

In part 2 our focus was not so much on the person of the Spirit (the theme of part 1) but on the work of the Spirit in OT perspective. God comes before us in the OT as the one who works by Word and Spirit. Creation and its sustenance are the work of the Spirit as the Spirit implements the divine purposes in nature and history. Nature too has a history. God has not left creation to look after itself. The OT is theistic, not deistic. But there are now distortions in creation. Sin is at work. The divine project promises to overcome the distortions and bring order back where it belongs. Israel is crucial to that project. As Jesus said, ". . . salvation is from the Jews" (John 4:22). Again, working by Word and Spirit, God creates a people for himself but does so with the whole world ultimately in mind (cf. Gen. 12:1–3 and Ex. 19:5–6). The Spirit was involved in the work of leaders like Moses, judges like Samson, prophets like Elijah, and kings like David. But like Adam before it, Israel failed to image God. But there was hope. God makes promises and keeps them. A time is coming when yet again by Word and Spirit—as the Prophets tell us—he will form his people afresh with new hearts, a new spirit within them, his Spirit placed within them in the setting of a recovered land, and finally a new heavens and new earth. This will not be the experience of a select few but of all God's people. A Spirit-anointed Messiah, servant, and proclaimer will be the crucial agent in bringing about the divine intent. History will once more be the arena of God's action. The God of the OT is no Manichee. Creation and history are not to be escaped from. Grace does not destroy nature but will transfigure it. The best is yet to be. Creation has a future.

Comparing the length of part 2, dealing with the OT ministry of the Holy Spirit, and part 3, treating the NT testimony to the Spirit's ministry, the disparity in length is patent. In the flow of redemptive history, when the NT era dawns and the Son of God walks the earth, the amount of revealed information makes a quantum leap in three key areas. The Old Testament says little about the Fatherhood of God, not so the New. The OT says little about Satan—the opponent of God's kingly rule—not so the New. And in the NT the Spirit's person and work come into prominence

THE MAGNIFICENCE OF DIVINE SELFLESSNESS □ 283

in a way that makes the OT presentation seem quite muted. Indeed, the incarnate Christ's ministry cannot be understood apart from the Spirit's empowering. The Spirit was integrally involved in Christ's conception, baptism, temptations, preaching, mighty works, death, and resurrection. These Christological mysteries or moments are pneumatological ones too. But with Pentecost a great reversal comes into view. The ascended and glorified Jesus as the Lord and Christ pours out the Spirit of OT promise. Thus he fulfills the prophecy of John the Baptist that, as the one greater than the Baptist, he would baptize with the Spirit. Moreover, the Spirit as the Paraclete promised by Jesus continues the witness of Christ through the disciples of Christ as the gospel is spread from Jerusalem to the ends of the earth, even to Rome itself. Furthermore, through the baptism with the Spirit believers are incorporated into the body of Christ. In fact, early Christianity is unintelligible apart from the Spirit's work in and through the body of Christ. But the Spirit may be grieved, quenched, and even blasphemed. Significantly, the gift of the Spirit is the believer's guarantee of a place with God in the new heavens and earth. Importantly, without the Spirit there is no real knowledge of God. He is the epistemic bond in the triune Godhead. He is the searcher of the depths. He also plays a crucial role in the Christian's assurance that he or she really is an adopted child of God and an heir of the good things that God has in store for his family. Indeed, without the Spirit we are left with only a decaffeinated faith. As Orthodox Metropolitan Ignatius Hazim argues, "Without the Holy Spirit, God is distant, Christ is in the past, the Gospel is a dead letter, the Church is simple organization, authority is domination, mission is propaganda, worship is the summoning of spirits, and Christian action is the morality of slaves."[2]

Importantly, we saw that the Spirit's own stories are never solo stories. When the Spirit is in view, so too is God per se, as in OT text after text; or the Father and/or the Son, in NT text after text. For example, there are Christological moments without any explicit reference to the Spirit, such as the transfiguration. However, there are no pneumatological moments without reference also to the Father and the Son. All this underscores the self-effacing character of the Spirit's ministry.[3] Even Pentecost is about God (Father), the Son, and the Spirit, with the focus on the risen Christ.

2. Quoted in Bishop Robert Morneau, "The Word of God Must Be Passed On," *The Compass,* May 4, 2001, http://www.thecompassnews.org/compass/2001-05-04/01cn0504c2.htm, accessed April 30, 2007.

3. Raymond E. Brown maintains that, "The Holy Spirit is the ultimate revelation of God" ("Diverse Views of the Spirit in the New Testament," *Worship* 77 no. 3 [May 1983]: 236). This is extraordinary. In the light of the canonical presentation of the Spirit, one might legitimately claim that the Spirit as the searcher of the depths is the ultimate revealer of God, but hardly the ultimate revelation. The Spirit points away from himself.

We have seen then that the Holy Spirit focuses not on himself but supremely on the Son. J. I. Packer captures this other-person focus by describing the Spirit's ministry as a floodlight ministry. He suggests,

> It is as if the Spirit stands behind us, throwing light over on Jesus, who stands facing us. The Spirit's message to us is never, "Look at me; listen to me; come to me; get to know me," but always, "Look at *him* and see *him*, and see his glory; get to know *him*, and hear his word; go to *him*, and have life; get to know *him*, and taste his gift of joy and peace."[4]

Finely said. A floodlight illuminates something other than itself. You do not go to the theater to stare at the spotlight—to alter the image slightly—but to watch the performance that the spotlight illuminates.

In so many sections of Western societies, magnificence lies in high visibility, whether of talent or power or wealth. A magnificent mansion, for example, is typically spectacular in size, style, and aesthetic worth. There is a road in greater Chicago that runs along part of Lake Michigan which has wonderful houses. Their magnificence is worth a drive to see and take visitors to enjoy. Paradoxically, however, in a world of self-promotion, the magnificence of the Spirit lies, not in self-display, but in self-abnegation. An increasing number of contemporary theologians have described this as the "kenosis" (self-emptying) of the Spirit.[5] I prefer "self-effacement" or "divine selflessness," since there is no pneumatological passage of Scripture comparable to the Philippians text (Phil. 2:5–11). The magnificence of the Spirit lies in this self-effacement or divine selflessness. For this reason believers are rightly called "Christians" not "Pneumians."

---

4. J. I. Packer, *Keep in Step with the Spirit* (Leicester, England: Inter-Varsity, 1984), 66, emphasis original.

5. See the discussion in D. Lyle Dabney, *"Pneumatologia Crucis*: Reclaiming *Theologia Crucis* for a Theology of the Spirit Today," *Scottish Journal of Theology* 53 no. 4 (2000): 511–524. The idea of a kenosis of the Holy Spirit is actually not new. H. Wheeler Robinson discussed it in the 1920s (*The Christian Experience of the Holy Spirit* [London: Nisbet, 1928], 83).

Accommodatio: Lat., "accommodation." The idea that God in communicating his will and ways to humanity stoops like a great rhetorician to our level in order to connect.

Ad extra: Lat., "to the outside." Refers to the Trinity's works of creation, revelation, and redemption.

Ad intra: Lat., "to the inside." Refers to the Trinity's works and relations within the Godhead without any reference to created reality (e.g., the Father's love for the Son within the triune Godhead).

Analogy of faith: Lat. *analogia fidei.* A Reformation hermeneutic that assumes a high view of Scripture and therefore, Scripture is to interpret Scripture, Scripture is never to be interpreted against Scripture, and plain Scripture is to interpret obscure Scripture.

Appropriations: The idea that, although the works of the Trinity in relation to creation, revelation, and redemption are undivided—Augustine's *omnia opera trinitatis ad extra indivisa sunt*—there is theological merit and biblical warrant for regarding some works as particularly appropriate for one Person of the Trinity rather than another: hence, the Father with creation, the Son with redemption, and the Holy Spirit with sanctification.

Arianism: Named after its progenitor, Arius. A heresy of the fourth century that argued that the one God created Jesus as the highest of creatures and that the Holy Spirit is divine energy. According to this view, Jesus is a demigod.

Biblical theology: In evangelical parlance the expression can mean either doctrine as proved by scriptural texts or a way of using the Bible that observes the Scripture's own canonical unfolding of its story and thus places texts when used for doctrinal purposes in their contexts in their rhetorical settings in their book in the canon in the light of the flow of redemptive history. Not to be confused with mid-twentieth century's "The Biblical Theology Movement," involving liberal mainline scholars, which had largely dissipated by the end of the 1960s.

Cessationism: The view that the sign gifts to the church were for its formative period only. According to this view, a number of the charismatic gifts (e.g., tongues) are not given to the church today.

Charismatic movement: Primarily refers to a movement within mainline churches and free churches beginning in the 1960s which maintains that the gifts of the Spirit spoken of in the NT are available for use by God's people today. Charismatics are continuationists.

Christological moments: (sometimes, Christological mysteries) A device for understanding Christology as presented in the Gospels by reference to the apparent nodal points in Christ's life and work. Traditionally there are seven such moments: birth, baptism, temptations, transfiguration, death, resurrection, and ascension.

Christology: The doctrine of Christ's person and work.

Common grace: God's unmerited favor as Creator shown to men and women as creatures, whether believer or unbelievers.

Complete sanctification: The climax of the progressive transformation of the believer into the likeness of Christ, which is also the believer's glorification.

Consequentialist ethics: The view that the moral value of an action depends upon its outcome.

Conservatio: Lat., "preservation." A subset of divine providence. The divine activity of preserving creatures in their ongoing existence. Other aspects of providence are *gubernatio* (the divine government of creatures) and *concursus* (the divine working together with the creature to achieve his purposes).

Continuationism: The view that none of the spiritual gifts given to the church in its formative period have been withdrawn. According to this view, the now controversial charismatic gifts (e.g., tongues) are for the church today.

Covenanted blessing: A blessing held out in the gospel by way of promise to all believers (e.g., the forgiveness of sins) (compare "Uncovenanted blessing").

Creatio ex nihilo: Lat., "creation out of nothing." According to this view, God did not bring about creatures from preexisting material (*creatio ex materia*), as with Plato's demiurge, nor from his own being (*creatio ex Deo*), as with Plotinus's "The One."

Deism: Primarily an eighteenth-century view that posited a creator God but not one who maintained ongoing interest in the created order. A deistic tendency is one that tends to remove God from active ongoing interaction with the created realm.

Deontological ethics: (from the Greek *deon*, "duty") An ethic that focuses on doing one's duty, which is to obey the moral law.

Docetism: A Christological heresy that denies the reality of the incarnation by arguing that Christ is a spirit who only appeared or seemed (Gk. *dokein*, "to seem") to have human flesh. The second-century gnostic teacher Basilides, for example, was a docetist.

Dynamic monarchianism: A church heresy of the second and third centuries that argued that Jesus was a mere man whom the one God, who alone has the rule (monarchy), adopted into the Godhead because of his virtue, and whom God endowed with the Holy Spirit as divine energy (hence, "dynamic"). In this Christology Jesus differs from other servants of God only in degree, not in kind.

Economic Trinity: Refers to the various roles of the members of the Trinity in the administration (economy) of the plan of salvation. Modalistic monarchians affirm an economic Trinity of sorts as a revealed phenomenon but deny the essential Trinity.

Economy: The administration of the plan of salvation.

Eighth Christological moment: Arguably, the seven traditional Christological moments, the final one of which is the ascension (see above), fail to reckon with the pouring out of the Spirit by the risen Christ at Pentecost—which therefore constitutes an eighth moment.

Enhypostasia: Gk., *en* "in," *hypostasis,* "person." An early-church concept that the individual human personhood of the Second Person of Trinity inheres—is "inpersoned"—within the divine Personhood. The notion is predicated on the idea that there is nothing in principle alien between human personhood in the divine image and the divine personhood. This view is contrasted with that of *anhypostasia,* which maintains that the human nature of Christ is generic and, therefore, impersonal.

Epiclesis: An invocation. In post–Vatican II Roman Catholic theology, refers to an invocation to the Holy Spirit to transform the bread and wine into the actual body and blood of Christ, and an invocation to the Holy Spirit to transform the partakers of the sacrament.

Eschatology: Gk. *eschaton,* "last." Traditionally, narrowly defined as the Four Last Things: death, resurrection, heaven, and hell. But increasingly a broader definition is in play, by which eschatology is the story of the unfolding of the divine purpose in time and space from creation through redemption to new creation.

Essential (or immanent) Trinity: The Trinity's own eternal, internal life as Father, Son, and Holy Spirit.

Evidence: Information that counts toward establishing the truth or falsity of a proposition.

Evidence-based approach: An epistemological protocol using evidence to support truth claims.

External call: God's call to repentance and faith through the preaching of the gospel.

Filioque: Lat., "and from the Son." Refers to the procession of the Spirit within the triune Godhead. Added to the Niceno-Constantinopolitan Creed in the West without Eastern Church approval. According to Eastern theology, the Spirit proceeds from the Father alone. A key point of contention between creedal Western churches and Eastern ones, especially since the split of A.D. 1054.

Futuristic eschatology: (sometimes, consistent eschatology) The view that the kingdom (the dynamic rule of God) is wholly a future reality and that suggestions otherwise misunderstand the Gospels.

General revelation: What God has made known about his reality and character to all peoples everywhere and at all times, through the created order (e.g., Ps. 19:1–6).

Heilsgeschichte: German for "salvation-history." See "Redemptive history."

Heurism: A decision making procedure that adopts a definition, set of categories, distinction, or methodology in order to see what may be discovered thereby.

Historia salutis: Lat., "history of salvation." Refers to those unique events that are integral to the provision of salvation, from the calling of Abraham on (e.g., election of Israel, incarnation).

Illumination: The idea that the Spirit has a special work of enlightening the believer so that he or she understands the inspired Scriptures.

Inaugurated eschatology: The view that the kingdom (the dynamic rule of God) is active now in a beginning way but that the best is yet to be.

Insufflation: The action of blowing air upon a person or object.

Internal call: The idea in Reformed thought that the Holy Spirit uses the external call (see above) to work in the hearts of the elect who hear, to bring about repentance and faith in the gospel.

Internal testimony of the Holy Spirit: Lat. *testimonium internum Spiritus Sancti.* The Spirit's witness within the believer as to the truth of scriptural revelation.

Logos Christology: A "Christology from above" that begins with Christ as the Logos (Word) of God who becomes incarnate in flesh, as in John 1:14 (compare "Spirit Christology").

Manicheism: Teaching of Mani (c. 215–276), a Persian religious teacher; advocates an extreme dualism of good and evil, in which salvation involves freedom from the material order.

Modalistic monarchianism: A heresy of the second and third centuries that argued that the one God, who alone has the rule (monarchy), reveals himself over time in three temporary modes (hence, "modalistic"): the Father mode, the Son mode, and the Spirit mode. According to this view, Jesus had no real humanity.

Natural theology: The attempt to determine, by unaided human reason, the reality of God or gods and something of the nature of divine character.

Norma normans: Lat., "norming norm" or "standardizing standard." The supreme authority, the final court of appeal. For evangelicals, it is Scripture.

Norma normata: Lat., "ruled norms" or "ruled standards." An authority that is subject to a higher authority. For evangelicals, e.g., reason and tradition can be authoritative but both are subject to the higher authority of Scripture.

Ordinance: A term used in some Christian traditions (especially free churches) for baptism and the Lord's Supper as dominically commanded practices. The term places the focus on the relationship of these practices to Christ.

Ordo salutis: Lat., "order of salvation." The order of the elements in the application of salvation to the individual, beginning with calling and culminating in glorification.

Pentecostalism: A renewal movement beginning in the early 1900s which teaches that Christians need a second work of grace (the baptism of the Spirit) beyond regeneration to be holy and/or have power for Christian service. For many Pentecostals, speaking in tongues provides initial evidence that the baptism of the Spirit has taken place. This movement has produced a number of present-day denominations. Pentecostals are continuationists.

Perfecting cause: The idea that God the Spirit leads creatures to their divinely appointed ends.

Pneumatological moments: Arguably there are pneumatological moments that parallel most if not all of the Christological moments (see above): the Spirit's role in the birth of the Messiah, the commissioning, the temptations, the mighty works, the passion, resurrection, and Pentecost. Much less certain, for lack of overt evidence, is the Spirit's role in the transfiguration and ascension.

Pneumatology: The doctrine of the Holy Spirit's person and work.

Positional sanctification: The monergistic act of God whereby believers are set apart for his good pleasure. Sometimes termed definitive sanctification.

Progressive sanctification: The process whereby the Holy Spirit transforms the believer into the likeness of Christ. The process is synergistic, with both God and the believer at work.

Proleptic: Anticipatory.

Rahner's Rule: The rule that the immanent Trinity is the economic Trinity. What is seen in history is true of eternity. Named after Roman Catholic theologian Karl Rahner.

Realized eschatology: The view that the kingdom (the dynamic rule of God) is fully existent at the present time.

Redemptive history: The plot line of the canonical revelation from old creation to new, from Genesis to Revelation, with its accent on redemption.

Revelation: What God has made known about his reality, character, will, and ways.

Sacrament: A term preferred in some Christian traditions for ecclesial practices such as baptism and the Lord's Supper (and up to five more such events), classically understood as "an outward and visible sign of an inward and invisible grace." The idea of sacrament puts the accent on the relationship between the practice, the Christian, and grace.

Salvation-history: See "Redemptive history."

Saving grace: God's unmerited favor shown in the salvation of sinners. Sometimes referred to as special grace.

Special revelation: What God has made known about his reality, character, will, and ways to certain people at certain times (e.g., Ps. 19:7–14; Heb. 1:1–2).

Spirit Christology: A "Christology from below" that understands Christ as a Spirit-filled and/or Spirit-inspired man (compare "Logos Christology").

Subsequence: The term used by some for the idea that, in Acts or Luke–Acts, there is a normative pattern of Spirit baptism or reception or release following conversion, as a distinct work of the Holy Spirit.

Third Wave: A renewal movement that began in the 1980s. This movement, like the Pentecostal (the First Wave) and charismatic (the Second Wave) movements before it, affirms that the gifts of the Holy Spirit are for today. But in addition, the Third Wave argues that evangelism ordinarily should be accompanied by "signs, wonders, and miracles."

Typology: The idea that persons (e.g., Moses), events (e.g., the exodus), and institutions (e.g., the temple) can—in the plan of God—prefigure a later stage in that plan and provide the conceptuality necessary for understanding the divine intent (e.g., the coming of Christ to be the new Moses, to effect the new exodus, and to be the new temple).

Uncovenanted blessing: A blessing from God which, in the good purposes of God, may or may not be experienced by the believer (e.g., a long life) (compare "Covenanted blessing").

Virtue ethics: A view that focuses on the human subject and his or her strength of character as a moral agent (habits, motivations, and intentions).

Witness of the Spirit: May refer to Paul's teaching in Romans 8 that the Spirit bears witness with the human spirit to the believer's status as an adopted child of God, or it may refer to the idea made famous by Calvin that the Spirit has a secret inward ministry of persuading the believer that Scripture is the authentic and hence authoritative Word of God.

Unlike in John Owen's day, we do not have to worry about our reputations if we are interested in the Holy Spirit. We won't be "deemed a fanatic, estranged from the conduct of reason, and all generous principles of conversation."[1] Indeed, today we may access many excellent books and articles on pneumatology: some ancient, some recent, and some contemporary. Indeed there is a cornucopia of books, articles, dissertations, and the like on the Holy Spirit.[2] In offering suggestions for "further reading," therefore, I'll need to be highly selective. From the early church period, Basil of Caesarea's *On the Holy Spirit* is a classic contribution to our understanding of the Spirit. Another classic, but from the much later Puritan period, is John Owen's *The Holy Spirit*. Abraham Kuyper's *The Work of the Holy Spirit* is yet another classic. Though somewhat quaint and not technical, it still repays careful reading. I have found particularly helpful Sinclair Ferguson's *The Holy Spirit*. His work is informed both by an acute sense of the importance of biblical theology in construing doctrine and by a keen Reformed theological sensibility. J. I. Packer's *Keep in Step with the Spirit* displays his usual acumen. His work is not only theologically informative but pastorally astute. Thomas Smail is an underrated theologian. His several works *Reflected Glory, The Forgotten Father,* and *The Giving Gift* are a stimulating blend of Reformed thought and charismatic sensibility. Likewise, Max Turner in several works and articles was of great use, especially his *The Holy Spirit and Spiritual Gifts: Then and Now.* Of similar value was D. A. Carson, *Showing the Spirit: A Theological Exposition of*

1. John Owen, *The Holy Spirit, His Gifts and Power: Exposition of the Spirit's Name, Nature, Personality, Operations, and Effects* (reprint, abridged, Grand Rapids, Mich.: Kregel, 1967), 9.

2. Craig S. Keener, *Three Crucial Questions about the Holy Spirit* (Grand Rapids, Mich.: Baker, 1996), 203, refers to Watson E. Mills, *The Holy Spirit: A Bibliography* (Peabody, Mass.: Hendrickson, 1988), which lists 2,098 items (203). Mills published nearly twenty years ago. The stream of publications has continued to flow since then, with few signs of slowing down. Keener, for example, has published at least three books on the Spirit since 1996, as well as articles.

1 Corinthians 12–14. John R. W. Stott's *Baptism and Fullness: The Work of the Holy Spirit Today* remains a classic. Worth reading is the volume *Perspectives on Spirit Baptism: Five Views,* edited by Chad Owen Brand. So too is *Are Miraculous Gifts for Today? Four Views,* edited by Wayne Grudem. Jürgen Moltmann's several works on the Spirit proved provocative and greatly stimulating as usual, in particular his *The Spirit of Life: A Universal Affirmation.* More generally, Charles H. H. Scobie's massive *The Ways of Our God: An Approach to Biblical Theology* provided many helpful insights into the text of Scripture when viewed in the light of the flow of redemptive history. Even more useful in that respect was William J. Dumbrell, *The Search for Order: Biblical Eschatology in Focus.* Special mention must be made of Bruce Demarest's *The Cross and Salvation: The Doctrine of Salvation.* Many of the pneumatological themes are addressed in this book (e.g., sanctification) with such clarity and competence that I found myself tempted simply to reproduce his treatment. It is no longer the case that the doctrine of the Spirit is a neglected theme in theology. The contemporary literature is vast, and I have had to be highly selective. As for the great ones of the theological past, many of their names appear in this study, especially Irenaeus, Basil, Augustine, and Calvin. From the foregoing it can be seen that my debts are numerous. Scores of other debts are to be seen in the footnotes. However, I have not hesitated to disagree where differences of opinion and controversy required a judgment call.

symbols of, 98n7, 99–100n20, 158n41; and the temptations of Jesus, 159–160; and the transfiguration of Jesus, 163–164; and the unity of Christ's body (the church), 219–221; and wisdom, 126n47; witness of, 30, 268–273; worship of, 72; and the worship by God's people, 234–236. See also *filioque* controversy; illumination; mystery

"Holy Spirit" (Montague), 165n64

Holy Spirit, The (Bloesch), 60n4

"Holy Spirit, The" (Coffey), 75n53

Holy Spirit, The (Ferguson), 60n3, 97n5, 224n60, 269n36

"Holy Spirit, The" (Grenz), 34n32

Holy Spirit, The (Montague), 96n4

"Holy Spirit, The" (Wainwright), 59n2

"Holy Spirit, The" (Welker), 41n1

Holy Spirit, The, His Gifts and Power (Owen), 30n20

Holy Spirit in Christian Theology, The (Hendry), 54n59, 95n1

"Holy Spirit in Christian Theology, The" (W. Menzies), 29n15, 31n22

Holy Teaching (Bauerschmidt), 74n45

Hook, Norman, 202n117

hope, 141–142; and covenant promise, 131–132; of glory, 238–240

Hosea–Jonah (Stuart), 140n42

How to Read Karl Barth (Hunsinger), 49

Humanity of God, The (Barth), 49

humility, 43, 51, 53, 56, 113–114

Hunsinger, George, 49

Hunt, Boyd, 34n33, 101, 175, 243–244, 249, 249n156

Idea of the Holy, The (Otto), 42n4

idolatry, 23, 45–46, 54, 62, 72

illumination, 265–266; and "understanding," 266

imago dei, 53n55, 66n19

imitation of Christ, 175–176

"Infancy Gospel of Thomas, The," 156n30

Inspiration and Incarnation (Enns), 110n74

Institutes of the Christian Religion (Calvin), 45, 216–217n31, 271–272

interpretation, Christian theological, 106–107

Irenaeus, 77, 79–80, 96, 108, 126–129, 230, 254, 264

Irving, Edwin, 173n104, 174n108

"Is Carl Henry a Modernist?" (Brand), 50n43

Islam: and the Holy Spirit, 69; and the Trinity, 61, 87–89

Israel: dispensationalism's focus on, 138n34; God's care for, 118–119; God's communication with, 121–124; as God's covenant people, 131–132; God's governance of, 119–121; God's presence with, 124–126; re-creation of by the Holy Spirit, 136–138

Jarrett, Narelle, 173n104

Jeffers, James S., 245n148

Jehovah's Witnesses, 69n29

Jensen, Peter, 189, 189n48, 204n119, 206–207, 251n168

Jesus, 46; ascension of, 169–171; baptism of, 156–159, 174, 175; boyhood of, 156; commissioning of his disciples (post-resurrection), 188–190; contrasted with Adam, 127, 160, 160n49; contrasted with Israel, 160; crucifixion of, 164–167; deity of, 59; glorification of, 183, 191; gnostic accounts of his boyhood, 156n30; as holy, 153, 155–156; incarnation of, 151–156, 173; lordship of, 171n93; messiahship of, 151–152, 163; mighty works of, 160–162; "Nazareth Manifesto" of, 161; and the New Testament infancy narratives, 153n15; as a Paraclete, 185n29; prayer to, 85; relationship of to the Holy Spirit during his earthly life, 173–176; resurrection of, 167–169; as the Son of God, 153; temptations of, 159–160; transfiguration of, 46, 163–164, 163n57; "virgin birth" of, 152–156, 153n16; as the Word of God, 262. *See also* Christological mysteries/moments; imitation of Christ

Jesus—God and Man (Pannenberg), 88n106

"Jesus' Vision for the Restoration of Israel" (Scott), 152n9

John Paul II (pope), 67, 177, 190n58

John the Baptist, 180–182, 196n83; geographic hub of his ministry, 157n32; prophetic ministry of, 156–157

Johnson, Elizabeth A., 79, 79n71, 80, 82n86

Johnson, Luke Timothy, 212n16

Joshua, 119n13, 122

Judaism, first-century, 152

Judaizers, 59

judges, the, 119–120

justification, 240

Justin Martyr, 108, 245